COLORING MANDAL

For Balance, Harmony, and Spiritual Well-Being

S U S A N N E   F.   F I N C H E R

SHAMBHALA
Boston & London
2004

form conflict into harmony. This growth process may be experienced as stressful and challenging to cherished ideas and beliefs. An urge to create mandalas arises as one of the psyche's natural self-regulating mechanisms for bringing about a sense of balance, order, and well-being. (Indeed, those who create and color mandalas often report feeling more relaxed afterward.)

Jung's patients brought him mandalas they had drawn or painted. Such mandalas often displayed patterns based on four: four objects, four colors, or four-armed crosses known as swastikas (in Sanskrit, *svastika*, an ancient solar symbol representing the cosmic wheel spinning on an axis). The appearance of these mandalas indicated to Jung that his patient was experiencing individuation and that a balancing of the personality was in process, in which previously unconscious parts of the personality emerged symbolically in dreams and artwork. When understood and accepted by the ego (the part of yourself you call "I"), these once-hidden aspects of self increase self-awareness and make identity more complex and stable.

Individuation is ultimately humbling because, if all goes well, the ego must accept nothing less than dethronement as the most important part of the psyche. We come to know that the true center of the psyche is not "I," the center of consciousness, but the Self, which is the center of the *whole* psyche, though it resides in the unconscious. Just as the earth circles around the sun, the ego is subject to the superior centering power of the Self. Through individuation we learn to value and accept the guidance of the Self given in dreams and spontaneous artwork, especially mandalas.

Jung was familiar with the fourfold patterns in the spontaneous mandalas that he associated with the process of individuation. Mandalas that did not fit this pattern were puzzling to him. In his case study of a "Miss X," Jung includes illustrations of her mandalas based on six, eight, twelve, and sixteen, though he chooses not to comment on them because, he said, he did not understand them properly. Jung further says that this case study "is not intended to demonstrate how an entire lifetime expresses itself in symbolic form. The individuation process has many stages and is subject to many vicissitudes" (*The Archetypes and the Collective Unconscious*, p. 348). It re-

mained for another researcher to see the implications in designs other than the fourfold mandala.

That researcher was Joan Kellogg, an American art therapist. In association with the psychiatrist Francisco DiLeo, she conceptualized the growth and development of the psyche as an ongoing cycle through twelve stages. Each stage encompasses certain developmental tasks and is characterized by a particular state of consciousness. The twelve stages are experienced many times in the course of a lifetime. Kellogg discovered that these twelve stages are associated with prototypical mandala forms.

In Kellogg's model, called the Archetypal Stages of the Great Round of Mandala (or "the Great Round" for short), the twelve stages encompass a complete cycle of inner growth that begins in formless unconsciousness and unfolds into greater and greater self-awareness and accomplishment. The cycle then transitions to the ending when things naturally fall apart, energy returns to the unconscious, and a new cycle begins. The twelve stages of the Great Round are called the Void, Bliss, Labyrinth, Beginning, Target, Dragon Fight, Squaring the Circle, Functioning Ego, Crystallization, Gates of Death, Fragmentation, and Transcendent Ecstasy. (Kellogg later found it necessary to add a Stage 0, Clear Light.)

Most stages are initially experienced in normal growth and development. We repeat cycles of the Great Round again and again as we live our lives. With each "visit" to a stage we have an opportunity to consolidate our mastery of the challenges and states of consciousness associated with that stage. We may also clarify our understanding of past experiences there, and resolve unfinished business associated with the stage, thereby releasing bound energy to focus on subsequent stages of the Great Round. (For more on the Great Round, see my book *Creating Mandalas*.)

With experience and maturity we can more easily access the state of consciousness inherent in each stage. We may eventually develop the capability to be aware of all stages simultaneously, and thereby forgo identification with only a few stages. This ability to see the big picture brings an experience of transcendence and a sense of connection to the deeper psyche. The capacity to consciously experience a psychological center that incorporates a connection to the deeper psyche is the most important task of individuation.

*The sacred Sri Yantra is a crystal-like Hindu mandala
representing the creative energies of the universe.*

It is not unlike the Buddhist goal of liberation from the karmic cycles of the Wheel of Life.

In this book we will focus on one of the twelve stages of the Great Round: Crystallization (Stage Nine). Crystallization is associated with the completion of a cycle of growth that began in the Void (Stage One). It is the point in the Great Round where growing energy is perfectly fulfilled in a unique creation. Imagine a fully opened rose in a sunny garden, releasing its fragrance as it gently bobs in a summer breeze. This is the feeling of the stage of Crystallization.

Crystallization is a time of reaping rewards and benefits from the work we have performed, of realizing and appreciating our achievements; of resting in the pleasure of having fulfilled a personal creative inspiration. Time seems to slow to a relaxed, enjoyable pace. Crystallization is also a time of significant spiritual understanding, when our spiritual nature comes together in harmony with our physical nature.

A profound synthesis is suggested in Crystallization mandalas. The Sri Yantra, a traditional Indian design, may be considered such a mandala. Upward- and downward-pointing triangles interpenetrate. The downward-pointing triangles symbolize Shakti, the female principle representing all that is active and creative. The upward-pointing triangles symbolize Shiva, the male principle and the essence of absolute consciousness that permeates all reality. In the Hindu tradition, the coming together of these two energies is thought to set in motion all of creation.

The sacred art of the world's great religions includes myriad Crystallization mandalas. Typically, Crystallization mandalas are symmetrical and emphasize the center point. They convey a feeling of balance, harmony, and rest. Paradoxically, they also suggest a pulsing energy. Crystallization mandalas may indeed resemble crystals. Their structure is based on even numbers greater than four (six, eight, ten, twelve, and so on).

I have chosen to focus on Crystallization mandalas in this book because they embody peace, joy, and fulfillment. Spending time with these mandalas can be relaxing. Coloring them can provide a soothing balance for hectic lifestyles. Interacting with Crystallization mandalas may also help you develop your ability to access a calm state of mind more easily, whenever you choose to. And some of you may look beyond the patterns you see in these mandalas to experience the spiritual energy that inspired them.

Seventy-two mandalas are included because 72 is a sacred number containing within it many combinations of sacred numbers, most notably one (symbolic of the One, or God), two (representing the duality of life as in yin/yang, male/female, light/dark), three (God as Father, Son, Holy Spirit; Goddess as Maiden, Mother, Crone), four (as in the four directions and the four elements of earth, air, fire, water)—and twelve, the basis of the Great Round (as in twelve apostles, twelve sun signs of the zodiac, and twelve months of the year). Many of the mandalas in this book were inspired by the sacred art of the East, the Middle East, and Europe. Photos of snowflakes provided a beginning point for several. The visual prayers of great souls inspired others. All were drawn by me after opening sacred space by lighting a candle and sitting for a few minutes in meditation. You might enjoy taking the same steps to prepare for coloring a mandala. Whatever approach you take, it is my hope that your time with these mandalas will be well spent.

Susanne F. Fincher
Atlanta, Georgia
2003

References

Bently, W. A. *Snowflakes in Photographs*. Mineola, NY: Dover Publications, 2000.

Bryant, Barry. *The Wheel of Time Sand Mandala: Visual Scriptures of Tibetan Buddhism*. San Francisco: HarperSanFrancisco, 1995.

Copony, Heita. *Mystery of Mandalas*. Wheaton, IL: Theosophical Publishing House, 1989.

Fincher, Susanne F. *Coloring Mandalas: For Insight, Healing, and Self-Expression*. Boston & London: Shambhala Publications, 2000.

——. *Creating Mandalas: For Insight, Healing, and Self-Expression*. Boston & London: Shambhala Publications, 1991.

Jung, Carl G. *The Archetypes and the Collective Unconscious*, 2nd ed. Princeton, NJ: Princeton University Press, 1990.

Kellogg, Joan. *Mandala: Path of Beauty*. Rev. ed. Williamsburg, VA: Privately published, 1997.

Kellogg, Joan, and F. B. DiLeo. "Archetypal Stages of the Great Round of Mandala." *Journal of Religion and Psychical Research* 5 (1982): 38–49.

Kluckhohn, Clyde, and Dorothea Leighton. *The Navaho*. Rev. ed. Garden City, NY: Doubleday & Company, 1962.

Sacred Symbols: Mandala. By the Editors of Thames & Hudson. New York: Thames and Hudson, 1995.

Tucci, Giuseppe. *Theory and Practice of the Mandala*. London: Rider and Company, 1961.

Wilson, Eva. *Diseños Islamicos*. Naucalpan, Mexico: Ediciones G. Gili, 2000.

Zaczek, Iain. *Celtic Design*. New York: Crescent Books, 1995.

Mandalas for Coloring

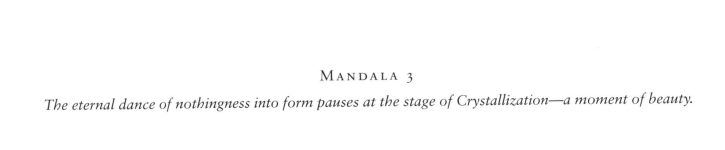

MANDALA 3

The eternal dance of nothingness into form pauses at the stage of Crystallization—a moment of beauty.

MANDALA 4

This mandala calls to mind a compass, a crystal, or perhaps a star blazing fervently beyond the limits of the human eye.

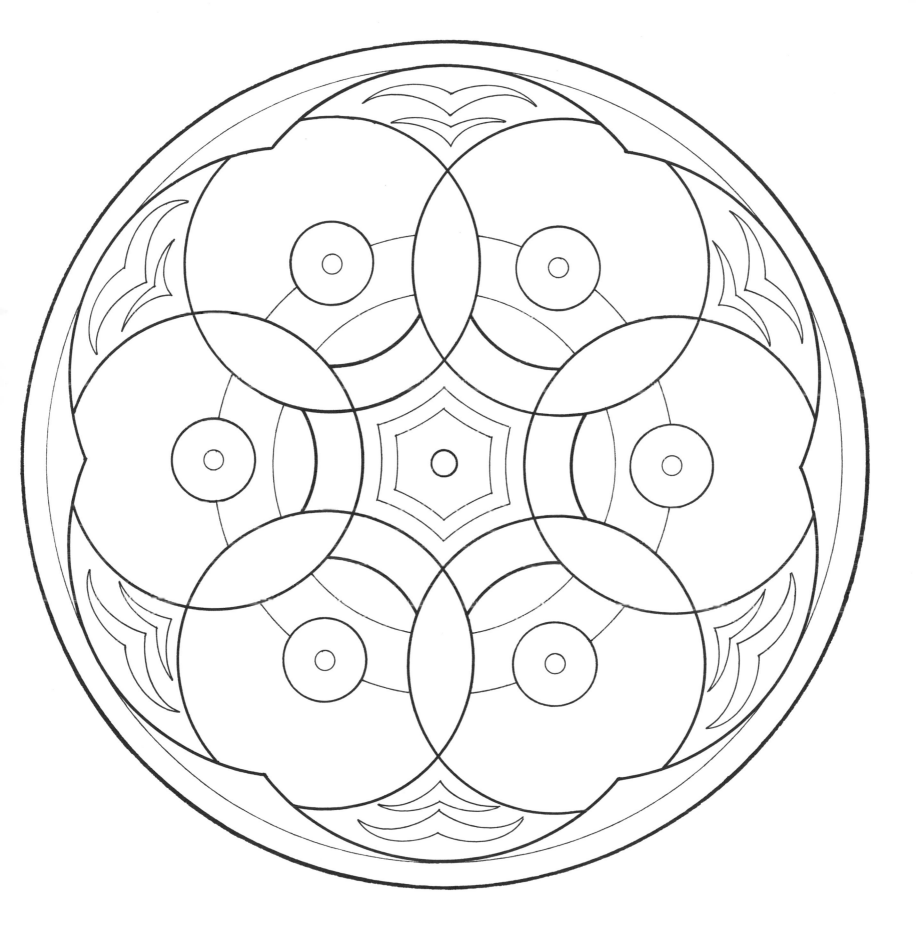

MANDALA 6

Rainbows, rising and setting suns, or stars with wings—all enfold the center where an eight-pointed form is crystallized.

MANDALA 8

Upward- and downward-pointing triangles rest upon the petals of a fully opened flower, the essence of the stage of Crystallization.

MANDALA 9

Layer upon layer of flower petals open around a center that, when left uncolored, suggests a gateway through to changes yet to come.

MANDALA 10

Interpenetrating triangles signify the coming together of opposites—dark/light, active/receptive, feeling/thinking.

MANDALA 12

The crystalline structure of a snowflake was the stimulus for this mandala that blooms like an exotic flower of flowers.

MANDALA 13

Dragonflies hover as strange blossoms—each supporting a pearl, or a moon, or a sun—neatly balance on the tips of a star.

The intricate patterns of this mandala suggest lit candles, a convivial gathering, or a grove of jeweled trees.

MANDALA 15

Resembling a multifaceted jewel, a seal of office, or an honorary medal bestowed for accomplishments, this mandala is based on a snowflake.

MANDALA 16

Fanlike forms unfolding evoke the quietly pulsing energy of Life experienced during the stage of Crystallization.

MANDALA 17

A splash of color, fanciful birds, or creatures on alert—what do you see in this mandala?

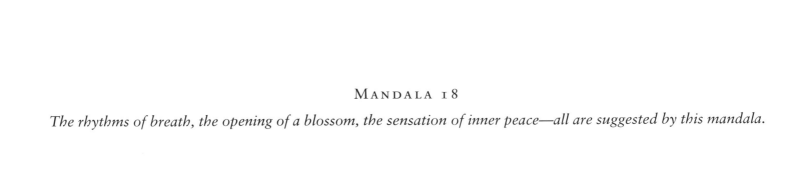

MANDALA 18

The rhythms of breath, the opening of a blossom, the sensation of inner peace—all are suggested by this mandala.

MANDALA 19

Inspired by the Buddhist Wheel of Life, this mandala alludes to repeating cycles of existence as well as the practice of meditation as a way to break free.

MANDALA 21

The rising and setting sun, the waxing and waning moon, or earth energy coursing along lines of natural magnetism: what do you imagine in this mandala?

MANDALA 22

A celestial rose supports the form created by two triangles coming together. In the Jewish tradition it is the Star of David, Solomon's Seal, or the symbol of God's union with the Shekhina, the feminine Divine Presence.

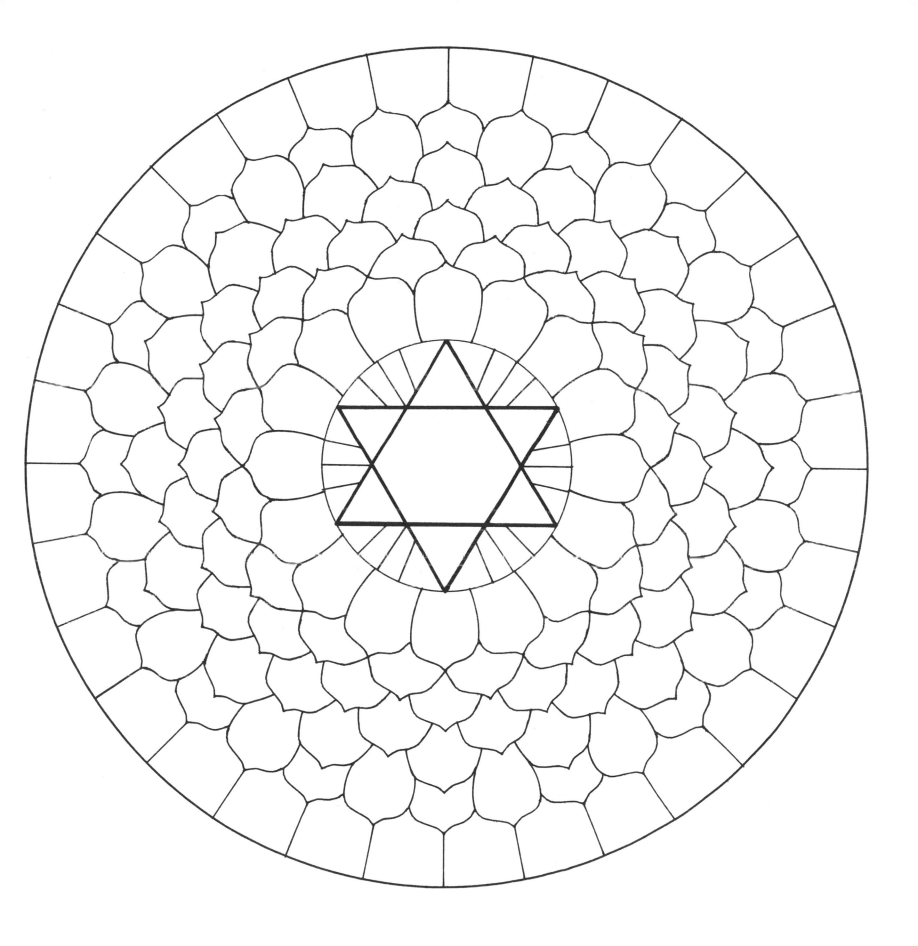

MANDALA 23

Lilies drink deep from wafting trails of fragrance linking them one to another. Inspired by the structure of a snowflake.

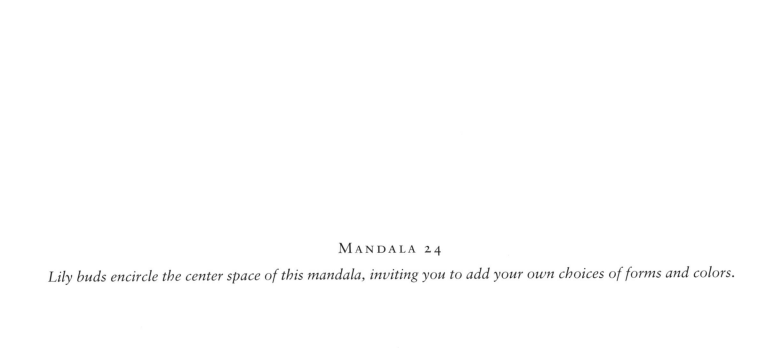

MANDALA 24

Lily buds encircle the center space of this mandala, inviting you to add your own choices of forms and colors.

MANDALA 25

The mandalas of Tibetan Buddhism often take the form of a palace or walled city enclosing a sacred inner precinct, as seen in this design.

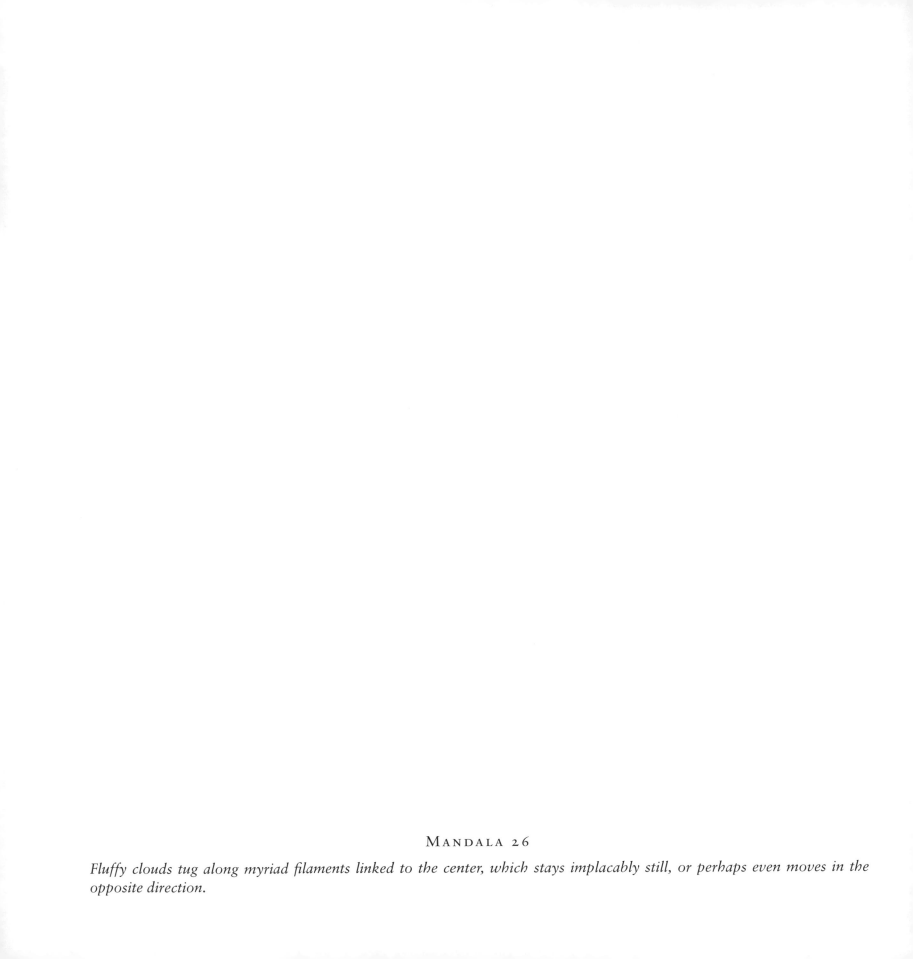

MANDALA 26

Fluffy clouds tug along myriad filaments linked to the center, which stays implacably still, or perhaps even moves in the opposite direction.

MANDALA 27

Star-gazing fish, lifted from the deep waters of the unconscious, converge on the center in a sprightly design based on a Celtic illumination.

MANDALA 28

This mandala calls to mind an arrangement of nectar-filled vases, flowers, and incense given as votive offerings.

MANDALA 29

Dynamic patterns frame an image of the Virgin Mary in this mandala based on a rose window in the Cathedral of Our Lady, Freiburg, Germany.

MANDALA 30

The wheel demonstrates that balance is possible between the quiet, still center and the quickly turning edge: each needs the other.

MANDALA 31

This mandala was inspired by an eighteenth-century Nepalese design utilized as an aid in grasping the unity of self and cosmos.

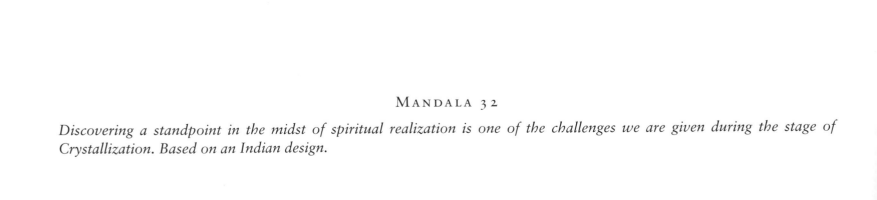

MANDALA 32

Discovering a standpoint in the midst of spiritual realization is one of the challenges we are given during the stage of Crystallization. Based on an Indian design.

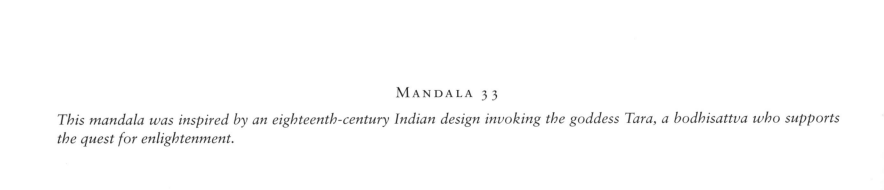

MANDALA 33

This mandala was inspired by an eighteenth-century Indian design invoking the goddess Tara, a bodhisattva who supports the quest for enlightenment.

Mandala 34

Petals spread out and out from the center, floating in the circular space of the mandala like a lily on a tranquil pond.

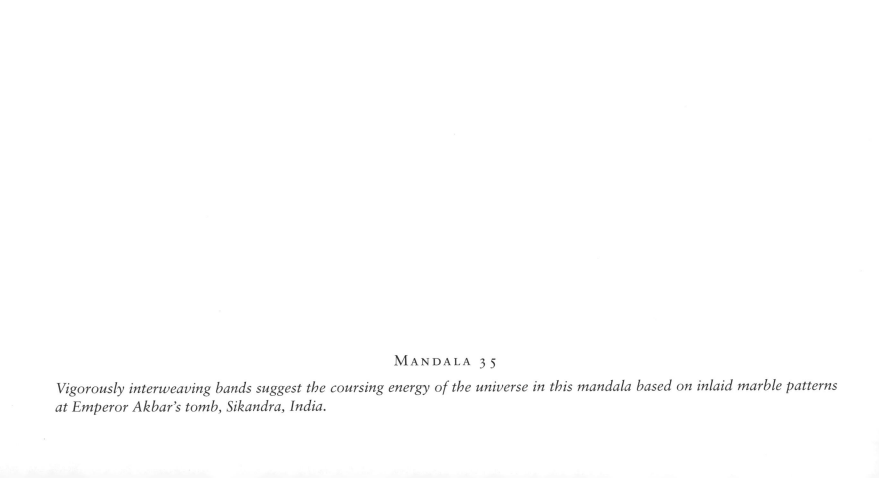

MANDALA 35

Vigorously interweaving bands suggest the coursing energy of the universe in this mandala based on inlaid marble patterns at Emperor Akbar's tomb, Sikandra, India.

MANDALA 36

Much of this complex design is comprised of a single strand, a visual teaching that the One and the many are the same. Inspired by designs at the tomb of Emperor Akbar.

MANDALA 37

Curving lines glide smoothly over and under, toward the center and away, in this feminine mandala drawn from an Islamic design.

MANDALA 38

A convoluted blossom fills the center of this mandala based on a sixteenth-century Iranian design.

MANDALA 39

Moving your gaze along the complicated pathways in this mandala can be so confusing that thought surrenders and calm prevails.

MANDALA 41

Just as naturally as planets orbit the sun, we experience the psyche's center of gravity as the Imago Dei, the inner Christ, the image of God within.

MANDALA 42

A meditating figure seems at home in the universe, seated at the center of this mandala inspired by a Buddhist thangka, or scroll painting.

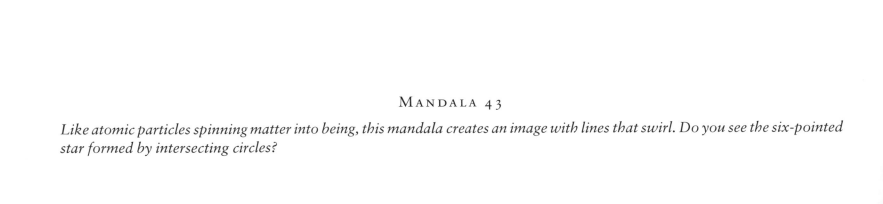

MANDALA 43

Like atomic particles spinning matter into being, this mandala creates an image with lines that swirl. Do you see the six-pointed star formed by intersecting circles?

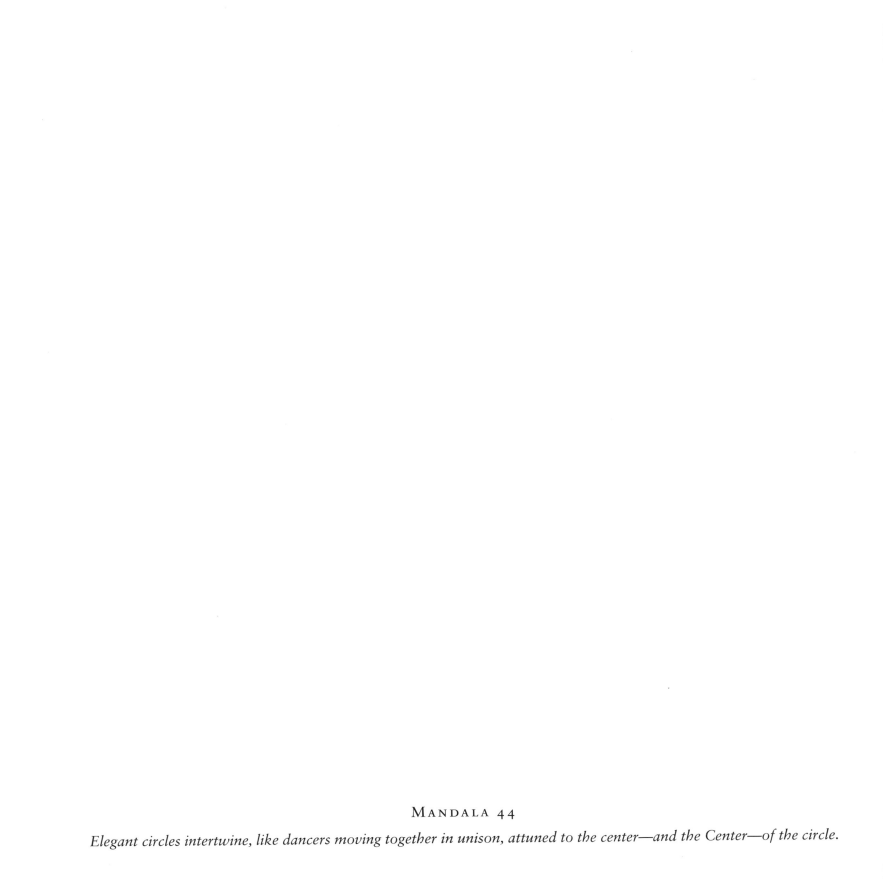

MANDALA 44

Elegant circles intertwine, like dancers moving together in unison, attuned to the center—and the Center—of the circle.

MANDALA 45

Triangles merge to create diamonds, a symbol of the synthesis experienced during the stage of Crystallization.

MANDALA 46

Pattern within pattern unfolds, alluding to the experience of deepening self-understanding.

MANDALA 47

An extravagant blossom with transparent petals—all the better to let in the light.

MANDALA 48

These winged circles await your colors to fully reveal the complexity of their relationships.

Four ribbons intertwine to create a dazzling star with twelve points. Inspired by an Egyptian design.

MANDALA 50

Odd numbers suggest energy, movement, and change. Even numbers connote balance, harmony, and completion. Forms defined by both types of numbers appear in this mandala based upon the numbers three, five, and ten. From an Islamic design.

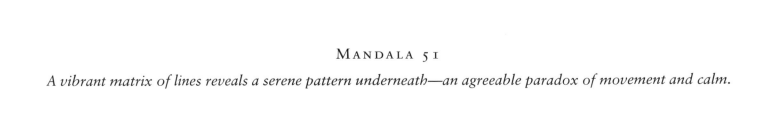

MANDALA 51

A vibrant matrix of lines reveals a serene pattern underneath—an agreeable paradox of movement and calm.

Like holographic images of the center, smaller flowers take form within spaces defined by intersecting lines.

MANDALA 53

During the stage of Crystallization, some experience understanding as resembling the discovery of a source of light within.

MANDALA 54

In the traditions of Islamic art, straight lines are masculine in quality, while curved lines are feminine. Both are brought together here, weaving a balanced and tranquil pattern.

Mandala 55

As suggested by the hearts in this mandala, the resolution of differences during the stage of Crystallization releases unconditional love.

MANDALA 56

Lines bound from side to side in the circle, creating almond-shaped spaces known as mandorlas. Within, a cosmic flower floats peacefully.

MANDALA 59

A wisdom figure meditates among celestial spheres, radiant light, and sacred fires in this mandala of the stage of Crystallization.

MANDALA 62

Simple bands and fancy flowers happily achieve a balance in this Crystallization mandala. Based on a Turkish design.

MANDALA 63

Triangles spin into labyrinths that amaze the eye. Drawn from an Islamic design.

MANDALA 64

Plump berries nestle among the leaves and petals of this flowerlike mandala, conveying the ripeness of the stage of Crystallization.

MANDALA 65

The theme of divine union between active and receptive qualities can be found in this delicate mandala inspired by an Islamic design.

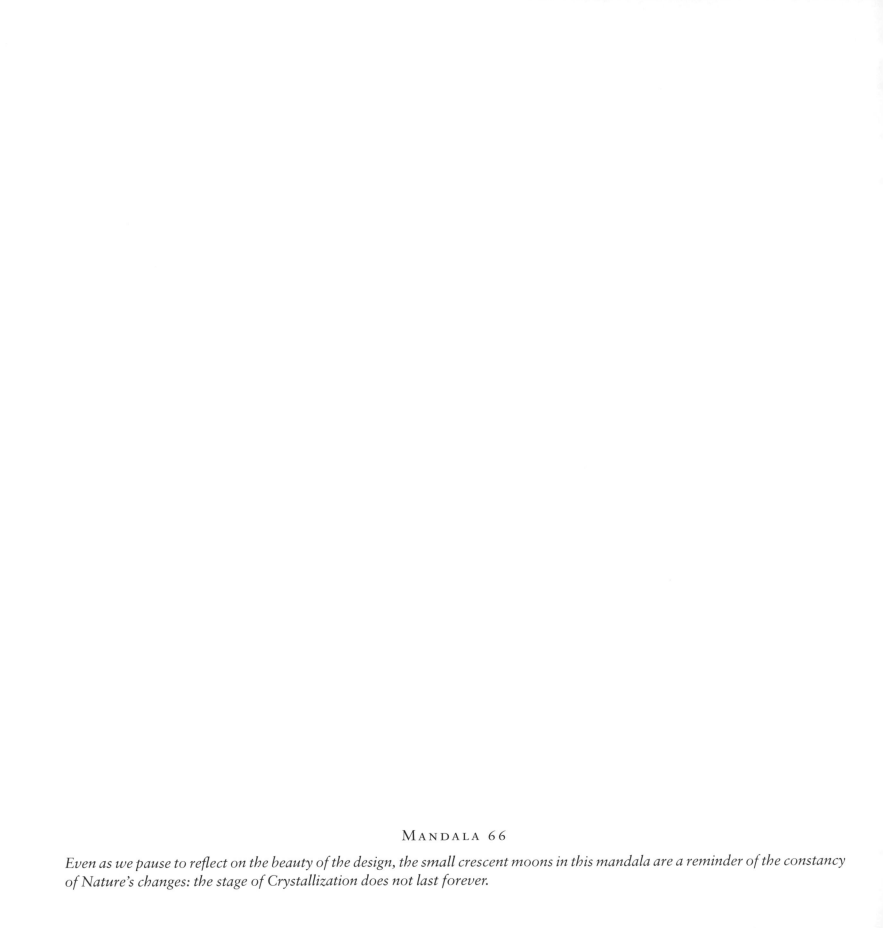

MANDALA 66

Even as we pause to reflect on the beauty of the design, the small crescent moons in this mandala are a reminder of the constancy of Nature's changes: the stage of Crystallization does not last forever.

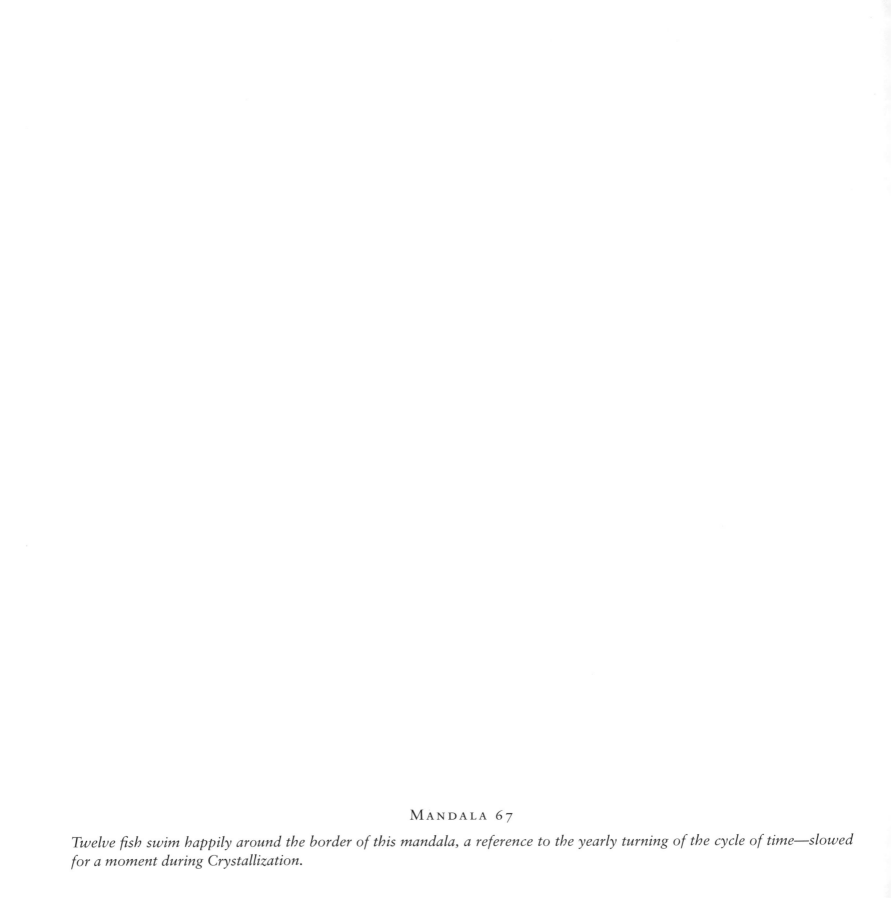

MANDALA 67

Twelve fish swim happily around the border of this mandala, a reference to the yearly turning of the cycle of time—slowed for a moment during Crystallization.

MANDALA 69

This jewel-like mandala is based on a nineteenth-century Nepalese thangka used for clearing and focusing one's awareness.

Arabesques of infinity signs, each one touching into the center, create vibrant patterns for coloring.

MANDALA 71

What comes after a flower is done with blooming? The return to the earth, as foreshadowed by the withering edges of this mandala.

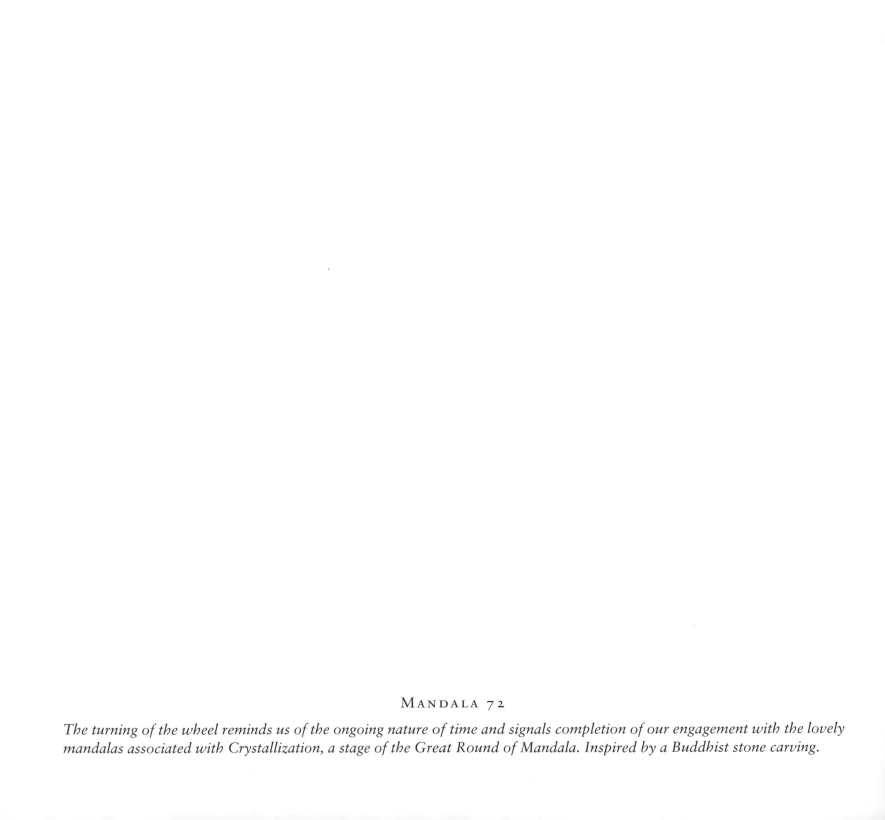

MANDALA 72

The turning of the wheel reminds us of the ongoing nature of time and signals completion of our engagement with the lovely mandalas associated with Crystallization, a stage of the Great Round of Mandala. Inspired by a Buddhist stone carving.

Create your own mandala design!

Better Homes and Gardens
BIGGEST BOOK OF
CHICKEN
RECIPES

Meredith® Books
Des Moines, Iowa

BETTER HOMES AND GARDENS®
BIGGEST BOOK OF CHICKEN RECIPES

Editor: Jan Miller
Contributing Project Editor: Spectrum Communication Services, Inc.
Contributing Graphic Designer: Joyce DeWitt
Copy Chief: Terri Fredrickson
Copy Editor: Kevin Cox
Publishing Operations Manager: Karen Schirm
Senior Editor, Asset & Information Management: Phillip Morgan
Edit and Design Production Coordinator: Mary Lee Gavin
Editorial Assistant: Cheryl Eckert
Book Production Managers: Pam Kvitne, Marjorie J. Schenkelberg,
   Rick von Holdt, Mark Weaver
Contributing Proofreaders: Jean Baker, Jill Blacksmith, Donna Segal
Test Kitchen Director: Lynn Blanchard
Test Kitchen Product Supervisor: Marilyn Cornelius
Test Kitchen Home Economists: Elizabeth Burt, R.D.,L.D.; Juliana Hale,
   Laura Harms, R.D.; Maryellyn Krantz; Greg Luna; Jill Moberly;
   Dianna Nolin; Colleen Weeden; Lori Wilson

Meredith® Books
Executive Director, Editorial: Gregory H. Kayko
Executive Director, Design: Matt Strelecki
Managing Editor: Amy Tincher-Durik
Executive Editor: Jennifer Darling
Senior Editor/Group Manager: Jan Miller
Marketing Product Manager: Toye Cody

Publisher and Editor in Chief: James D. Blume
Editorial Director: Linda Raglan Cunningham
Executive Director, Marketing: Kevin Kacere
Executive Director, New Business Development: Todd M. Davis
Executive Director, Sales: Ken Zagor
Director, Operations: George A. Susral
Director, Production: Douglas M. Johnston
Director, Marketing & Publicity: Amy Nichols
Business Director: Jim Leonard

Vice President and General Manager: Douglas J. Guendel

Better Homes and Gardens® Magazine
Editor in Chief: Gayle Goodson Butler
Deputy Editor, Food and Entertaining: Nancy Hopkins

Meredith Publishing Group
President: Jack Griffin
Senior Vice President: Karla Jeffries

Meredith Corporation
Chairman of the Board: William T. Kerr
President and Chief Executive Officer: Stephen M. Lacy

In Memoriam: E.T. Meredith III (1933–2003)

All of us at Meredith® Books are dedicated to providing you with the information and ideas you need to create delicious foods. We welcome your comments and suggestions. Write to us at: Meredith Books, Cookbook Editorial Department, 1716 Locust St., Des Moines, IA 50309-3023.

Our Better Homes and Gardens® Test Kitchen seal on the back cover of this book assures you that every recipe in *Biggest Book of Chicken Recipes* has been tested in the Better Homes and Gardens® Test Kitchen. This means that each recipe is practical and reliable, and meets our high standards of taste appeal. We guarantee your satisfaction with this book for as long as you own it.

TABLE OF CONTENTS

INTRODUCTION

Satisfying Meals for All Occasions

In the ever-changing world of cooking, one thing remains the same—good cooks turn to chicken when they want to serve hearty, delicious meals. Whether it's stuffed chicken breasts for a special party or a quick-fix sandwich on a busy weeknight, there's a way to cook chicken that fits every schedule and lifestyle.

The *Biggest Book of Chicken Recipes* brings you more than 360 of the best poultry recipes ever. These ideas make the most of whole birds and poultry pieces as well as ground or cooked chicken and turkey. From tried-and-true classics to ethnic favorites to the latest innovations, these recipes are just what you need for sensational meals.

Take a look inside. You'll discover a tantalizing collection of appetizers, including enticing new takes on Buffalo wings. Plus there are soul-warming soups and refreshing salads that are sure to please. For days when you're on the go, you'll find one of the no-tend slow-cooked dishes, 30-minute quick fixes, easy pizzas, or no-fuss sandwiches is a terrific solution to feeding the family. And when you have more time, try your hand at a succulent roasted whole bird, an appealing dinnertime delight, or a great-tasting grilled favorite.

No matter how you like your chicken, you'll find a creative idea to tempt you in the *Biggest Book of Chicken Recipes*. Say goodbye to those ho-hum meals and treat your family to one of these exceptional chicken dishes soon.

WINGS & THINGS

Kick off your next get-together with one or more of these irresistible appetizers including Buffalo wings, stuffed mushrooms, meatballs, spring rolls, and more.

For a simple presentation, make a double recipe of the sauce and spoon it into tall, yet small cups. This way each skewer can be dunked deep enough so all of the chicken gets coated with this cool, creamy sauce.

CHICKEN SOUVLAKI SKEWERS

PREP: *25 minutes*
MARINATE: *4 to 24 hours*
GRILL: *8 minutes*
MAKES: *16 skewers*

4	skinless, boneless chicken breast halves (about 1¼ pounds total)
2	tablespoons olive oil
2	tablespoons white wine vinegar
1	teaspoon finely shredded lemon peel
1	tablespoon lemon juice
2	cloves garlic, minced
1	teaspoon salt
1	teaspoon snipped fresh oregano or ¼ teaspoon dried oregano, crushed
1	teaspoon snipped fresh thyme or ¼ teaspoon dried thyme, crushed
¼	teaspoon black pepper
1	recipe Onion-Yogurt Sauce

1 Cut chicken lengthwise into 16 strips. Place chicken in a resealable plastic bag set in a shallow bowl.

2 For marinade, in a small bowl combine olive oil, vinegar, lemon peel, lemon juice, garlic, salt, oregano, thyme, and pepper. Pour over chicken. Seal bag; turn to coat chicken. Marinate in the refrigerator for 4 to 24 hours, turning bag occasionally.

3 Drain chicken, discarding marinade. On sixteen 6-inch skewers,* thread chicken, accordion-style.

4 Place skewers on the rack of an uncovered grill directly over medium coals. Grill for 8 to 10 minutes or until chicken is no longer pink, turning once halfway through grilling.

5 Serve skewers warm with Onion-Yogurt Sauce.

ONION-YOGURT SAUCE: In a small bowl stir together one 6-ounce carton plain yogurt, 2 tablespoons thinly sliced green onion or snipped fresh chives, 2 teaspoons grated onion, and ⅛ teaspoon salt.

Per skewer: 64 cal., 2 g total fat (0 g sat. fat), 21 mg chol., 195 mg sodium, 1 g carbo., 0 g fiber, 9 g pro.

BROILER DIRECTIONS: Preheat broiler. Place skewers on the unheated rack of a broiler pan. Broil 3 to 4 inches from the heat for 8 to 10 minutes or until chicken is no longer pink, turning once halfway through broiling.

*****TEST KITCHEN TIP:** If you use wooden skewers, soak them in water for 30 minutes before you thread the chicken onto the skewers (this prevents the skewers from burning during cooking).

Finely crushed pork rinds add delightful crunch to these nuggets. Look for pork rinds near the potato chips in the supermarket.

CHICKEN NUGGETS WITH CILANTRO CREAM

¼   cup finely crushed pork rinds (about ½ ounce)

1   tablespoon chili powder

¼   teaspoon salt

¼   teaspoon black pepper

⅛   teaspoon cayenne pepper

1   pound skinless, boneless chicken breasts, cut into 1-inch pieces

2   tablespoons butter or margarine, melted

½   cup dairy sour cream

2   tablespoons snipped fresh cilantro

PREP: *20 minutes*
BAKE: *8 minutes*
MAKES: *4 servings*

1 Preheat oven to 400°F. In a plastic bag combine pork rinds, chili powder, salt, black pepper, and cayenne pepper.

2 In a medium bowl combine chicken pieces and melted butter; toss to coat. Place in bag with pork rind mixture. Seal bag and shake until chicken is well coated.

3 Place chicken pieces in a single layer on a lightly greased baking sheet. Bake for 8 to 10 minutes or until chicken is no longer pink, turning pieces once.

4 Meanwhile, for cilantro cream, in a small bowl stir together sour cream and cilantro. Serve chicken pieces with cilantro cream.

Per serving: 259 cal., 14 g total fat (8 g sat. fat), 96 mg chol., 367 mg sodium, 2 g carbo., 1 g fiber, 30 g pro.

For some people, it just isn't a party without chicken wings. If you're in that crowd, try this whiskey-laced twist on the classic.

CHICKEN WINGS IN MAPLE-WHISKEY SAUCE

PREP: *20 minutes*

BAKE: *20 minutes*

COOK: *4 to 5 hours on low-heat setting or 2 to 2½ hours on high-heat setting*

MAKES: *16 servings*

3 pounds chicken wings (about 16)

½ cup pure maple syrup or maple-flavored syrup

½ cup whiskey or orange juice

2 tablespoons butter or margarine, melted

1 Preheat oven to 375°F. If desired, using a sharp knife, carefully cut off tips of chicken wings; discard wing tips. In a foil-lined 15×10×1-inch baking pan arrange chicken wings in a single layer. Bake for 20 minutes. Drain well.

2 For sauce, in a 3½- or 4-quart slow cooker combine maple syrup, whiskey or orange juice, and melted butter. Add chicken wings, stirring to coat with sauce.

3 Cover and cook on low-heat setting for 4 to 5 hours or on high-heat setting for 2 to 2½ hours.

4 Serve immediately or keep warm on low-heat setting for up to 2 hours.

Per serving: 180 cal., 11 g total fat (3 g sat. fat), 62 mg chol., 67 mg sodium, 7 g carbo., 0 g fiber, 10 g pro.

Southeast Asian flavors add zing to recipes. Here a taste of Thailand imbues ever-popular Buffalo wings.

THAI CHICKEN WINGS

24   chicken drummettes (about 2¼ pounds total)

½   cup purchased salsa

2   tablespoons creamy peanut butter

1   tablespoon lime juice

2   teaspoons soy sauce

2   teaspoons grated fresh ginger

¼   cup sugar

¼   cup creamy peanut butter

3   tablespoons soy sauce

3   tablespoons water

2   cloves garlic, minced

PREP: *20 minutes*

COOK: *5 to 6 hours on low-heat setting or 2½ to 3 hours on high-heat setting*

MAKES: *12 servings*

1 Place drummettes in a 3½- or 4-quart slow cooker. In a small bowl combine salsa, the 2 tablespoons peanut butter, the lime juice, the 2 teaspoons soy sauce, and the ginger. Pour over drummettes; toss to coat.

2 Cover and cook on low-heat setting for 5 to 6 hours or on high-heat setting for 2½ to 3 hours.

3 Meanwhile, for the peanut sauce, in a small saucepan whisk together sugar, the ¼ cup peanut butter, the 3 tablespoons soy sauce, the water, and garlic. Cook over medium-low heat until sugar is dissolved and mixture is smooth; set aside (mixture will thicken as it cools).

4 Drain drummettes, discarding cooking liquid. Return drummettes to slow cooker. Gently stir in peanut sauce. Serve immediately or keep warm in a covered slow cooker on low-heat setting for up to 2 hours.

Per serving: 189 cal., 13 g total fat (3 g sat. fat), 58 mg chol., 392 mg sodium, 6 g carbo., 1 g fiber, 12 g pro.

Honey and pineapple juice partner in a delicious marinade that doubles as a gorgeous glaze.

POLYNESIAN CHICKEN WINGS

PREP: *25 minutes*

COOL: *30 minutes*

MARINATE: *6 to 24 hours*

GRILL: *20 minutes*

MAKES: *12 servings*

½ cup unsweetened pineapple juice

¼ cup honey

¼ cup Worcestershire sauce

1 tablespoon grated fresh ginger or 1 teaspoon ground ginger

4 cloves garlic, minced

1 teaspoon salt

12 chicken wings (about 2½ pounds total)

1 fresh pineapple, cored, halved lengthwise, and cut into ½-inch-thick slices

1 For marinade, in a small saucepan stir together pineapple juice, honey, Worcestershire sauce, ginger, garlic, and salt. Bring to boiling; reduce heat. Simmer, uncovered, about 12 minutes or until marinade is reduced to ½ cup; stir occasionally. Cool about 30 minutes or until room temperature.

2 Bend the sections of each chicken wing back and forth at the large joint, breaking the cartilage connecting them. Use a knife or cleaver to cut through the cartilage and skin, cutting each wing into 2 sections. Place chicken pieces in a resealable plastic bag set in a shallow dish. Pour marinade over chicken pieces. Seal bag; turn to coat chicken. Marinate in the refrigerator for 6 to 24 hours, turning bag occasionally.

3 Drain chicken pieces, reserving marinade. For a charcoal grill, arrange medium-hot coals around a drip pan. Test for medium heat above pan. Place chicken pieces, bone sides down, on grill rack over pan. Cover and grill for 20 to 25 minutes or until chicken is no longer pink, brushing with reserved marinade during the first 15 minutes of grilling. Discard any remaining marinade.

4 Halve pineapple slices. Place on grill rack directly over the coals for the last 5 minutes of grilling; turn once. (For a gas grill, preheat grill. Reduce heat to medium. Adjust for indirect cooking. Place chicken [and later pineapple] on rack. Grill as above.)

Per serving: 167 cal., 8 g total fat (2 g sat. fat), 39 mg chol., 291 mg sodium, 14 g carbo., 1 g fiber, 10 g pro.

If you'd like to serve wine at your party, try a Shiraz. The deep, dark, fruity wine will bring forward the plum and ginger notes in this sophisticated take on drummies.

CHICKEN DRUMMETTES WITH PLUM SAUCE

¾ cup bottled plum sauce

¼ cup honey

¼ cup red wine vinegar

1 tablespoon sesame seeds, toasted*

1 tablespoon grated fresh ginger

2 cloves garlic, minced

36 chicken wing drummettes (about 3½ pounds total)

1 to 1¼ teaspoons five-spice powder

1 teaspoon salt

½ teaspoon black pepper

2 tablespoons olive oil

Blanched fresh pea pods (optional)

PREP: *35 minutes*

BAKE: *15 minutes*

MAKES: *36 drummettes*

1 For sauce, in a small saucepan combine plum sauce, honey, vinegar, sesame seeds, ginger, and garlic. Bring to boiling over medium heat, stirring occasionally; reduce heat. Simmer, uncovered, for 3 minutes to blend flavors. Remove from heat; set aside.

2 Preheat oven to 400°F. Spread drummettes in an even layer in a 15×10×1 inch baking pan. In a small bowl combine five-spice powder, salt, and pepper; sprinkle over drummettes in baking pan.

3 In a 12-inch nonstick skillet heat oil over medium heat. Add half of the drummettes to hot oil; cook about 10 minutes or until browned, turning occasionally to brown all sides. Return drummettes to the baking pan. Repeat with remaining drummettes.

4 Drizzle ⅔ cup of the sauce over drummettes. Bake for 15 to 20 minutes or until chicken is no longer pink. Reheat the remaining sauce and serve with hot drummettes. If desired, garnish with pea pods.

Per drummette: 87 cal., 5 g total fat (1 g sat. fat), 29 mg chol., 124 mg sodium, 5 g carbo., 0 g fiber, 4 g pro.

*TEST KITCHEN TIP: To toast sesame seeds, place seeds in a dry skillet. Cook over medium heat until seeds are golden brown, shaking skillet occasionally. Remove from heat.

In this tantalizing appetizer, flecks of dried cranberries add a colorful note to the lean rounds of homemade chicken sausage while the sour cream topper contributes just the right tang.

CRANBERRY CHICKEN PATTIES

PREP: *25 minutes*

BAKE: *20 minutes*

MAKES: *16 patties*

1	egg, lightly beaten
¾	cup fine dry bread crumbs
¼	cup snipped dried cranberries
2	tablespoons snipped fresh sage
½	teaspoon salt
1	pound uncooked ground chicken or ground turkey
1	recipe Sage Cream
¼	cup whole cranberry sauce

1 Preheat oven to 400°F. Line a 15×10×1-inch baking pan with foil; set aside. In a medium bowl combine egg, bread crumbs, dried cranberries, snipped sage, and salt. Add chicken; mix well. Form the mixture into sixteen 2-inch-wide patties. Place patties on prepared baking pan.

2 Bake about 20 minutes or until patties are done (165°F),* turning once. Serve warm with Sage Cream and cranberry sauce.

SAGE CREAM: In a small bowl stir together one 8-ounce carton dairy sour cream and 2 tablespoons snipped fresh sage or 1 teaspoon dried sage, crushed. Cover and chill until serving time.

Per patty: 104 cal., 6 g total fat (2 g sat. fat), 20 mg chol., 199 mg sodium, 7 g carbo., 0 g fiber, 6 g pro.

MAKE-AHEAD DIRECTIONS: Prepare as directed through Step 1. Cover and refrigerate for up to 24 hours. Continue as directed in Steps 2 and 3, except bake about 25 minutes or until patties are done (165°F),* turning once.

*****TEST KITCHEN TIP:** The internal color of a burger is not a reliable doneness indicator. A chicken or turkey patty cooked to 165°F is safe, regardless of color. To measure the doneness of a patty, insert an instant-read thermometer through the side of the patty to the center.

To make the meatballs even more healthful, ask your butcher for ultra-lean ground turkey breast.

CREOLE TURKEY MEATBALLS

Nonstick cooking spray
1 medium onion, chopped
1 medium green sweet pepper, chopped
½ cup quick-cooking rolled oats
1 egg, beaten
2 tablespoons milk
2 cloves garlic, minced
1 teaspoon dried Italian seasoning, crushed
1 teaspoon salt-free seasoning blend
1 teaspoon Creole seasoning
1 pound uncooked ground turkey or ground chicken

PREP: *25 minutes*
BAKE: *25 minutes*
MAKES: *10 servings*

1 Preheat oven to 375°F. Lightly coat a 15×10×1-inch baking pan with nonstick cooking spray; set aside. In a large bowl combine onion, sweet pepper, rolled oats, egg, milk, garlic, Italian seasoning, salt-free seasoning blend, and Creole seasoning. Add turkey; mix well.

2 Using a small ice cream scoop or slightly rounded measuring tablespoon, shape turkey mixture into 1¼-inch balls. Arrange in prepared pan. Bake about 25 minutes or until done (165°F).*

Per serving: 98 cal., 5 g total fat (1 g sat. fat), 57 mg chol., 52 mg sodium, 5 g carbo., 1 g fiber, 9 g pro.

MAKE-AHEAD DIRECTIONS: Prepare as directed through Step 2. Cover and chill for up to 24 hours. Uncover; bake as directed.

*TEST KITCHEN TIP: The internal color of a meatball is not a reliable doneness indicator. A turkey or chicken meatball cooked to 165°F is safe, regardless of color. To measure the doneness of a meatball, insert an instant-read thermometer into the center of the meatball.

Add color to the pizza toppings with thin slices of unpeeled green apple.

BARBECUED CHICKEN, APPLE & ONION PIZZA

PREP: *20 minutes*
BAKE: *10 minutes per batch*
MAKES: *32 wedges*

2   tablespoons butter or margarine

1   tart cooking apple, cored and thinly sliced

1   medium sweet onion (such as Vidalia, Maui, or Walla Walla), halved lengthwise and thinly sliced

2   10-ounce packages 8-inch Italian bread shells (such as Boboli brand) (4 shells) or four 8-inch Italian flatbreads (focaccia)

½   cup bottled barbecue sauce

2   cups shredded cooked chicken or turkey*

1   tablespoon snipped fresh oregano or thyme

1½   cups shredded Gouda or fontina cheese (6 ounces)

1 Preheat oven to 425°F. In a large skillet melt butter over medium heat. Add apple and onion; cook just until apple and onion are tender, stirring occasionally. Remove from heat.

2 Place bread shells or flatbreads on two large baking sheets. Spread barbecue sauce over bread shells. Divide chicken evenly among bread shells. Arrange apple and onion slices over top. Sprinkle with oregano; top with cheese.

3 Bake, one sheet at a time, about 10 minutes or until edges are lightly browned and chicken is hot. Cut each pizza into eight wedges.

Per wedge: 95 cal., 4 g total fat (1 g sat. fat), 17 mg chol., 185 mg sodium, 9 g carbo., 0 g fiber, 6 g pro.

*TEST KITCHEN TIP: Cook the chicken 24 hours ahead; cover and chill. Or purchase a roasted chicken from the supermarket or use leftover cooked turkey.

Sweet dried fruit, spicy salsa, and salty olives make this an out-of-the-ordinary pizza-style appetizer. (Recipe pictured on page 97.)

PICADILLO CHICKEN PIZZETTAS

1	6- or 6½-ounce package pizza crust mix
1	cup purchased salsa
¼	teaspoon ground cinnamon
¼	teaspoon ground cumin
2	cups sliced or chopped cooked chicken or turkey
½	cup dried cranberries or raisins
½	cup pimiento-stuffed green olives, coarsely chopped
¼	cup sliced green onions or chopped onion
1	tablespoon sliced almonds
1	cup shredded manchego or Monterey Jack cheese (4 ounces)
1	tablespoon snipped fresh cilantro

PREP: *25 minutes*
BAKE: *15 minutes*
MAKES: *24 servings*

1 Preheat oven to 425°F. Prepare pizza crust according to package directions. Pat dough into a greased 15×10×1-inch baking pan (crust will be thin). Bake for 5 minutes.

2 In a small bowl combine salsa, cinnamon, and cumin; spread evenly over crust. Top with chicken, cranberries or raisins, olives, green onion or onion, and almonds. Sprinkle with cheese.

3 Bake about 15 minutes or until edges of crust are golden brown. Remove from oven; sprinkle with cilantro. Cut into 12 pieces; cut each piece in half diagonally.

Per serving: 87 cal., 4 g total fat (1 g sat. fat), 15 mg chol., 226 mg sodium, 8 g carbo., 1 g fiber, 6 g pro.

If you can't find mini sweet peppers, plum tomatoes are an excellent alternative. Or spoon the chicken salad into halved regular-size peppers or tomatoes.

PESTO CHICKEN SALAD IN MINI PEPPERS

START TO FINISH:
35 minutes
MAKES: *20 servings*

20   mini sweet peppers (each 1½ to 2 inches long)

1   cup chopped cooked chicken or turkey (5 ounces)

2   tablespoons finely chopped onion

3   tablespoons purchased pesto

2   tablespoons mayonnaise or salad dressing

⅛   teaspoon black pepper

1 To make pepper shells, cut peppers lengthwise, removing the top one-third of each pepper and leaving stem on the other portion. Finely chop 2 tablespoons of the removed pepper and use for the salad (reserve remaining sweet pepper for another use). Remove seeds and membranes from pepper shells.

2 For chicken salad, in a small bowl combine chicken, onion, and the chopped sweet pepper. In a small bowl stir together pesto, mayonnaise, and black pepper. Add mayonnaise mixture to chicken mixture, stirring to combine.

3 To serve, divide chicken mixture among pepper shells. Arrange on a serving platter.

Per serving: 41 cal., 3 g total fat (1 g sat. fat), 7 mg chol., 35 mg sodium, 2 g carbo., 1 g fiber, 3 g pro.

PESTO CHICKEN SALAD IN TOMATO SHELLS: Cut 8 to 10 small plum tomatoes in half lengthwise. Scoop out and discard the tomato pulp, leaving ¼-inch-thick shells. Place tomato shells, cut sides down, on paper towels to drain. Let stand for 30 minutes. Just before serving, divide chicken mixture among tomato shells. Arrange on a serving platter. Makes 16 to 20 servings.

Per serving: 51 cal., 3 g total fat (1 g sat. fat), 9 mg chol., 45 mg sodium, 2 g carbo., 1 g fiber, 3 g pro.

MAKE-AHEAD DIRECTIONS: Prepare filled vegetables as directed. Arrange on a serving platter. Cover with plastic wrap; chill peppers in the refrigerator for up to 2 hours or tomatoes for up to 1 hour.

Cooked chicken, smoky-flavored almonds, Parmesan cheese, and golden raisins fill these plump, tender mushroom morsels with irresistible flavor.

CHICKEN & RAISIN-STUFFED MUSHROOMS

15	large fresh mushrooms (each 2½ to 3 inches in diameter)
2	green onions, thinly sliced
1	clove garlic, minced
3	tablespoons butter or margarine
¾	cup finely chopped cooked chicken or turkey (about 4 ounces)
2	tablespoons chopped golden raisins
2	tablespoons finely chopped smoky-flavored almonds
2	tablespoons fine dry bread crumbs
2	tablespoons freshly grated Parmesan cheese
1	tablespoon snipped fresh parsley
	Olive oil

PREP: *45 minutes*
BAKE: *13 minutes*
MAKES: *15 mushrooms*

1 Preheat oven to 425°F. Clean mushrooms with a damp paper towel. If desired, remove and discard stems from mushrooms. Set caps aside.

2 For filling, in a small saucepan cook green onions and garlic in hot butter about 2 minutes or until tender. Remove from heat. Stir in chicken, raisins, almonds, bread crumbs, Parmesan cheese, and parsley. Set filling aside.

3 Place mushrooms, stem sides down, in a 15×10×1-inch baking pan (if using mushrooms with stems intact, place stem sides up and omit the turning step). Bake for 5 minutes. Turn mushrooms stem sides up. Brush mushrooms with oil. Divide filling among mushrooms. Bake for 8 to 10 minutes more or until heated through. Serve immediately.

Per stuffed mushroom: 60 cal., 4 g total fat (2 g sat. fat), 13 mg chol., 65 mg sodium, 3 g carbo., 0 g fiber, 3 g pro.

Serve these as the opening act for your favorite stir-fry. Then round out the meal with hot tea and fortune cookies.

CHICKEN & RICE-FILLED SPRING ROLLS

PREP: *25 minutes*

CHILL: *1 to 2 hours*

MAKES: *24 servings*

8	8-inch dried rice papers
16	fresh thin asparagus spears, trimmed
1	cup finely chopped cooked chicken or turkey (5 ounces)
1	cup cooked long grain rice
¾	cup bottled sweet and sour sauce

1 Place some warm water in a shallow dish. Dip each rice paper in the warm water and then place between damp towels for 5 minutes.

2 Meanwhile, in a covered large saucepan cook asparagus spears in lightly salted boiling water for 3 minutes. Drain; rinse with cold water. Drain again.

3 In a medium bowl stir together chicken, rice, and ¼ cup of the sweet and sour sauce. Place two of the asparagus spears about 1 inch from the bottom edge of one of the rice papers. Place ¼ cup of the chicken mixture on top of the asparagus. Fold up the bottom edge of the rice paper over the filling. Fold in sides. Roll up. Repeat with remaining rice papers, asparagus, and chicken mixture.

4 Cover and chill spring rolls for 1 to 2 hours. Cut each spring roll into thirds. Serve with the remaining ½ cup sweet and sour sauce.

Per serving: 56 cal., 1 g total fat (0 g sat. fat), 5 mg chol., 35 mg sodium, 12 g carbo., 1 g fiber, 3 g pro.

On the hotness scale, poblano peppers fall in the mild to medium range. Larger than many chile peppers, poblanos grow up to 5 inches long. Look for them in Mexican markets and large supermarkets.

CHICKEN & POBLANO-STUFFED BUNS

1	tablespoon olive oil or cooking oil
1	medium fresh poblano chile pepper, seeded and chopped* (½ cup)
⅓	cup chopped onion
1	clove garlic, minced
1½	cups finely chopped cooked chicken or turkey (about 8 ounces)
1	large tomato, peeled, seeded, and chopped (about 1 cup)
1	teaspoon vinegar
¼	teaspoon salt
¼	teaspoon ground cumin
¼	teaspoon black pepper
1	16-ounce package frozen white roll dough (12 rolls), thawed
¾	cup shredded asadero or Monterey Jack cheese (3 ounces)
	Yellow cornmeal (optional)

PREP: *35 minutes*

RISE: *30 minutes*

BAKE: *18 minutes*

MAKES: *12 buns*

1 For filling, in a large skillet heat oil over medium heat. Add chile pepper, onion, and garlic; cook until tender. Stir in chicken, tomato, vinegar, salt, cumin, and black pepper. Cook and stir about 4 minutes or until no liquid remains. Remove from heat. Set aside.

2 On a lightly floured surface, roll each dough ball into a 5-inch circle. Spoon 2 tablespoons of the filling onto each dough circle. Sprinkle cheese over filling. Lightly brush edges of dough with water. Bring up sides of dough around filling; pinch edges of dough to seal.

3 Place buns, seam sides down, on greased baking sheet. Cover; let rise in a warm place until puffed (about 30 minutes). (Or cover and chill for 2 to 8 hours; let stand at room temperature 20 minutes before baking.)

4 Meanwhile, preheat oven to 375°F. Lightly brush the bun tops with water. If desired, sprinkle with cornmeal. Bake for 18 to 20 minutes or until golden brown. Serve immediately.

Per bun: 173 cal., 6 g total fat (2 g sat. fat), 23 mg chol., 289 mg sodium, 20 g carbo., 1 g fiber, 9 g pro.

*TEST KITCHEN TIP: Because chile peppers contain volatile oils that can burn your skin and eyes, avoid direct contact with them as much as possible. When working with chile peppers, wear plastic or rubber gloves. If your bare hands do touch the peppers, wash your hands and nails well with soap and warm water.

If you don't have any leftover cooked chicken, stop by your supermarket's deli counter and pick up a whole roasted chicken. It yields about 2 cups of cooked chicken. Freeze half for another time.

CHICKEN-PESTO TRIANGLES

PREP: *30 minutes*

BAKE: *15 minutes*

MAKES: *16 triangles*

1   15-ounce package rolled refrigerated unbaked piecrust (2 crusts)

1   cup diced cooked chicken or turkey (5 ounces)

¼   cup slivered almonds or pine nuts, toasted and coarsely chopped

⅓   cup purchased pesto

2   tablespoons butter or margarine, melted

1   tablespoon sesame seeds or snipped fresh parsley

1 Let piecrusts stand at room temperature according to package directions. Preheat oven to 400°F.

2 For filling, in a medium bowl stir together chicken and nuts. Add pesto; toss until moistened.

3 Unroll one piecrust on a lightly floured surface; press flat with your fingers. Cut piecrust into eight wedges. Spoon 1 tablespoon of the filling onto each pastry wedge, placing filling near rounded edge. Brush edges of pastry wedges with water. Fold the pointed end of each pastry wedge over filling, then fold the two corners over filling, pressing gently to seal. Place filled triangles on an ungreased baking sheet. Brush with melted butter; sprinkle with sesame seeds or parsley. Repeat with remaining piecrust and filling.

4 Bake for 15 to 18 minutes or until pastry is golden brown. Serve warm.

Per triangle: 193 cal., 13 g total fat (4 g sat. fat), 14 mg chol., 180 mg sodium, 14 g carbo., 0 g fiber, 4 g pro.

CHICKEN-PESTO TARTS: For tart shells, use a 2-inch round cutter to cut piecrust dough into rounds; press rounds into 1¾-inch muffin pans to make shells. Spoon filling into shells. Bake as directed. Makes 48 tarts.

Per tart: 64 cal., 4 g total fat (1 g sat. fat), 5 mg chol., 60 mg sodium, 5 g carbo., 0 g fiber, 1 g pro.

Because English cucumber slices have very few seeds, they make the ideal base for these lively turkey-and-nut canapés. (Recipe pictured on page 98.)

MACADAMIA TURKEY SALAD ON CUCUMBER SLICES

½   cup finely chopped cooked turkey or chicken
     (about 3 ounces)

½   of a small apple, chopped

2   tablespoons mayonnaise dressing

1   tablespoon bottled chutney (snip any large fruit pieces)

1   tablespoon snipped fresh chives or sliced green onion

½   teaspoon grated fresh ginger or ⅛ teaspoon ground ginger

¼   cup chopped macadamia nuts, cashews, or peanuts

24   ¼-inch-thick cucumber slices

PREP: *25 minutes*
CHILL: *2 hours*
MAKES: *12 servings*

1 In a small bowl combine turkey, apple, mayonnaise dressing, chutney, chives or green onion, and ginger. Cover and chill for 2 hours. Just before serving, stir in half of the nuts.

2 To serve, spoon a scant tablespoon of the turkey mixture onto each cucumber slice. Sprinkle with remaining nuts.

Per serving: 54 cal., 4 g total fat (0 g sat. fat), 5 mg chol., 35 mg sodium, 2 g carbo., 0 g fiber, 2 g pro.

These turkey-and-tortilla wraps slice into festive bite-size rounds for party nibbling.

TURKEY-MANGO PINWHEELS

PREP: *20 minutes*

CHILL: *30 minutes to 4 hours*

MAKES: *16 servings*

6 ounces soft goat cheese (chèvre)

⅓ cup mango chutney (snip any large fruit pieces)

4 10-inch flour tortillas

8 ounces thinly sliced smoked turkey breast or smoked chicken breast

2 cups arugula leaves or fresh spinach leaves

8 refrigerated mango slices, drained and patted dry

1 In a small bowl stir together goat cheese and mango chutney. Spread goat cheese mixture onto tortillas, leaving a 1-inch space along one edge of each tortilla.

2 Arrange turkey slices on goat cheese mixture. Top with arugula leaves. Cut any large mango slices in half lengthwise. Place mango slices on arugula along the edge opposite the 1-inch space. Roll up tortillas, starting with the edge with the mango. Cover and chill for 30 minutes to 4 hours.

3 To serve, cut diagonally into ¾-inch-thick slices.

Per serving: 104 cal., 3 g total fat (2 g sat. fat), 11 mg chol., 242 mg sodium, 13 g carbo., 0 g fiber, 6 g pro.

Excellent chutney choices for these mini sandwiches are cranberry, apple-curry, and mango.

TINY TURKEY TEA SANDWICHES

1	recipe Tiny Sweet Potato Biscuits
⅔	cup fruit chutney (snip any large fruit pieces)
1	cup mesclun, fresh baby spinach, or arugula, stems trimmed
3	ounces thinly sliced Havarti or Muenster cheese, cut to fit biscuits
6	ounces thinly sliced smoked turkey or smoked chicken, cut and folded to fit biscuits

PREP: *35 minutes*
BAKE: *12 minutes*
MAKES: *24 sandwiches*

1 Prepare Tiny Sweet Potato Biscuits. Use a fork to split the cooled biscuits in half.

2 To assemble sandwiches, spread chutney on the cut sides of each biscuit. Top each biscuit bottom with 1 or 2 mesclun leaves, some of the cheese, and some of the turkey. Place biscuit tops on top of turkey. If necessary, use a sandwich pick to hold each sandwich together.

TINY SWEET POTATO BISCUITS: Preheat oven to 425°F. In a large bowl stir together 1½ cups all-purpose flour, 1 tablespoon sugar, 1 teaspoon baking powder, ½ teaspoon baking soda, and ½ teaspoon salt. Using a pastry blender, cut in ¼ cup cold butter until mixture resembles coarse crumbs. Make a well in the center of the flour mixture. In a small bowl stir together ½ cup buttermilk and ½ cup mashed cooked sweet potato. Add sweet potato mixture to flour mixture, stirring just until combined. Turn out dough onto a well-floured surface. Knead by folding and gently pressing dough for 10 to 12 strokes. Lightly roll or pat dough until ½ inch thick. Using a floured 1½-inch biscuit cutter, cut dough into circles. Place biscuits 1 inch apart on an ungreased large baking sheet. Reroll scraps. Bake for 12 to 14 minutes or until biscuits are light brown. Transfer biscuits to a wire rack and let cool. Makes 24 biscuits.

Per sandwich: 90 cal., 4 g total fat (1 g sat. fat), 15 mg chol., 216 mg sodium, 10 g carbo., 1 g fiber, 4 g pro.

MAKE-AHEAD DIRECTIONS: Prepare and bake biscuits as directed; cool completely. Place biscuits in a freezer container or bag. Seal and freeze for up to 3 months. Thaw at room temperature.

This appetizer holds well for up to an hour—but it's so good, it will likely be long gone before then!

TURKEY KIELBASA BITES

PREP: *10 minutes*

COOK: *3 to 4 hours on low-heat setting or 1½ to 2 hours on high-heat setting*

MAKES: *10 to 12 servings*

1   16-ounce package cooked turkey kielbasa, cut into 1-inch pieces

1   12-ounce carton cranberry-orange or cranberry-raspberry crushed fruit

1   tablespoon Dijon-style mustard

¼   teaspoon crushed red pepper

1 In a 1½-quart slow cooker combine kielbasa, cranberry-orange crushed fruit, Dijon mustard, and crushed red pepper.

2 Cover and cook on low-heat setting for 3 to 4 hours or on high-heat setting for 1½ to 2 hours. If no heat setting is available, cook for 2½ to 3 hours.

3 Serve immediately or keep warm, covered, on warm setting or low-heat setting (if available) for up to 1 hour. Serve kielbasa with wooden toothpicks.

Per serving: 126 cal., 4 g total fat (1 g sat. fat), 28 mg chol., 441 mg sodium, 15 g carbo., 0 g fiber, 7 g pro.

A CHICKEN IN EVERY POT

2

No matter whether it's chicken and
noodle, chili, or chowder, each of these
hearty soups and stews is delicious
spoonful after spoonful.

The thickening mixture of flour and oil is called a roux. It should be cooked to a coppery color, similar to that of a tarnished penny. Getting just the right color takes a while, so be patient and keep stirring!

CHICKEN-SAUSAGE GUMBO

PREP: *45 minutes*
COOK: *1 hour*
MAKES: *10 servings*

1   cup all-purpose flour
⅔   cup cooking oil
1   cup sliced celery
1   cup chopped green sweet pepper
½   cup chopped onion
2   cloves garlic, minced
8   ounces cooked smoked sausage, cut into 1-inch pieces
8   ounces andouille sausage, cut into ½-inch pieces
2   pounds meaty chicken pieces (breast halves, thighs, and/or drumsticks), skinned if desired
5   cups water
1   teaspoon salt
¼   to ½ teaspoon cayenne pepper
¼   teaspoon black pepper
      Hot cooked rice (optional)

1 For roux, in large heavy Dutch oven stir together flour and oil until smooth. Cook over medium-high heat for 5 minutes. Reduce heat to medium. Cook and stir for 10 to 15 minutes or until roux is reddish brown in color (the deeper the color, the richer and more flavorful the gumbo will be). Stir in celery, sweet pepper, onion, and garlic; cook for 5 minutes more, stirring occasionally. Add sausages and cook until lightly browned.

2 Add chicken, the water, salt, cayenne pepper, and black pepper to sausage mixture. Bring to boiling; reduce heat. Cover and simmer about 1 hour or until chicken is tender and no longer pink (170°F for breasts; 180°F for thighs and drumsticks).

3 Skim off fat. Remove chicken from sausage mixture in Dutch oven; let cool slightly. When chicken is cool enough to handle, remove meat from bones; discard bones. Coarsely chop chicken and return to sausage mixture. Cook for 2 to 3 minutes or until chicken is heated through. If desired, serve with rice.

Per serving: 460 cal., 34 g total fat (9 g sat. fat), 72 mg chol., 961 mg sodium, 12 g carbo., 1 g fiber, 25 g pro.

With the rich hues of red, green, and yellow, this beautiful chowder is as pleasing to the eye as it is to the palate. Aromatic cumin and coriander add great depth to the flavor.

CHICKEN CHOWDER

1   tablespoon olive oil or cooking oil

1   pound skinless, boneless chicken breasts, cut into cubes

1   medium onion, chopped

1   medium red, green, or yellow sweet pepper, coarsely chopped

3   cloves garlic, minced

2   or 3 fresh jalapeño chile peppers, seeded and finely chopped (see tip, page 19)

2   small zucchini and/or yellow summer squash, coarsely chopped

2   14-ounce cans reduced-sodium chicken broth

1   10-ounce package frozen baby lima beans or one 12-ounce package frozen sweet soybeans (edamame)

2   teaspoons ground cumin

2   teaspoons ground coriander

¼   teaspoon salt

¼   teaspoon black pepper

1   8-ounce carton dairy sour cream

2   tablespoons all-purpose flour

Salt

Black pepper

1 In a 4-quart Dutch oven heat oil over medium heat. Add chicken, onion, sweet pepper, garlic, and chile peppers; cook and stir until chicken is browned and vegetables are tender. Add zucchini; cook for 2 minutes more. Add chicken broth, lima beans or soybeans, cumin, coriander, the ¼ teaspoon salt, and the ¼ teaspoon black pepper. Bring to boiling; reduce heat. Simmer, uncovered, for 5 minutes.

2 In a small bowl stir together sour cream and flour. Whisk into soup mixture. Cook and stir until thickened and bubbly; cook and stir for 1 minute more. Season to taste with additional salt and black pepper.

Per serving: 291 cal., 12 g total fat (6 g sat. fat), 62 mg chol., 730 mg sodium, 21 g carbo., 5 g fiber, 25 g pro.

MAKE-AHEAD DIRECTIONS: Prepare chowder as directed through Step 1. Transfer chowder to a freezer container. Cover and freeze for up to 1 month. To serve, thaw chowder in refrigerator for 24 hours. Transfer chowder to a 4-quart Dutch oven. Bring to boiling, stirring frequently. Continue with Step 2.

This chicken-and-vegetable soup owes its extraordinary flavor to Yukon gold potato, artichoke hearts, and a blend of seasonings.

CHICKEN & ARTICHOKE SOUP

PREP: *40 minutes*
COOK: *55 minutes*
MAKES: *5 or 6 servings*

3	tablespoons butter
1	large onion, finely chopped
1	stalk celery, sliced
2	cloves garlic, minced
3	tablespoons all-purpose flour
2	14-ounce cans reduced-sodium chicken broth
2	cups water
8	ounces skinless, boneless chicken breasts, cut into 1-inch pieces
1	large Yukon gold potato, peeled and chopped (1 cup)
1	medium carrot, sliced
1	14½-ounce can diced tomatoes
1½	teaspoons snipped fresh rosemary or ½ teaspoon dried rosemary, crushed
1½	teaspoons snipped fresh thyme or ½ teaspoon dried thyme, crushed
1½	teaspoons snipped fresh parsley or ½ teaspoon dried parsley flakes
½	teaspoon salt
¼	teaspoon black pepper
¼	teaspoon cayenne pepper
1	14-ounce can artichoke hearts, drained and quartered
2	tablespoons grated Parmesan cheese

1 In a 4-quart Dutch oven melt butter over medium heat. Add onion and celery; cook about 4 minutes or until tender. Add garlic; cook for 1 minute more. Stir in flour; cook for 1 minute. Stir in chicken broth, the water, chicken, potato, carrot, undrained tomatoes, dried herbs (if using), salt, black pepper, and cayenne pepper. Bring to boiling; reduce heat. Cover and simmer for 55 minutes.

2 Stir in artichoke hearts and fresh herbs (if using). Heat through. Sprinkle individual servings with Parmesan cheese.

Per serving: 237 cal., 8 g total fat (5 g sat. fat), 46 mg chol., 1,141 mg sodium, 23 g carbo., 5 g fiber, 17 g pro.

Gravy mix and cheese spread give this chicken-and-potato medley delightful body and creaminess.

TEX-MEX CHEESY CHICKEN CHOWDER

1   tablespoon cooking oil

1   large onion, chopped

1   cup thinly sliced celery

2   cloves garlic, minced

1½   pounds skinless, boneless chicken breasts,
     cut into bite-size pieces

1   32-ounce package frozen diced hash brown potatoes

2   14-ounce cans chicken broth

1   2.64-ounce package country gravy mix

2   cups milk

1   16-ounce jar chunky salsa

1   8-ounce package pasteurized prepared cheese product,
     cut into chunks

1   4-ounce can diced green chile peppers

     Corn chips

START TO FINISH:
45 minutes

MAKES: *16 servings*

1 In a 6-quart Dutch oven heat oil over medium heat. Add onion, celery, and garlic; cook about 5 minutes or until onion is tender. Add chicken; cook and stir for 2 to 3 minutes or until chicken is no longer pink. Add potatoes and chicken broth. Bring to boiling; reduce heat. Cover and simmer for 12 to 15 minutes or until potatoes are tender, stirring occasionally.

2 In a medium bowl dissolve gravy mix in milk; stir into chicken mixture. Stir in salsa, cheese, and chile peppers; reduce heat to low. Cook and stir until cheese is melted. Serve with corn chips.

Per serving: 303 cal., 15 g total fat (5 g sat. fat), 35 mg chol., 857 mg sodium, 26 g carbo., 2 g fiber, 16 g pro.

Garlic, ginger, red curry paste, cumin, basil, and cilantro blend with coconut milk and soy sauce to give this Asian-style meal-in-a-bowl fabulous flavor. (Recipe pictured on page 99.)

CONFETTI CHICKEN SOUP

START TO FINISH:
40 minutes

MAKES: *6 servings*

2   tablespoons cooking oil

1   pound skinless, boneless chicken breasts, cut into 1-inch cubes

8   cloves garlic, minced

4   teaspoons minced fresh ginger

1   tablespoon red curry paste or ¼ teaspoon cayenne pepper

1   teaspoon ground cumin

4   cups water

1   14-ounce can unsweetened coconut milk

2   cups shredded carrot

2   cups small broccoli florets

1   medium red sweet pepper, cut into bite-size strips

2   3-ounce packages chicken-flavor ramen noodles, coarsely broken

2   cups fresh pea pods, halved crosswise

2   tablespoons soy sauce

4   teaspoons lime juice

1   cup slivered fresh basil

⅓   cup snipped fresh cilantro

1 In a 4-quart Dutch oven heat 1 tablespoon of the oil over medium-high heat. Add chicken; cook for 3 to 4 minutes or until no longer pink and lightly browned. Remove chicken and set aside.

2 Add the remaining 1 tablespoon oil to Dutch oven. Add garlic, ginger, curry paste or cayenne pepper, and cumin; cook and stir for 30 seconds. Stir in the water, coconut milk, carrot, broccoli, sweet pepper, and noodles (set seasoning packets aside).

3 Bring to boiling; reduce heat. Cover and simmer for 3 minutes. Stir in cooked chicken, contents of the seasoning packets, pea pods, soy sauce, and lime juice. Stir in basil and cilantro.

Per serving: 454 cal., 25 g total fat (12 g sat. fat), 44 mg chol., 1,087 mg sodium, 33 g carbo., 4 g fiber, 26 g pro.

If you have some cooked chicken left over from a prior meal, skip cooking the chicken in Step 1 and add the chicken to the soup in Step 2. Doing so shaves minutes off the prep time.

CHICKEN SOUP WITH BARLEY

12	ounces skinless, boneless chicken breasts or thighs or turkey breast tenderloins, cut into bite-size pieces
1	tablespoon cooking oil
½	cup chopped onion
½	cup chopped red or green sweet pepper
1	clove garlic, minced
2	14-ounce cans reduced-sodium chicken broth
1½	cups loose-pack frozen cut green beans
1	cup loose-pack frozen whole kernel corn or one 8-ounce can whole kernel corn, drained
⅓	cup quick-cooking barley
2	tablespoons snipped fresh basil or 1½ teaspoons dried basil, crushed
¼	teaspoon salt
¼	teaspoon black pepper

PREP: *35 minutes*
COOK: *10 minutes*
MAKES: *4 servings*

1 In a Dutch oven cook and stir chicken in hot oil for 5 minutes. Using a slotted spoon, remove chicken from Dutch oven, reserving drippings. In pan drippings, cook onion, sweet pepper, and garlic for 3 minutes, stirring occasionally. Drain off fat.

2 Return chicken to Dutch oven. Add chicken broth, green beans, corn, uncooked barley, dried basil (if using), salt, and black pepper. Bring to boiling; reduce heat. Cover and simmer for 10 to 15 minutes or until barley is cooked. Stir in fresh basil (if using).

Per serving: 253 cal., 7 g total fat (1 g sat. fat), 60 mg chol., 686 mg sodium, 26 g carbo., 4 g fiber, 24 g pro.

Chase away the cold with this salsa-spiked bowl of red. Let each person dress up the chili by choosing from the variety of toppers.

CHICKEN SALSA CHILI

PREP: *25 minutes*

COOK: *25 minutes*

MAKES: *6 to 8 servings*

3	tablespoons olive oil
1½	cups chopped yellow onion
6	cloves garlic, minced
1	pound skinless, boneless chicken breasts, cut into bite-size pieces
2	15-ounce cans dark red kidney beans, rinsed and drained
1	29-ounce can tomato puree
1	28-ounce can whole peeled tomatoes, cut up
1	15-ounce can garbanzo beans (chickpeas), rinsed and drained
1	14-ounce can chicken broth
2	to 3 tablespoons salt-free chili powder or chili powder
2	teaspoons finely chopped fresh jalapeño chile pepper (see tip, page 19)
½	teaspoon crushed red pepper
⅓	cup snipped fresh cilantro
2	tablespoons lime juice
	Salt
	Black pepper
	Dairy sour cream (optional)
	Finely chopped red onion (optional)
	Shredded cheddar cheese (optional)
	Corn chips (optional)

1 In a 4-quart Dutch oven heat oil over medium-high heat. Add onion and garlic; cook about 5 minutes or until tender. Add chicken; cook and stir for 2 minutes more. Stir in kidney beans, tomato puree, undrained tomatoes, garbanzo beans, chicken broth, chili powder, chile pepper, and crushed red pepper. Bring to boiling; reduce heat. Cover and simmer for 20 minutes. Uncover and simmer for 5 minutes more. Remove from heat; stir in cilantro and lime juice. Season to taste with salt and black pepper.

2 If desired, top individual servings with sour cream, chopped red onion, cheese, and corn chips. Serve immediately.

Per serving: 423 cal., 10 g total fat (1 g sat. fat), 45 mg chol., 1,095 mg sodium, 55 g carbo., 15 g fiber, 35 g pro.

Israeli couscous is larger and has a slightly more "toothy" texture than other couscous. It is available in many grocery stores and specialty food shops. You can make this stew with all chicken pieces: Substitute 12 chicken thighs for the duck and cook the thighs along with the drumsticks.

CHICKEN & DUCK STEW

12	chicken drumsticks (about 3 pounds total), skinned if desired
3	boneless duck breast halves, skinned and quartered
¼	cup olive oil
3	cups assorted sliced fresh mushrooms (such as cremini, shiitake, oyster, and/or button)
2	medium onions, sliced
3	cloves garlic, minced
6	medium tomatoes, seeded and chopped (about 3 cups)
3	medium green sweet peppers, cut into 1-inch pieces
1½	cups dry Marsala or beef broth
1	6-ounce can tomato paste
¾	cup pitted kalamata olives and/or green olives
2	tablespoons balsamic vinegar
1	teaspoon salt
¼	teaspoon black pepper
¼	cup snipped fresh oregano or marjoram
2	tablespoons snipped fresh rosemary
6	cups hot cooked Israeli couscous or couscous

PREP: *1 hour*
COOK: *45 minutes*
MAKES: *12 servings*

1 In a 6-quart Dutch oven cook chicken drumsticks and duck, half at a time, in hot oil about 15 minutes or until lightly browned, turning to brown evenly. Remove poultry from Dutch oven, reserving drippings in the Dutch oven; set chicken aside. Cover and chill the duck portions in the refrigerator while cooking vegetables and chicken.

2 Add mushrooms, onions, and garlic to drippings in Dutch oven. Cook and stir about 5 minutes or just until vegetables are tender. Return chicken to Dutch oven.

3 Meanwhile, in a large bowl combine tomatoes, sweet peppers, Marsala, tomato paste, olives, balsamic vinegar, salt, and black pepper. Pour over chicken in Dutch oven. Bring to boiling; reduce heat. Cover and simmer for 20 minutes. Add duck. Return to boiling; reduce heat. Cover and simmer for 25 to 30 minutes more or until poultry is tender. Stir in oregano and rosemary. Serve stew with couscous.

Per serving: 393 cal., 14 g total fat (3 g sat. fat), 129 mg chol., 407 mg sodium, 28 g carbo., 3 g fiber, 33 g pro.

Quinoa, a staple in South American cooking, is a cream-colored, bead-shaped grain that's a tasty replacement for rice in soups and stews such as this one.

PERUVIAN CHICKEN RAGOUT

PREP: *35 minutes*
COOK: *15 minutes*
MAKES: *6 servings*

1	pound skinless, boneless chicken thighs, cut into 1-inch pieces
2	tablespoons all-purpose flour
1	teaspoon chili powder
½	teaspoon salt
½	teaspoon black pepper
1	tablespoon cooking oil
1	medium onion, chopped
1	clove garlic, minced
1	28-ounce can diced tomatoes
1	14-ounce can chicken broth
1	medium potato, peeled and diced
1	cup loose-pack frozen whole kernel corn
½	cup quinoa
2	cups packed fresh spinach leaves
	Finely shredded lemon peel (set aside)
2	tablespoons lemon juice

1 In a large resealable plastic bag combine chicken, flour, chili powder, salt, and pepper. Seal and shake to coat.

2 In a 4- to 6-quart Dutch oven heat oil over medium heat. Add chicken mixture, onion, and garlic; cook until browned, stirring occasionally. Add undrained tomatoes, chicken broth, potato, corn, and quinoa. Bring to boiling; reduce heat. Cover and simmer for 15 to 20 minutes or until potato and quinoa are tender.

3 Stir in spinach and lemon juice; cook just until spinach is wilted. Sprinkle individual servings with shredded lemon peel.

Per serving: 262 cal., 7 g total fat (1 g sat. fat), 63 mg chol., 761 mg sodium, 30 g carbo., 4 g fiber, 20 g pro.

Dress up this stew by topping it with toasted slices of Parmesan cheese-sprinkled French bread. (Recipe pictured on page 99.)

CARAWAY CHICKEN STEW

PREP: *45 minutes*
COOK: *50 minutes*
MAKES: *6 servings*

3	pounds chicken thighs and/or bone-in chicken breasts, skinned and fat removed
3¾	cups water
2	teaspoons instant chicken bouillon granules
1	teaspoon salt
1	teaspoon caraway seeds, crushed
¼	teaspoon black pepper
8	ounces fresh green beans, trimmed and cut into 2-inch-long pieces
2	medium carrots, peeled and cut into ¾-inch chunks
2	stalks celery, bias-cut into ½-inch-thick slices
2	cups sliced fresh shiitake, cremini, oyster, and/or button mushrooms
1	cup pearl onions, peeled
¼	cup all-purpose flour
¼	cup cold water

1 In a 4-quart Dutch oven combine chicken, the 3¾ cups water, the bouillon granules, salt, caraway seeds, and pepper. Bring to boiling; reduce heat. Cover and simmer for 40 minutes. Stir in green beans, carrots, celery, mushrooms, and pearl onions. Return to boiling; reduce heat. Cover and simmer about 10 minutes or until chicken is tender and no longer pink.

2 Remove chicken pieces from the stew; let cool slightly. When cool enough to handle, remove meat from bones; discard bones. Cut up the meat; add to vegetable mixture in Dutch oven. In a small bowl combine flour and the ¼ cup cold water; whisk until smooth. Add to stew. Cook and stir until thickened and bubbly. Cook and stir for 1 minute more.

Per serving: 229 cal., 5 g total fat (1 g sat. fat), 107 mg chol., 783 mg sodium, 18 g carbo., 4 g fiber, 28 g pro.

Besides the familiar onions, this soup contains three other members of the onion family—leeks, green onions, and shallots.

TURKEY ONION SOUP

PREP: *45 minutes*

COOK: *1 hour*

MAKES: *6 servings*

1	tablespoon cooking oil
3	medium onions, chopped
3	medium leeks, chopped
3	carrots, sliced
3	stalks celery, sliced
1	bunch green onions, sliced
3	shallots, finely chopped
1	2½-pound turkey breast half, skinned
5½	cups water
¼	cup snipped fresh parsley
1½	teaspoons dried oregano, crushed
1½	teaspoons dried Greek seasoning
1	teaspoon salt
1	teaspoon fennel seeds, crushed
½	teaspoon freshly ground black pepper
2	bay leaves

1 In a 4-quart Dutch oven heat oil over medium-high heat. Add onions, leeks, carrots, celery, green onions, and shallots; cook for 7 to 10 minutes or until tender. Add turkey breast half, the water, parsley, oregano, Greek seasoning, salt, fennel seeds, pepper, and bay leaves. Bring to boiling; reduce heat. Cover and simmer for 1 to 2 hours or until turkey breast is tender.

2 Remove turkey from Dutch oven; let cool slightly. When cool enough to handle, remove meat from bones; discard bones. Chop meat and return to Dutch oven. Discard bay leaves.

Per serving: 227 cal., 5 g total fat (1 g sat. fat), 80 mg chol., 522 mg sodium, 12 g carbo., 3 g fiber, 33 g pro.

Purchased salsa saves you the effort of chopping tomatoes, onions, and peppers for this chili.

ZESTY BLACK BEAN CHILI

PREP: *10 minutes*
COOK: *20 minutes*
MAKES: *4 servings*

8	ounces cooked turkey kielbasa, halved lengthwise and sliced
1	16-ounce jar thick and chunky salsa
1	15- to 16-ounce can black beans, rinsed and drained
1½	cups vegetable juice or hot-style vegetable juice
¼	cup water
2	teaspoons chili powder
2	cloves garlic, minced, or ¼ teaspoon garlic powder
	Dairy sour cream or plain low-fat yogurt (optional)
	Sliced green onion and/or chopped red onion (optional)
	Chopped avocado (optional)

1 In a large saucepan stir together turkey kielbasa, salsa, black beans, vegetable juice, the water, chili powder, and garlic. Bring to boiling; reduce heat. Cover and simmer for 20 minutes, stirring occasionally. If desired, top individual servings with sour cream, onion, and avocado.

Per serving: 219 cal., 6 g total fat (2 g sat. fat), 35 mg chol., 1,891 mg sodium, 33 g carbo., 6 g fiber, 16 g pro.

For a little extra flavor, use fire-roasted diced tomatoes or diced tomatoes with Italian herbs.

GROUND CHICKEN & BARLEY SOUP

PREP: *25 minutes*

COOK: *1 hour*

MAKES: *6 servings*

Nonstick cooking spray

1 pound uncooked ground chicken or turkey

5 cups water

1 14½-ounce can diced tomatoes

1 cup vegetable juice or hot-style vegetable juice

⅓ cup quick-cooking barley

⅓ cup dry split peas, rinsed and drained

¾ teaspoon salt

½ teaspoon dried oregano, crushed

¼ teaspoon dried basil, crushed

¼ teaspoon black pepper

1 bay leaf

2 stalks celery with leaves, cut into ½-inch pieces

1 medium carrot, cut into ½-inch pieces

Salt (optional)

1 Lightly coat an unheated 4-quart Dutch oven or pot with nonstick cooking spray. Preheat Dutch oven over medium heat. Add ground chicken to hot Dutch oven; cook about 5 minutes or until no longer pink, stirring occasionally. Drain off fat. Stir in the water, undrained tomatoes, vegetable juice, uncooked barley, split peas, the ¾ teaspoon salt, the oregano, basil, black pepper, and bay leaf. Bring to boiling; reduce heat. Cover and simmer for 30 minutes.

2 Stir in celery and carrot. Cover and simmer about 30 minutes more or until vegetables and barley are tender. Discard bay leaf. If desired, season to taste with additional salt.

Per serving: 243 cal., 10 g total fat (0 g sat. fat), 0 mg chol., 585 mg sodium, 19 g carbo., 5 g fiber, 17 g pro.

Using no-salt-added tomatoes and rinsing the beans and hominy help keep the sodium levels in this lively chili in check.

CHIPOTLE CHILI WITH HOMINY

Nonstick cooking spray

8	ounces uncooked ground chicken or turkey breast
1	cup chopped onion
1½	teaspoons ground cumin
½	teaspoon dried oregano, crushed
2	14½-ounce cans no-salt-added stewed tomatoes
1	15-ounce can red beans, rinsed and drained
1	15-ounce can yellow hominy, rinsed and drained
1	small green or red sweet pepper, chopped
½	cup water
1	to 2 teaspoons chopped canned chipotle chile peppers in adobo sauce (see tip, page 19)
6	tablespoons shredded cheddar cheese (optional)

START TO FINISH:
30 minutes

MAKES: *6 servings*

1 Lightly coat an unheated large saucepan with nonstick cooking spray. Preheat saucepan over medium heat. Add ground chicken and onion; cook until browned. If necessary, drain off fat. Stir cumin and oregano into chicken mixture; cook for 1 minute more. Add undrained tomatoes, red beans, hominy, sweet pepper, the water, and chile peppers. Bring to boiling; reduce heat. Cover and simmer for 5 minutes.

2 If desired, sprinkle individual servings with cheese.

Per serving: 239 cal., 6 g total fat (0 g sat. fat), 0 mg chol., 474 mg sodium, 35 g carbo., 9 g fiber, 13 g pro.

There's no need to head to a Mexican restaurant when you can have this hearty, satisfying Tex-Mex favorite on your table in minutes.

CHICKEN TORTILLA SOUP

START TO FINISH:
30 minutes

MAKES: *6 servings*

1   2- to 2¼-pound purchased roasted chicken

2   14-ounce cans chicken broth with roasted garlic

1   15-ounce can chopped tomatoes and green chile peppers

1   11-ounce can whole kernel corn with sweet peppers, drained

1   small fresh jalapeño chile pepper, seeded and finely chopped (see tip, page 19)

1   teaspoon ground cumin

2   tablespoons snipped fresh cilantro

1   tablespoon lime juice

Tortilla chips with lime or regular tortilla chips, broken

1 Remove meat from chicken; discard skin and bones. Shred enough of the meat to measure 2 cups; set aside. Refrigerate any remaining meat for another use.

2 In a large saucepan combine chicken broth, undrained tomatoes, corn, chile pepper, and cumin. Bring to boiling; reduce heat. Cover and simmer for 10 minutes. Stir in shredded chicken, cilantro, and lime juice. Heat through. Top individual servings with tortilla chips.

Per serving: 183 cal., 5 g total fat (1 g sat. fat), 43 mg chol., 1,080 mg sodium, 18 g carbo., 2 g fiber, 16 g pro.

You'll find two kinds of sesame oil at the supermarket. Light-colored sesame oil is mild in flavor and is used as a cooking oil. Toasted sesame oil has a deep, nutty flavor and is used in small amounts for seasoning. Look for toasted sesame oil in the Asian food section.

CHICKEN & VEGETABLE SOUP

2	14-ounce cans chicken broth
2	cups loose-pack frozen stir-fry vegetables (any combination)
1	9-ounce package refrigerated or frozen chopped cooked chicken breast
1	tablespoon soy sauce
1	to 2 teaspoons hot chili sauce
½	teaspoon toasted sesame oil
¼	teaspoon ground ginger
1	3-ounce package chicken-flavor ramen noodles, broken
2	tablespoons sliced green onion

START TO FINISH:
25 minutes

MAKES: *4 servings*

1 In a large saucepan combine chicken broth, frozen vegetables, chicken, soy sauce, chili sauce, sesame oil, and ginger. Bring to boiling; reduce heat. Cover and simmer for 5 minutes.

2 Stir in ramen noodles (discard seasoning packet). Return to boiling; reduce heat. Cover and simmer about 3 minutes more or until vegetables and noodles are tender. Top individual servings with green onion.

Per serving: 251 cal., 7 g total fat (2 g sat. fat), 74 mg chol., 1,126 mg sodium, 20 g carbo., 2 g fiber, 26 g pro.

The flavors of the Mediterranean shine in this combination of zucchini, garlic, fresh herb, and Madeira. It's a sunny twist on old-fashioned chicken and rice soup.

WILD RICE CHICKEN SOUP

START TO FINISH:
25 minutes

MAKES: *6 servings*

1	6.2-ounce package quick-cooking long grain and wild rice mix
2	14-ounce cans reduced-sodium chicken broth
1	tablespoon snipped fresh thyme or 1 teaspoon dried thyme, crushed
4	cloves garlic, minced
4	cups chopped tomatoes
1	9-ounce package frozen chopped cooked chicken
1	cup finely chopped zucchini
¼	teaspoon freshly ground black pepper
1	tablespoon Madeira or dry sherry

1 Prepare rice mix according to package directions, except omit the seasoning packet and the margarine.

2 Meanwhile, in a Dutch oven combine chicken broth, dried thyme (if using), and garlic; bring to boiling. Stir in tomato, chicken, zucchini, pepper, and fresh thyme (if using). Return to boiling; reduce heat. Cover and simmer for 5 minutes. Stir in cooked rice and Madeira. Heat through.

Per serving: 223 cal., 4 g total fat (1 g sat. fat), 38 mg chol., 793 mg sodium, 30 g carbo., 3 g fiber, 18 g pro.

There are dozens of versions of mulligatawny soup, a curry-seasoned favorite from Southern India. This one features tart apples and carrot.

MULLIGATAWNY SOUP

1	tablespoon cooking oil
1	cup chopped onion
1	cup coarsely chopped carrot
1	cup sliced celery
1⅓	cups chopped tart apples
2	to 3 teaspoons curry powder
¼	teaspoon salt
3	cups reduced-sodium chicken broth
3	cups water
1	14½-ounce can no-salt-added stewed tomatoes
2	cups chopped cooked chicken or turkey (10 ounces)

PREP: *40 minutes*
COOK: *20 minutes*
MAKES: *6 servings*

1 In a Dutch oven heat oil over medium heat. Add onion, carrot, and celery; cook and stir about 10 minutes or until crisp-tender. Reduce heat to medium-low; add apple, curry powder, and salt. Cover and cook for 5 minutes.

2 Stir in chicken broth, the water, and undrained tomatoes. Bring to boiling; reduce heat. Simmer, uncovered, for 10 minutes. Stir in cooked chicken; simmer for 10 minutes more.

Per serving: 173 cal., 6 g total fat (1 g sat. fat), 42 mg chol., 498 mg sodium, 14 g carbo., 3 g fiber, 16 g pro.

Great Northern beans and a hint of half-and-half make this sophisticated chili different from the traditional bowl of red.

WHITE BEAN CHILI

START TO FINISH:
50 minutes

MAKES: *8 servings*

1	tablespoon butter
1½	cups finely chopped celery
1	cup finely chopped onion
1	cup finely chopped green sweet pepper
3	cloves garlic, minced
2	15- to 16-ounce cans Great Northern or white kidney beans (cannellini beans), rinsed and drained
2	14-ounce cans chicken broth
3	cups cubed cooked chicken or turkey (about 1 pound)
1	cup purchased salsa
2	teaspoons ground cumin
2	bay leaves
½	cup half-and-half, light cream, or whipping cream
2	tablespoons cornstarch
	Salt
	Black pepper
	Purchased salsa (optional)
	Sliced green onions (optional)

1 In a 4-quart Dutch oven melt butter over medium heat. Add celery, onion, sweet pepper, and garlic; cook until tender. Add beans, chicken broth, chicken, the 1 cup salsa, the cumin, and bay leaves. Bring to boiling; reduce heat. Simmer, uncovered, for 10 minutes.

2 In a screw-top jar combine half-and-half and cornstarch. Cover and shake well; stir into chili. Cook and stir until slightly thickened and bubbly. Cook and stir for 2 minutes more. Season to taste with salt and black pepper. Discard bay leaves.

3 If desired, top individual servings with additional salsa and sliced green onion.

Per serving: 298 cal., 8 g total fat (3 g sat. fat), 57 mg chol., 746 mg sodium, 32 g carbo., 7 g fiber, 25 g pro.

Leafy green kale, red lentils, and tomato add nutrients as well as great taste to this homey soup.

KALE, LENTIL & CHICKEN SOUP

1 tablespoon olive oil

1 cup chopped onion

1 cup coarsely chopped carrot

2 cloves garlic, minced

6 cups reduced-sodium chicken broth

1 tablespoon snipped fresh basil or 1 teaspoon dried basil, crushed

4 cups coarsely chopped kale (about 8 ounces)

½ teaspoon salt

⅛ teaspoon black pepper

1½ cups cubed cooked chicken or turkey (about 8 ounces)

1 medium tomato, seeded and chopped

½ cup dry red lentils*

PREP: *35 minutes*

COOK: *25 minutes*

MAKES: *6 servings*

1 In a large saucepan heat oil over medium low heat. Add onion, carrot, and garlic. Cover and cook for 5 to 7 minutes or until vegetables are nearly tender, stirring occasionally.

2 Add chicken broth and dried basil (if using) to vegetable mixture. Bring to boiling; reduce heat. Cover and simmer for 10 minutes. Stir in kale, salt, and pepper. Return to boiling; reduce heat. Cover and simmer for 10 minutes.

3 Stir in cooked chicken, tomato, red lentils, and fresh basil (if using). Cover and simmer for 5 to 10 minutes more or until kale and lentils are tender.

Per serving: 199 cal., 5 g total fat (1 g sat. fat), 31 mg chol., 833 mg sodium, 20 g carbo., 5 g fiber, 18 g pro.

*TEST KITCHEN TIP: If you wish to substitute brown or yellow lentils for the red lentils, you'll need to increase the cooking time. Check package directions for cooking times and add the lentils in Step 2.

To speed up the last-minute preparation, bake the butternut squash ahead of time and store it, covered, in the refrigerator overnight.

CURRIED SQUASH & CHICKEN BISQUE

PREP: *35 minutes*

BAKE: *50 minutes*

MAKES: *5 or 6 servings*

2 pounds butternut squash

1 medium onion, chopped

1 tablespoon olive oil

2 cloves garlic, minced

2 tablespoons grated fresh ginger

2 cups cubed cooked chicken or turkey (10 ounces)

1 14-ounce can chicken broth

1 13½-ounce can unsweetened coconut milk

¼ cup water

2 to 3 teaspoons curry powder

½ teaspoon salt

⅛ teaspoon black pepper

2 cups hot cooked brown rice

¼ cup snipped fresh cilantro

¼ cup chopped cashews

1 Preheat oven to 350°F. Cut squash in half lengthwise; remove and discard seeds. Arrange the squash halves, cut sides down, in a 3-quart rectangular baking dish. Bake for 30 minutes. Turn squash halves cut sides up. Bake, covered, for 20 to 25 minutes more or until squash is tender. Let cool slightly. Carefully scoop the pulp from squash halves into a medium bowl; discard shells. Mash squash slightly with a potato masher; set aside.

2 In a large saucepan cook onion in hot oil for 3 to 4 minutes or until tender. Add garlic and ginger; cook and stir for 1 minute more. Carefully stir in mashed squash, chicken, chicken broth, coconut milk, the water, curry powder, salt, and pepper. Cook over medium heat until heated through, stirring occasionally.

3 To serve, spoon hot rice and chicken mixture into bowls. Sprinkle with cilantro and cashews.

Per serving: 465 cal., 26 g total fat (15 g sat. fat), 50 mg chol., 684 mg sodium, 37 g carbo., 4 g fiber, 24 g pro.

You won't have to call your children twice when you serve this creamy carrot- and rice-loaded chicken soup for dinner. They'll be asking for seconds.

CREAMY CHICKEN & RICE SOUP

1	tablespoon butter or margarine
½	cup chopped onion
½	cup sliced celery
½	cup sliced carrot or fresh mushrooms
1	14-ounce can reduced-sodium chicken broth
1	10¾-ounce can reduced-fat and reduced-sodium condensed cream of chicken soup
1	cup water
1	6¼-ounce package chicken-flavor rice pilaf mix
⅛	teaspoon black pepper
2½	cups milk
2	cups chopped cooked chicken or turkey (10 ounces)
	Snipped fresh parsley (optional)

PREP: *35 minutes*
COOK: *20 minutes*
MAKES: *6 servings*

1 In a large saucepan melt butter over medium heat. Add onion, celery, and carrot or mushrooms; cook until tender.

2 Add chicken broth, cream of chicken soup, and the water. Stir in pilaf mix with the seasoning packet and pepper. Bring to boiling; reduce heat. Cover and simmer about 20 minutes or until rice is tender, stirring occasionally.

3 Stir in milk and cooked chicken; heat through. If desired, sprinkle individual servings with snipped parsley.

Per serving: 303 cal., 9 g total fat (4 g sat. fat), 60 mg chol., 979 mg sodium, 34 g carbo., 1 g fiber, 22 g pro.

Tailor this soup to your family's tastes. Just add whichever vegetables everybody likes best.

CHOOSE-A-VEGETABLE CHICKEN SOUP

START TO FINISH:
40 minutes

MAKES: *6 servings*

2   14-ounce cans reduced-sodium chicken broth

2   cups water

¼   teaspoon black pepper

1   cup dried twisted spaghetti or broken fusilli pasta

3   cups vegetable pieces (such as thinly sliced carrots, small broccoli florets, chopped green or red sweet pepper, and/or fresh or frozen whole kernel corn)

1½   cups cubed cooked chicken or turkey (about 8 ounces)

1   tablespoon snipped fresh basil

¼   cup finely shredded Parmesan cheese (1 ounce)

1 In a Dutch oven combine chicken broth, the water, and black pepper; bring to boiling. Stir in the uncooked pasta. Return to boiling; reduce heat. Cover and simmer for 5 minutes. Stir in vegetables. Return to boiling; reduce heat. Cover and simmer for 5 to 8 minutes more or until vegetables and pasta are tender. Stir in chicken and basil; heat through. Sprinkle individual servings with Parmesan cheese.

Per serving: 172 cal., 4 g total fat (2 g sat. fat), 35 mg chol., 447 mg sodium, 18 g carbo., 2 g fiber, 16 g pro.

Bits of spinach, carrot, and artichoke color this creamy chicken soup. Serve it as a main dish for four or as an elegant first course for eight.

CHICKEN, ARTICHOKE & BRIE SOUP

¼	cup butter or margarine
1	cup chopped carrot
1	cup sliced celery
1	cup chopped onion
2	cloves garlic, minced
2	14-ounce cans chicken broth
½	teaspoon white pepper
¼	teaspoon salt
2	cups half-and-half, light cream, or whole milk
¼	cup all-purpose flour
1½	cups cubed cooked chicken or turkey (about 8 ounces)
1	cup whipping cream
½	of a 10-ounce package frozen chopped spinach, thawed and well drained
½	of an 8- or 9-ounce package frozen artichoke hearts, thawed and cut into bite-size pieces
1	4½-ounce round Brie or Camembert cheese, rind removed and cut up
	Purchased croutons (optional)

START TO FINISH:
45 minutes

MAKES: *4 main-dish or 8 appetizer servings*

1 In a large saucepan melt butter over medium heat. Add carrot, celery, onion, and garlic; cook and stir until tender. Add chicken broth, white pepper, and salt. Bring to boiling; reduce heat. Simmer, uncovered, for 15 minutes.

2 In a large screw-top jar combine half-and-half and flour; cover and shake well. Stir into soup. Cook and stir until thickened and bubbly.

3 Stir in chicken, whipping cream, spinach, artichoke hearts, and Brie. Cook and stir over medium-low heat about 5 minutes more or until heated through and cheese is melted. (Stir constantly to make sure soup doesn't scorch on bottom of saucepan.) If desired, serve topped with croutons.

Per serving: 770 cal., 61 g total fat (36 g sat. fat), 238 mg chol., 1,449 mg sodium, 25 g carbo., 5 g fiber, 31 g pro.

A south-of-the-border flavor dominates this thick, savory chowder. Green chile peppers provide a kick, and cilantro, a prominent herb in Mexican foods, adds an air of authenticity.

CHICKEN & CORN CHOWDER

START TO FINISH:
40 minutes

MAKES: *4 servings*

½	cup chopped onion
1	tablespoon butter or margarine
2	cups fresh or frozen whole kernel corn
1½	cups reduced-sodium chicken broth
1½	cups chopped, peeled potato
1	4-ounce can diced green chile peppers, drained
¼	teaspoon coarsely ground black pepper
2	cups milk
2	tablespoons all-purpose flour
5	ounces cooked chicken, cut into thin strips
2	tablespoons snipped fresh cilantro or 2 teaspoons snipped fresh oregano

1 In a large saucepan cook onion in hot butter for 3 to 4 minutes or until tender. Add corn, chicken broth, potato, chile peppers, and black pepper. Bring to boiling; reduce heat. Cover and simmer about 15 minutes or until potato is tender, stirring occasionally.

2 In a screw-top jar combine milk and flour; cover and shake well. Add to potato mixture. Cook and stir until thickened and bubbly. Add chicken and cilantro. Heat through.

Per serving: 311 cal., 9 g total fat (4 g sat. fat), 49 mg chol., 446 mg sodium, 40 g carbo., 4 g fiber, 20 g pro.

This soup combines nutty wild rice with a rich, creamy blend of chicken, mushrooms, and whipping cream.

VEGETABLE-WILD RICE SOUP

3	14-ounce cans chicken broth
1	cup chopped carrot
½	cup wild rice, rinsed and drained
½	cup chopped celery
½	cup chopped onion
2	cups sliced fresh mushrooms
2	tablespoons butter
¼	cup all-purpose flour
¼	teaspoon salt
¼	teaspoon black pepper
1	cup whipping cream
2	cups chopped cooked chicken or turkey (10 ounces)
	Snipped fresh chives (optional)

PREP: *30 minutes*
COOK: *35 minutes*
MAKES: *6 to 8 servings*

1 In a 4-quart Dutch oven combine two cans of the broth, the carrot, uncooked wild rice, celery, and onion. Bring to boiling; reduce heat. Cover and simmer for 35 to 40 minutes or until wild rice is tender but still chewy, adding mushrooms for the last 5 minutes of cooking.

2 Meanwhile, in a medium saucepan melt butter over medium heat. Stir in flour, salt, and pepper. Add the remaining one can broth. Cook and stir until thickened and bubbly. Cook and stir for 1 minute more; stir in whipping cream.

3 Add whipping cream mixture to wild rice mixture, stirring constantly. Stir in chicken; heat through. If desired, garnish with chives.

Per serving: 364 cal., 24 g total fat (12 g sat. fat), 109 mg chol., 1,016 mg sodium, 20 g carbo., 2 g fiber, 20 g pro.

Need a quick meal? Dress up cooked turkey or chicken with cheese ravioli, veggies, and Italian seasoning. (Recipe pictured on page 100.)

TURKEY RAVIOLI SOUP

START TO FINISH:
30 minutes

MAKES: *6 servings*

6 cups reduced-sodium chicken broth

¾ cup chopped red sweet pepper

½ cup chopped onion

1½ teaspoons dried Italian seasoning, crushed

1 9-ounce package refrigerated light cheese ravioli

1½ cups cooked turkey or chicken cut into bite-size pieces (about 8 ounces)

2 cups shredded fresh spinach

Shredded Parmesan cheese (optional)

1 In a Dutch oven combine chicken broth, sweet pepper, onion, and Italian seasoning. Bring to boiling; reduce heat. Cover and simmer for 5 minutes. Add ravioli and turkey. Return to boiling; reduce heat. Simmer, uncovered, about 6 minutes or just until ravioli is tender. Stir in spinach. If desired, sprinkle individual servings with Parmesan cheese.

Per serving: 246 cal., 7 g total fat (3 g sat. fat), 48 mg chol., 879 mg sodium, 24 g carbo., 2 g fiber, 22 g pro.

Queso fresco is a mild Mexican cheese with a crumbly texture similar to that of feta or farmer's cheese. Look for it at Hispanic food markets or larger supermarkets.

YUCATAN-STYLE TURKEY SOUP

PREP: *50 minutes*
COOK: *15 minutes*
MAKES: *6 servings*

1	medium onion, thinly sliced
3	or 4 cloves garlic
1	tablespoon cooking oil
2	canned chipotle chile peppers in adobo sauce, drained and chopped (see tip, page 19)
2	medium carrots, chopped
5	cups reduced-sodium chicken broth or turkey stock
2	cups coarsely chopped tomatoes
1/8	teaspoon salt
1	pound cooked turkey or chicken, cubed or shredded (about 3 cups)
2	small zucchini, chopped (2 cups)
2	tablespoons snipped fresh cilantro
1	avocado, halved, seeded, peeled, and chopped
1	lime, cut into wedges
1/3	cup crumbled queso fresco or feta cheese
6	fresh cilantro sprigs

1 In a dry medium skillet combine onion slices and unpeeled garlic cloves; cook and stir for 3 to 5 minutes or until edges are brown. Chop onion; peel and slice garlic cloves.

2 In a 4-quart Dutch oven heat oil over medium-high heat. Add chopped onion, sliced garlic, and chipotle peppers. Cook and stir for 3 minutes. Add carrots. Cook and stir for 3 minutes more.

3 Add chicken broth, tomato, and salt. Bring to boiling; reduce heat. Cover and simmer for 10 minutes. Add turkey, zucchini, and snipped cilantro; cover and cook for 5 minutes more.

4 Serve with avocado, lime wedges, queso fresco, and cilantro sprigs.

Per serving: 229 cal., 8 g total fat (2 g sat. fat), 65 mg chol., 609 mg sodium, 12 g carbo., 4 g fiber, 27 g pro.

This recipe is a terrific way to use leftover turkey. But if you don't have any, buy a cooked turkey breast half or refrigerated or frozen chopped cooked chicken.

TURKEY & SWEET POTATO CHOWDER

PREP: *35 minutes*

COOK: *12 minutes*

MAKES: *5 servings*

1 large potato, peeled if desired and chopped (about 1½ cups)

1 14-ounce can reduced-sodium chicken broth

2 small ears frozen corn-on-the-cob, thawed, or 1 cup loose-pack frozen whole kernel corn

12 ounces cooked turkey breast or cooked chicken breast, cut into ½-inch cubes

1½ cups milk

1 large sweet potato, peeled and cut into ¾-inch cubes (about 1½ cups)

⅛ to ¼ teaspoon black pepper

¼ cup coarsely snipped fresh flat-leaf parsley

1 In a large saucepan combine chopped potato and chicken broth. Bring to boiling; reduce heat. Simmer, uncovered, about 12 minutes or until potato is tender, stirring occasionally. Remove from heat. Do not drain. Using a potato masher, mash potato until mixture is thickened and nearly smooth.

2 If using corn-on-the-cob, cut the kernels from one of the ears of corn. Carefully cut the second ear of corn crosswise into ½-inch-thick slices.

3 Stir corn, turkey, milk, sweet potato, and pepper into potato mixture in saucepan. Bring to boiling; reduce heat. Cover and simmer for 12 to 15 minutes or until sweet potato is tender.

4 Sprinkle individual servings with parsley.

Per serving: 250 cal., 4 g total fat (2 g sat. fat), 53 mg chol., 293 mg sodium, 27 g carbo., 3 g fiber, 27 g pro.

This soup makes a great nutritious meal—it's filling, satisfying, and low in calories and fat.

TURKEY & RICE SOUP

2	14-ounce cans reduced-sodium chicken broth
1½	cups water
1	teaspoon snipped fresh rosemary or ¼ teaspoon dried rosemary, crushed
¼	teaspoon black pepper
½	cup thinly sliced carrot
½	cup thinly sliced celery
⅓	cup chopped onion
1	cup instant rice
½	cup loose-pack frozen cut green beans
2	cups chopped cooked turkey or chicken (10 ounces)
1	14½-ounce can diced tomatoes
	Fresh rosemary sprigs (optional)

START TO FINISH:
45 minutes

MAKES: *6 servings*

1 In a large saucepan or Dutch oven combine chicken broth, the water, snipped or dried rosemary, and pepper. Add carrot, celery, and onion. Bring to boiling.

2 Stir in uncooked rice and green beans. Return to boiling; reduce heat. Cover and simmer for 10 to 12 minutes or until vegetables are tender. Stir in turkey and undrained tomatoes; heat through. If desired, garnish with rosemary sprigs.

Per serving: 177 cal., 2 g total fat (1 g sat. fat), 35 mg chol., 500 mg sodium, 20 g carbo., 1 g fiber, 17 g pro.

It's hard to guess what you'll enjoy more—how easy this soup is to assemble or its smoky, Southwestern flavor!

SMOKED TURKEY CHUCKWAGON SOUP

START TO FINISH:
20 minutes

MAKES: *4 servings*

2   14-ounce cans reduced-sodium chicken broth

1   15-ounce can white hominy, drained

1   11-ounce can condensed tomato rice soup

2   cups chopped smoked turkey (10 ounces)

½   cup chopped yellow sweet pepper

⅓   cup purchased salsa

1   teaspoon ground cumin

1½   cups crushed tortilla chips (2½ ounces)

    Dairy sour cream (optional)

1 In a large saucepan combine chicken broth, hominy, tomato rice soup, smoked turkey, sweet pepper, salsa, and cumin. Bring to boiling; reduce heat. Simmer, uncovered, about 5 minutes or until sweet pepper is tender.

2 Top individual servings with tortilla chips and, if desired, sour cream.

Per serving: 318 cal., 10 g total fat (2 g sat. fat), 38 mg chol., 2,013 mg sodium, 39 g carbo., 5 g fiber, 20 g pro.

GARDEN-FRESH SALADS

There's nothing better than one
of these tempting poultry salads
when you want a meal
that's light yet satisfying.

For an even quicker dish, replace the green beans and edamame with 8 cups torn romaine lettuce.

SPICED CHICKEN & BEAN SALAD

START TO FINISH:
30 minutes

MAKES: *4 servings*

2   tablespoons olive oil

1   teaspoon ground coriander

1   teaspoon ground cumin

½   teaspoon salt

½   teaspoon ground cinnamon

¼   teaspoon cayenne pepper

1¼   pounds skinless, boneless chicken thighs

1   cup fresh or frozen green and/or wax beans

1   cup frozen edamame (green soy beans) or lima beans

1   avocado, halved, seeded, peeled, and sliced

3   ounces blue cheese, broken into chunks

¼   cup bottled creamy garlic, cucumber ranch, or Italian vinaigrette salad dressing

1 Heat a nonstick or well-seasoned grill pan on range top over medium heat. In a small bowl combine oil, coriander, cumin, salt, cinnamon, and cayenne pepper. Trim fat from chicken thighs. Brush oil mixture on both sides of chicken thighs.

2 Place chicken on hot grill pan. Cook about 12 minutes or until chicken is tender and no longer pink (180°F), turning once. Transfer chicken to a cutting board. Cut each chicken thigh into three pieces.

3 Meanwhile, in a covered large saucepan cook fresh green and/or wax beans in enough boiling water to cover for 10 to 15 minutes or until crisp-tender. (If using frozen green and/or wax beans, cook for 5 to 10 minutes or until crisp-tender.) Using a slotted spoon,* remove beans and set aside. Add edamame or lima beans to boiling water. Cover and cook for 4 to 6 minutes or until tender. Drain well.

4 Arrange chicken, green and/or wax beans, edamame or lima beans, avocado, and cheese on salad plates or a platter. Drizzle with dressing.

Per serving: 543 cal., 35 g total fat (9 g sat. fat), 129 mg chol., 880 mg sodium, 15 g carbo., 7 g fiber, 43 g pro.

*TEST KITCHEN TIP: If you do not have a slotted spoon, place green and/or wax beans in a heatproof strainer. Lower strainer into boiling water and cook as directed above. Lift strainer out of water to drain. Cook edamame or lima beans as directed above.

You can blend this great-tasting homemade berry dressing in minutes. Frozen raspberries are the foundation for its delicious flavor.

CHICKEN SALAD WITH BERRY DRESSING

PREP: *25 minutes*

BROIL: *12 minutes*

MAKES: *4 servings*

1   10-ounce package frozen red raspberries, thawed

2   tablespoons olive oil or salad oil

2   tablespoons lemon juice

1   clove garlic, minced

4   skinless, boneless chicken breast halves
    (about 1¼ pounds total)

2   tablespoons honey mustard

7   cups torn mixed salad greens

2   medium oranges, peeled and sectioned

1   avocado, halved, seeded, peeled, and sliced lengthwise

1   pink grapefruit, peeled and sectioned

2   green onions, thinly bias-sliced

1 Preheat broiler. For raspberry dressing, in a blender or food processor combine raspberries, oil, lemon juice, and garlic. Cover and blend or process until smooth. Strain dressing through a sieve; discard seeds. Cover and chill dressing until serving time.

2 Place chicken on the unheated rack of a broiler pan. Broil 4 to 5 inches from the heat for 12 to 15 minutes or until tender and no longer pink (170°F), turning once and brushing with honey mustard during the last 2 minutes of broiling. Cool chicken slightly; slice into ¼-inch-wide strips.

3 In a large bowl toss together chicken, greens, oranges, avocado, and grapefruit. Divide greens mixture among four dinner plates. Sprinkle with green onions. Drizzle salads with raspberry dressing.

Per serving: 475 cal., 16 g total fat (2 g sat. fat), 82 mg chol., 155 mg sodium, 49 g carbo., 8 g fiber, 36 g pro.

Personalize this simple salad with your favorite salad dressing.

CHICKEN TOSSED SALAD

START TO FINISH:
30 minutes

MAKES: *4 servings*

4 skinless, boneless chicken breast halves (about 1¼ pounds total)

1 tablespoon olive oil

¼ teaspoon garlic-pepper blend

8 cups torn mixed salad greens

1 medium yellow or red sweet pepper, cut into bite-size strips

1 medium tomato, cut into wedges

½ cup bottled salad dressing (such as a berry or roasted garlic vinaigrette or Parmesan-basil Italian)

¼ cup crumbled feta cheese (1 ounce)

¼ cup purchased croutons

1 Brush chicken breasts with olive oil; sprinkle with garlic-pepper blend. In a medium nonstick skillet cook chicken over medium heat for 10 to 12 minutes or until no longer pink (170°F), turning once. Cool chicken slightly; cut into bite-size strips. Set aside.

2 In a large serving bowl toss greens, sweet pepper, and tomato; add dressing and toss to coat. Top with chicken, feta cheese, and croutons.

Per serving: 321 cal., 13 g total fat (2 g sat. fat), 88 mg chol., 320 mg sodium, 16 g carbo., 2 g fiber, 36 g pro.

This main-dish mango-dressed salad makes a spectacular showing on a buffet table. Remember it the next time you're planning a buffet-style meal.

MANGO CHICKEN SALAD

2	mangoes, seeded, peeled, and coarsely chopped
⅓	cup olive oil
2	tablespoons sherry vinegar or red wine vinegar
½	teaspoon sugar
4	skinless, boneless chicken breast halves (about 1¼ pounds total)
8	cups torn mixed salad greens
½	cup coarsely chopped pecans, walnuts, or almonds or ¼ cup pine nuts, toasted
3	green onions, cut diagonally into ½-inch-long pieces
3	slices bacon, crisp-cooked, drained, and crumbled
¼	cup olive oil
1	tablespoon sherry vinegar or red wine vinegar
½	teaspoon sea salt or kosher salt
¼	teaspoon freshly ground black pepper

PREP: *25 minutes*
BROIL: *12 minutes*
MAKES: *6 servings*

1 Preheat broiler. For mango vinaigrette, in a food processor or blender combine chopped mangoes, the ⅓ cup oil, the 2 tablespoons sherry vinegar, and the sugar. Cover; process or blend until mixture is smooth. Cover and chill in the refrigerator while preparing salad.

2 Place chicken on the unheated rack of a broiler pan. Broil 4 to 5 inches from the heat for 12 to 15 minutes or until chicken is tender and no longer pink (170°F), turning once halfway through broiling.

3 Meanwhile, in a large bowl combine greens, nuts, green onions, and bacon. Toss gently to mix. In a small bowl whisk together the ¼ cup oil, the 1 tablespoon sherry vinegar, the salt, and pepper. Drizzle over salad mixture. Toss gently to mix. Arrange on a large serving platter.

4 Cut chicken into bite-size strips. Arrange chicken on top of the greens mixture. Stir chilled mango vinaigrette; spoon over chicken.

Per serving: 437 cal., 31 g total fat (4 g sat. fat), 59 mg chol., 288 mg sodium, 16 g carbo., 3 g fiber, 25 g pro.

GRILLING DIRECTIONS: For a charcoal grill, place chicken on the rack of an uncovered grill directly over medium coals. Grill for 12 to 15 minutes or until chicken is tender and no longer pink (170°F), turning once halfway through grilling. (For a gas grill, preheat grill. Reduce heat to medium. Place chicken on rack over heat. Cover and grill as above.)

A sprinkle of chopped peanuts adds extra crunch to the spicy chicken strips and red onion nestled in lettuce leaves. The spiciness of this dish depends on the brand of Thai dressing you use.

THAI CHICKEN IN LETTUCE CUPS

START TO FINISH:
25 minutes

MAKES: *4 servings*

12	ounces chicken breast tenderloins
¼	cup bottled Thai ginger salad dressing and marinade
½	cup thinly sliced red onion
4	butterhead (Boston or Bibb) lettuce cups
3	tablespoons coarsely chopped dry roasted peanuts

1 In a medium bowl combine chicken and salad dressing; toss to coat. Let stand at room temperature for 10 minutes.

2 Heat a large skillet over medium-high heat for 2 minutes; add undrained chicken mixture and red onion. Cook and stir for 3 to 5 minutes or until chicken is tender and no longer pink and onion is tender.

3 Divide chicken mixture among lettuce cups. Sprinkle with peanuts.

Per serving: 156 cal., 5 g total fat (1 g sat. fat), 49 mg chol., 392 mg sodium, 6 g carbo., 0 g fiber, 22 g pro.

Shortcut the preparation time by using seasoned cooked or grilled chicken strips, available in your grocer's refrigerated section.

SESAME VEGETABLE SALAD

1 pound chicken breast tenderloins, halved crosswise

 Salt

 Black pepper

1 tablespoon olive oil or cooking oil

1 pound fresh asparagus, trimmed

1 pound fresh sugar snap peas or pea pods, trimmed

6 cups watercress, tough stems removed

2 medium yellow sweet peppers, cut into thin strips

1 cup grape tomatoes

1 recipe Garlic Ginger Soy Dressing

1 tablespoon sesame seeds, toasted

PREP: *35 minutes*

CHILL: *1 hour*

MAKES: *12 servings*

1 Sprinkle chicken lightly with salt and pepper. In a large skillet heat oil over medium-high heat. Add chicken; cook for 6 to 8 minutes or until chicken is tender and no longer pink, turning to brown evenly. Remove chicken from skillet and cool slightly; place in an airtight container. Chill for 1 hour.

2 In a covered large saucepan cook asparagus and sugar snap peas in a small amount of boiling salted water for 2 to 4 minutes or until crisp-tender. Drain; rinse with cold water. Drain well.

3 To serve, in a very large bowl toss together chilled chicken, asparagus, sugar snap peas, watercress, sweet peppers, and tomatoes. Add Garlic Ginger Soy Dressing; toss well. Sprinkle with sesame seeds.

GARLIC GINGER SOY DRESSING: In a screw-top jar combine ½ cup rice vinegar; ⅓ cup olive oil; 1 clove garlic, minced; 2 teaspoons honey; 2 teaspoons soy sauce; 1 teaspoon sesame seeds, toasted; ¾ teaspoon ground ginger; ¼ teaspoon salt; and ⅛ teaspoon black pepper. Cover and shake well.

Per serving: 158 cal., 8 g total fat (1 g sat. fat), 22 mg chol., 159 mg sodium, 9 g carbo., 2 g fiber, 11 g pro.

MAKE-AHEAD DIRECTIONS: Prepare as directed through Step 2. Chill chicken and vegetables separately for up to 48 hours. Prepare dressing as directed; cover and chill for up to 1 week. Serve as directed in Step 3, shaking dressing before using.

The tang from the lime juice in the dressing counterbalances the heat from the chili powder. (Recipe pictured on page 101.)

CHILI-LIME CHICKEN SALAD

START TO FINISH:
25 minutes

MAKES: *4 servings*

1   pound chicken breast tenderloins*

2   teaspoons chili powder

⅛   teaspoon salt

⅛   teaspoon black pepper

1   tablespoon olive oil

¼   cup olive oil or salad oil

3   tablespoons lime juice

2   tablespoons snipped fresh cilantro

1   tablespoon white wine vinegar

¼   teaspoon salt

    Dash black pepper

6   cups torn romaine lettuce

8   cherry tomatoes, halved or quartered

½   of a medium avocado, halved, seeded, peeled, and sliced

1 In a medium bowl toss chicken breast tenderloins with chili powder, the ⅛ teaspoon salt, and the ⅛ teaspoon pepper. In a large skillet heat the 1 tablespoon oil over medium-high heat. Add chicken mixture; reduce heat to medium. Cook for 8 to 12 minutes or until chicken is no longer pink, turning once.

2 Meanwhile, for dressing, in a screw-top jar combine the ¼ cup oil, the lime juice, cilantro, white wine vinegar, the ¼ teaspoon salt, and the dash pepper. Cover and shake well.

3 Arrange romaine on four salad plates. Top with chicken, tomatoes, and avocado. Drizzle with dressing.

Per serving: 284 cal., 20 g total fat (3 g sat. fat), 55 mg chol., 278 mg sodium, 8 g carbo., 4 g fiber, 20 g pro.

***TEST KITCHEN TIP:** If you can't find chicken breast tenderloins at the supermarket, make your own by cutting skinless, boneless chicken breasts lengthwise into strips.

Chicken breast strips double-dipped in a lemon-and-herb flour then flash-fried in a skillet have all the crunch of traditional fried chicken, yet they're ready in half the time. (Recipe pictured on page 101.)

QUICK-FRIED CHICKEN SALAD

¾   cup all-purpose flour

4   tablespoons snipped fresh purple or green basil

1   tablespoon finely shredded lemon peel

2   eggs, beaten

1   pound skinless, boneless chicken breast strips

2   tablespoons cooking oil

4   cups mixed spring salad greens

1   head radicchio, torn into bite-size pieces

2   cups sliced fresh strawberries

½   cup bottled balsamic vinaigrette salad dressing

6   butterhead (Bibb or Boston) lettuce leaves

     Fresh purple or green basil leaves (optional)

START TO FINISH:
30 minutes

MAKES: *6 servings*

1 In a shallow dish combine flour, 2 tablespoons of the snipped basil, and the lemon peel. Place eggs in another shallow dish. Dip chicken into flour mixture, then into the eggs, and then again into flour mixture to coat.

2 In a 12-inch heavy skillet heat oil over medium-high heat. Add chicken breast strips; cook for 6 to 8 minutes or until chicken is no longer pink, turning once. (If necessary, reduce heat to medium to prevent overbrowning and add more oil as needed during cooking.) Cool slightly.

3 Meanwhile, in a large bowl toss together greens, radicchio, strawberries, and the remaining 2 tablespoons snipped basil. Drizzle vinaigrette over greens mixture; toss gently to coat.

4 To serve, line six bowls with lettuce leaves. Add greens mixture. Top with chicken and, if desired, basil leaves.

Per serving: 261 cal., 13 g total fat (2 g sat. fat), 79 mg chol., 295 mg sodium, 16 g carbo., 2 g fiber, 21 g pro.

A chile pepper, red onion, and fresh mango salsa make the perfect partners for turkey breast slices.

SPICED JERK TURKEY WITH SALSA

START TO FINISH:
35 minutes

MAKES: *4 servings*

4	teaspoons Jamaican jerk seasoning
1	teaspoon ground cumin
½	teaspoon salt
½	teaspoon ground ginger
⅛	teaspoon cayenne pepper
1	tablespoon olive oil
2	cloves garlic, minced
8	2-ounce turkey breast slices, cut ¼ to ⅜ inch thick
1	cup chopped, peeled mango, peeled peach, or nectarine
¼	cup finely chopped red sweet pepper
¼	cup finely chopped red onion
2	tablespoons snipped fresh cilantro
1	tablespoon lime juice
1	teaspoon finely chopped, seeded fresh serrano chile pepper (see tip, page 19)
1	tablespoon olive oil
6	cups torn mixed salad greens

1 In a small bowl combine Jamaican jerk seasoning, cumin, salt, ginger, and cayenne pepper; reserve 1 teaspoon of the cumin mixture for salsa. Add 1 tablespoon oil and the garlic to the remaining cumin mixture. Use your fingers to rub mixture evenly onto both sides of each turkey slice. Set aside.

2 For salsa, in a small bowl stir together mango, sweet pepper, red onion, cilantro, lime juice, chile pepper, and the reserved 1 teaspoon cumin mixture. Set aside.

3 In a large skillet heat 1 tablespoon oil over medium heat. Add half of the turkey slices; cook for 4 to 6 minutes or until turkey is no longer pink, turning once. Repeat with remaining turkey slices. (Add more oil if necessary during cooking.) If desired, cut turkey into bite-size strips. Serve turkey on salad greens; top with salsa.

Per serving: 243 cal., 8 g total fat (1 g sat. fat), 70 mg chol., 648 mg sodium, 13 g carbo., 3 g fiber, 30 g pro.

Pile this salad in a bowl or cup or encase it in a flavored tortilla. Kids will love the tropical twist in this 15-minute meal. If you like, skip toasting the coconut.

POPCORN CHICKEN WITH COCONUT SLAW

1   10- to 12-ounce package frozen cooked, breaded
      popcorn chicken

½   of a 16-ounce package (4 cups) shredded cabbage with carrot
      (coleslaw mix)

1   cup mango pieces or quartered strawberries

½   cup raw coconut chips and/or shredded coconut, toasted*

⅓   cup bottled citrus vinaigrette salad dressing or bottled
      Italian salad dressing

      Salt

      Black pepper

      Raw coconut chips and/or shredded coconut, toasted*

START TO FINISH:
15 minutes

MAKES: *4 servings*

1 Cook popcorn chicken in the microwave oven according to package directions. Meanwhile, in a large bowl combine shredded cabbage, mango pieces or strawberries, and the ½ cup coconut. Add vinaigrette; toss to coat. Add cooked chicken and toss.

2 Divide chicken mixture among four goblets or bowls. Season to taste with salt and pepper. If desired, top with additional coconut.

Per serving: 331 cal., 19 g total fat (8 g sat. fat), 17 mg chol., 720 mg sodium, 32 g carbo., 5 g fiber, 9 g pro.

***TEST KITCHEN TIP:** To toast coconut, preheat oven to 350°F. Place coconut in a shallow baking pan. Bake, uncovered, for 5 to 10 minutes or until toasted, stirring once or twice.

This tempting, fuss-free salad goes together in a flash. The hardest part is cooking the pasta.

PASTA CHICKEN CAESAR SALAD

START TO FINISH:
20 minutes

MAKES: *4 servings*

6   ounces dried radiatore or large bow tie pasta
    (about 2¼ cups)

1   10-ounce package Caesar salad kit
    (includes lettuce, dressing, croutons, and cheese)

1   cup cherry tomatoes, halved

1   9-ounce package refrigerated cooked chicken breast strips

1 Cook pasta according to package directions; drain well. Rinse with cold water; drain again.

2 In a very large bowl combine cooked pasta, entire contents of the salad package, and the tomatoes; toss to combine. Divide among four serving bowls. Top with chicken strips.

Per serving: 377 cal., 14 g total fat (3 g sat. fat), 49 mg chol., 868 mg sodium, 40 g carbo., 3 g fiber, 22 g pro.

The subtly sweet flavor of white balsamic vinegar fuses deliciously with basil, orange juice, and honey in the refreshing homemade vinaigrette that flavors this barley, chicken, and fruit combo.

ORANGE-BARLEY CHICKEN SALAD

½ cup quick-cooking barley

1 9-ounce package frozen cooked chicken breast strips, thawed

1½ cups cubed fresh pineapple

1 cup halved seedless grapes

Leaf lettuce

1 recipe Orange-Basil Vinaigrette

2 tablespoons chopped pecans, toasted

PREP: *25 minutes*

CHILL: *1 hour*

MAKES: *4 servings*

1 Cook barley according to package directions. Drain. Rinse under cold water; drain again. Cover; chill for at least 1 hour.

2 Stir chicken, pineapple, and grapes into barley. Line four dinner plates with lettuce. Top with chicken mixture. Shake Orange-Basil Vinaigrette; drizzle over salads. Top with pecans.

ORANGE-BASIL VINAIGRETTE: In a screw-top jar combine 1 teaspoon finely shredded orange peel; ¼ cup orange juice; ¼ cup salad oil; 2 tablespoons white balsamic vinegar or white wine vinegar; 2 tablespoons snipped fresh basil or 1 teaspoon dried basil, crushed; and 1 tablespoon honey. Cover and shake well. Makes ½ cup.

Per serving: 381 cal., 20 g total fat (3 g sat. fat), 45 mg chol., 379 mg sodium, 36 g carbo., 4 g fiber, 19 g pro.

Couscous is a tiny grain-shaped pasta made from semolina flour. Once cooked and fluffed up, it's a good substitute for rice. You'll find couscous near the rice and dried beans at your grocery store. (Recipe pictured on page 102.)

COUSCOUS CHICKEN SALAD

START TO FINISH:
20 minutes

MAKES: *4 servings*

1	14-ounce can reduced-sodium chicken broth
1¼	cups quick-cooking couscous
½	cup mango chutney (cut up large fruit pieces)
¼	cup bottled olive oil and vinegar salad dressing, white wine vinaigrette salad dressing, or roasted garlic vinaigrette salad dressing
1	6-ounce package refrigerated cooked lemon-pepper or Italian-style chicken breast strips, cut into bite-size pieces (about 1½ cups)
1	cup coarsely chopped, seeded cucumber or radish
½	cup golden raisins
	Salt
	Black pepper
1	small cucumber, cut into spears

1 In a medium saucepan bring chicken broth to boiling. Stir in couscous. Cover and remove from heat. Let stand for 5 minutes. Fluff couscous lightly with a fork.

2 In a medium bowl combine mango chutney and salad dressing. Add couscous, chicken, chopped cucumber or radish, and raisins; toss to coat. Season to taste with salt and pepper. Serve with cucumber spears.

Per serving: 418 cal., 10 g total fat (1 g sat. fat), 28 mg chol., 873 mg sodium, 62 g carbo., 4 g fiber, 19 g pro.

All you need is a skillet and four simple ingredients, and you can treat your family to a mouthwatering salad meal.

WARM CHICKEN & WILTED GREENS

2   cups frozen (yellow, green, and red) peppers
    and onion stir-fry vegetables

1   9-ounce package frozen chopped cooked
    chicken breast, thawed

¼   cup bottled sesame salad dressing

6   cups fresh baby spinach and/or torn leaf lettuce

1 In a 12-inch skillet prepare frozen stir-fry vegetables according to package directions. Stir in chicken and salad dressing; heat through. Add spinach and/or lettuce. Toss mixture in skillet for 30 to 60 seconds or just until spinach is wilted.

Per serving: 153 cal., 6 g total fat (1 g sat. fat), 34 mg chol., 309 mg sodium, 8 g carbo., 2 g fiber, 17 g pro.

START TO FINISH:
25 minutes

MAKES: *4 servings*

Rip open a bag of crisp greens and arrange them on a platter along with flavor-packed extras such as chicken, fresh berries, cheese, and nuts. Then add a splash of dressing. What could be easier?

SPRING GREENS & ROASTED CHICKEN

START TO FINISH:
25 minutes

MAKES: *6 servings*

1 2¼-pound purchased roasted chicken, chilled

1 5-ounce package mixed spring salad greens (about 8 cups)

2 cups sliced fresh strawberries or fresh blueberries

4 ounces Gorgonzola or blue cheese, crumbled (1 cup)

½ cup honey-roasted cashews or peanuts

1 lemon, halved

3 tablespoons olive oil

¼ teaspoon salt

¼ teaspoon black pepper

1 Remove string from chicken, if present. Remove and discard skin from chicken. Pull meat from bones, discarding bones. Shred meat (you should have about 3½ cups).

2 Place greens on a serving platter. Top with chicken, berries, cheese, and nuts. Drizzle with juice from lemon and oil; sprinkle with salt and pepper.

Per serving: 376 cal., 27 g total fat (8 g sat. fat), 81 mg chol., 454 mg sodium, 9 g carbo., 2 g fiber, 27 g pro.

Deli-roasted chicken teamed with fresh fruit, jicama, and bottled dressing is an easy dinnertime fix. The salad holds well overnight too, so you can enjoy any leftovers the next day.

CHICKEN & GRAPE PASTA SALAD

1	2- to 2½-pound purchased roasted chicken or 3 cups chopped cooked chicken or turkey
1½	cups dried radiatore, mostaccioli, and/or medium shell macaroni
3	cups assorted grapes, halved and seeded, if necessary
1½	cups halved small fresh strawberries
1	cup chopped, peeled jicama or one 8-ounce can sliced water chestnuts, drained
⅔	cup bottled cucumber ranch salad dressing
⅛	teaspoon cayenne pepper
1	to 2 tablespoons milk (optional)
	Leaf lettuce
	Purchased sugared sliced almonds (optional)

PREP: *40 minutes*

CHILL: *4 to 24 hours*

MAKES: *6 servings*

1 Remove string from chicken, if present. Remove and discard skin from chicken. Remove meat from bones, discarding bones. Tear meat into bite-size pieces. Cook pasta according to package directions; drain. Rinse with cold water; drain again.

2 In a large salad bowl combine chicken, cooked pasta, grapes, strawberries, and jicama or water chestnuts.

3 For dressing, in a small bowl stir together ranch salad dressing and cayenne pepper. Pour dressing over chicken mixture. Toss lightly to coat. Cover and chill for 4 to 24 hours.

4 Before serving, if necessary, stir in enough of the milk to moisten. Serve salad in lettuce-lined bowls and, if desired, sprinkle with almonds.

Per serving: 455 cal., 20 g total fat (3 g sat. fat), 67 mg chol., 269 mg sodium, 43 g carbo., 3 g fiber, 27 g pro.

Crème fraîche is a thickened cream with a tangy flavor that's often used in French cooking. If you can't find it at your supermarket, sour cream will work just fine.

SOUTHERN CHICKEN SALAD

START TO FINISH:
25 minutes

MAKES: *4 servings*

½ cup purchased crème fraîche or dairy sour cream

¼ cup white wine vinegar

3 to 4 tablespoons Dijon-style mustard

2 cloves garlic, minced

½ teaspoon salt

¼ teaspoon black pepper

6 cups torn mixed salad greens (such as romaine lettuce, spinach, and/or baby mustard greens)

½ cup lightly packed small fresh mint leaves

2 tablespoons shredded fresh basil or marjoram leaves

4 slices Texas toast or large slices sourdough bread, toasted

2 to 4 tablespoons honey butter

1 2- to 2½-pound purchased roasted chicken, quartered*

4 medium peaches or nectarines, pitted and sliced

1 For dressing, in a small bowl whisk together crème fraîche, vinegar, mustard, garlic, salt, and pepper; set aside.

2 In a large bowl toss together greens, mint, and basil. Spread toast slices with honey butter; place one slice on each of four serving plates. Top toast slices with greens mixture. Arrange chicken and peaches on top of greens mixture. Drizzle with dressing.

Per serving: 677 cal., 36 g total fat (13 g sat. fat), 218 mg chol., 965 mg sodium, 37 g carbo., 3 g fiber, 52 g pro.

*TEST KITCHEN TIP: The roasted chicken can be warm or chilled for this salad.

For a special touch, make this salad with ruby red blood oranges instead of regular oranges.

ORANGE-CHICKEN SALAD

2	large oranges
1	cup mayonnaise or salad dressing
¾	teaspoon lemon-pepper seasoning
5	cups cubed or shredded cooked chicken or turkey
½	cup chopped pecans or walnuts, toasted

PREP: *20 minutes*

CHILL: *2 to 4 hours*

MAKES: *6 servings*

1 Finely shred 1 teaspoon peel from one of the oranges. Cut orange in half; squeeze orange until you have 2 tablespoons juice. Peel and section the remaining orange; cut sections into bite-size pieces.

2 In a medium bowl combine orange peel, orange juice, mayonnaise, and lemon-pepper seasoning. Stir in orange sections, chicken, and nuts. Cover and chill for 2 to 4 hours before serving.

Per serving: 558 cal., 44 g total fat (7 g sat. fat), 117 mg chol., 436 mg sodium, 3 g carbo., 1 g fiber, 35 g pro.

If you opt for the fiery fresh jalapeño rather than the chipotles, this salad really can pack some heat.

SANTA FE CHICKEN SALAD

PREP: *25 minutes*

CHILL: *1 to 4 hours*

MAKES: *4 servings*

½ cup mayonnaise or salad dressing

1 tablespoon lime juice

2 teaspoons finely chopped canned chipotle chile peppers in adobo sauce or finely chopped, seeded, fresh jalapeño chile pepper (see tip, page 19)

2½ cups chopped cooked chicken or turkey (about 12 ounces)

¼ cup finely chopped celery

¼ cup snipped fresh cilantro

3 tablespoons thinly sliced green onions

3 tablespoons finely chopped yellow sweet pepper

3 tablespoons finely chopped red sweet pepper

⅛ teaspoon salt

⅛ teaspoon black pepper

Tortilla salad cups, shredded lettuce, tostada shells, flour tortillas, or tortilla chips

1 For dressing, in a small bowl stir together mayonnaise, lime juice, and chile pepper. Set aside.

2 In a medium bowl combine chicken, celery, cilantro, green onion, sweet peppers, salt, and black pepper. Pour dressing over chicken mixture; toss to coat. Cover; chill for 1 to 4 hours.

3 Serve salad in tortilla salad cups or spoon it over shredded lettuce, tostada shells, flour tortillas, or tortilla chips.

Per serving: 435 cal., 29 g total fat (5 g sat. fat), 88 mg chol., 359 mg sodium, 15 g carbo., 2 g fiber, 27 g pro.

This satisfying blend of chicken, olives, walnuts, artichokes, and fresh spinach boasts a bold Mediterranean flavor. It's a well-rounded meal when served with warm pita bread rounds.

MEDITERRANEAN CHICKEN SALAD

START TO FINISH:
30 minutes

MAKES: *6 servings*

1   pound cooked chicken or turkey, shredded or cut into bite-size strips (about 3 cups)

1   13¾-ounce can artichoke hearts, drained and quartered

1   cup chopped celery

½   of a medium cucumber, halved lengthwise, seeded, and sliced

½   cup sliced pitted kalamata olives

½   cup chopped walnuts

⅓   cup sliced green onions

½   of a small lemon, seeded and cut into 6 wedges

½   cup olive oil

¼   cup sugar

¼   cup sherry vinegar or white wine vinegar

½   teaspoon salt

¼   teaspoon black pepper

2   cups fresh spinach leaves

Snipped fresh parsley (optional)

1 In a very large bowl combine chicken, artichokes, celery, cucumber, olives, walnuts, and green onion. Set aside.

2 For dressing, in a blender or food processor combine lemon (including peel), olive oil, sugar, vinegar, salt, and pepper; cover and blend or process until nearly smooth. Pour dressing over chicken mixture; toss to coat.

3 Serve salad on spinach leaves. If desired, sprinkle with parsley.

Per serving: 451 cal., 32 g total fat (5 g sat. fat), 67 mg chol., 628 mg sodium, 17 g carbo., 5 g fiber, 25 g pro.

When retesting this decades-old recipe, our Test Kitchen tasters thought it needed more zip. So instead of using just one Anaheim pepper as the original recipe did, this version calls for a whole can of chile peppers. This salad is probably the forerunner of what is now known as the taco salad.

MEXICAN CHEF'S SALAD

START TO FINISH:
25 minutes

MAKES: *6 servings*

2 cups red and/or yellow cherry tomatoes, quartered

1 cup sliced celery

1 cup bite-size strips cooked ham

1 cup bite-size strips cooked chicken or turkey

3 tablespoons thinly sliced green onions

1 8-ounce bottle honey Dijon salad dressing

1 4-ounce can diced green chile peppers, drained

3 tablespoons sliced pitted ripe olives

1 12-ounce package torn mixed salad greens

1 cup shredded carrot

2 cups corn chips and/or tortilla chips (optional)

1 In a large bowl combine cherry tomatoes, celery, ham, chicken, and green onion.

2 In a small bowl combine salad dressing, chile peppers, and olives. Add dressing mixture to tomato mixture; toss gently to coat.

3 To serve, divide salad greens and carrot among six dinner plates. Top with tomato mixture. Serve immediately. If desired, serve with corn chips.

Per serving: 287 cal., 20 g total fat (3 g sat. fat), 34 mg chol., 584 mg sodium, 16 g carbo., 3 g fiber, 13 g pro.

The next time you're roasting or grilling chicken for dinner, cook a few extra pieces so there's some left over. Tuck the leftovers into the freezer and you'll always have cooked chicken on hand for this garden-fresh spinach salad.

CITRUS CHICKEN SALAD

2   cups fresh baby spinach

1   11-ounce can mandarin orange sections, drained

½   cup loose-pack frozen whole kernel corn

6   ounces cooked chicken breast or turkey breast, shredded, or one 6-ounce package refrigerated cooked chicken breast strips*

2   tablespoons white wine vinegar or cider vinegar

1   tablespoon Dijon-style mustard

2   teaspoons snipped fresh oregano or ½ teaspoon dried oregano, crushed

2   teaspoons orange marmalade

2   teaspoons salad oil

⅛   teaspoon salt

⅛   teaspoon black pepper

START TO FINISH:
20 minutes

MAKES: *2 servings*

1 In a serving bowl toss together spinach, mandarin orange sections, and corn. Top with chicken.

2 For dressing, in a screw-top jar combine vinegar, mustard, oregano, orange marmalade, oil, salt, and pepper; cover and shake well.

3 Pour dressing over chicken and spinach mixture; toss to coat.

Per serving: 312 cal., 8 g total fat (2 g sat. fat), 72 mg chol., 426 mg sodium, 29 g carbo., 3 g fiber, 30 g pro.

*__TEST KITCHEN TIP:__ If using the packaged refrigerated cooked chicken breast strips, omit the ⅛ teaspoon salt from the dressing.

Dress up leftover cooked chicken with this fabulous peanut butter, soy sauce, and ginger dressing.

CHICKEN SALAD WITH PEANUTTY DRESSING

START TO FINISH:
25 minutes
MAKES: *4 servings*

6 cups cut-up romaine lettuce or napa cabbage

2 cups chopped cooked chicken breast or turkey breast (10 ounces)

1 small apple, cored and cut into chunks

½ cup green and/or red seedless grapes, halved

3 tablespoons water

2 tablespoons creamy peanut butter

2 teaspoons reduced-sodium soy sauce

¼ teaspoon ground ginger (optional)

1 On four salad plates arrange romaine or napa cabbage, chicken, apple, and grapes.

2 In a small bowl whisk together the water, peanut butter, soy sauce, and, if desired, ginger. Drizzle peanut butter mixture over salad.

Per serving: 210 cal., 7 g total fat (2 g sat. fat), 60 mg chol., 192 mg sodium, 13 g carbo., 3 g fiber, 25 g pro.

When you need something quick for lunch, this salad is it. The greens are torn and ready to use. The dressing and oranges add a distinctly Asian flavor. (Recipe pictured on page 102.)

ASIAN CHICKEN SALAD

1 10-ounce package torn mixed salad greens

8 ounces cooked chicken or turkey, cut into bite-size pieces

⅓ cup bottled Asian vinaigrette salad dressing

1 11-ounce can mandarin orange sections, drained

3 tablespoons sliced almonds, toasted

1 In a large bowl combine greens and chicken. Add salad dressing; toss to coat. Divide greens mixture among four salad plates. Top with mandarin orange sections and almonds. Serve immediately.

Per serving: 218 cal., 9 g total fat (1 g sat. fat), 50 mg chol., 502 mg sodium, 15 g carbo., 2 g fiber, 19 g pro.

START TO FINISH:
15 minutes

MAKES: *4 servings*

Soft cream cheese with chives and onion serves as the dressing in this savory chicken salad. Roasted red sweet peppers and green olives add a touch of color.

CHICKEN SALAD WITH OLIVES & PEPPERS

PREP: *15 minutes*

CHILL: *2 to 24 hours*

MAKES: *4 servings*

2 cups chopped cooked chicken or turkey (10 ounces)

¼ cup chopped walnuts, toasted

¼ cup chopped bottled roasted red sweet peppers

¼ cup sliced pimiento-stuffed green olives

½ of an 8-ounce tub cream cheese with chives and onion

Black pepper

1 In a medium bowl combine chicken, walnuts, roasted red peppers, and olives. Add cream cheese, stirring until combined. Season to taste with black pepper. Cover and chill for 2 to 24 hours before serving.

Per serving: 229 cal., 16 g total fat (7 g sat. fat), 61 mg chol., 501 mg sodium, 4 g carbo., 1 g fiber, 17 g pro.

Made with two forms of mustard, coarse-grain brown mustard and creamy Dijon-style mustard blend, this chicken salad gets its crunch from celery and pine nuts.

MUSTARD-DRESSED CHICKEN SALAD

¼ cup mayonnaise or salad dressing

2 tablespoons creamy Dijon-style mustard blend

2 tablespoons coarse-grain brown mustard

2½ cups chopped cooked chicken or turkey (about 12 ounces)

¼ cup finely chopped celery

¼ cup thinly sliced green onions

2 tablespoons pine nuts, toasted

1 tablespoon snipped fresh parsley

1 tablespoon drained and finely chopped oil-packed dried tomatoes

Salt

Black pepper

Leaf lettuce

PREP: *25 minutes*

CHILL: *1 to 4 hours*

MAKES: *4 servings*

1 For dressing, in a small bowl stir together mayonnaise, creamy mustard blend, and brown mustard. Set aside.

2 In a medium bowl combine chicken, celery, green onion, pine nuts, parsley, and dried tomato. Season to taste with salt and pepper. Spoon dressing over chicken mixture; toss to coat. Cover; chill for 1 to 4 hours.

3 Serve on four lettuce-lined salad plates.

Per serving: 320 cal., 21 g total fat (4 g sat. fat), 83 mg chol., 448 mg sodium, 4 g carbo., 1 g fiber, 27 g pro.

Yogurt and ranch dressing top chicken, broccoli, carrot, and nuts. This salad is a surefire winner.

CHICKEN, BROCCOLI & CARROT SALAD

START TO FINISH:
15 minutes

MAKES: *4 servings*

¼ cup plain low-fat yogurt

¼ cup bottled ranch salad dressing

1½ cups chopped cooked chicken or turkey (about 8 ounces)

½ cup chopped broccoli

¼ cup shredded carrot

¼ cup chopped pecans or walnuts (optional)

1 In a small bowl stir together yogurt and ranch salad dressing.

2 In a medium bowl combine chicken, broccoli, carrot, and, if desired, nuts. Pour yogurt mixture over chicken mixture; toss to coat. If desired, cover and chill for up to 24 hours.

Per serving: 184 cal., 11 g total fat (2 g sat. fat), 52 mg chol., 179 mg sodium, 4 g carbo., 1 g fiber, 17 g pro.

How do you turn baby spinach into a meal? Add cubed turkey, grapefruit and orange sections, and almond slices to the spinach and toss them all together with a fresh poppy seed dressing. (Recipe pictured on page 103.)

TURKEY & SPINACH SALAD

8	cups fresh baby spinach or torn fresh spinach leaves
8	ounces cooked turkey or chicken, cubed
2	grapefruit, peeled and sectioned
2	oranges, peeled and sectioned
¼	cup orange juice
2	tablespoons olive oil
1	teaspoon honey
½	teaspoon poppy seeds
¼	teaspoon salt
¼	teaspoon dry mustard
2	tablespoons sliced almonds, toasted (optional)

START TO FINISH: *25 minutes*

MAKES: *4 servings*

1 Place spinach in a large bowl. Add turkey, grapefruit sections, and orange sections.

2 For dressing, in a screw-top jar combine orange juice, oil, honey, poppy seeds, salt, and dry mustard. Cover and shake well. Pour dressing over salad; toss gently. If desired, sprinkle with almonds.

Per serving: 228 cal., 10 g total fat (2 g sat. fat), 43 mg chol., 261 mg sodium, 16 g carbo., 8 g fiber, 20 g pro.

Fruit, turkey, and nuts are a tasty trio, especially when combined with a tangy buttermilk dressing. (Recipe pictured on page 103.)

TURKEY-PEAR SALAD

START TO FINISH:
25 minutes

MAKES: *4 servings*

½   cup buttermilk

2   tablespoons mayonnaise or salad dressing

1   tablespoon frozen apple juice concentrate or frozen orange juice concentrate, thawed

1   teaspoon Dijon-style mustard

6   cups torn mixed salad greens

8   ounces cooked turkey or chicken, cut into bite-size strips

2   medium pears and/or apples, sliced

¼   cup broken walnuts, toasted (optional)

1 For dressing, in a small bowl stir together buttermilk, mayonnaise, apple juice concentrate, and mustard.

2 In a salad bowl combine salad greens, turkey, and pear and/or apple slices. Drizzle with dressing; toss to coat. If desired, sprinkle with walnuts.

Per serving: 227 cal., 9 g total fat (2 g sat. fat), 47 mg chol., 150 mg sodium, 19 g carbo., 4 g fiber, 19 g pro.

FROM THE SLOW COOKER

With these foolproof slow-cooker
recipes, you can enjoy
great-tasting meals anytime.

What to do with the extra chipotle chile peppers? Pack them in a freezer container, covered with the sauce from the can. Seal, label, and freeze them for up to 2 months. When you need the peppers, thaw them in the refrigerator.

SWEET & SMOKY CHICKEN

PREP: *15 minutes*

COOK: *6 to 7 hours on low-heat setting or 3 to 3½ hours on high-heat setting*

MAKES: *4 to 6 servings*

2½ to 3 pounds meaty chicken pieces (breast halves, thighs, and/or drumsticks), skinned and fat removed

¼ teaspoon salt

⅛ teaspoon black pepper

1 cup chicken broth

½ cup seedless raspberry jam

½ cup snipped dried apricots

1 to 2 canned chipotle chile peppers in adobo sauce, chopped, plus 1 tablespoon adobo sauce (see tip, page 19)

1 tablespoon quick-cooking tapioca, finely ground

1 Place chicken in a 3½- or 4-quart slow cooker. Sprinkle with salt and black pepper. For sauce, in a small bowl stir together chicken broth, raspberry jam, dried apricots, chipotle peppers and adobo sauce, and tapioca. Pour over chicken.

2 Cover and cook on low-heat setting for 6 to 7 hours or on high-heat setting for 3 to 3½ hours. Using a slotted spoon, transfer chicken to a serving platter. Serve sauce over chicken.

Per serving: 412 cal., 10 g total fat (3 g sat. fat), 115 mg chol., 549 mg sodium, 41 g carbo., 2 g fiber, 38 g pro.

Serve an Italian dressing-topped salad and crusty Italian bread with this creamy chicken and you have a first-rate meal that requires little work.

DRIED TOMATO CHICKEN ALFREDO

1	medium onion, halved and thinly sliced
2½	pounds meaty chicken pieces (breast halves, thighs, and/or drumsticks), skinned and fat removed
	Salt
	Black pepper
½	cup dried tomatoes (not oil-packed), cut into strips or chopped
1	4-ounce can (drained weight) sliced mushrooms, drained
1	16-ounce jar light Parmesan Alfredo pasta sauce
1	9-ounce package frozen artichoke hearts, thawed and drained
	Hot cooked pasta
1	ounce Parmesan cheese, shaved

1 Place onion in a 3½- or 4-quart slow cooker. Top with chicken; sprinkle lightly with salt and pepper. Top chicken with dried tomatoes and drained mushrooms; pour Alfredo sauce over.

2 Cover and cook on low-heat setting for 5½ to 6 hours or on high-heat setting for 3 hours.

3 Add artichoke hearts to slow cooker; cover and cook for 30 minutes more. Serve chicken, vegetables, and sauce over pasta. Top with shaved Parmesan cheese.

Per serving: 576 cal., 23 g total fat (11 g sat. fat), 167 mg chol., 1,419 mg sodium, 38 g carbo., 7 g fiber, 50 g pro.

PREP: *15 minutes*

COOK: *5½ to 6 hours on low-heat setting or 3 hours on high-heat setting; plus 30 minutes*

MAKES: *4 servings*

Cinnamon, cloves, golden raisins, and dried apricots add a spicy-sweet twist to this saucy chicken dish.

MOROCCAN CHICKEN

PREP: *20 minutes*

COOK: *6 to 7 hours on low-heat setting or 3 to 3½ hours on high-heat setting*

MAKES: *4 servings*

2½ pounds meaty chicken pieces
   (breast halves, thighs, and/or drumsticks),
   skinned and fat removed

½ teaspoon salt

½ teaspoon black pepper

¼ teaspoon ground cinnamon

⅛ teaspoon ground cloves or ground allspice

1 14½-ounce can diced tomatoes with onions and garlic

½ cup golden raisins

½ cup dried apricots, snipped

1 tablespoon quick-cooking tapioca

2 cups hot cooked couscous

1 Place chicken in a 3½- or 4-quart slow cooker. In a small bowl combine salt, pepper, cinnamon, and cloves; sprinkle over chicken. In a medium bowl combine undrained tomatoes, golden raisins, apricots, and tapioca; pour over chicken.

2 Cover and cook on low-heat setting for 6 to 7 hours or on high-heat setting for 3 to 3½ hours.

3 To serve, divide couscous among four dinner plates; top with chicken. Skim fat from tomato mixture in slow cooker. Spoon tomato mixture over chicken and couscous.

Per serving: 474 cal., 10 g total fat (3 g sat. fat), 115 mg chol., 900 mg sodium, 54 g carbo., 4 g fiber, 43 g pro.

If you prefer, use nonalcoholic beer instead of ale.

CHICKEN IN ALE

4	medium potatoes, peeled and thinly sliced
3	leeks, thinly sliced
1	medium onion, cut into thin wedges
1	teaspoon salt
¼	teaspoon black pepper
2½	pounds meaty chicken pieces (breast halves, thighs, and/or drumsticks), skinned and fat removed
½	cup ale or nonalcoholic beer
½	cup chicken broth
2	tablespoons brown mustard
1	tablespoon packed brown sugar
1	tablespoon quick-cooking tapioca
½	teaspoon dried thyme, crushed

PREP: *30 minutes*

COOK: *6 to 7 hours on low-heat setting or 3 to 3½ hours on high-heat setting*

MAKES: *4 servings*

1 In a 5- to 6-quart slow cooker combine potatoes, leeks, and onion; sprinkle with half of the salt and pepper. Add chicken; sprinkle with remaining salt and pepper. In a medium bowl combine ale, chicken broth, mustard, brown sugar, tapioca, and thyme; pour over chicken.

2 Cover and cook on low-heat setting for 6 to 7 hours or on high-heat setting for 3 to 3½ hours.

Per serving: 403 cal., 10 g total fat (3 g sat. fat), 115 mg chol., 923 mg sodium, 34 g carbo., 3 g fiber, 41 g pro.

Capers and olives give this sauce its spirited Southern Italian flavor. If you prefer, substitute your favorite pasta for the almond-shaped orzo.

PUTTANESCA CHICKEN

PREP: *20 minutes*

COOK: *6 to 7 hours on low-heat setting or 3 to 3½ hours on high-heat setting*

MAKES: *6 servings*

2½ to 3 pounds meaty chicken pieces (breast halves, thighs, and/or drumsticks), skinned and fat removed

¼ teaspoon salt

⅛ teaspoon black pepper

1 26-ounce jar pasta sauce with olives

2 tablespoons drained capers

1 teaspoon finely shredded lemon peel

3 cups hot cooked orzo pasta (rosamarina)

1 Place chicken in a 3½- or 4-quart slow cooker. Sprinkle with salt and pepper. For sauce, in a medium bowl stir together pasta sauce, capers, and lemon peel. Pour over chicken.

2 Cover and cook on low-heat setting for 6 to 7 hours or on high-heat setting for 3 to 3½ hours. Serve chicken and sauce over hot cooked orzo.

Per serving: 315 cal., 8 g total fat (2 g sat. fat), 77 mg chol., 678 mg sodium, 30 g carbo., 3 g fiber, 30 g pro.

If you think chutney sounds like one of those hard-to-find ingredients you have to drive all over town to find, think again! These days, the condiment is widely available at supermarkets.

BARBECUE-CHUTNEY CHICKEN

1	medium onion, cut into wedges
3	pounds meaty chicken pieces (breast halves, thighs, and/or drumsticks), skinned and fat removed
¼	teaspoon salt
⅛	teaspoon black pepper
⅔	cup bottled barbecue sauce
½	cup mango chutney (large fruit pieces cut up)
1	teaspoon curry powder
2	to 3 cups hot cooked rice

PREP: *15 minutes*

COOK: *6 to 7 hours on low-heat setting or 3 to 3½ hours on high-heat setting*

MAKES: *4 to 6 servings*

1 Place onion in a 3½- or 4-quart slow cooker. Add chicken; sprinkle with salt and pepper. In a small bowl stir together barbecue sauce, chutney, and curry powder. Pour over chicken.

2 Cover and cook on low-heat setting for 6 to 7 hours or on high-heat setting for 3 to 3½ hours. Serve chicken and chutney mixture with hot cooked rice.

Per serving: 538 cal., 12 g total fat (3 g sat. fat), 138 mg chol., 647 mg sodium, 57 g carbo., 2 g fiber, 48 g pro.

Why stop for take-out when you can head directly home knowing that this Asian favorite is ready and waiting in your slow cooker?

MOO SHU-STYLE CHICKEN

PREP: *20 minutes*

COOK: *6 to 7 hours on low-heat setting or 3 to 3½ hours on high-heat setting*

MAKES: *4 servings*

2½ to 3 pounds meaty chicken pieces (breast halves, thighs, and/or drumsticks), skinned and fat removed

¼ teaspoon salt

⅛ teaspoon black pepper

½ cup water

¼ cup soy sauce

2 teaspoons toasted sesame oil

¾ teaspoon ground ginger

8 7- to 8-inch flour tortillas

½ cup bottled hoisin sauce

2 cups packaged shredded broccoli (broccoli slaw mix) or packaged shredded cabbage with carrot (coleslaw mix)

1 Place chicken in a 3½- or 4-quart slow cooker. Sprinkle with salt and pepper. In a small bowl stir together the water, soy sauce, sesame oil, and ginger. Pour over chicken.

2 Cover and cook on low-heat setting for 6 to 7 hours or on high-heat setting for 3 to 3½ hours.

3 Using a slotted spoon, remove chicken from slow cooker, reserving cooking liquid. When cool enough to handle, remove chicken from bones; discard bones. Using two forks, pull chicken apart into shreds. Return chicken to slow cooker; heat through.

4 To serve, spread each tortilla with 1 tablespoon of the hoisin sauce. Using a slotted spoon, spoon shredded chicken just below centers of tortillas. Top with shredded broccoli. Fold bottom edge of each tortilla up and over filling. Fold in opposite sides; roll up from bottom.

Per serving: 520 cal., 18 g total fat (4 g sat. fat), 115 mg chol., 1,315 mg sodium, 44 g carbo., 3 g fiber, 44 g pro.

Feta cheese and fresh parsley make a pretty garnish on this Mediterranean-inspired chicken dish.

FETA-TOPPED CHICKEN

1	teaspoon finely shredded lemon peel
1	teaspoon dried basil, crushed
1	teaspoon dried rosemary, crushed
½	teaspoon salt
¼	teaspoon black pepper
2	cloves garlic, minced
3½	to 4 pounds meaty chicken pieces (breast halves, thighs, and/or drumsticks), skinned and fat removed
½	cup reduced-sodium chicken broth
½	cup crumbled feta cheese (2 ounces)
2	tablespoons snipped fresh flat-leaf parsley

PREP: *20 minutes*

COOK: *5 to 6 hours on low-heat setting or 2½ to 3 hours on high-heat setting*

MAKES: *6 servings*

1 In a small bowl combine lemon peel, basil, rosemary, salt, pepper, and garlic. Sprinkle lemon peel mixture over chicken pieces; rub in with your fingers. Place chicken in a 4- to 5-quart slow cooker. Add chicken broth.

2 Cover and cook on low-heat setting for 5 to 6 hours or on high-heat setting for 2½ to 3 hours.

3 Transfer chicken to a serving platter. Discard cooking liquid. Sprinkle chicken with feta cheese and parsley.

Per serving: 179 cal., 6 g total fat (2 g sat. fat), 97 mg chol., 425 mg sodium, 1 g carbo., 0 g fiber, 29 g pro.

Pepperoni isn't just for pizza! Here a little adds bold flavor to a zesty pasta topper. Save the extra pepperoni to fold into an omelet or toss into a salad.

PEPPERONI CHICKEN

PREP: *15 minutes*

COOK: *6 to 7 hours on low-heat setting or 3 to 3½ hours on high-heat setting*

MAKES: *4 to 6 servings*

2½ to 3 pounds meaty chicken pieces (breast halves, thighs, and/or drumsticks), skinned and fat removed

⅛ teaspoon black pepper

1 15-ounce container refrigerated marinara sauce or 2 cups desired tomato-based pasta sauce

½ of a 3-ounce package sliced pepperoni, halved

½ cup pitted kalamata or ripe olives, halved

8 ounces dried mostaccioli pasta

1 Place chicken in a 3½- or 4-quart slow cooker. Sprinkle with pepper. For sauce, in a medium bowl stir together marinara sauce, pepperoni, and olives. Pour over chicken.

2 Cover and cook on low-heat setting for 6 to 7 hours or on high-heat setting for 3 to 3½ hours.

3 Cook pasta according to package directions; drain. Serve chicken and sauce over hot cooked pasta.

Per serving: 595 cal., 20 g total fat (5 g sat. fat), 124 mg chol., 1,041 mg sodium, 52 g carbo., 4 g fiber, 48 g pro.

**PICADILLO
CHICKEN
PIZZETTAS**

(Recipe on page 15)

WINGS & THINGS

**MACADAMIA
TURKEY
SALAD ON
CUCUMBER
SLICES**

(Recipe on page 21)

A CHICKEN IN EVERY POT

CONFETTI CHICKEN SOUP

(Recipe on page 30)

CARAWAY CHICKEN STEW

(Recipe on page 35)

A CHICKEN IN EVERY POT

TURKEY RAVIOLI SOUP

(Recipe on page 52)

GARDEN-FRESH SALADS

**CHILI-
LIME
CHICKEN
SALAD**

(Recipe on page 64)

**QUICK-
FRIED
CHICKEN
SALAD**

(Recipe on page 65)

GARDEN-FRESH SALADS

**COUSCOUS
CHICKEN
SALAD**

(Recipe on page 70)

**ASIAN
CHICKEN
SALAD**

(Recipe on page 81)

GARDEN-FRESH SALADS

TURKEY & SPINACH SALAD

(Recipe on page 85)

TURKEY-PEAR SALAD

(Recipe on page 86)

FROM THE SLOW COOKER

CREAMY CURRY SOUP

(Recipe on page 145)

SPINACH, CHICKEN & WILD RICE SOUP

(Recipe on page 161)

QUICK FIXES

SWEET & SOUR CHICKEN

(Recipe on page 171)

CREAMY RANCH CHICHEN

(Recipe on page 178)

QUICK FIXES

MEDITERRANEAN
PIZZA
SKILLET

(Recipe on page 181)

QUICK FIXES

LEMON-TARRAGON CHICKEN TOSS

(Recipe on page 185)

SHORTCUT CHICKEN MOLE

(Recipe on page 189)

CHICKEN, GOAT CHEESE & GREENS

(Recipe on page 201)

QUICK FIXES

CHICKEN LINGUINE WITH PESTO SAUCE

(Recipe on page 203)

QUICK FIXES

CHICKEN & SLAW TOSTADAS

(Recipe on page 214)

PEANUT-CHICKEN BOWL

(Recipe on page 215)

For the stuffing, be sure to use a hard-crusted, dense sourdough loaf. It will give a better texture than lighter bread.

CHICKEN WITH SOURDOUGH STUFFING

6	cups crusty, open-textured, rustic-style sourdough bread cut into 1-inch cubes
1⅓	cups chopped tomatoes
1	cup finely chopped carrot
½	cup chicken broth
1½	teaspoons dried thyme, crushed
¼	teaspoon coarsely ground black pepper
6	small whole chicken legs (drumstick and thigh) (3¾ to 4½ pounds total)
⅓	cup thinly sliced leek or chopped onion

PREP: *25 minutes*

COOK: *6 to 6½ hours on low-heat setting or 3 to 3½ hours on high-heat setting*

MAKES: *6 servings*

1 For stuffing, in a large bowl combine bread cubes, tomato, and carrot. In a small bowl combine chicken broth, thyme, and pepper. Drizzle broth mixture over bread cube mixture, lightly tossing to mix. (Stuffing will not be completely moistened.) Place chicken in a 4 to 5 quart slow cooker. Add leek. Lightly pack stuffing on top of chicken and leek.

2 Cover and cook on low-heat setting for 6 to 6½ hours or on high-heat setting for 3 to 3½ hours.

3 Using a slotted spoon, transfer stuffing and chicken to a serving platter.

Per serving: 412 cal., 17 g total fat (5 g sat. fat), 105 mg chol., 409 mg sodium, 28 g carbo., 1 g fiber, 35 g pro.

Rely on this recipe when your schedule is jam-packed—just put three ingredients into the cooker and you can be on your way.

ITALIAN CHICKEN & VEGETABLES

PREP: *15 minutes*

COOK: *6 to 7 hours on low-heat setting or 3 to 3½ hours on high-heat setting*

MAKES: *4 servings*

4   small whole chicken legs (drumstick and thigh) (2½ to 3 pounds total), skinned and fat removed

1   26-ounce jar roasted garlic pasta sauce

1   16-ounce package frozen (yellow, green, and red) peppers and onion stir-fry vegetables

3   cups hot cooked noodles

⅓   cup shredded mozzarella cheese or finely shredded Parmesan cheese

1 Place chicken in a 3½- or 4-quart slow cooker. Add pasta sauce and frozen vegetables.

2 Cover and cook on low-heat setting for 6 to 7 hours or on high-heat setting for 3 to 3½ hours.

3 Serve the chicken and vegetable mixture with hot cooked noodles. Sprinkle with mozzarella cheese.

Per serving: 500 cal., 12 g total fat (3 g sat. fat), 174 mg chol., 796 mg sodium, 52 g carbo., 6 g fiber, 45 g pro.

This one-dish meal is dressed up with fresh gremolata, which is a lemon peel, parsley, and chopped walnut topping. It gives the dish a fantastic citrusy flavor. (Recipe pictured on page 104.)

CHICKEN WITH MUSHROOM STUFFING

Nonstick cooking spray

2	tablespoons finely shredded lemon peel
1	tablespoon ground sage
1	tablespoon seasoned salt
1½	teaspoons freshly ground black pepper
8	small whole chicken legs (drumstick and thigh) (about 5 pounds total), skinned and fat removed
¼	cup butter
4	cups quartered or sliced fresh cremini, baby portobello, shiitake, and/or button mushrooms
2	cloves garlic, thinly sliced
8	cups sourdough baguette cut into 1-inch pieces (12 to 14 ounces)
1	cup coarsely shredded carrot
1	cup chicken broth
¼	cup chopped walnuts, toasted
¼	cup snipped fresh flat-leaf parsley

PREP: *40 minutes*

COOK: *4 to 5 hours on high-heat setting*

MAKES: *8 servings*

1 Lightly coat the inside of a 6-quart slow cooker with nonstick cooking spray. Set aside 1 teaspoon of the lemon peel. In a small bowl combine the remaining 5 teaspoons lemon peel, the sage, seasoned salt, and pepper. Remove three-quarters of the sage mixture; sprinkle over chicken legs and rub in with your fingers. Place chicken in prepared slow cooker.

2 Meanwhile, for stuffing, in a large skillet melt butter over medium heat. Add mushrooms and garlic; cook and stir for 3 to 5 minutes or just until tender. Stir in remaining sage mixture. In a large bowl combine bread and carrot; add mushroom mixture. Drizzle with chicken broth, tossing gently.

3 Lightly pack stuffing on top of chicken. Cover and cook on high-heat setting for 4 to 5 hours.

4 Using a slotted spoon, transfer stuffing and chicken to a serving platter; discard juices in slow cooker.

5 In a small bowl combine the reserved 1 teaspoon lemon peel, the walnuts, and parsley; sprinkle over chicken and stuffing.

Per serving: 412 cal., 17 g total fat (5 g sat. fat), 146 mg chol., 1,450 mg sodium, 27 g carbo., 3 g fiber, 39 g pro.

You'll have plenty of the rich, creamy sauce—ladle this hearty dish over pasta or brown rice.

CHICKEN BREASTS WITH BRANDY SAUCE

PREP: *20 minutes*

COOK: *5 to 6 hours on low-heat setting or 2½ to 3 hours on high-heat setting*

MAKES: *6 servings*

2	cups quartered fresh mushrooms
6	medium bone-in chicken breast halves (about 3 pounds total), skinned and fat removed
¼	teaspoon black pepper
3	ounces thinly sliced prosciutto, cut into thin strips
¼	cup reduced-sodium chicken broth
¼	cup brandy
½	teaspoon dried thyme, crushed
2	tablespoons cornstarch
2	tablespoons cold water
½	of an 8-ounce package reduced-fat cream cheese (Neufchâtel), cubed
½	cup half-and-half

1 Place mushrooms in a 4½- to 6-quart slow cooker. Sprinkle chicken with pepper. Add chicken to slow cooker. Top with prosciutto. In a small bowl combine chicken broth, brandy, and thyme; pour over chicken mixture.

2 Cover and cook on low-heat setting for 5 to 6 hours or on high-heat setting for 2½ to 3 hours.

3 Transfer chicken and mushrooms to a serving platter, reserving cooking liquid. Cover chicken and mushrooms; keep warm.

4 For sauce, pour cooking liquid into a medium saucepan. In a small bowl combine cornstarch and the cold water; add to liquid in saucepan. Cook and stir over medium-high heat until thickened and bubbly. Cook and stir for 2 minutes more. Add cream cheese and half-and-half, whisking until smooth. Serve sauce with chicken.

Per serving: 445 cal., 23 g total fat (9 g sat. fat), 147 mg chol., 583 mg sodium, 5 g carbo., 0 g fiber, 45 g pro.

Look for sweet smoked paprika at food specialty shops or in the seasoning aisle of larger supermarkets.

CHICKEN WITH SMOKY PAPRIKA SAUCE

1	6-ounce jar (drained weight) sliced mushrooms, drained
2	small onions, cut into very thin wedges
1	small fennel bulb, very thinly sliced
6	small bone-in chicken breast halves (about 3 pounds total), skinned if desired
½	teaspoon salt
⅛	teaspoon black pepper
1	10-ounce container refrigerated Alfredo pasta sauce
1½	teaspoons sweet smoked paprika
6	ounces dried angel hair pasta
1	3-ounce package cream cheese, cubed and softened
2	tablespoons sliced almonds, toasted

PREP: *25 minutes*

COOK: *5 to 6 hours on low-heat setting or 2½ to 3 hours on high-heat setting*

MAKES: *6 servings*

1 In a 4- to 5-quart slow cooker combine drained mushrooms, onions, and fennel. Arrange chicken on top of vegetables; sprinkle with salt and pepper. In a small bowl stir together Alfredo pasta sauce and paprika; spoon over chicken.

2 Cover and cook on low-heat setting for 5 to 6 hours or on high-heat setting for 2½ hours.

3 Cook pasta according to package directions; drain. Remove chicken from slow cooker. Stir cooked pasta and cream cheese into vegetable mixture; transfer to a serving platter. Arrange chicken on top of pasta mixture; sprinkle with almonds.

Per serving: 464 cal., 24 g total fat (4 g sat. fat), 112 mg chol., 605 mg sodium, 29 g carbo., 3 g fiber, 38 g pro.

Be sure to sprinkle the bacon on just before serving so it stays nice and crisp.

JALAPEÑO & BACON CHICKEN BREASTS

PREP: *20 minutes*

COOK: *5 to 6 hours on low-heat setting or 2½ to 3 hours on high-heat setting; plus 15 minutes on high-heat setting*

MAKES: *6 servings*

6   medium bone-in chicken breast halves (about 3 pounds total), skinned and fat removed

1   tablespoon chili powder
     Salt

½   cup reduced-sodium chicken broth

2   tablespoons lemon juice

⅓   cup bottled pickled jalapeño chile pepper slices, drained

1   tablespoon cornstarch

1   tablespoon cold water

1   8-ounce package reduced-fat cream cheese (Neufchâtel), softened and cut into cubes

2   slices bacon or turkey bacon, crisp-cooked, drained, and crumbled

1 Sprinkle chicken with chili powder and salt. Place chicken, bone sides down, in a 4½- to 6-quart slow cooker. Pour chicken broth and lemon juice around chicken in slow cooker. Top with chile pepper slices.

2 Cover and cook on low-heat setting for 5 to 6 hours or on high-heat setting for 2½ to 3 hours.

3 Transfer chicken and chile peppers to a serving platter, reserving cooking liquid. Cover chicken with foil; keep warm.

4 If using low-heat setting, turn to high-heat setting. For sauce, in a small bowl combine cornstarch and the cold water; stir into reserved cooking liquid in slow cooker. Add cream cheese, whisking until combined. Cover and cook about 15 minutes more or until thickened. Serve sauce with chicken. Sprinkle with bacon.

Per serving: 429 cal., 26 g total fat (10 g sat. fat), 147 mg chol., 639 mg sodium, 5 g carbo., 1 g fiber, 43 g pro.

Calling all blue cheese lovers! This dish will become addictive. For added crunch, top with toasted walnuts.

BLUE CHEESE CHICKEN

8   medium bone-in chicken breast halves
     (about 4 pounds total), skinned and fat removed

½   teaspoon salt

¼   teaspoon black pepper

¾   cup reduced-sodium chicken broth

⅓   cup finely crumbled blue cheese (1 ounce)

⅔   cup half-and-half

2   teaspoons cornstarch

2   tablespoons finely chopped walnuts, toasted (optional)
     Finely crumbled blue cheese (optional)

PREP: *20 minutes*

COOK: *5 hours on low-heat setting or 2½ hours on high-heat setting*

MAKES: *8 servings*

1 Place chicken in a 5- to 6-quart slow cooker. Sprinkle with salt and pepper. Pour chicken broth over chicken; sprinkle with the ⅓ cup blue cheese.

2 Cover and cook on low-heat setting for 5 hours or on high-heat setting for 2½ hours.

3 Transfer chicken to a serving platter; discard cooking liquid. Cover chicken to keep warm.

4 For sauce, in a small saucepan combine half-and-half and cornstarch. Cook and stir over medium heat until thickened and bubbly. Cook and stir for 2 minutes more. Spoon sauce over chicken. If desired, sprinkle with nuts and additional blue cheese.

Per serving: 343 cal., 19 g total fat (7 g sat. fat), 125 mg chol., 348 mg sodium, 2 g carbo., 0 g fiber, 39 g pro.

Dressed up with pepper strips, this hearty dish satisfies the desire for food that is colorful.

TEX-MEX CHICKEN OVER RED BEANS & RICE

PREP: *15 minutes*

COOK: *4 to 5 hours on low-heat setting or 2 to 2½ hours on high-heat setting*

MAKES: *4 servings*

1   16-ounce package frozen (yellow, green, and red) peppers and onion stir-fry vegetables

1   pound skinless, boneless chicken breasts and/or thighs, cut into bite-size strips

1   12-ounce jar chicken gravy

1   cup purchased salsa with chipotles

1   7-ounce package red beans and rice mix

1 In a 3½- or 4-quart slow cooker combine frozen vegetables, chicken strips, gravy, and salsa.

2 Cover and cook on low-heat setting for 4 to 5 hours or on high-heat setting for 2 to 2½ hours.

3 Cook red beans and rice according to package directions. To serve, divide red beans and rice among four shallow bowls. Using a slotted spoon, spoon chicken and vegetable mixture over the beans and rice.

Per serving: 399 cal., 7 g total fat (2 g sat. fat), 68 mg chol., 1,480 mg sodium, 49 g carbo., 6 g fiber, 35 g pro.

Don't skimp on the 12 cloves of garlic. Gentle simmering in the slow cooker transforms their flavor from pungent and harsh to mellow and smooth.

ROSEMARY CHICKEN

Nonstick cooking spray

1½ pounds skinless, boneless chicken breasts or thighs

1 8- or 9-ounce package frozen artichoke hearts

½ cup chopped onion

12 cloves garlic, minced

½ cup reduced-sodium chicken broth

2 teaspoons dried rosemary, crushed

1 teaspoon finely shredded lemon peel

½ teaspoon black pepper

1 tablespoon cornstarch

1 tablespoon cold water

Lemon wedges (optional)

PREP: *25 minutes*

COOK: *6 to 7 hours on low-heat setting or 3 to 3½ hours on high-heat setting; plus 15 minutes on high-heat setting*

MAKES: *6 servings*

1 Coat an unheated large nonstick skillet with nonstick cooking spray. Preheat over medium heat. Brown chicken, half at a time, in hot skillet.

2 In a 3½- or 4-quart slow cooker combine frozen artichoke hearts, onion, and garlic. In a small bowl combine chicken broth, rosemary, lemon peel, and pepper. Pour over vegetables in slow cooker. Add browned chicken; spoon some of the artichoke mixture over chicken.

3 Cover and cook on low-heat setting for 6 to 7 hours or on high-heat setting for 3 to 3½ hours.

4 Using a slotted spoon, transfer chicken and artichokes to a serving platter, reserving cooking liquid. Cover chicken and artichokes with foil; keep warm.

5 If using low-heat setting, turn to high-heat setting. For sauce, in a small bowl combine cornstarch and the cold water. Stir into liquid in slow cooker. Cover and cook about 15 minutes more or until slightly thickened. Spoon sauce over chicken and artichokes. If desired, serve with lemon wedges.

Per serving: 161 cal., 2 g total fat (0 g sat. fat), 66 mg chol., 126 mg sodium, 8 g carbo., 2 g fiber, 28 g pro.

This dish is patterned after an ever-favorite oven casserole. Because the chicken is cut into spoonable bite-size pieces, it's just right for a potluck buffet.

CHICKEN, BROCCOLI & RICE

PREP: *20 minutes*

COOK: *4 to 5 hours on low-heat setting or 2 to 2½ hours on high-heat setting; plus 30 minutes on high-heat setting*

MAKES: *8 servings*

2   pounds skinless, boneless chicken breasts and/or thighs, cut into bite-size pieces

¾   cup chopped onion

2   10¾-ounce cans condensed cream of mushroom soup

1   14-ounce can chicken broth

1   8-ounce package shredded American cheese

½   teaspoon black pepper

1   16-ounce package frozen cut broccoli, thawed and well drained

2¼   cups instant white rice

1 In a 4- to 5-quart slow cooker combine chicken and onion. In a medium bowl stir together cream of mushroom soup, chicken broth, cheese, and pepper. Pour over chicken mixture.

2 Cover and cook on low-heat setting for 4 to 5 hours or on high-heat setting for 2 to 2½ hours.

3 If using low-heat setting, turn to high-heat setting. Stir in broccoli and uncooked rice. Cover and cook for 30 minutes more.

Per serving: 428 cal., 15 g total fat (7 g sat. fat), 85 mg chol., 1,149 mg sodium, 34 g carbo., 3 g fiber, 37 g pro.

A wonderful blend of tangy and sweet makes a winning sauce for chicken and wild rice. Save time by leaving the apple wedges unpeeled; they'll retain their shape better too.

CRANBERRY CHICKEN

2	medium apples, cored and cut into wedges
1	medium onion, thinly sliced
1	16-ounce can whole cranberry sauce
¼	cup frozen lemonade concentrate, thawed
2	tablespoons quick-cooking tapioca
2	tablespoons honey
¼	teaspoon salt
6	skinless, boneless chicken breast halves (about 2 pounds total)
2	6-ounce packages long grain and wild rice mix

PREP: *20 minutes*

COOK: *6 to 7 hours on low-heat setting or 3 to 3½ hours on high-heat setting*

MAKES: *6 servings*

1 In a 3½- or 4-quart slow cooker combine apples and onion. In a medium bowl combine cranberry sauce, lemonade concentrate, tapioca, honey, and salt. Add chicken breasts, one at a time, to cranberry mixture, turning to coat. Place chicken on top of apple mixture. Pour cranberry mixture over chicken.

2 Cover and cook on low-heat setting for 6 to 7 hours or on high-heat setting for 3 to 3½ hours.

3 In a large saucepan prepare long grain and wild rice with seasoning packets according to package directions. Serve with chicken and sauce.

Per serving: 565 cal., 2 g total fat (1 g sat. fat), 88 mg chol., 993 mg sodium, 96 g carbo., 4 g fiber, 40 g pro.

Some say the secret to good cooking is good ingredients. In this slow-simmered pleaser, you'll find four classic Greek ingredients: chicken, feta, olives, and pine nuts.

GREEK CHICKEN WITH COUSCOUS

PREP: *15 minutes*

COOK: *5 to 6 hours on low-heat setting or 2½ to 3 hours on high-heat setting*

STAND: *5 minutes*

MAKES: *8 servings*

2 pounds skinless, boneless chicken breasts, cut into ½-inch pieces

2 14½-ounce cans diced tomatoes with basil, oregano, and garlic

1½ cups water

2 6-ounce packages couscous with toasted pine nut mix

1 cup crumbled feta cheese (4 ounces)

½ cup pitted kalamata olives, coarsely chopped

1 Place chicken in a 3½- or 4-quart slow cooker. Add undrained tomatoes and the water.

2 Cover and cook on low-heat setting for 5 to 6 hours or on high-heat setting for 2½ to 3 hours. Remove liner from slow cooker, if possible, or turn off cooker. Stir in couscous. Cover and let stand for 5 minutes. Fluff couscous mixture with a fork.

3 To serve, spoon couscous mixture onto eight dinner plates. Sprinkle with feta cheese and olives.

Per serving: 377 cal., 8 g total fat (4 g sat. fat), 82 mg chol., 1,226 mg sodium, 41 g carbo., 3 g fiber, 36 g pro.

Legend has it that chicken tetrazzini was created for a famous opera singer—but that doesn't stop this dish from being wonderfully homey, crowd-pleasing fare!

EASY CHICKEN TETRAZZINI

2½	pounds skinless, boneless chicken breasts and/or thighs, cut into 1-inch pieces
2	4½-ounce jars (drained weight) sliced mushrooms, drained
1	16-ounce jar Alfredo pasta sauce
¼	cup chicken broth or water
2	tablespoons dry sherry (optional)
¼	teaspoon black pepper
¼	teaspoon ground nutmeg
10	ounces broken dried spaghetti or linguine
¾	cup thinly sliced green onions
⅔	cup grated Parmesan cheese

PREP: *20 minutes*

COOK: *5 to 6 hours on low-heat setting or 2½ to 3 hours on high-heat setting*

MAKES: *8 servings*

1 In a 3½- or 4-quart slow cooker combine chicken and mushrooms. In a medium bowl stir together Alfredo sauce, chicken broth, sherry (if desired), pepper, and nutmeg. Pour over chicken mixture.

2 Cover and cook on low-heat setting for 5 to 6 hours or on high-heat setting for 2½ to 3 hours.

3 Cook pasta according to package directions; drain. Stir hot cooked pasta, green onion, and ½ cup of the Parmesan cheese into chicken mixture in slow cooker.

4 To serve, sprinkle with remaining Parmesan cheese.

Per serving: 433 cal., 14 g total fat (7 g sat. fat), 120 mg chol., 701 mg sodium, 31 g carbo., 2 g fiber, 43 g pro.

Serve this chili in bread bowls if your supermarket bakery sells them or spoon it over corn bread.

CHICKEN CHILI

PREP: *25 minutes*

COOK: *5 to 6 hours on low-heat setting or 2½ to 3 hours on high-heat setting*

MAKES: *2 servings*

Nonstick cooking spray

8 ounces skinless, boneless chicken breasts, cut into 1-inch pieces

1 15-ounce can white kidney beans (cannellini beans) or Great Northern beans, rinsed and drained

1¼ cups reduced-sodium chicken broth

⅓ cup chopped green sweet pepper

¼ cup chopped onion

½ of a small fresh jalapeño chile pepper, seeded and finely chopped (see tip, page 19)

¼ teaspoon ground cumin

¼ teaspoon dried oregano, crushed

⅛ teaspoon white pepper

1 clove garlic, minced

¼ cup shredded Monterey Jack cheese (1 ounce) (optional)

1 Lightly coat an unheated medium skillet with nonstick cooking spray. Preheat skillet over medium-high heat. Brown chicken in hot skillet; drain off fat.

2 In a 1½-quart slow cooker combine chicken, beans, chicken broth, sweet pepper, onion, chile pepper, cumin, oregano, white pepper, and garlic.

3 Cover and cook on low-heat setting for 5 to 6 hours or on high-heat setting for 2½ to 3 hours. If no heat setting is available, cook for 4 to 5 hours. If desired, sprinkle individual servings with cheese.

Per serving: 275 cal., 2 g total fat (0 g sat. fat), 66 mg chol., 750 mg sodium, 33 g carbo., 11 g fiber, 40 g pro.

Garam masala is a blend of ground spices that's used in Indian cooking. Look for it in the seasoning section of larger supermarkets or at specialty food shops.

TANDOORI CHICKEN & VEGETABLES

3	carrots, thinly sliced
1	onion, halved and thinly sliced
1½	teaspoons garam masala
½	teaspoon garlic salt
¼	teaspoon ground ginger
¼	teaspoon ground turmeric
6	skinless, boneless chicken breast halves (about 2¼ pounds total) or 2¼ to 2½ pounds skinless, boneless chicken thighs
1	14½-ounce can diced tomatoes with basil, oregano, and garlic
	Hot cooked rice

PREP: *20 minutes*

COOK: *4 to 5 hours on low-heat setting or 2 to 2½ hours on high-heat setting*

MAKES: *6 servings*

1 In a 4- to 5-quart slow cooker combine carrots and onion; set aside.

2 In a small bowl combine garam masala, garlic salt, ginger, and turmeric; sprinkle evenly over chicken. Place chicken on top of vegetables in slow cooker. Pour undrained tomatoes over chicken.

3 Cover and cook on low-heat setting for 4 to 5 hours or on high-heat setting for 2 to 2½ hours.

4 Serve chicken and vegetables with hot cooked rice. Spoon cooking liquid over chicken and rice to moisten.

Per serving: 343 cal., 3 g total fat (1 g sat. fat), 99 mg chol., 549 mg sodium, 33 g carbo., 2 g fiber, 43 g pro.

With moist chicken, earthy mushrooms, and sour cream spooned over soft noodles, stroganoff is satisfying comfort food.

CHICKEN STROGANOFF

PREP: *20 minutes*

COOK: *6 to 7 hours on low-heat setting or 3 to 3½ hours on high-heat setting*

MAKES: *6 to 8 servings*

2   pounds skinless, boneless chicken breasts and/or thighs, cut into 1-inch pieces

1   cup chopped onion

2   10¾-ounce cans condensed cream of mushroom soup with roasted garlic

⅓   cup water

12   ounces dried wide egg noodles

1   8-ounce carton dairy sour cream

    Freshly ground black pepper (optional)

1 In a 3½- or 4-quart slow cooker combine chicken and onion. In a medium bowl stir together cream of mushroom soup with roasted garlic and the water. Pour over chicken and onion.

2 Cover and cook on low-heat setting for 6 to 7 hours or on high-heat setting for 3 to 3½ hours.

3 Cook noodles according to package directions; drain. Just before serving, stir sour cream into chicken mixture. To serve, spoon chicken mixture over hot cooked noodles. If desired, sprinkle with black pepper.

Per serving: 532 cal., 14 g total fat (6 g sat. fat), 162 mg chol., 775 mg sodium, 54 g carbo., 3 g fiber, 46 g pro.

These succulent drumsticks, with an innovative blend of lemonade concentrate and hoisin sauce, are all but impossible to resist.

LEMON-HOISIN CHICKEN DRUMSTICKS

4	pounds chicken drumsticks, skinned and fat removed
½	teaspoon five spice powder
¼	teaspoon salt
⅛	teaspoon cayenne pepper
⅓	cup frozen lemonade concentrate, thawed
¼	cup hoisin sauce
¼	cup rice vinegar or cider vinegar
2	tablespoons cornstarch
2	tablespoons cold water
⅓	cup thinly sliced green onions
1	tablespoon sesame seeds, toasted

PREP: *20 minutes*

COOK: *6 to 7 hours on low-heat setting or 3 to 3½ hours on high-heat setting*

MAKES: *6 servings*

1 Place chicken in a 3½- or 4-quart slow cooker. In a small bowl combine five spice powder, salt, and cayenne pepper; sprinkle over chicken. In a medium bowl combine lemonade concentrate, hoisin sauce, and vinegar; pour over chicken.

2 Cover and cook on low-heat setting for 6 to 7 hours or on high-heat setting for 3 to 3½ hours.

3 Using a slotted spoon, transfer chicken to a serving platter; cover and keep warm. Strain cooking juices; skim off fat. Transfer 1½ cups of the cooking juices to a small saucepan. In a small bowl combine cornstarch and the cold water; add to saucepan along with green onion. Cook and stir until thickened and bubbly; cook and stir for 2 minutes more. Spoon over chicken; sprinkle with sesame seeds.

Per serving: 272 cal., 7 g total fat (2 g sat. fat), 130 mg chol., 355 mg sodium, 14 g carbo., 0 g fiber, 36 g pro.

The superb balance of tomato, ginger, garlic, and crushed red pepper will make this dish a favorite. (Recipe pictured on page 104.)

ZESTY GINGER-TOMATO CHICKEN

PREP: *20 minutes*

COOK: *6 to 7 hours on low-heat setting or 3 to 3½ hours on high-heat setting*

MAKES: *6 servings*

2½   to 3 pounds chicken drumsticks and/or thighs, skinned and fat removed

2   14½-ounce cans diced tomatoes

2   tablespoons quick-cooking tapioca

1   tablespoon grated fresh ginger

1   tablespoon snipped fresh cilantro or parsley

4   cloves garlic, minced

½   teaspoon crushed red pepper

½   teaspoon salt

3   cups hot cooked quinoa or brown rice

     Snipped fresh cilantro or parsley (optional)

1 Place chicken in a 3½- or 4-quart slow cooker. Drain one can of the tomatoes. In a medium bowl combine drained and undrained tomatoes, the tapioca, ginger, the 1 tablespoon cilantro, the garlic, crushed red pepper, and salt. Pour over chicken.

2 Cover and cook on low-heat setting for 6 to 7 hours or on high-heat setting for 3 to 3½ hours.

3 Skim off fat. Serve with hot cooked quinoa. If desired, sprinkle with additional cilantro.

Per serving: 302 cal., 6 g total fat (1 g sat. fat), 81 mg chol., 549 mg sodium, 35 g carbo., 4 g fiber, 28 g pro.

Chicken thighs and drumsticks generally are a meat-department bargain. Cooked in a robust barbecue sauce, they're as tasty as they are economical.

BARBECUE-STYLE CHICKEN

2	medium potatoes, cut into ½-inch pieces
1	large green sweet pepper, cut into strips
1	medium onion, sliced
1	tablespoon quick-cooking tapioca
2	pounds chicken thighs or drumsticks, skinned and fat removed
1	8-ounce can tomato sauce
2	tablespoons packed brown sugar
1	tablespoon Worcestershire sauce
1	tablespoon yellow mustard
1	clove garlic, minced
¼	teaspoon salt

PREP: *25 minutes*

COOK: *10 to 12 hours on low-heat setting or 5 to 6 hours on high-heat setting*

MAKES: *4 or 5 servings*

1 In a 3½- or 4-quart slow cooker combine potatoes, sweet pepper, and onion. Sprinkle tapioca over potato mixture. Place chicken on top of the vegetables. For sauce, in a small bowl stir together tomato sauce, brown sugar, Worcestershire sauce, mustard, garlic, and salt. Pour sauce over chicken.

2 Cover and cook on low-heat setting for 10 to 12 hours or on high-heat setting for 5 to 6 hours.

3 Transfer chicken and vegetables to a large serving bowl. Skim fat from sauce. Spoon sauce over chicken and vegetables.

Per serving: 267 cal., 4 g total fat (1 g sat. fat), 98 mg chol., 594 mg sodium, 27 g carbo., 2 g fiber, 29 g pro.

Chicken, eggplant, and olives are common in both Greek and Italian cuisines, so either the Greek or Italian seasoning is a delightful choice for this fresh-tasting dish.

MEDITERRANEAN CHICKEN THIGHS

PREP: *20 minutes*

COOK: *5 to 6 hours on low-heat setting or 2½ to 3 hours on high-heat setting*

MAKES: *6 servings*

½ of a medium eggplant, peeled and cubed (8 ounces)

1 medium onion, cut into wedges

¼ cup pitted ripe olives, halved

2 cloves garlic, minced

3 pounds chicken thighs, skinned and fat removed

2 teaspoons finely shredded lemon peel

1 teaspoon dried Greek seasoning or Italian seasoning, crushed

¼ teaspoon black pepper

⅛ teaspoon salt

⅓ cup reduced-sodium chicken broth

⅔ cup coarsely chopped plum tomatoes

½ cup shredded Parmesan cheese (2 ounces) (optional)

1 In a 4- to 5-quart slow cooker combine eggplant, onion, olives, and garlic. Top with chicken. Sprinkle chicken with lemon peel, Greek seasoning, pepper, and salt. Pour chicken broth over chicken.

2 Cover and cook on low-heat setting for 5 to 6 hours or on high-heat setting for 2½ to 3 hours.

3 Using a slotted spoon, transfer chicken and eggplant mixture to a serving platter. Discard cooking liquid. Sprinkle chicken with tomato and, if desired, Parmesan cheese.

Per serving: 179 cal., 6 g total fat (1 g sat. fat), 107 mg chol., 234 mg sodium, 5 g carbo., 2 g fiber, 26 g pro.

Here's a mild sweet-sour chicken dish made with mango chutney and chili sauce. Serve rice alongside to soak up every last drop of the sauce. (Recipe pictured on page 105.)

GINGER CHICKEN

½	cup mango chutney (large fruit pieces cut up)
¼	cup bottled chili sauce
2	tablespoons quick-cooking tapioca
1½	teaspoons grated fresh ginger or ½ teaspoon ground ginger
12	chicken thighs (about 4 pounds total), skinned and fat removed
	Hot cooked brown rice (optional)
	Sliced green onions (optional)

PREP: *15 minutes*

COOK: *5 to 6 hours on low-heat setting or 2½ to 3 hours on high-heat setting*

MAKES: *6 servings*

1 In a 4- to 5-quart slow cooker combine chutney, chili sauce, tapioca, and ginger. Add chicken, turning to coat.

2 Cover and cook on low-heat setting for 5 to 6 hours or on high-heat setting for 2½ to 3 hours. If desired, serve chicken over rice and sprinkle with green onion.

Per serving: 264 cal., 7 g total fat (2 g sat. fat), 143 mg chol., 494 mg sodium, 16 g carbo., 1 g fiber, 34 g pro.

There's no need to cook the rice separately. Simply stir it into the chicken mixture and cook it in the sauce for a convenient one-dish dinner.

EASY CHICKEN & RICE

PREP: *20 minutes*

COOK: *5 to 6 hours on low-heat setting or 2½ to 3 hours on high-heat setting; plus 10 minutes on high-heat setting*

MAKES: *4 servings*

2	cups sliced fresh mushrooms
1	cup sliced celery
½	cup chopped onion
1½	teaspoons dried dill
¼	teaspoon black pepper
2	pounds chicken thighs, skinned and fat removed
1	10¾-ounce can condensed cream of mushroom or cream of chicken soup
¾	cup chicken broth
1½	cups instant rice

1 In a 3½- or 4-quart slow cooker combine mushrooms, celery, onion, dill, and pepper. Place chicken on top of mushroom mixture. In a small bowl combine cream of mushroom soup and chicken broth. Pour over chicken.

2 Cover and cook on low-heat setting for 5 to 6 hours or on high-heat setting for 2½ to 3 hours.

3 If using low-heat setting, turn to high-heat setting. Stir uncooked rice into mushroom mixture. Cover and cook for 10 minutes more.

Per serving: 516 cal., 12 g total fat (3 g sat. fat), 108 mg chol., 840 mg sodium, 66 g carbo., 3 g fiber, 34 g pro.

In this luscious recipe, already creamy Alfredo sauce gets a little extra richness from cream cheese.

BASIL-CREAM CHICKEN THIGHS

2½	pounds chicken thighs, skinned and fat removed
¼	teaspoon black pepper
1	3-ounce package cream cheese, cubed
1	10-ounce container refrigerated Alfredo pasta sauce
¼	cup water
1	teaspoon dried basil, crushed
1	16-ounce package loose-pack frozen broccoli, cauliflower, and carrots
3	cups hot cooked fettuccine

PREP: *15 minutes*

COOK: *6 to 7 hours on low-heat setting or 3 to 3½ hours on high-heat setting*

MAKES: *6 servings*

1 Place chicken in a 3½- or 4-quart slow cooker. Sprinkle with pepper. Add cream cheese. In a small bowl stir together Alfredo sauce, the water, and basil. Pour over chicken mixture. Top with frozen vegetables.

2 Cover and cook on low-heat setting for 6 to 7 hours or on high-heat setting for 3 to 3½ hours. Transfer chicken to a serving platter. Stir vegetable mixture; serve over chicken and hot cooked fettuccine.

Per serving: 456 cal., 24 g total fat (12 g sat. fat), 136 mg chol., 415 mg sodium, 27 g carbo., 4 g fiber, 30 g pro.

*Look for lemongrass in the produce aisle of most supermarkets or your local Asian market.
If you can't find it, substitute an equal amount of shredded lemon peel.*

THAI CHICKEN & VEGETABLE SOUP

PREP: *30 minutes*

COOK: *7 to 8 hours on
low-heat setting or 3½ to 4 hours
on high-heat setting*

STAND: *15 minutes*

MAKES: *6 servings*

1½	pounds skinless, boneless chicken thighs, cut into 1-inch pieces
3	cups cauliflower florets
2	cups bias-sliced carrot
¾	cup chopped onion
1	8-ounce can bamboo shoots, drained
3	tablespoons finely chopped lemongrass
3	tablespoons grated fresh ginger
4	cloves garlic, minced
½	teaspoon crushed red pepper
2	14-ounce cans reduced-sodium chicken broth
1	15-ounce can unsweetened light coconut milk
2	cups fresh pea pods, trimmed and halved
3	fresh serrano chile peppers, seeded and chopped (see tip, page 19)
1	tablespoon finely shredded lime peel

1 In a 4- to 5-quart slow cooker combine chicken, cauliflower, carrot, onion, bamboo shoots, lemongrass, ginger, garlic, and crushed red pepper. Pour chicken broth over chicken mixture.

2 Cover and cook on low-heat setting for 7 to 8 hours or on high-heat setting for 3½ to 4 hours.

3 Stir in coconut milk, pea pods, chile peppers, and lime peel. Remove liner from slow cooker, if possible, or turn off cooker. Cover and let stand for 15 minutes.

Per serving: 260 cal., 9 g total fat (4 g sat. fat), 91 mg chol., 460 mg sodium, 16 g carbo., 4 g fiber, 27 g pro.

Red sweet pepper pieces, cilantro, and corn make this a colorful south-of-the-border home-style soup.

MEXICAN CHICKEN SOUP

Nonstick cooking spray

2 skinless, boneless chicken thighs, cut into 1-inch pieces (about 6 ounces total)

1 small skinless, boneless chicken breast half, cut into 1-inch pieces (about 4 ounces)

1¼ cups reduced-sodium chicken broth

¾ cup coarsely chopped red or green sweet pepper

½ cup loose-pack frozen whole kernel corn

¼ cup chopped onion

1 small fresh jalapeño chile pepper, seeded and finely chopped (see tip, page 19)

½ teaspoon ground cumin

⅛ teaspoon salt

⅛ teaspoon black pepper

1 clove garlic, minced

1 tablespoon snipped fresh cilantro

2 tablespoons shredded Monterey Jack cheese or Monterey Jack cheese with jalapeño chile peppers

PREP: *25 minutes*

COOK: *5 to 6 hours on low-heat setting or 2½ to 3 hours on high-heat setting*

MAKES: *2 servings*

1 Lightly coat an unheated medium skillet with nonstick cooking spray. Preheat skillet over medium-high heat. Add chicken to hot skillet; cook and stir until browned. Drain off fat.

2 In a 1½ quart slow cooker combine chicken, chicken broth, sweet pepper, corn, onion, chile pepper, cumin, salt, black pepper, and garlic.

3 Cover and cook on low-heat setting for 5 to 6 hours or on high-heat setting for 2½ to 3 hours. If no heat setting is available, cook for 4 to 5 hours.

4 Stir in cilantro. Sprinkle individual servings with cheese.

Per serving: 271 cal., 7 g total fat (3 g sat. fat), 107 mg chol., 634 mg sodium, 16 g carbo., 3 g fiber, 36 g pro.

Although chicken soup is touted as having tremendous comforting powers when you're under the weather, don't wait until you're sick to enjoy this version. It's terrific anytime.

HERBED CHICKEN NOODLE SOUP

PREP: *25 minutes*

COOK: *6 to 7 hours on low-heat setting or 3 to 3½ hours on high-heat setting; plus 1 hour on high-heat setting*

MAKES: *6 servings*

1   pound boneless, skinless chicken thighs, cut into 1-inch pieces

1   10¾-ounce can condensed cream of chicken soup

2   stalks celery, thinly sliced

2   medium carrots, thinly sliced

1   medium onion, chopped

1   4½-ounce can (drained weight) sliced mushrooms, drained

1   clove garlic, minced

½   teaspoon dried sage, crushed

½   teaspoon dried thyme, crushed

¼   teaspoon dried rosemary, crushed

⅛   teaspoon black pepper

2   14-ounce cans chicken broth

½   of a 16-ounce package frozen home-style egg noodles (about 3 cups)

1 In a 3½- or 4-quart slow cooker combine chicken, cream of chicken soup, celery, carrots, onion, drained mushrooms, garlic, sage, thyme, rosemary, and pepper. Pour chicken broth over chicken mixture.

2 Cover and cook on low-heat setting for 6 to 7 hours or on high-heat setting for 3 to 3½ hours.

3 If using low-heat setting, turn to high-heat setting. Stir in frozen noodles. Cover and cook for 1 hour more.

Per serving: 241 cal., 8 g total fat (2 g sat. fat), 103 mg chol., 1,115 mg sodium, 22 g carbo., 2 g fiber, 20 g pro.

For ages, Italians have been savoring the creamy richness white kidney beans bring to cooking. Follow their lead and give the beans a go in this hearty and satisfying dish. Serve it in shallow bowls with crusty bread.

ITALIAN CHICKEN WITH WHITE BEANS

1	cup chopped onion
1	cup chopped carrot
½	cup thinly sliced celery
3	cloves garlic, minced
2	pounds skinless, boneless chicken thighs
¼	teaspoon salt
⅛	teaspoon black pepper
1	14½-ounce can diced tomatoes
½	cup chicken broth
½	cup dry white wine
1½	teaspoons dried Italian seasoning, crushed
1	15- or 19-ounce can white kidney beans (cannellini beans), rinsed and drained
	Grated Parmesan cheese

PREP: *20 minutes*

COOK: *6 to 7 hours on low-heat setting or 3 to 3½ hours on high-heat setting*

STAND: *10 minutes*

MAKES: *6 to 8 servings*

1 In a 3½- or 4-quart slow cooker combine onion, carrot, celery, and garlic. Add chicken; sprinkle with salt and pepper. In a medium bowl stir together undrained tomatoes, chicken broth, wine, and Italian seasoning. Pour over chicken mixture.

2 Cover and cook on low-heat setting for 6 to 7 hours or on high-heat setting for 3 to 3½ hours. Remove liner from slow cooker, if possible, or turn off cooker. Stir beans into chicken mixture. Cover and let stand for 10 minutes.

3 Using a slotted spoon, transfer chicken and vegetables to a serving dish, reserving cooking liquid. Drizzle chicken and vegetables with enough of the cooking liquid to moisten. Sprinkle individual servings with Parmesan cheese.

Per serving: 296 cal., 7 g total fat (2 g sat. fat), 123 mg chol., 577 mg sodium, 19 g carbo., 5 g fiber, 37 g pro.

Rice and two kinds of beans make this South American–style meal especially hearty. You'll love the contrast of sweet cranberry and hot chipotle pepper.

CRANBERRY-CHIPOTLE CHICKEN

PREP: *30 minutes*

COOK: *6 to 7 hours on low-heat setting or 3 to 3½ hours on high-heat setting*

MAKES: *6 servings*

1 16-ounce can whole cranberry sauce

1 canned chipotle chile pepper in adobo sauce, finely chopped (see tip, page 19)

1 tablespoon lime juice

¼ teaspoon salt

8 ounces bacon, cut into 1-inch pieces

1 cup chopped onion

1 15½-ounce can black beans, rinsed and drained

1 15½-ounce can white kidney beans (cannellini beans), rinsed and drained

1 cup chopped plum tomatoes

½ cup long grain rice

½ cup chicken broth

3 cloves garlic, minced

½ teaspoon salt

½ teaspoon ground cumin

¼ teaspoon ground cinnamon

1 pound skinless, boneless chicken thighs

Avocado slices (optional)

Sliced green onions (optional)

1 For sauce, in a small bowl combine cranberry sauce, chile pepper, lime juice, and the ¼ teaspoon salt; set aside.

2 In a large skillet cook bacon and onion until bacon is crisp. Drain off fat.

3 In a 3½- or 4-quart slow cooker combine bacon mixture, black beans, white kidney beans, tomato, uncooked rice, chicken broth, garlic, the ½ teaspoon salt, the cumin, and cinnamon. Top with chicken. Pour sauce over chicken.

4 Cover and cook on low-heat setting for 6 to 7 hours or on high-heat setting for 3 to 3½ hours.

5 If desired, top individual servings with avocado slices and sprinkle with sliced green onion.

Per serving: 517 cal., 14 g total fat (3 g sat. fat), 72 mg chol., 1,137 mg sodium, 71 g carbo., 11 g fiber, 28 g pro.

If you enjoy really zesty Cajun food, splash on some bottled hot pepper sauce. (Recipe pictured on page 105.)

JAMBALAYA-STYLE CHICKEN & SHRIMP

1	pound skinless, boneless chicken thighs, cut into bite-size pieces
4	ounces smoked turkey sausage, halved lengthwise and cut into ½-inch-thick slices
1½	cups chopped red, yellow, and/or green sweet pepper
1	cup thinly sliced celery
1	cup chopped onion
1	14½-ounce can no-salt-added diced tomatoes
1	10-ounce can chopped tomatoes and green chile peppers
2	tablespoons quick-cooking tapioca
1	teaspoon dried basil, crushed
¼	teaspoon cayenne pepper
4	ounces frozen peeled and deveined medium shrimp with tails, thawed
2	cups loose-pack frozen cut okra
3	cups hot cooked brown rice

PREP: *30 minutes*

COOK: *6 to 8 hours on low-heat setting or 3 to 4 hours on high-heat setting; plus 30 minutes on high-heat setting*

MAKES: *6 servings*

1 In a 3½- or 4-quart slow cooker combine chicken, sausage, sweet pepper, celery, and onion. Stir in undrained diced tomatoes, undrained chopped tomatoes and green chile peppers, tapioca, basil, and cayenne pepper.

2 Cover and cook on low-heat setting for 6 to 8 hours or on high-heat setting for 3 to 4 hours.

3 If using low-heat setting, turn to high-heat setting. Stir in shrimp and okra. Cover and cook about 30 minutes more or until shrimp are opaque. Serve with hot cooked brown rice.

Per serving: 322 cal., 6 g total fat (2 g sat. fat), 101 mg chol., 496 mg sodium, 40 g carbo., 5 g fiber, 27 g pro.

Mashed potatoes—with all that peeling, boiling, and mashing—didn't used to qualify as hassle-free fare. Nowadays they do, thanks to refrigerated mashed potatoes, which make a satisfying topper for this casserole-style medley.

POTATO-TOPPED CHICKEN & VEGETABLES

PREP: *20 minutes*

COOK: *7 to 8 hours on low-heat setting or 3½ to 4 hours on high-heat setting; plus 30 minutes on low-heat setting*

MAKES: *6 servings*

1	16-ounce package peeled baby carrots
1	medium onion, cut into wedges
2	pounds skinless, boneless chicken thighs
1	10¾-ounce can condensed cream of chicken or cream of mushroom soup
1	teaspoon dried basil, crushed
¼	teaspoon black pepper
1	20-ounce package refrigerated mashed potatoes
½	cup shredded cheddar cheese (2 ounces)
4	cloves garlic, minced

1 In a 3½- to 4½-quart slow cooker combine carrots and onion. Add chicken. In a medium bowl combine cream of chicken soup, basil, and pepper. Spoon over chicken mixture.

2 Cover and cook on low-heat setting for 7 to 8 hours or on high-heat setting for 3½ to 4 hours.

3 If using high-heat setting, turn to low-heat setting. In a large bowl stir together mashed potatoes, cheese, and garlic. Spoon over chicken mixture. Cover and cook about 30 minutes more or until potatoes are heated through. (Do not overcook or potatoes will become too soft.)

Per serving: 393 cal., 14 g total fat (5 g sat. fat), 135 mg chol., 707 mg sodium, 27 g carbo., 4 g fiber, 37 g pro.

You'll taste a hint of exotic Asian cooking in this blend of licorice-flavored anise seeds, plums, and oranges. The couscous is a snap to prepare; just stir it into boiling water about 5 minutes before serving time.

CHICKEN WITH ORANGE COUSCOUS

¾ cup bottled plum sauce

⅓ cup orange juice

¼ cup orange marmalade

2 tablespoons quick-cooking tapioca

¼ teaspoon anise seeds, crushed

2½ to 2¾ pounds skinless, boneless chicken thighs

2¼ cups water

1 tablespoon orange marmalade

1 10-ounce package quick-cooking couscous

¼ teaspoon salt

Orange peel strips and orange slices (optional)

PREP: *15 minutes*

COOK: *5 to 6 hours on low-heat setting or 2½ to 3 hours on high-heat setting*

MAKES: *6 servings*

1 For sauce, in a small bowl combine plum sauce, orange juice, the ¼ cup orange marmalade, the tapioca, and anise seeds. Place chicken in a 3½- or 4-quart slow cooker. Pour sauce over chicken.

2 Cover and cook on low-heat setting for 5 to 6 hours or on high-heat setting for 2½ to 3 hours. Remove chicken; keep warm. Skim fat from sauce.

3 In a medium saucepan combine the water and the 1 tablespoon orange marmalade; bring to boiling. Remove from heat. Stir in couscous and salt. Cover; let stand for 5 minutes. Fluff couscous with a fork just before serving. Serve chicken and sauce with couscous. If desired, garnish chicken with orange peel strips and couscous with orange slices.

Per serving: 534 cal., 8 g total fat (2 g sat. fat), 157 mg chol., 404 mg sodium, 70 g carbo., 3 g fiber, 44 g pro.

This Tex-Mex take on a one-dish meal has everything—bread, chicken, beans, and salad—all stacked up on one plate. Customize this meal with your favorite salsa.

CHICKEN TOSTADAS

PREP: *30 minutes*

COOK: *5 to 6 hours on low-heat setting or 2½ to 3 hours on high-heat setting*

MAKES: *10 servings*

2   fresh jalapeño chile peppers, seeded and finely chopped (see tip, page 19)

8   cloves garlic, minced

3   tablespoons chili powder

3   tablespoons lime juice

¼   teaspoon bottled hot pepper sauce

1   medium onion, sliced and separated into rings

2   pounds skinless, boneless chicken thighs

1   16-ounce can refried beans

10   purchased tostada shells

1½   cups shredded cheddar cheese (6 ounces)

2   cups shredded lettuce

1¼   cups purchased salsa

¾   cup dairy sour cream

¾   cup sliced ripe olives (optional)

1 In a 3½- to 5-quart slow cooker combine chile peppers, garlic, chili powder, lime juice, and hot pepper sauce. Add onion; top with chicken.

2 Cover and cook on low-heat setting for 5 to 6 hours or on high-heat setting for 2½ to 3 hours.

3 Remove chicken and onion from slow cooker, reserving ½ cup of the cooking liquid. Using two forks, pull chicken apart into shreds. In a medium bowl combine shredded chicken, onion, and the reserved ½ cup cooking liquid.

4 Spread refried beans on tostada shells. Top with hot chicken mixture and shredded cheese. Serve with lettuce, salsa, sour cream, and, if desired, olives.

Per serving: 333 cal., 16 g total fat (7 g sat. fat), 100 mg chol., 574 mg sodium, 21 g carbo., 5 g fiber, 27 g pro.

It's the coconut milk and curry powder that give this lush soup its exotic flair. Top it with peanuts and toasted coconut and serve it with wedges of pita bread—perfect for mopping up the last few drops. (Recipe pictured on page 106.)

CREAMY CURRY SOUP

1	10¾-ounce can condensed cream of chicken or cream of celery soup
1	cup water
2	teaspoons curry powder
1¼	pounds skinless, boneless chicken thighs or breasts, cut into ¾-inch pieces
2	cups sliced carrots
1	13½-ounce can unsweetened coconut milk
1	red sweet pepper, cut into thin bite-size strips
½	cup sliced green onions
	Chopped peanuts (optional)
	Toasted coconut (optional)

PREP: *20 minutes*

COOK: *4 to 5 hours on low-heat setting or 2 to 2½ hours on high-heat setting; plus 15 minutes on low-heat setting*

MAKES: *6 servings*

1 In a 3½- to 4½-quart slow cooker combine cream of chicken soup and the water. Stir in curry powder. Stir in chicken and carrot.

2 Cover and cook on low-heat setting for 4 to 5 hours or on high-heat setting for 2 to 2½ hours.

3 If using high-heat setting, turn to low-heat setting. Stir in coconut milk, sweet pepper, and green onion. Cover and cook for 15 minutes more. If desired, garnish with chopped peanuts and/or toasted coconut.

Per serving: 309 cal., 19 g total fat (12 g sat. fat), 80 mg chol., 479 mg sodium, 13 g carbo., 2 g fiber, 22 g pro.

Traditionally made with lamb or mutton, shepherd's pie works equally well with turkey in this slow-cooked version. Dried thyme contributes an herbal note.

TURKEY SHEPHERD'S PIE

PREP: *15 minutes*

COOK: *6 to 7 hours on low-heat setting or 3 to 3½ hours on high-heat setting; plus 10 minutes on high-heat setting*

MAKES: *4 servings*

1 10-ounce package loose-pack frozen mixed vegetables

12 ounces turkey breast tenderloins or skinless, boneless chicken breasts, cut into ½-inch-wide strips

1 12-ounce jar turkey or chicken gravy

1 teaspoon dried thyme, crushed

1 20-ounce package refrigerated mashed potatoes

1 Place frozen vegetables in a 3½- or 4-quart slow cooker. Top with turkey strips. In a small bowl stir together gravy and thyme; pour over turkey.

2 Cover and cook on low-heat setting for 6 to 7 hours or on high-heat setting for 3 to 3½ hours.

3 If using low-heat setting, turn to high-heat setting. Using a spoon, drop mashed potatoes into eight small mounds on top of turkey mixture. Cover and cook for 10 minutes more. To serve, spoon some of the turkey mixture and two of the potato mounds into each of four shallow bowls.

Per serving: 297 cal., 5 g total fat (1 g sat. fat), 51 mg chol., 781 mg sodium, 33 g carbo., 4 g fiber, 27 g pro.

Quartered refrigerated biscuits make easy dumplings for this turkey-and-vegetable combination.

TURKEY & DUMPLINGS

1½   cups thinly sliced carrot

1½   cups thinly sliced celery

2   small onions, cut into very thin wedges

1½   pounds turkey breast tenderloins, cut into ¾-inch cubes

1   14-ounce can reduced-sodium chicken broth

1   10¾-ounce can condensed cream of chicken soup

2   teaspoons dried sage leaves, crushed

¼   teaspoon black pepper

¼   cup all-purpose flour

1   6-ounce package (5) refrigerated biscuits, cut into quarters

PREP: *25 minutes*

COOK: *6 to 7 hours on low-heat setting or 3 to 3½ hours on high-heat setting; plus 45 minutes on high-heat setting*

STAND: *15 minutes*

MAKES: *5 or 6 servings*

1 In a 4- to 5-quart slow cooker combine carrot, celery, and onions; stir in turkey. Set aside ½ cup of the chicken broth. In a medium bowl combine the remaining chicken broth, the cream of chicken soup, sage, and pepper; stir into turkey mixture.

2 Cover and cook on low-heat setting for 6 to 7 hours or on high-heat setting for 3 to 3½ hours.

3 If using low-heat setting, turn to high-heat setting. In a small bowl whisk together the reserved ½ cup chicken broth and the flour; stir into turkey mixture. Arrange quartered biscuits on top of turkey mixture. Cover and cook for 45 minutes more.

4 Remove liner from slow cooker, if possible, or turn off slow cooker. Cover and let stand for 15 minutes.

Per serving: 359 cal., 8 g total fat (2 g sat. fat), 95 mg chol., 1,070 mg sodium, 30 g carbo., 3 g fiber, 39 g pro.

Texans love black-eyed peas. There's no better way to discover this Southwestern favorite than in this tasty dish.

TEXAS TURKEY BONANZA

PREP: *35 minutes*

COOK: *8 to 10 hours on low-heat setting or 4 to 5 hours on high-heat setting; plus 30 minutes on high-heat setting*

MAKES: *6 servings*

2   cups dry black-eyed peas

5   cups water

3   cups water

1   to 3 fresh jalapeño chile peppers, seeded and quartered lengthwise (see tip, page 19)

1½ teaspoons dried sage leaves, crushed

1   teaspoon salt

1   pound turkey breast tenderloins, cut into 1½-inch pieces

2   medium yellow summer squash, cut into wedges

½   cup finely chopped red onion

Snipped fresh cilantro

1   recipe Lime Sour Cream (optional)

Finely chopped fresh jalapeño chile pepper (see tip, page 19) (optional)

1 Sort through black-eyed peas to remove any pebbles or other foreign matter. Rinse black-eyed peas. In a large saucepan combine black-eyed peas and the 5 cups water. Bring to boiling; reduce heat. Cook, uncovered, for 10 minutes. Remove from heat. Drain and rinse black-eyed peas.

2 In a 4- or 4½-quart slow cooker combine black-eyed peas, the 3 cups water, the quartered chile peppers, the sage, and salt. Top with turkey.

3 Cover and cook on low-heat setting for 8 to 10 hours or on high-heat setting for 4 to 5 hours.

4 If using low-heat setting, turn to high-heat setting. Stir squash into stew. Cover and cook for 30 minutes more. Sprinkle individual servings with red onion and cilantro. If desired, top with Lime Sour Cream and finely chopped chile pepper.

Per serving: 144 cal., 1 g total fat (0 g sat. fat), 47 mg chol., 423 mg sodium, 13 g carbo., 4 g fiber, 21 g pro.

LIME SOUR CREAM: In a small bowl combine ½ cup dairy sour cream, ½ teaspoon finely shredded lime peel, and 1 tablespoon lime juice. Cover and chill before serving.

This creamy stew is extra satisfying, thanks to a double dose of turkey—both turkey breast tenderloins and turkey kielbasa. The vinegar adds a pleasantly tangy note.

TURKEY & SAUSAGE STEW

2   14-ounce cans reduced-sodium chicken broth

1   pound turkey breast tenderloins, cut into 1½-inch pieces

8   ounces cooked turkey kielbasa, cut into 1-inch pieces

¼   cup bottled clear Italian salad dressing

2   tablespoons vinegar

3   cups shredded cabbage

1   cup shredded Swiss cheese (4 ounces) (optional)

½   cup dairy sour cream (optional)

1 In a 3½- or 4-quart slow cooker combine chicken broth, turkey breast, kielbasa, salad dressing, and vinegar.

2 Cover and cook on low-heat setting for 5 hours or on high-heat setting for 2½ hours. Stir in cabbage. If desired, top individual servings with Swiss cheese and sour cream.

Per serving: 189 cal., 7 g total fat (1 g sat. fat), 45 mg chol., 870 mg sodium, 4 g carbo., 1 g fiber, 27 g pro.

PREP: *20 minutes*

COOK: *5 hours on low-heat setting or 2½ hours on high-heat setting*

MAKES: *6 servings*

The perfectly balanced spice blend really brings the turkey and sweet potatoes alive in this anything but ho-hum soup.

TURKEY & SWEET POTATO SOUP

PREP: *25 minutes*

COOK: *6 to 8 hours on low-heat setting or 3 to 4 hours on high-heat setting*

MAKES: *6 servings*

1 pound turkey breast tenderloins, cut into ¾-inch pieces

4 cups peeled sweet potatoes cut into bite-size pieces

2 14-ounce cans chicken broth

1 cup chopped onion

1 cup thinly sliced celery

1 tablespoon red curry powder

½ teaspoon salt

⅛ teaspoon crushed red pepper

2 cloves garlic, minced

1 13½-ounce can unsweetened coconut milk

1 In a 3½- or 4-quart slow cooker combine turkey, sweet potato, chicken broth, onion, celery, curry powder, salt, crushed red pepper, and garlic.

2 Cover and cook on low-heat setting for 6 to 8 hours or on high-heat setting for 3 to 4 hours. Stir in coconut milk.

Per serving: 333 cal., 15 g total fat (12 g sat. fat), 47 mg chol., 843 mg sodium, 28 g carbo., 4 g fiber, 23 g pro.

A down-home favorite goes uptown! Here, smoked salmon and dill add a gourmet angle to creamed turkey and mushrooms.

CREAMED TURKEY & SALMON

2	pounds turkey breast tenderloins, cut into 1-inch pieces
8	ounces fresh mushrooms, quartered
⅓	cup water
1	teaspoon salt
½	teaspoon dried dill, crushed
¼	teaspoon black pepper
¾	cup half-and-half
2	tablespoons cornstarch
4	ounces smoked salmon (not lox-style), skinned and flaked
¼	cup sliced green onions

1 In a 3½- or 4-quart slow cooker combine turkey and mushrooms. Stir in the water, salt, dill, and pepper.

2 Cover and cook on low-heat setting for 3½ hours or on high-heat setting for 1½ hours.

3 If using low-heat setting, turn to high-heat setting. In a small bowl combine half-and-half and cornstarch. Stir into turkey mixture. Cover and cook for 15 minutes more. Stir in salmon and green onion.

Per serving: 254 cal., 7 g total fat (3 g sat. fat), 106 mg chol., 623 mg sodium, 5 g carbo., 1 g fiber, 41 g pro.

PREP: *20 minutes*

COOK: *3½ hours on low-heat setting or 1½ hours on high-heat setting; plus 15 minutes on high-heat setting*

MAKES: *6 servings*

This recipe makes enough for a crowd. Refrigerate leftover filling for another meal. Another time, slip the savory filling into buns instead of tortillas.

SESAME-GINGER TURKEY

PREP: *20 minutes*

COOK: *6 to 7 hours on low-heat setting or 3 to 3½ hours on high-heat setting*

STAND: *5 minutes*

MAKES: *12 servings*

Nonstick cooking spray

3½ to 4 pounds turkey thighs, skinned and fat removed

1 cup bottled sesame-ginger stir-fry sauce

¼ cup water

1 16-ounce package shredded broccoli (broccoli slaw mix)

12 8-inch flour tortillas, warmed*

¾ cup sliced green onions

1 Lightly coat a 3½- or 4-quart slow cooker with nonstick cooking spray. Place turkey thighs in slow cooker. In a small bowl stir together stir-fry sauce and the water. Pour over turkey.

2 Cover and cook on low-heat setting for 6 to 7 hours or on high-heat setting for 3 to 3½ hours.

3 Using a slotted spoon, remove turkey from slow cooker. When cool enough to handle, remove turkey from bones; discard bones. Using two forks, pull turkey apart into bite-size pieces.

4 Remove liner from slow cooker, if possible, or turn off cooker. Place broccoli in sauce mixture in slow cooker. Stir to coat; cover. Let stand for 5 minutes. Using a slotted spoon, remove broccoli mixture from slow cooker.

5 To assemble, divide turkey among tortillas. Top with broccoli mixture and green onion. Spoon some of the sauce from slow cooker on top of green onion. Roll up and serve immediately.

Per serving: 207 cal., 5 g total fat (1 g sat. fat), 67 mg chol., 422 mg sodium, 20 g carbo., 2 g fiber, 20 g pro.

*TEST KITCHEN TIP: To warm tortillas, preheat oven to 350°F. Stack tortillas and wrap tightly in foil. Bake about 10 minutes or until tortillas are heated through.

Accent the flavor of cranberries with chili sauce for a tender turkey dish that's luscious with mashed sweet or white potatoes.

CRANBERRY-SAUCED TURKEY THIGHS

1	16-ounce can jellied cranberry sauce
½	cup bottled chili sauce
1	tablespoon vinegar
¼	teaspoon pumpkin pie spice
2½	to 3 pounds turkey thighs (2 or 3 thighs), skinned and fat removed

PREP: *10 minutes*

COOK: *9 to 10 hours on low-heat setting or 4½ to 5 hours on high-heat setting*

MAKES: *4 to 6 servings*

1 In a 3½- or 4-quart slow cooker stir together cranberry sauce, chili sauce, vinegar, and pumpkin pie spice. Place turkey thighs, meaty sides down, on top of sauce mixture.

2 Cover and cook on low-heat setting for 9 to 10 hours or on high-heat setting for 4½ to 5 hours.

3 Transfer turkey to a serving dish. Skim fat from sauce. Serve sauce with turkey.

Per serving: 388 cal., 5 g total fat (2 g sat. fat), 145 mg chol., 300 mg sodium, 46 g carbo., 2 g fiber, 37 g pro.

Diced hash brown potatoes bring rib-sticking goodness to this filling stew—with no peeling or slicing involved. You'll also appreciate the nice smoky flavor the sausage brings to the mix.

EASY SAUSAGE & CHICKEN STEW

PREP: *15 minutes*

COOK: *8 to 10 hours on low-heat setting or 4 to 5 hours on high-heat setting; plus 30 minutes on high-heat setting*

MAKES: *6 to 8 servings*

1   pound cooked smoked turkey sausage, halved lengthwise and sliced

2   cups packaged peeled baby carrots

1   14-ounce can reduced-sodium chicken broth

1½   cups loose-pack frozen diced hash brown potatoes

1   10¾-ounce can condensed cream of chicken soup

1   teaspoon dried oregano, crushed

2   cups chopped cooked chicken or turkey (10 ounces)

1   9-ounce package frozen cut green beans, thawed

1 In a 3½- or 4-quart slow cooker combine turkey sausage, carrots, chicken broth, hash brown potatoes, cream of chicken soup, and oregano.

2 Cover and cook on low-heat setting for 8 to 10 hours or on high-heat setting for 4 to 5 hours.

3 If using low-heat setting, turn to high-heat setting. Stir in chicken and green beans. Cover and cook for 30 minutes more.

Per serving: 477 cal., 30 g total fat (13 g sat. fat), 79 mg chol., 1,238 mg sodium, 25 g carbo., 4 g fiber, 27 g pro.

To keep the meat mixture from sticking to your hands, wet them with cold water before shaping the meatballs.

SAUCY CHICKEN & RICE BALLS

1	egg, beaten
½	cup finely chopped onion
1	teaspoon salt
1	teaspoon dried Italian seasoning, crushed
¼	teaspoon black pepper
1½	pounds uncooked ground chicken or turkey
⅔	cup long grain rice
2	tablespoons cooking oil
1	medium onion, cut into thin wedges
2	medium zucchini, halved lengthwise and sliced
1	medium yellow summer squash, halved lengthwise and sliced
1	15-ounce container refrigerated marinara sauce
1	8-ounce can tomato sauce
1	tablespoon quick-cooking tapioca
¼	cup grated Parmesan cheese
¼	cup slivered fresh basil (optional)

PREP: *45 minutes*

COOK: *6 to 7 hours on low-heat setting or 3 to 3½ hours on high-heat setting*

MAKES: *6 servings*

1 In a large bowl combine egg, the chopped onion, the salt, Italian seasoning, and pepper. Add chicken and uncooked rice; mix well. Shape into 24 meatballs. In an extra-large skillet heat oil over medium heat. Add meatballs; cook about 10 minutes or until browned, turning occasionally.

2 Meanwhile, place onion wedges in a 4- to 6-quart slow cooker. Transfer browned meatballs to slow cooker. Top with zucchini and squash. In a medium bowl combine marinara sauce, tomato sauce, and tapioca; spoon over vegetables.

3 Cover and cook on low-heat setting for 6 to 7 hours or on high-heat setting for 3 to 3½ hours.

4 To serve, top with Parmesan cheese and, if desired, sprinkle with basil.

Per serving: 441 cal., 23 g total fat (2 g sat. fat), 38 mg chol., 960 mg sodium, 31 g carbo., 2 g fiber, 27 g pro.

Sloppy Joes can be more than ground beef; chicken can get sloppy too! Sneak some veggies in for great flavor.

SLOPPY CHICKEN PIZZA JOES

PREP: *20 minutes*

COOK: *6 to 8 hours on low-heat setting or 3 to 4 hours on high-heat setting*

BROIL: *1 minute*

MAKES: *8 sandwiches*

Nonstick cooking spray

3 pounds uncooked ground chicken or turkey

2 14-ounce jars pizza sauce

2 cups frozen (yellow, green, and red) peppers and onion stir-fry vegetables, thawed and chopped

8 hoagie rolls

8 slices mozzarella or provolone cheese (8 ounces)

1 Coat an unheated large skillet with nonstick cooking spray. Preheat the skillet over medium-high heat. Add chicken to hot skillet; cook until no longer pink.

2 In a 3½- or 4-quart slow cooker stir together pizza sauce and chopped vegetables. Stir in cooked chicken.

3 Cover and cook on low-heat setting for 6 to 8 hours or on high-heat setting for 3 to 4 hours.

4 Preheat broiler. Arrange split rolls, cut sides up, on an unheated broiler pan. Broil 3 inches from the heat for 1 to 2 minutes or until toasted. Spoon chicken mixture onto toasted roll bottoms. Top with cheese and roll tops.

Per sandwich: 641 cal., 24 g total fat (3 g sat. fat), 16 mg chol., 1,132 mg sodium, 58 g carbo., 2 g fiber, 47 g pro.

Mediterranean can mean many things—but it usually means you're in for a treat! Here, cinnamon and feta give this dish an intriguing Greek angle.

MEDITERRANEAN CHICKEN & PASTA

1	pound uncooked ground chicken or turkey
1	14½-ounce can diced tomatoes with basil, oregano, and garlic
1½	cups tomato juice
1½	cups water
2	medium carrots, very thinly sliced
1	medium onion, cut into wedges
1	stalk celery, finely chopped
1	teaspoon dried Italian seasoning, crushed
½	teaspoon salt
½	teaspoon ground cinnamon
1	cup dried medium shell pasta
1	cup crumbled feta cheese (4 ounces)

PREP: *25 minutes*

COOK: *4½ to 5½ hours on low-heat setting or 2¼ to 2¾ hours on high-heat setting; plus 30 minutes on high-heat setting*

MAKES: *4 to 6 servings*

1 In a large skillet cook chicken until no longer pink. Drain off fat.

2 Transfer chicken to a 3½- or 4-quart slow cooker. Stir in undrained tomatoes, tomato juice, the water, carrots, onion, celery, Italian seasoning, salt, and cinnamon.

3 Cover and cook on low-heat setting for 4½ to 5½ hours or on high-heat setting for 2¼ to 2¾ hours.

4 If using low-heat setting, turn to high-heat setting. Stir in uncooked pasta. Cover and cook for 30 to 45 minutes more or until pasta is tender. Sprinkle individual servings with feta cheese.

Per serving: 437 cal., 18 g total fat (6 g sat. fat), 33 mg chol., 1,650 mg sodium, 39 g carbo., 4 g fiber, 31 g pro.

A can of cola moistens and slightly sweetens this sandwich filling. Slather mustard on the buns and serve these sandwiches with forks just in case some of the filling escapes the buns.

CHICKEN SLOPPY JOES

PREP: *25 minutes*

COOK: *6 to 7 hours on low-heat setting or 3 to 3½ hours on high-heat setting*

MAKES: *10 to 12 servings*

2	pounds uncooked ground chicken or turkey
1½	cups finely chopped celery
1	cup finely chopped onion
1	12-ounce can cola
2	teaspoons dry mustard
½	teaspoon salt
½	teaspoon black pepper
¼	teaspoon cayenne pepper (optional)
	Yellow mustard
10	to 12 hamburger buns, split and toasted
	Dill pickle slices
	Chopped onion

1 In a large skillet cook chicken, celery, and the 1 cup onion until chicken is no longer pink, stirring often to break into small pieces. Drain off fat. Transfer chicken mixture to a 3½- or 4-quart slow cooker. In a small bowl combine cola, dry mustard, salt, black pepper, and, if desired, cayenne pepper. Pour over chicken mixture; stir to combine.

2 Cover and cook on low-heat setting for 6 to 7 hours or on high-heat setting for 3 to 3½ hours.

3 Spread yellow mustard on bottom halves of buns. Using a slotted spoon, place chicken mixture on bun bottoms. Top with pickle slices and additional chopped onion. Add bun tops.

Per serving: 284 cal., 10 g total fat (1 g sat. fat), 0 mg chol., 415 mg sodium, 28 g carbo., 2 g fiber, 20 g pro.

Smoked chicken and cheese give this creamy comfort food impressive flavor.

SMOKY CHICKEN & POTATO CASSEROLE

Nonstick cooking spray

1 10¾-ounce can condensed cream of chicken with herbs soup

1 8-ounce carton dairy sour cream

6 ounces smoked cheddar cheese, shredded (1½ cups)

1 28-ounce package frozen loose-pack diced hash brown potatoes with onion and peppers, thawed

3 cups chopped smoked or roasted chicken or turkey (about 1 pound)

Crushed croutons (optional)

1 Lightly coat a 3½- or 4-quart slow cooker with nonstick cooking spray. In the slow cooker combine cream of chicken with herbs soup, sour cream, and cheese. Stir in potatoes and chicken.

2 Cover and cook on low-heat setting for 5 to 6 hours. If desired, top individual servings with crushed croutons.

Per serving: 399 cal., 20 g total fat (12 g sat. fat), 80 mg chol., 1,313 mg sodium, 31 g carbo., 3 g fiber, 25 g pro.

PREP: *15 minutes*

COOK: *5 to 6 hours on low-heat setting*

MAKES: *6 servings*

Here's a light soup that's crowded with tender noodles and vegetables. A few drops of soy or teriyaki sauce adds another layer of flavor.

ASIAN CHICKEN NOODLE SOUP

PREP: *15 minutes*

COOK: *5 to 6 hours on low-heat setting or 2½ to 3 hours on high-heat setting; plus 10 minutes on high-heat setting*

MAKES: *6 servings*

6	cups water
2	3-ounce packages chicken-flavor ramen noodles
1	teaspoon grated fresh ginger
2	cups chopped cooked chicken or turkey (10 ounces)
1	16-ounce package frozen broccoli stir-fry vegetables
¼	cup sliced green onions
	Crushed red pepper (optional)
	Soy sauce or teriyaki sauce (optional)

1 In a 3½- to 4½-quart slow cooker combine the water, seasoning packets from ramen noodles (reserve ramen noodles), and ginger. Add chicken and frozen vegetables.

2 Cover and cook on low-heat setting for 5 to 6 hours or on high-heat setting for 2½ to 3 hours.

3 If using low-heat setting, turn to high-heat setting. Stir in ramen noodles. Cover and cook for 10 to 15 minutes more or just until noodles are tender. Stir in green onion. If desired, sprinkle individual servings with crushed red pepper and serve with soy sauce.

Per serving: 180 cal., 1 g total fat (0 g sat. fat), 23 mg chol., 782 mg sodium, 26 g carbo., 2 g fiber, 15 g pro.

To round out the meal, bake up a can of refrigerated biscuits and serve crisp greens tossed with citrus slices and your favorite vinaigrette. (Recipe pictured on page 106.)

SPINACH, CHICKEN & WILD RICE SOUP

3   cups water

1   14-ounce can reduced-sodium chicken broth

1   10¾-ounce can condensed cream of chicken soup

⅔   cup wild rice, rinsed and drained

½   teaspoon dried thyme, crushed

¼   teaspoon black pepper

3   cups chopped cooked chicken or turkey (about 1 pound)

2   cups shredded fresh spinach

PREP: *15 minutes*

COOK: *7 to 8 hours on low-heat setting or 3½ to 4 hours on high-heat setting*

MAKES: *6 servings*

1 In a 3½- or 4-quart slow cooker combine the water, chicken broth, cream of chicken soup, uncooked wild rice, thyme, and pepper.

2 Cover and cook on low-heat setting for 7 to 8 hours or on high-heat setting for 3½ to 4 hours.

3 Stir in cooked chicken and shredded spinach.

Per serving: 237 cal., 6 g total fat (2 g sat. fat), 64 mg chol., 589 mg sodium, 19 g carbo., 2 g fiber, 27 g pro.

If you're going to a "bring a dish" gathering with people you don't know, don't worry. Chicken and stuffing always satisfies!

CHICKEN & STUFFING CASSEROLE

PREP: *30 minutes*

COOK: *4½ to 5 hours on low-heat setting*

MAKES: *16 to 20 servings*

½	cup butter or margarine
1	cup thinly sliced celery
¾	cup chopped onion
	Nonstick cooking spray
1	6-ounce package long grain and wild rice mix
1	14-ounce package herb-seasoned stuffing croutons
4	cups cubed cooked chicken or turkey (20 ounces)
1	8-ounce can (drained weight) sliced mushrooms, drained
¼	cup snipped fresh parsley
1½	teaspoons poultry seasoning
¼	teaspoon black pepper
2	eggs, lightly beaten
2	14-ounce cans reduced-sodium chicken broth
1	10¾-ounce can reduced-fat and reduced-sodium condensed cream of chicken or cream of mushroom soup

1 In a large skillet melt butter over medium heat. Add celery and onion; cook about 5 minutes or until vegetables are tender. Set aside.

2 Lightly coat a 5½- or 6-quart slow cooker with nonstick cooking spray. Add rice mix (reserve seasoning packet). Using a slotted spoon, transfer vegetables to slow cooker, reserving butter. Stir to combine.

3 Place croutons in a very large bowl. Stir in reserved butter from cooking vegetables, the chicken, mushrooms, parsley, poultry seasoning, pepper, and seasoning packet from rice mix.

4 In a medium bowl combine eggs, chicken broth, and cream of chicken soup. Pour over crouton mixture; toss gently to moisten. Transfer crouton mixture to slow cooker.

5 Cover and cook on low-heat setting for 4½ to 5 hours. Stir gently before serving.

Per serving: 287 cal., 11 g total fat (5 g sat. fat), 76 mg chol., 903 mg sodium, 31 g carbo., 3 g fiber, 16 g pro.

QUICK FIXES

These no-fuss, family-pleasing chicken and turkey dishes are ready to eat in 30 minutes or less.

5

These butterflied chicken breasts cook in a flash in hot butter. Choose large chicken breast halves so you can butterfly them easily.

APPLE-DIJON CHICKEN

START TO FINISH:
30 minutes

MAKES: *4 servings*

4   large skinless, boneless chicken breast halves
     (about 1½ pounds total)

     Salt

     Black pepper

2   tablespoons butter

1   medium tart cooking apple (such as Granny Smith),
     cored and thinly sliced

⅓   cup whipping cream

2   tablespoons Dijon-style mustard

1 Butterfly each chicken breast half by cutting horizontally from one long side of the breast almost to, but not through, the opposite long side of the breast. Lay the breast open. Sprinkle both sides of each chicken breast with salt and pepper.

2 In a large skillet melt 1 tablespoon of the butter over medium-high heat. Add chicken, half at a time, and cook for 4 to 6 minutes or until tender and no longer pink (170°F), turning to brown evenly. Remove from skillet; keep warm.

3 Add the remaining 1 tablespoon butter to skillet. Add sliced apple; cook and stir about 3 minutes or until tender. Add whipping cream and mustard to skillet. Cook and stir until heated through and thickened slightly. Season to taste with additional salt and pepper. Serve sauce and apples over chicken.

Per serving: 342 cal., 16 g total fat (9 g sat. fat), 142 mg chol., 407 mg sodium, 6 g carbo., 1 g fiber, 40 g pro.

If you like, substitute red kidney beans for the black beans.

ZESTY CHICKEN WITH BLACK BEANS & RICE

2	tablespoons cooking oil
1	pound skinless, boneless chicken breasts, cut into 2-inch pieces
1	6- to 7.4-ounce package Spanish rice mix
1¾	cups water
1	15-ounce can black beans, rinsed and drained
1	14½-ounce can diced tomatoes
	Dairy sour cream, sliced green onions, and/or lime wedges (optional)

1 In a large skillet heat 1 tablespoon of the oil over medium heat. Add chicken; cook until brown. Remove chicken from skillet; keep warm.

2 Add rice mix and the remaining 1 tablespoon oil to skillet; cook and stir over medium heat for 2 minutes. Stir in seasoning packet from rice mix, the water, black beans, and undrained tomatoes; add chicken. Bring to boiling; reduce heat. Cover and simmer for 15 to 20 minutes or until rice is tender and chicken is tender and no longer pink.

3 If desired, serve with sour cream, green onion, and/or lime wedges.

Per serving: 424 cal., 9 g total fat (2 g sat. fat), 66 mg chol., 1,080 mg sodium, 52 g carbo., 6 g fiber, 37 g pro.

START TO FINISH:
30 minutes

MAKES: *4 servings*

This stir-fry features a diverse mix of ingredients, including fish sauce, lemongrass, pineapple, cucumber, and jalapeño chile peppers. If you've never tried fish sauce, don't be deterred by its pungent odor; its flavor greatly enhances this dish.

BANGKOK STIR-FRY

START TO FINISH:
30 minutes

MAKES: *4 servings*

2 tablespoons fish sauce (nam pla)

1 tablespoon lime juice

2 teaspoons minced fresh lemongrass or 1 teaspoon finely shredded lemon peel

4 teaspoons cooking oil

1 large red onion, halved lengthwise and sliced

3 cloves garlic, minced

¼ of a fresh pineapple, peeled, cored, and cut into ¼-inch-thick wedges

1 small cucumber, cut into thin bite-size strips

1 or 2 fresh jalapeño chile peppers, seeded and finely chopped (see tip, page 19)

12 ounces skinless, boneless chicken breasts, cut into bite-size strips

3 cups hot cooked aromatic rice (such as jasmine or basmati)

Snipped fresh cilantro or parsley (optional)

1 For sauce, in a small bowl stir together fish sauce, lime juice, and lemongrass or lemon peel; set aside.

2 Pour 2 teaspoons of the oil into a wok or large skillet. Heat wok or skillet over medium-high heat. Stir-fry onion and garlic in hot oil for 2 minutes. Add pineapple, cucumber, and chile peppers. Stir-fry for 2 minutes more. Remove from wok.

3 Add the remaining 2 teaspoons oil to hot wok. Add chicken. Stir-fry for 2 to 3 minutes or until chicken is tender and no longer pink. Return onion mixture to wok. Add sauce. Cook and stir about 1 minute more or until heated through. Serve immediately over rice. If desired, sprinkle with snipped cilantro.

Per serving: 345 cal., 6 g total fat (1 g sat. fat), 49 mg chol., 747 mg sodium, 46 g carbo., 2 g fiber, 25 g pro.

Cooking the broccoli with the linguine minimizes the number of pans needed.

TARRAGON CHICKEN LINGUINE

6	ounces dried linguine or fettuccine
2	cups broccoli florets
½	cup reduced-sodium chicken broth
2	teaspoons cornstarch
¼	teaspoon lemon-pepper seasoning or black pepper
12	ounces skinless, boneless chicken breasts, cut into bite-size strips
2	teaspoons olive oil or cooking oil
1	tablespoon snipped fresh tarragon or dill or ½ teaspoon dried tarragon or dill, crushed

START TO FINISH:
25 minutes

MAKES: *4 servings*

1 Cook pasta according to package directions, adding broccoli for the last 4 minutes of cooking. Drain; keep warm.

2 In a small bowl combine chicken broth, cornstarch, and lemon-pepper seasoning or pepper; set aside.

3 In a large nonstick skillet cook chicken in hot oil about 4 minutes or until tender and no longer pink, stirring often.

4 Stir cornstarch mixture; add to skillet. Cook and stir until thickened. Stir in tarragon or dill; cook for 2 minutes more. Serve over hot pasta-broccoli mixture.

Per serving: 293 cal., 4 g total fat (1 g sat. fat), 49 mg chol., 153 mg sodium, 36 g carbo., 2 g fiber, 27 g pro.

Skip the fast-food chicken fingers. These homemade morsels are crunchy, juicy, and delicious. Plus, they're baked instead of fried! Try honey mustard, buttermilk salad dressing, or sweet-and-sour sauce for dipping.

CHICKEN FINGERS

PREP: *15 minutes*
BAKE: *12 minutes*
MAKES: *4 servings*

12	ounces skinless, boneless chicken breasts
1	egg, lightly beaten
1	tablespoon honey
1	teaspoon yellow mustard
1	cup packaged cornflake crumbs or 2 cups cornflakes, finely crushed
	Dash black pepper
	Purchased dipping sauce (optional)

1 Preheat oven to 450°F. Cut chicken into 3×¾-inch strips. In a shallow dish combine egg, honey, and mustard. In another shallow dish stir together cornflake crumbs and pepper. Dip chicken strips into the egg mixture; roll in crumb mixture to coat.

2 Arrange chicken strips on an ungreased baking sheet. Bake about 12 minutes or until golden and chicken is tender and no longer pink. If desired, serve with your favorite dipping sauce.

Per serving: 212 cal., 3 g total fat (1 g sat. fat), 102 mg chol., 236 mg sodium, 23 g carbo., 0 g fiber, 23 g pro.

Szechwan Chinese cuisine is known for its hot, spicy dishes. While chile oil spikes up the heat in this recipe, the sweetness from the apricot preserves tempers it.

SZECHWAN-FRIED CHICKEN BREASTS

1	tablespoon reduced-sodium soy sauce
1	teaspoon grated fresh ginger
1	teaspoon chile oil
½	teaspoon sugar
½	cup all-purpose flour
4	skinless, boneless chicken breast halves (about 1¼ pounds total)
1	tablespoon cooking oil
¼	cup apricot preserves
¼	cup reduced-sodium chicken broth
	Hot cooked rice (optional)
	Shredded orange peel (optional)

START TO FINISH:
30 minutes

MAKES: *4 servings*

1 In a small bowl stir together soy sauce, ginger, ½ teaspoon of the chile oil, and the sugar; set aside.

2 Place flour in a shallow bowl. Brush both sides of each chicken breast half with the soy sauce mixture; dip in flour to coat. In a large nonstick skillet heat cooking oil over medium-high heat. Add chicken; cook for 12 to 14 minutes or until tender and no longer pink (170°F), turning once. Remove chicken from skillet; cover and keep warm.

3 For sauce, add apricot preserves, chicken broth, and the remaining ½ teaspoon chile oil to skillet. Cook and stir over medium heat until preserves melt and mixture is heated through. Spoon sauce over chicken. If desired, serve with hot cooked rice and sprinkle with orange peel.

Per serving: 314 cal., 7 g total fat (1 g sat. fat), 82 mg chol., 267 mg sodium, 26 g carbo., 1 g fiber, 35 g pro.

For a special presentation, spoon the sauce onto dinner plates, slice the chicken breasts, reassemble them on the sauce, and garnish with sprigs of fresh tarragon or dill.

CHICKEN MEDALLIONS WITH MUSTARD SAUCE

START TO FINISH:
25 minutes

MAKES: *4 servings*

4   skinless, boneless chicken breast halves
    (about 1¼ pounds total)

    Salt

    Black pepper

2   tablespoons olive oil or cooking oil

¼   cup dry white wine

2   tablespoons crème fraîche

2   tablespoons tarragon mustard or dill mustard

1 Place each chicken breast half between two pieces of plastic wrap. Using the flat side of a meat mallet, pound chicken lightly into rectangles about ½ inch thick. Remove plastic wrap. Sprinkle chicken with salt and pepper.

2 In a 12-inch skillet heat oil over medium-high heat. Add chicken breast halves, two at a time, and cook for 6 to 8 minutes or until golden brown, turning once. Transfer chicken to a serving platter; keep warm.

3 For sauce, carefully add wine to hot skillet. Cook until bubbly, stirring to loosen any browned bits in bottom of skillet. Add crème fraîche and mustard to skillet; stir with a wire whisk until combined. Spoon sauce over chicken.

Per serving: 255 cal., 11 g total fat (3 g sat. fat), 92 mg chol., 306 mg sodium, 1 g carbo., 0 g fiber, 33 g pro.

A perennial favorite of all ages, sweet-and-sour chicken can be made quickly—without deep frying—if you use this recipe! (Recipe pictured on page 107.)

SWEET & SOUR CHICKEN

1	8-ounce can pineapple chunks (juice pack)
½	cup bottled sweet-and-sour sauce
12	ounces skinless, boneless chicken breasts, cut into 1-inch pieces
1	tablespoon reduced-sodium soy sauce
4	teaspoons cooking oil
1	medium red sweet pepper, cut into bite-size strips
½	cup thinly sliced carrot
1	cup fresh pea pods, tips and stems removed
2	cups hot cooked rice

START TO FINISH:
25 minutes

MAKES: *4 or 5 servings*

1 Drain pineapple, reserving 2 tablespoons of the juice; set pineapple chunks aside. In a small bowl stir together the reserved pineapple juice and the sweet-and-sour sauce; set aside. In a medium bowl toss chicken with soy sauce; set aside.

2 In a large nonstick skillet heat 1 tablespoon of the oil over medium-high heat. Add sweet pepper and carrot; cook and stir for 3 minutes. Add pea pods. Cook and stir about 1 minute more or until vegetables are crisp-tender. Remove from skillet; set aside.

3 Add the remaining 1 teaspoon oil to skillet. Using a slotted spoon, add chicken to skillet. Cook and stir for 3 to 4 minutes or until chicken is tender and no longer pink. Add sweet-and-sour sauce mixture, vegetable mixture, and pineapple chunks; heat through. Serve chicken mixture with hot cooked rice.

Per serving: 337 cal., 6 g total fat (1 g sat. fat), 49 mg chol., 297 mg sodium, 46 g carbo., 3 g fiber, 23 g pro.

The zesty flavors of artichokes, wine, and garlic combine with the crunch of chopped pistachios in this sophisticated chicken dish.

CHICKEN VENETO

START TO FINISH:
30 minutes

MAKES: *4 servings*

8	ounces dried fettuccine or linguine
12	ounces skinless, boneless chicken breasts
2	tablespoons olive oil
¼	cup butter
3	cloves garlic, minced
1	9-ounce package frozen artichoke hearts, thawed and quartered
¾	cup dry white wine
¼	cup coarsely chopped pistachios
¼	teaspoon salt
2	tablespoons snipped fresh flat-leaf parsley
	Cracked black pepper

1 Cook pasta according to package directions. Drain; keep warm.

2 Meanwhile, cut chicken into bite-size strips. In a large skillet heat oil over medium-high heat. Add chicken; cook and stir for 3 to 4 minutes or until chicken is tender and no longer pink. Using a slotted spoon, remove chicken from skillet; discard pan drippings.

3 In the same skillet melt butter over medium heat. Add garlic; cook and stir for 15 seconds. Remove from heat. Add artichokes, wine, and pistachios. Return to heat. Bring to boiling; reduce heat. Simmer, uncovered, for 5 minutes. Stir in salt. Return chicken to the skillet. Cook for 1 to 2 minutes more or until heated through.

4 To serve, arrange the pasta on four dinner plates or a large platter. Spoon the chicken mixture over the pasta. Sprinkle with parsley and cracked black pepper to taste. Serve immediately.

Per serving: 583 cal., 25 g total fat (8 g sat. fat), 82 mg chol., 325 mg sodium, 51 g carbo., 6 g fiber, 31 g pro.

Look for sweet ginger stir-fry sauce in the Asian food section of larger supermarkets or at Asian food stores.

SWEET GINGER STIR-FRY

START TO FINISH:
20 minutes

MAKES: *4 servings*

2	tablespoons cooking oil
2	cups loose-pack frozen mixed vegetables
12	ounces skinless, boneless chicken breasts or skinless, boneless chicken thighs, cut into 1-inch pieces
½	cup purchased sweet ginger stir-fry sauce
2	cups hot cooked rice

1 Pour oil into a wok or large skillet. Heat over medium-high heat. Add frozen vegetables; stir-fry about 3 minutes or until vegetables are crisp-tender. Remove vegetables from wok.

2 Add chicken to hot wok. (Add more oil if necessary.) Stir-fry for 3 to 4 minutes or until chicken is no longer pink. Push chicken from center of the wok. Add stir-fry sauce to center of the wok. Cook and stir until bubbly. Return cooked vegetables to wok. Stir to coat. Cook and stir about 1 minute more or until heated through. Serve over hot cooked rice.

Per serving: 382 cal., 9 g total fat (1 g sat. fat), 49 mg chol., 879 mg sodium, 50 g carbo., 3 g fiber, 24 g pro.

This version of the classic chicken and grape combo substitutes a sauce of butter and sherry vinegar for the traditional cream sauce. If your grapes have seeds, halve them and remove the seeds with the tip of a spoon.

CHICKEN VÉRONIQUE

START TO FINISH:
20 minutes

MAKES: *4 servings*

4   skinless, boneless chicken breast halves (about 1¼ pounds total)

¼   teaspoon salt

¼   teaspoon black pepper

¼   cup butter

1   cup seedless red grapes, halved

3   tablespoons sherry vinegar or red wine vinegar

¼   teaspoon dried thyme, crushed

1 Sprinkle chicken with salt and pepper. In a large skillet melt 2 tablespoons of the butter over medium-high heat. Add chicken; cook for 8 to 10 minutes or until tender and no longer pink (170°F), turning once. Transfer to a serving platter; keep warm.

2 For sauce, add the remaining 2 tablespoons butter, the grapes, vinegar, and thyme to hot skillet. Cook until slightly thickened, stirring to loosen any browned bits in bottom of skillet. Serve sauce over chicken.

Per serving: 301 cal., 15 g total fat (8 g sat. fat), 115 mg chol., 348 mg sodium, 7 g carbo., 0 g fiber, 33 g pro.

If you have the time, cook some jasmine or basmati rice to serve with this fresh-tasting stir-fry.

PINEAPPLE-CHICKEN STIR-FRY

4	teaspoons cooking oil
1	medium red onion, halved lengthwise and sliced
¼	of a fresh pineapple, peeled, cored, and cut into bite-size pieces
¾	cup zucchini cut into thin bite-size strips
¾	cup trimmed fresh pea pods
12	ounces skinless, boneless chicken breasts, cut into thin bite-size strips
3	tablespoons bottled stir-fry sauce
	Fresh pineapple wedges (optional)

START TO FINISH:
25 minutes

MAKES: *4 servings*

1 Pour 2 teaspoons of the oil into a wok or large skillet. Heat over medium-high heat. Add red onion; stir-fry for 2 minutes. Add bite-size pineapple pieces, zucchini, and pea pods. Stir-fry for 2 minutes more. Remove onion mixture from wok.

2 Add the remaining 2 teaspoons oil to hot wok. Add chicken. Stir-fry for 2 to 3 minutes or until chicken is tender and no longer pink. Return onion mixture to wok. Add stir-fry sauce. Cook and stir about 1 minute more or until heated through. If desired, serve with fresh pineapple wedges.

Per serving: 181 cal., 6 g total fat (1 g sat. fat), 49 mg chol., 440 mg sodium, 11 g carbo., 1 g fiber, 21 g pro.

Save time by picking up a package of sliced mushrooms in your supermarket's produce section.

CHICKEN WITH CREAMY MUSHROOMS

START TO FINISH:
30 minutes

MAKES: *6 servings*

3   tablespoons butter

1   pound sliced fresh mushrooms (such as button or shiitake)

6   purchased Italian-marinated skinless, boneless chicken breast halves (about 2 pounds total)

3   tablespoons rice vinegar or white wine vinegar

1½   cups whipping cream

3   tablespoons capers, rinsed and drained

¼   teaspoon freshly ground black pepper

     Steamed fresh vegetables (optional)

1 In a 12-inch skillet melt 1 tablespoon of the butter over medium-high heat. Add mushrooms; cook about 5 minutes or until tender. Remove mushrooms from skillet. Set aside.

2 Reduce heat to medium. Add the remaining 2 tablespoons butter and the chicken breast halves to skillet. Cook for 8 to 12 minutes or until tender and no longer pink (170°F), turning once. Remove chicken from skillet; keep warm.

3 Remove skillet from heat; add vinegar, stirring to loosen browned bits in bottom of skillet. Return skillet to heat. Stir in whipping cream, capers, and pepper. Bring to boiling; boil gently, uncovered, for 2 to 3 minutes or until sauce is slightly thickened. Return mushrooms to skillet; heat through.

4 If desired, cut each chicken piece in half horizontally. Top chicken with mushroom sauce. If desired, serve with steamed vegetables.

Per serving: 456 cal., 34 g total fat (19 g sat. fat), 183 mg chol., 967 mg sodium, 7 g carbo., 1 g fiber, 33 g pro.

Pounding the chicken breasts to an even thickness helps them cook quickly and evenly.

CHICKEN PICCATA

3	tablespoons all-purpose flour
½	teaspoon kosher salt
¼	teaspoon freshly ground black pepper
4	skinless, boneless chicken breast halves (about 1¼ pounds total)
⅓	cup dry white wine or chicken broth
3	tablespoons lemon juice
2	tablespoons capers, rinsed and drained
⅛	teaspoon kosher salt
⅛	teaspoon freshly ground black pepper
3	tablespoons butter
2	cloves garlic, minced
2	tablespoons snipped fresh flat-leaf parsley
	Lemon slices, halved (optional)

START TO FINISH:
25 minutes

MAKES: *4 servings*

1 In a shallow bowl stir together flour, the ½ teaspoon salt, and the ¼ teaspoon pepper; set aside. Place each chicken breast half between two pieces of plastic wrap. Using the flat side of a meat mallet, lightly pound chicken into rectangles about ¼ inch thick. Remove plastic wrap. Lightly coat chicken pieces with flour mixture, turning to coat evenly; shake off excess.

2 For sauce, in a small bowl stir together wine, lemon juice, capers, the ⅛ teaspoon salt, and the ⅛ teaspoon pepper. Set aside.

3 In a 12-inch skillet melt 2 tablespoons of the butter over medium-high heat. Add chicken; cook for 5 to 6 minutes or until browned, turning to brown evenly. Remove from skillet, reserving drippings in skillet.

4 Add the remaining 1 tablespoon butter and the garlic to drippings in skillet. Cook and stir for 1 minute. Stir sauce. Carefully add sauce to the skillet. Cook for 30 to 60 seconds or until sauce is bubbly and reduces slightly, scraping up the browned bits from the bottom of the skillet. Return chicken to the skillet. Cook for 2 to 3 minutes more or until heated through. Sprinkle with parsley. If desired, garnish with lemon slices. Serve immediately.

Per serving: 281 cal., 11 g total fat (5 g sat. fat), 106 mg chol., 573 mg sodium, 6 g carbo., 0 g fiber, 34 g pro.

Round out this comforting chicken-and-pasta meal with a tossed salad and some crusty bread. (Recipe pictured on page 107.)

CREAMY RANCH CHICKEN

START TO FINISH:
30 minutes

MAKES: *4 servings*

6   slices bacon

4   skinless, boneless chicken breast halves (about 1¼ pounds total), cut into bite-size pieces

2   tablespoons all-purpose flour

2   tablespoons dry ranch salad dressing mix

1¼ cups milk

3   cups dried medium noodles

1   tablespoon finely shredded Parmesan cheese

1 Cut bacon into narrow strips. In a large skillet cook bacon over medium heat until crisp. Drain bacon on paper towels; discard all but 2 tablespoons of the drippings.

2 In the same skillet cook and stir chicken in reserved drippings until tender and no longer pink. Sprinkle flour and dry salad dressing mix over chicken in skillet; stir well. Stir in milk. Cook and stir until thickened and bubbly. Cook and stir for 1 minute more. Stir in bacon.

3 Meanwhile, cook noodles according to package directions. Serve chicken mixture with noodles; sprinkle with Parmesan cheese.

Per serving: 488 cal., 18 g total fat (7 g sat. fat), 137 mg chol., 574 mg sodium, 27 g carbo., 1 g fiber, 45 g pro.

For a colorful presentation, mix green, yellow, and red sweet pepper strips.

PEPPER & PEACH FAJITA CHICKEN

4	skinless, boneless chicken breast halves (about 1¼ pounds total)
1½	teaspoons fajita seasoning
2	tablespoons olive oil or butter
1½	cups sweet pepper strips (any color)
1	medium fresh peach or nectarine, cut into thin slices, or 1 cup frozen unsweetened peach slices, thawed

START TO FINISH:
30 minutes

MAKES: *4 servings*

1 Sprinkle both sides of each chicken breast half with the fajita seasoning. In a large skillet heat 1 tablespoon of the oil or butter over medium heat. Add chicken; cook for 12 to 14 minutes or until chicken is tender and no longer pink (170°F), turning once. Transfer chicken to a serving platter and keep warm.

2 Add the remaining 1 tablespoon oil or butter to skillet. Add sweet pepper strips. Cook and stir about 3 minutes or until peppers are crisp-tender. Gently stir in peach or nectarine slices. Cook for 1 to 2 minutes more or until heated through. Spoon pepper strips and peach mixture over chicken.

Per serving: 243 cal., 9 g total fat (1 g sat. fat), 82 mg chol., 150 mg sodium, 7 g carbo., 2 g fiber, 33 g pro.

Dijon-style mustard, which contains white wine and seasonings, adds a sharp flavor and a little French refinement to this dish.

DIJON CHICKEN & MUSHROOMS

START TO FINISH:
30 minutes

MAKES: *4 servings*

3   tablespoons butter or margarine

2   cups sliced fresh mushrooms

4   skinless, boneless chicken breast halves
    (about 1¼ pounds total)

1   10¾-ounce can condensed cream of chicken soup

¼   cup dry white wine

¼   cup water

2   tablespoons Dijon-style mustard

½   teaspoon dried thyme or tarragon, crushed

    Hot cooked pasta

1 In a large skillet melt 1 tablespoon of the butter over medium-high heat. Add mushrooms; cook for 3 to 4 minutes or until tender. Remove mushrooms from skillet. In the same skillet cook chicken in the remaining 2 tablespoons butter for 8 to 10 minutes or until tender and no longer pink (170°F), turning once.

2 Meanwhile, in a small bowl stir together cream of chicken soup, wine, the water, mustard, and thyme.

3 Return mushrooms to skillet; add soup mixture. Bring to boiling; reduce heat. Simmer, uncovered, for 2 minutes. Serve chicken and soup mixture over hot cooked pasta.

Per serving: 498 cal., 18 g total fat (8 g sat. fat), 112 mg chol., 947 mg sodium, 37 g carbo., 2 g fiber, 41 g pro.

Garlic, plum tomatoes, artichokes, ripe olives, Italian seasoning, and feta cheese add up to a terrific Mediterranean spin for chicken. (Recipe pictured on page 108.)

MEDITERRANEAN PIZZA SKILLET

2	tablespoons olive oil
3	skinless, boneless chicken breast halves (about 1 pound total), cut into ¾-inch pieces
2	cloves garlic, minced
4	plum tomatoes, chopped
1	14-ounce can artichoke hearts, drained and quartered
1	2¼-ounce can sliced pitted ripe olives, drained
½	teaspoon dried Italian seasoning, crushed
¼	teaspoon black pepper
2	cups romaine lettuce or hearty mesclun, chopped
1	cup crumbled feta cheese (4 ounces)
⅓	cup fresh basil leaves, torn or shredded
	Sliced crusty Italian or French bread

PREP: *20 minutes*
COOK: *11 minutes*
MAKES: *4 servings*

1 In a large skillet heat oil over medium-high heat. Add chicken and garlic; cook and stir until chicken is brown. Stir in tomatoes, artichoke hearts, olives, Italian seasoning, and pepper. Bring to boiling; reduce heat. Cover and simmer about 10 minutes or until chicken is no longer pink.

2 Top chicken mixture with romaine and feta cheese. Cook, covered, for 1 to 2 minutes more or until romaine starts to wilt. Sprinkle with basil and serve on or with bread.

Per serving: 395 cal., 17 g total fat (6 g sat. fat), 82 mg chol., 1,003 mg sodium, 27 g carbo., 6 g fiber, 33 g pro.

Bring fresh and bold Asian flavors to your table with this fruit and chicken stir-fry. If you prefer, use peaches or plums in place of the nectarines.

FRUIT & CHICKEN STIR-FRY

START TO FINISH:
25 minutes

MAKES: *4 servings*

3	tablespoons reduced-sodium soy sauce
4	teaspoons honey
4	teaspoons red wine vinegar
½	teaspoon cornstarch
½	teaspoon curry powder
¼	teaspoon bottled hot pepper sauce
	Dash ground allspice
1	tablespoon cooking oil
1	pound skinless, boneless chicken breasts, cut into bite-size strips
1	small red sweet pepper, cut into thin bite-size strips
2	medium green onions, bias-sliced
2	nectarines, pitted and cut into ½-inch-thick slices
2	cups hot cooked couscous or rice

1 For sauce, in a small bowl stir together soy sauce, honey, red wine vinegar, cornstarch, curry powder, hot pepper sauce, and allspice; set aside.

2 Pour oil into a large wok or skillet. Heat over medium-high heat. Add chicken, sweet pepper, and green onions to wok; cook and stir for 3 to 4 minutes or until chicken is no longer pink. Push chicken mixture from center of wok. Stir sauce; add to center of wok. Cook and stir until thickened and bubbly. Stir to coat all ingredients.

3 Add nectarine slices to chicken mixture. Cook and stir for 1 to 2 minutes more or until heated through. Serve over hot cooked couscous or rice.

Per serving: 319 cal., 6 g total fat (1 g sat. fat), 66 mg chol., 501 mg sodium, 35 g carbo., 3 g fiber, 31 g pro.

This special-day dish features oodles of noodles, pan-fried chicken, and a medley of peppers—ingredients that are sure to please everyone around the table.

MAPLE CHICKEN FETTUCCINE

START TO FINISH: *30 minutes*

MAKES: *5 servings*

10	ounces dried fettuccine
5	skinless, boneless chicken breast halves (about 1½ pounds total)
	Salt
	Black pepper
1	tablespoon olive oil
1	16-ounce package frozen (yellow, green, and red) peppers and onion stir-fry vegetables
¾	cup chicken broth
1	tablespoon cornstarch
1	teaspoon snipped fresh rosemary
⅛	teaspoon black pepper
¼	cup maple syrup

1 Cook pasta according to package directions; drain. Set aside and keep warm.

2 Meanwhile, sprinkle chicken with salt and black pepper. In a large skillet heat oil over medium heat. Add chicken; cook for 12 to 14 minutes or until tender and no longer pink (170°F), turning once. Remove chicken from skillet; keep warm.

3 Increase heat to medium-high. Add stir-fry vegetables to skillet; cook and stir for 6 to 8 minutes or until vegetables are crisp-tender.

4 In a small bowl stir together broth, cornstarch, rosemary, and the ⅛ teaspoon black pepper. Add to skillet. Cook and stir until thickened and bubbly. Cook and stir for 1 minute more. Stir in maple syrup.

5 To serve, arrange hot pasta in five shallow bowls or on five dinner plates. Top with chicken. Spoon vegetable mixture over chicken.

Per serving: 465 cal., 6 g total fat (1 g sat. fat), 79 mg chol., 285 mg sodium, 60 g carbo., 2 g fiber, 40 g pro.

Team this easy-to-fix chicken with corn muffins and green beans for a palate-pleasing meal.

HONEYED CRANBERRY CHICKEN

START TO FINISH:
20 minutes

MAKES: *4 servings*

1   tablespoon butter

4   skinless, boneless chicken breast halves
    (about 1¼ pounds total)

½   cup whole cranberry sauce

2   tablespoons honey

½   teaspoon finely shredded lemon peel

1   tablespoon lemon juice

1 In a large skillet melt butter over medium heat. Add chicken; cook about 10 minutes or until tender and no longer pink (170°F), turning once. Transfer to a serving platter; reserve drippings in skillet. Cover chicken to keep warm.

2 Stir cranberry sauce, honey, lemon peel, and lemon juice into the reserved drippings in skillet. Cook and stir until heated through. Spoon over chicken.

Per serving: 275 cal., 5 g total fat (2 g sat. fat), 90 mg chol., 103 mg sodium, 23 g carbo., 1 g fiber, 33 g pro.

A small amount of honey lends a sweet dimension to this lemon-spiked chicken. (Recipe pictured on page 109.)

LEMON-TARRAGON CHICKEN TOSS

6	ounces dried fettuccine or linguine
2	cups broccoli or cauliflower florets
½	cup reduced-sodium chicken broth
3	tablespoons lemon juice
1	tablespoon honey
2	teaspoons cornstarch
¼	teaspoon white pepper
2	teaspoons olive oil or cooking oil
12	ounces skinless, boneless chicken breasts, cut into bite-size strips
½	cup shredded carrot
1	tablespoon snipped fresh tarragon or ½ teaspoon dried tarragon, crushed
	Lemon slices, halved (optional)

START TO FINISH:
20 minutes

MAKES: *4 servings*

1 Cook pasta according to package directions, adding the broccoli or cauliflower for the last 4 minutes of cooking. Drain.

2 Meanwhile, in a small bowl combine chicken broth, lemon juice, honey, cornstarch, and white pepper; set aside.

3 In a large nonstick skillet heat oil over medium-high heat. Add chicken; cook and stir for 3 to 4 minutes or until no longer pink. Stir cornstarch mixture; add to skillet. Cook and stir until thickened and bubbly. Add carrot and tarragon; cook for 1 minute more.

4 To serve, spoon chicken mixture over pasta. If desired, garnish with halved lemon slices. Serve immediately.

Per serving: 320 cal., 4 g total fat (1 g sat. fat), 49 mg chol., 143 mg sodium, 43 g carbo., 3 g fiber, 27 g pro.

This sweet, crunchy chicken is sure to be a favorite with kids.

HULA STIR-FRY

START TO FINISH:
25 minutes

MAKES: *4 servings*

1   tablespoon cooking oil

1   pound skinless, boneless chicken breasts, cut into bite-size pieces

1   16-ounce package frozen stir-fry vegetables

1   8-ounce can pineapple chunks (juice pack)

2   3-ounce packages ramen noodles (any flavor), broken

⅔   cup purchased stir-fry sauce

½   cup water

1 In a large skillet heat oil over medium-high heat. Add chicken; cook and stir about 6 minutes or until no longer pink. Add vegetables to the skillet. Cover and cook for 5 to 7 minutes or until vegetables are tender but still slightly crunchy.

2 Stir undrained pineapple chunks, ramen noodles (discard seasoning packets), stir-fry sauce, and the water into chicken mixture in skillet. Bring to boiling; reduce heat to medium-low. Cover and cook about 3 minutes more or until noodles are tender, stirring occasionally.

Per serving: 471 cal., 14 g total fat (1 g sat. fat), 67 mg chol., 1,103 mg sodium, 49 g carbo., 3 g fiber, 37 g pro.

This meal is quick, easy, and satisfying—perfect for the end of a busy workday.

ITALIAN CHICKEN SKILLET

2	tablespoons olive oil
1½	pounds skinless, boneless chicken breasts, cut into thin bite-size strips
¼	teaspoon salt
⅛	teaspoon black pepper
1	14½-ounce can diced tomatoes with basil, garlic, and oregano, drained
2	tablespoons snipped fresh basil
1	10-ounce package fresh spinach
1	cup shredded mozzarella cheese (4 ounces)

START TO FINISH:
25 minutes

MAKES: *4 servings*

1 In a 12-inch skillet heat oil over medium-high heat. Add chicken, half at a time; cook and stir until no longer pink. Drain off fat. Return all chicken to skillet. Sprinkle chicken with salt and pepper.

2 Add drained tomatoes and basil to skillet. Bring to boiling. Add spinach to skillet, half at a time, tossing with tongs just until wilted. Remove from heat. Sprinkle with cheese. Let stand for 3 to 5 minutes or until cheese is melted.

Per serving: 380 cal., 14 g total fat (4 g sat. fat), 116 mg chol., 998 mg sodium, 12 g carbo., 2 g fiber, 50 g pro.

Take care not to overcook the cucumber. Cook it just until it begins to soften but still has a bit of crispness. If you like, seed the cucumber before chopping it.

LEMON~DILL BUTTER CHICKEN & CUCUMBERS

PREP: *10 minutes*
BROIL: *12 minutes*
MAKES: *4 servings*

4   skinless, boneless chicken breast halves (about 1¼ pounds total)
1   medium lemon
3   tablespoons butter
½   teaspoon dried dill
¼   teaspoon salt
¼   teaspoon black pepper
1½   cups coarsely chopped cucumber or zucchini

1 Preheat broiler. Place chicken on the unheated rack of a broiler pan. Broil 4 to 5 inches from the heat for 12 to 15 minutes or until tender and no longer pink (170°F), turning once halfway through broiling.

2 Meanwhile, finely shred ½ teaspoon peel from the lemon. Cut lemon in half; squeeze lemon until you have 2 tablespoons juice.

3 In a small skillet melt butter over medium heat. Stir in lemon peel, lemon juice, dill, salt, and pepper. Stir in cucumber. Cook and stir over medium heat for 3 to 4 minutes or just until cucumber is tender. Spoon cucumber mixture over chicken.

Per serving: 244 cal., 11 g total fat (6 g sat. fat), 107 mg chol., 477 mg sodium, 2 g carbo., 0 g fiber, 33 g pro.

Depending on the type of chile peppers available, traditional mole sauces vary in color and kick. However, they always have one thing in common, and that's chocolate. This version relies on salsa for bite and cocoa powder for richness. (Recipe pictured on page 109.)

SHORTCUT CHICKEN MOLE

START TO FINISH:
15 minutes

MAKES: *4 servings*

1½   cups instant rice

1   tablespoon cooking oil

12   ounces skinless, boneless chicken strips

1   tablespoon unsweetened cocoa powder

1   teaspoon ground cumin

1   16-ounce jar thick and chunky salsa

½   of a 16-ounce package (2 cups) frozen (yellow, green, and red) peppers and onion stir-fry vegetables

    Fresh herb sprigs (optional)

1 Cook rice according to package directions.

2 Meanwhile, in a large skillet heat oil over medium-high heat. Add chicken strips; cook and stir for 2 to 3 minutes or until light brown. Drain off fat.

3 Sprinkle chicken with cocoa powder and cumin; stir to combine. Stir in salsa and frozen peppers. Bring to boiling; reduce heat. Cover and simmer about 5 minutes or just until peppers are tender.

4 Serve chicken mixture with hot cooked rice. If desired, garnish with fresh herb sprigs.

Per serving: 334 cal., 5 g total fat (1 g sat. fat), 49 mg chol., 549 mg sodium, 44 g carbo., 3 g fiber, 26 g pro.

For a speedier version, substitute leftover cooked chicken strips or cooked chicken breast strips from your supermarket's meat case. Dip and coat them as directed and simply reheat them in the oven for about 5 minutes.

TWO-STEP CRUNCHY CHICKEN STRIPS

PREP: *10 minutes*

BAKE: *10 minutes*

MAKES: *4 to 6 servings*

Nonstick cooking spray

2½ cups crushed bite-size cheddar fish-shaped crackers and/or pretzels

⅔ cup bottled buttermilk ranch salad dressing or honey Dijon-style mustard

1 pound chicken breast tenderloins

Bottled buttermilk ranch salad dressing or honey Dijon-style mustard (optional)

1 Preheat oven to 425°F. Line a 15×10×1-inch baking pan with foil; lightly coat foil with nonstick cooking spray. Set aside.

2 Place the crushed crackers or pretzels in a shallow dish. Place the ⅔ cup ranch dressing or mustard in another shallow dish. Dip chicken tenderloins into the dressing or mustard, allowing excess to drip off; dip into crushed crackers or pretzels to coat. Arrange chicken in prepared pan. Bake for 10 to 15 minutes or until chicken is tender and no longer pink (170°F). If desired, serve with additional ranch dressing or mustard.

Per serving: 517 cal., 21 g total fat (2 g sat. fat), 66 mg chol., 1,060 mg sodium, 51 g carbo., 2 g fiber, 33 g pro.

Serve this exceptional dish with steamed broccoli, asparagus, or Brussels sprouts. The tasty juices and crusty flavor bits left in the pan after cooking the turkey jump-start a snappy pan sauce.

TURKEY PICCATA WITH FETTUCCINE

6	ounces dried fettuccine or linguine
¼	cup all-purpose flour
½	teaspoon lemon-pepper seasoning or black pepper
2	turkey breast tenderloins (about 1 pound total)
2	tablespoons olive oil or cooking oil
⅓	cup dry white wine
2	tablespoons lemon juice
2	tablespoons water
½	teaspoon instant chicken bouillon granules
1	tablespoon capers, rinsed and drained (optional)
2	tablespoons snipped fresh parsley
	Lemon wedges (optional)
	Fresh parsley sprigs (optional)

START TO FINISH:
30 minutes

MAKES: *4 servings*

1 Cook pasta according to package directions; drain.

2 Meanwhile, in a shallow bowl stir together flour and lemon-pepper seasoning; set aside. Split each turkey tenderloin in half horizontally to make a total of four ½-inch-thick portions. Dip turkey portions in flour mixture to coat.

3 In a large skillet heat oil over medium-high heat. Add turkey; cook for 6 to 10 minutes or until light golden brown and no longer pink (170°F), turning once. Remove turkey from skillet; cover and keep warm.

4 For sauce, add wine, lemon juice, the water, and bouillon granules to skillet, scraping up browned bits from bottom of skillet. If desired, stir in capers. Bring to boiling; reduce heat. Simmer, uncovered, for 2 minutes. Remove from heat; stir in snipped parsley.

5 To serve, divide pasta among four dinner plates. Place turkey on top of pasta. Spoon sauce over all. If desired, serve with lemon wedges and garnish with parsley sprigs.

Per serving: 377 cal., 9 g total fat (2 g sat. fat), 68 mg chol., 301 mg sodium, 36 g carbo., 1 g fiber, 33 g pro.

In this recipe a small amount of honey and crushed red pepper combine with the delightful flavor of balsamic vinegar, resulting in a tantalizing spicy-sweet blend.

BALSAMIC TURKEY WITH ZUCCHINI

START TO FINISH:
25 minutes

MAKES: *4 servings*

2 tablespoons balsamic vinegar

2 tablespoons cooking oil

1 tablespoon honey

⅛ to ¼ teaspoon crushed red pepper

2 turkey breast tenderloins (about 1 pound total)

Salt

Black pepper

2 medium zucchini, halved lengthwise and cut into ¼-inch-thick slices

2 cups hot cooked pasta or rice

½ cup chopped tomato

Shredded fresh basil

1 For dressing, in a small bowl stir together balsamic vinegar, 1 tablespoon of the oil, the honey, and crushed red pepper; set aside. Split each turkey breast tenderloin in half horizontally to make a total of four ½-inch-thick portions. Lightly sprinkle turkey with salt and pepper.

2 In a large nonstick skillet heat the remaining 1 tablespoon oil over medium-high heat. Add turkey; cook for 8 to 10 minutes or until tender and no longer pink (170°F), turning once. Remove from skillet; cover and keep warm.

3 Add zucchini to skillet; cook and stir about 3 minutes or until crisp-tender. Cut turkey into bite-size pieces. In a large bowl combine turkey, zucchini, and dressing. Spoon over hot cooked pasta. Sprinkle with chopped tomato and basil.

Per serving: 328 cal., 9 g total fat (2 g sat. fat), 68 mg chol., 96 mg sodium, 30 g carbo., 2 g fiber, 31 g pro.

Cooking with bold ingredients ensures flavor-packed meals. The lively tastes of garlic, sage, and apple jelly meld into an impressive brush-on glaze.

APPLE-GLAZED TURKEY

2   turkey breast tenderloins (about 1 pound total)

1   tablespoon lemon juice

1   tablespoon olive oil or cooking oil

½   teaspoon seasoned salt

½   teaspoon dried sage leaves, crushed

4   cloves garlic, minced

2   tablespoons apple jelly, melted

     Fresh sage leaves (optional)

     Apple slices (optional)

PREP: *10 minutes*

BROIL: *9 minutes*

MAKES: *4 servings*

1 Preheat broiler. Split each turkey breast tenderloin in half horizontally to make a total of four ½-inch-thick portions. Place turkey portions on the unheated rack of a broiler pan. In a small bowl combine lemon juice, oil, seasoned salt, dried sage, and garlic. Brush sage mixture on both sides of each turkey portion.

2 Broil turkey 4 to 5 inches from the heat for 5 minutes. Turn turkey; broil for 2 minutes more. Using a clean brush, brush with apple jelly. Broil for 2 to 3 minutes more or until tender and no longer pink (170°F). Slice the turkey. If desired, garnish with fresh sage leaves and apple slices.

Per serving: 192 cal., 5 g total fat (1 g sat. fat), 68 mg chol., 247 mg sodium, 8 g carbo., 0 g fiber, 27 g pro.

The contrast of sweet and hot peppers makes this skillet dish scrumptious. Serve the turkey slices over rice to soak up the flavorful juices.

TURKEY & PEPPERS

START TO FINISH:
25 minutes

MAKES: *4 servings*

4 ¼- to ⅜-inch-thick turkey breast slices (about 12 ounces total)

   Salt

   Black pepper

1 tablespoon olive oil

2 medium red, yellow, and/or green sweet peppers, cut into thin bite-size strips

1 medium onion, halved lengthwise and sliced

1 fresh jalapeño chile pepper, seeded and thinly sliced (see tip, page 19)

¾ cup chicken broth

1 tablespoon all-purpose flour

1 teaspoon paprika

   Hot cooked rice (optional)

1 Sprinkle turkey lightly with salt and black pepper. In a large nonstick skillet heat oil over medium-high heat. Add turkey; cook for 4 to 5 minutes or until turkey is tender and no longer pink (170°F), turning once. (If necessary, reduce heat to medium to prevent overbrowning.) Transfer turkey to a serving platter; cover and keep warm.

2 Add sweet peppers, onion, and chile pepper to skillet. Cook, covered, for 4 to 5 minutes or until vegetables are crisp-tender, stirring occasionally.

3 In a screw-top jar combine chicken broth, flour, and paprika; shake well. Add to sweet pepper mixture. Cook and stir over medium heat until thickened and bubbly. Cook and stir for 1 minute more. If desired, serve turkey over hot cooked rice. Spoon the sweet pepper mixture over turkey and rice.

Per serving: 167 cal., 5 g total fat (1 g sat. fat), 51 mg chol., 260 mg sodium, 8 g carbo., 2 g fiber, 22 g pro.

The mini burgers bake in just 12 minutes, so give the waffle fries a head start in the oven before popping in the burgers.

BBQ CHICKEN BURGERS & WAFFLE FRIES

⅓   cup bottled barbecue sauce

⅓   cup grape jelly or seedless raspberry jam

3   cups frozen waffle-cut or thick-cut french fried potatoes

4   slices packaged ready-to-serve cooked bacon, chopped

2   tablespoons fine dry bread crumbs

2   tablespoons finely chopped honey-roasted walnuts or almonds

1   tablespoon bottled barbecue sauce

½   teaspoon poultry seasoning

¼   teaspoon salt

⅛   teaspoon black pepper

8   ounces uncooked ground chicken or ground turkey

½   cup shredded Italian-blend cheese, Monterey Jack cheese with jalapeño chile peppers, or Gorgonzola cheese

     Snipped fresh chives

     Lettuce

8   dinner rolls or cocktail-size hamburger buns, split

     Tomato slices

START TO FINISH:
30 minutes

MAKES: *4 servings*

1 Preheat oven to 425°F. In a small bowl whisk together the ⅓ cup barbecue sauce and the jelly until smooth. Set aside.

2 Arrange waffle-cut potatoes in a single layer on an ungreased baking sheet. Sprinkle with chopped bacon. Bake for 8 minutes.

3 Meanwhile, in a medium bowl combine bread crumbs, nuts, the 1 tablespoon barbecue sauce, the poultry seasoning, salt, and black pepper. Add ground chicken; mix well. Shape into eight balls; place 2 inches apart on greased shallow baking pan. Moisten the bottom of a glass and press each ball to about ¼-inch thickness.

4 Place pan of burgers in oven. Bake burgers and potatoes for 5 minutes. Stir potatoes; turn burgers. Bake burgers and potatoes for 5 minutes more.

5 Sprinkle cheese over potatoes. Brush barbecue sauce-jelly mixture on burgers. Bake burgers and potatoes about 2 minutes more or until burgers are no longer pink in center and cheese is melted on potatoes.

6 To serve, sprinkle potatoes with snipped chives. Place lettuce and burgers on the bottom halves of dinner rolls. Spoon the remaining jelly mixture over burgers. Add tomato slices and top halves of rolls.

Per serving: 537 cal., 21 g total fat (7 g sat. fat), 20 mg chol., 902 mg sodium, 66 g carbo., 4 g fiber, 22 g pro.

All the goodness of Thanksgiving dinner comes together in this healthful entrée that features cranberry sauce, turkey, stuffing, and sage.

TURKEY BURGERS WITH CRANBERRY SAUCE

PREP: *12 minutes*

BROIL: *11 minutes*

MAKES: *4 servings*

⅓	cup herb-seasoned stuffing mix, crushed (¼ cup)
2	tablespoons milk
1	tablespoon snipped fresh sage or ½ teaspoon dried sage, crushed
¼	teaspoon salt
1	pound uncooked ground turkey or ground chicken
1	cup torn mixed salad greens, watercress leaves, or shredded fresh spinach
4	whole wheat hamburger buns, split and toasted
½	cup whole cranberry sauce

1 Preheat broiler. In a large bowl combine stuffing mix, milk, sage, and salt. Add ground turkey; mix well. Shape into four ½-inch-thick patties. Place patties on the unheated rack of a broiler pan. Broil 4 to 5 inches from the heat for 11 to 13 minutes or until done (165°F),* turning once halfway through broiling.

2 To serve, divide greens among bottom halves of buns; top with patties and cranberry sauce. Add top halves of buns.

Per serving: 350 cal., 11 g total fat (3 g sat. fat), 71 mg chol., 503 mg sodium, 37 g carbo., 3 g fiber, 28 g pro.

*TEST KITCHEN TIP: The internal color of a burger is not a reliable doneness indicator. A turkey or chicken patty cooked to 165°F is safe, regardless of color. To measure the doneness of a patty, insert an instant-read thermometer through the side of the patty to a depth of 2 to 3 inches.

Kids of all ages will love these protein-rich turkey burgers.

SAUCY TURKEY BURGERS

¼ cup fine dry bread crumbs

3 tablespoons ketchup

4 teaspoons dill or sweet pickle relish

1 clove garlic, minced

¼ teaspoon salt

¼ teaspoon black pepper

1 pound uncooked ground turkey or ground chicken

⅓ cup low-fat mayonnaise dressing or salad dressing

4 romaine lettuce or green leaf lettuce leaves

8 tomato slices

4 whole wheat hamburger buns, split and toasted

PREP: *15 minutes*

BROIL: *14 minutes*

MAKES: *4 servings*

1 Preheat broiler. In a large bowl combine bread crumbs, 2 tablespoons of the ketchup, 2 teaspoons of the pickle relish, the garlic, salt, and ⅛ teaspoon of the pepper. Add ground turkey; mix well. Shape into four ¾-inch-thick patties.

2 In a small bowl combine mayonnaise dressing, the remaining 1 tablespoon ketchup, the remaining 2 teaspoons pickle relish, and the remaining ⅛ teaspoon pepper; set aside.

3 Place patties on the unheated rack of a broiler pan. Broil 4 to 5 inches from the heat for 14 to 18 minutes or until done (165°F),* turning once halfway through broiling.

4 To serve, place lettuce leaves and tomato slices on the bottom halves of buns; top with burgers. Spoon mayonnaise mixture over burgers. Add top halves of buns.

Per serving: 343 cal., 12 g total fat (3 g sat. fat), 74 mg chol., 953 mg sodium, 33 g carbo., 3 g fiber, 29 g pro.

*TEST KITCHEN TIP: The internal color of a burger is not a reliable doneness indicator. A turkey or chicken patty cooked to 165°F is safe, regardless of color. To measure the doneness of a patty, insert an instant read thermometer through the side of the patty to a depth of 2 to 3 inches.

This recipe gives burgers Asian flair by using Thai seasoning and peanut sauce.

THAI TURKEY BURGERS

PREP: *15 minutes*

BROIL: *14 minutes*

MAKES: *4 servings*

1	egg, beaten
¼	cup fine dry bread crumbs
1	teaspoon Thai seasoning
1	pound uncooked ground turkey or ground chicken
4	kaiser rolls or hamburger buns, split and toasted
¾	cup fresh basil leaves
2	tablespoons purchased peanut dipping sauce
	Green onions, bias-sliced (optional)

1 Preheat broiler. In a medium bowl combine egg, bread crumbs, and Thai seasoning. Add ground turkey; mix well. Shape into four ¾-inch-thick patties.

2 Place patties on the unheated rack of a broiler pan. Broil 3 to 4 inches from the heat for 14 to 18 minutes or until done (165°F),* turning once halfway through broiling.

3 To serve, top bottom halves of buns with basil; add patties. Spoon peanut dipping sauce over patties. If desired, garnish with green onions. Add top halves of buns.

Per serving: 389 cal., 13 g total fat (3 g sat. fat), 123 mg chol., 739 mg sodium, 36 g carbo., 2 g fiber, 31 g pro.

*TEST KITCHEN TIP: The internal color of a burger is not a reliable doneness indicator. A turkey or chicken patty cooked to 165°F is safe, regardless of color. To measure the doneness of a patty, insert an instant-read thermometer through the side of the patty to a depth of 2 to 3 inches.

Use your favorite pasta sauce in this dish, which is quick, easy, and, best of all, great tasting.

SPICY TURKEY OVER PASTA

1   9-ounce package refrigerated fettuccine or linguine

8   ounces uncooked Italian turkey sausage
     (remove casings, if present)

1   cup cut-up pattypan squash or yellow summer squash

1   small red sweet pepper, cut into thin strips

¼   cup chopped red onion

1   14-ounce jar pasta sauce

2   tablespoons shredded Parmesan cheese (optional)

1 Cook pasta according to package directions; drain.

2 Meanwhile, in a large skillet cook sausage, squash, sweet pepper, and onion over medium heat until sausage is brown; drain off fat. Stir pasta sauce into sausage mixture in skillet; heat through.

3 Serve sausage mixture over hot pasta. If desired, sprinkle with Parmesan cheese.

Per serving: 350 cal., 10 g total fat (3 g sat. fat), 115 mg chol., 866 mg sodium, 49 g carbo., 5 g fiber, 20 g pro.

START TO FINISH:
25 minutes

MAKES: *4 servings*

A handful of ingredients makes this time-efficient meal a breeze. Toasted almonds or pine nuts add a special touch.

POLENTA WITH TURKEY SAUSAGE FLORENTINE

START TO FINISH:
25 minutes

MAKES: *2 servings*

1   9- or 10-ounce package frozen creamed spinach

8   ounces uncooked bulk turkey sausage

1   tablespoon olive oil

½   of a 16-ounce tube refrigerated cooked polenta with wild mushrooms, cut into ¾-inch-thick slices

2   tablespoons sliced almonds or pine nuts, toasted

1 Cook the spinach according to package directions. Meanwhile, in a medium skillet cook sausage until brown; drain in colander. In the same skillet heat oil over medium heat. Add polenta slices; cook about 6 minutes or until golden brown, turning once. Divide polenta between two dinner plates.

2 Stir cooked sausage into hot creamed spinach; heat through and spoon over polenta. Sprinkle with toasted nuts.

Per serving: 607 cal., 41 g total fat (8 g sat. fat), 119 mg chol., 1,586 mg sodium, 33 g carbo., 6 g fiber, 28 g pro.

With this recipe, a fabulous dinner is a cinch to make, especially when you pick up a ready-to-eat chicken on your way home from work. (Recipe pictured on page 110.)

CHICKEN, GOAT CHEESE & GREENS

1½	pounds Swiss chard, beet greens, and/or mustard greens, trimmed and washed
1	2- to 2½-pound purchased roasted chicken
3	tablespoons olive oil
2	tablespoons lemon juice
2	tablespoons snipped fresh dill, oregano, and/or sage
¼	teaspoon sea salt, kosher salt, or salt
⅛	teaspoon cracked black pepper
1	3- to 4-ounce log goat cheese (chèvre), sliced into rounds or coarsely crumbled
⅛	teaspoon cracked black pepper

PREP: *15 minutes*
BAKE: *15 minutes*
MAKES: *4 servings*

1 Preheat oven to 350°F. Reserve one or two small leaves of the Swiss chard. Tear remaining Swiss chard and place in a 3-quart rectangular baking dish. Remove string from chicken; use the string to tie the chicken legs together. Place chicken on Swiss chard in dish. In a small bowl combine oil and lemon juice. Drizzle oil mixture over chicken and Swiss chard in dish. Sprinkle 1 tablespoon of the snipped herbs over the chicken and Swiss chard. Sprinkle salt and ⅛ teaspoon pepper over Swiss chard only.

2 Loosely cover baking dish with foil. Bake for 15 to 20 minutes or until Swiss chard is tender. Meanwhile, sprinkle goat cheese with the remaining 1 tablespoon snipped herbs and ⅛ teaspoon pepper.

3 Transfer chicken to a serving platter. Place some of the goat cheese on top of the chicken. Add reserved Swiss chard leaves on top of chicken. Toss cooked Swiss chard in dish to evenly coat with cooking liquid. Serve cooked Swiss chard and the remaining cheese with chicken.

Per serving: 542 cal., 36 g total fat (10 g sat. fat), 143 mg chol., 620 mg sodium, 7 g carbo., 3 g fiber, 48 g pro.

TEST KITCHEN TIP: This recipe doubles easily to serve 8. Double the ingredients and prepare as directed above, except place all the greens and both chickens in a large shallow roasting pan. Bake as above.

Purchased pesto and roasted chicken help get this pasta on the table in a mere 25 minutes.

PESTO PENNE WITH ROASTED CHICKEN

START TO FINISH:
25 minutes

MAKES: *4 servings*

8	ounces dried penne, mostaccioli, or bow tie pasta (4 cups)
2	cups broccoli florets
1	7-ounce container refrigerated basil pesto (about ¾ cup)
2½	cups bite-size slices purchased roasted chicken, refrigerated cooked chicken breast strips, or bite-size slices leftover cooked chicken (about 12 ounces)
1	7-ounce jar roasted red sweet peppers, drained and cut into strips (about 1 cup)
¼	cup finely shredded Parmesan cheese
	Finely shredded Parmesan cheese (optional)
½	teaspoon coarsely ground black pepper

1 Cook pasta according to package directions, adding broccoli for the last 2 minutes of cooking. Drain, reserving ½ cup of the pasta water. Return drained pasta and broccoli to hot saucepan.

2 In a small bowl combine pesto and the reserved ½ cup pasta water. Add chicken, roasted red sweet peppers, and pesto mixture to pasta and broccoli in saucepan. Toss gently to coat. Heat through over medium heat. Add the ¼ cup Parmesan cheese to pasta mixture; toss to combine.

3 Divide cooked pasta among four warm pasta bowls. If desired, sprinkle with additional Parmesan cheese. Sprinkle with coarsely ground black pepper. Serve immediately.

Per serving: 601 cal., 28 g total fat (2 g sat. fat), 69 mg chol., 1,168 mg sodium, 56 g carbo., 3 g fiber, 33 g pro.

Purchased roasted chicken and pesto as well as refrigerated Alfredo sauce make this sophisticated pasta super easy. (Recipe pictured on page 111.)

CHICKEN LINGUINE WITH PESTO SAUCE

8	ounces dried linguine
1	10-ounce package frozen broccoli, cauliflower, and carrots
1	10-ounce container refrigerated Alfredo pasta sauce or 1 cup bottled Alfredo pasta sauce
⅓	cup purchased basil pesto
¼	cup milk
½	of a 2- to 2¼-pound purchased roasted chicken
	Milk (optional)
	Grated Parmesan cheese

START TO FINISH:
20 minutes

MAKES: *4 servings*

1 In a 4- to 5-quart Dutch oven cook pasta according to package directions, adding vegetables for the last 5 minutes of cooking. Drain. Return to hot Dutch oven.

2 While pasta is cooking, in a small bowl combine Alfredo sauce, pesto, and the ¼ cup milk; set aside. Remove meat from chicken; discard skin and bones. Shred or chop meat.

3 Add chicken to pasta and vegetables in Dutch oven. Add Alfredo sauce mixture; toss gently to coat. Heat through over medium-low heat. If necessary, stir in enough additional milk to reach desired consistency. Sprinkle individual servings with cheese.

Per serving: 801 cal., 48 g total fat (4 g sat. fat), 109 mg chol., 546 mg sodium, 54 g carbo., 3 g fiber, 37 g pro.

If you enjoy quesadillas with a kick, use shredded Monterey Jack cheese with jalapeño chile peppers and hot-style salsa.

CHICKEN QUESADILLAS

START TO FINISH:
25 minutes

MAKES: *4 servings*

1　2½-pound purchased roasted chicken

4　8- to 10-inch flour tortillas

1　cup fresh spinach leaves

1　8-ounce can (drained weight) sliced mushrooms, drained

2　cups shredded Monterey Jack cheese (8 ounces)

　　Purchased salsa (optional)

　　Purchased guacamole (optional)

1 Remove meat from chicken; discard skin and bones. Chop meat; reserve 2 cups. Cover and chill or freeze remaining chicken for another use.

2 Spoon the 2 cups chicken evenly onto bottom halves of tortillas. Top with spinach and mushrooms. Sprinkle cheese evenly over mushrooms. Fold tortillas in half.

3 Heat quesadillas on a griddle over medium heat until browned on both sides and cheese is melted, turning once. If desired, serve with salsa and guacamole.

Per serving: 573 cal., 28 g total fat (13 g sat. fat), 144 mg chol., 857 mg sodium, 28 g carbo., 1 g fiber, 50 g pro.

The lime peel and tequila give the Alfredo sauce a Tex-Mex attitude.

TEQUILA-LIME CHICKEN

1   9-ounce package refrigerated fettuccine

1   lime

1   10-ounce container refrigerated regular or light Alfredo pasta sauce

¼   cup tequila or milk

1   9-ounce package refrigerated cooked grilled chicken breast strips

1 Cook fettuccine according to package directions; drain.

2 Meanwhile, finely shred enough peel from the lime to equal 1 teaspoon. Cut lime into wedges and set aside. In a medium saucepan combine lime peel, Alfredo sauce, and tequila; cook and stir just until boiling. Stir in chicken strips; heat through. Toss sauce with hot fettuccine. Serve with lime wedges.

Per serving: 528 cal., 24 g total fat (1 g sat. fat), 123 mg chol., 853 mg sodium, 39 g carbo., 2 g fiber, 11 g pro.

START TO FINISH:
15 minutes

MAKES: *4 servings*

Be sure to use a skillet that can withstand the heat of the oven. A cast-iron skillet does the job nicely.

PUFFY OMELET WITH CHEESY CHICKEN FILLING

START TO FINISH:
25 minutes

MAKES: *2 servings*

4   egg whites

¼   teaspoon salt

⅛   teaspoon black pepper

2   tablespoons water

4   egg yolks, beaten

1   tablespoon butter

⅔   cup shredded Monterey Jack cheese with jalapeño chile peppers or cheddar cheese

1   6-ounce package refrigerated cooked southwestern-style chicken breast strips, chopped

2   tablespoons purchased salsa or picante sauce

     Purchased salsa or picante sauce (optional)

1 Preheat oven to 350°F. In a medium bowl beat egg whites, salt, and pepper with an electric mixer on medium to high speed until frothy. Add the water; continue beating for 1 to 2 minutes or until stiff peaks form (tips stand straight). Fold in yolks.

2 In a large ovenproof skillet heat butter over medium-high heat until a drop of water sizzles. Spread egg mixture in skillet. Cook about 3 minutes or just until bottom is golden. Bake for 3 to 4 minutes or until top is dry and edge is light brown.

3 Using a metal spatula, loosen the omelet from the side of the skillet. Make a shallow cut slightly off center across the omelet. Sprinkle cheese over the larger side. Top with chicken and the 2 tablespoons salsa. Fold smaller side of omelet over larger side. Cut omelet in half. If desired, serve with additional salsa.

Per serving: 464 cal., 31 g total fat (16 g sat. fat), 537 mg chol., 1,540 mg sodium, 3 g carbo., 0 g fiber, 41 g pro.

Leftover grilled chicken or turkey is an appetizing option for the purchased refrigerated chicken strips.

CHICKEN IN A PHYLLO NEST

Nonstick cooking spray

10	sheets frozen phyllo dough (14×9-inch rectangles), thawed
2	tablespoons olive oil
1	cup 2-inch-long pieces green onions
12	ounces refrigerated grilled chicken breast strips (3 cups)
1	6-ounce package fresh baby spinach
¾	cup cherry tomatoes, halved or quartered (optional)
1	tablespoon snipped fresh tarragon
¼	teaspoon freshly ground black pepper
½	cup bottled balsamic vinaigrette salad dressing

START TO FINISH:
25 minutes

MAKES: *6 servings*

1 Preheat oven to 425°F. Lightly coat a 15×10×1-inch baking pan with nonstick cooking spray; set aside. Roll stack of phyllo sheets into a cylinder shape. With a sharp knife cut phyllo roll crosswise into ¼- to ½-inch-wide strips. Gently separate phyllo strips and spread evenly in the prepared baking pan. Coat phyllo generously with additional nonstick cooking spray. Bake for 8 to 10 minutes or until phyllo strips are golden brown.

2 Meanwhile, in a 12-inch skillet heat oil over medium-high heat. Add green onion; cook about 1 minute or just until tender. Add chicken; cook and stir until heated through. Remove skillet from heat. Add spinach, cherry tomatoes (if desired), tarragon, and pepper. Toss to combine.

3 Divide phyllo among six bowls. Spoon chicken mixture over phyllo. Drizzle with balsamic vinaigrette. Serve immediately.

Per serving: 197 cal., 10 g total fat (2 g sat. fat), 40 mg chol., 760 mg sodium, 14 g carbo., 1 g fiber, 14 g pro.

Microwaving the frozen chicken just a tad allows the skewers to be inserted easily. Instead of chicken, you can opt for thick slices of fully cooked smoked turkey sausage. Thread it onto the skewers with the biscuit dough and bake as directed.

CHICKEN & BISCUIT KABOBS

START TO FINISH:
20 minutes

MAKES: *4 servings*

½   of a 13½-ounce package (12) frozen cooked breaded chicken breast chunks

1   4½-ounce package (6) refrigerated buttermilk or country biscuits

1   medium zucchini and/or yellow summer squash, cut into 3×¾-inch strips

⅓   cup butter, melted*

3   tablespoons honey*

1 Preheat oven to 400°F. Arrange chicken chunks in a single layer on a microwave-safe plate. Microwave, uncovered, on 100% power (high) for 1 minute (chicken will not be heated through).

2 Use kitchen scissors to snip each biscuit in half. On each of four wooden or metal skewers alternately thread chicken pieces, biscuit halves, and squash, leaving a ¼-inch space between pieces. Place on ungreased baking sheet. Bake about 10 minutes or until biscuits are golden brown and chicken is heated through.

3 Meanwhile, whisk together melted butter and honey. Drizzle some over kabobs. Pass remainder for dipping.

Per serving: 376 cal., 22 g total fat (9 g sat. fat), 57 mg chol., 649 mg sodium, 37 g carbo., 1 g fiber, 10 g pro.

*TEST KITCHEN TIP: You can substitute ½ cup honey-butter for the melted butter and honey. Place in a microwave-safe bowl and microwave, uncovered, on 100% power (high) for 35 to 45 seconds or until melted.

Here's a chance to pile on extra veggies if you think your kids won't notice. For an extra taste of Mexican-style flavor, top each tostada with a spoonful of light dairy sour cream.

TOWERING TOSTADAS

START TO FINISH:
15 minutes

MAKES: *4 servings*

1¼ cups taco sauce with shredded chicken
(½ of an 18-ounce tub)

4 6-inch tostada shells

¾ cup shredded, peeled jicama; shredded carrot;
packaged shredded broccoli (broccoli slaw mix);
and/or canned black beans, rinsed and drained

⅓ cup shredded colby and Monterey Jack cheese

1 In a small saucepan cook shredded chicken until heated through. Divide evenly among tostada shells. Top with vegetables and/or beans and cheese.

Per serving: 174 cal., 8 g total fat (3 g sat. fat), 40 mg chol., 645 mg sodium, 14 g carbo., 2 g fiber, 9 g pro.

Dip the quesadilla wedges into green onion-topped sour cream and salsa. Or spoon the sour cream and salsa over the quesadillas and eat them with a knife and fork.

BBQ CHICKEN & CHEESE QUESADILLAS

PREP: *20 minutes*

COOK: *4 minutes per batch*

MAKES: *4 servings*

4   7- or 8-inch flour tortillas
     Nonstick cooking spray

1   cup shredded Mexican-blend cheese or extra-sharp cheddar cheese (4 ounces)

1   18-ounce tub refrigerated shredded chicken with barbecue sauce (2 cups)

1   4-ounce can diced green chile peppers, drained

1   cup purchased salsa

¼   cup dairy sour cream

¼   cup sliced green onions
     Shredded Mexican-blend cheese or extra-sharp cheddar cheese

1 Preheat oven to 300°F. Coat one side of each tortilla with nonstick cooking spray. Place tortillas, coated sides down, on cutting board or waxed paper. Sprinkle ¼ cup of the cheese onto half of each tortilla. Top with barbecued chicken and chile peppers. Fold tortillas in half, pressing gently.

2 Heat a 10-inch nonstick skillet over medium heat. Add two of the quesadillas to hot skillet; cook for 4 to 6 minutes or until light brown, turning once. Remove quesadillas from skillet; place on a baking sheet. Keep warm in oven. Repeat with remaining quesadillas. To serve, cut each quesadilla into three wedges. Serve with salsa, sour cream, green onion, and additional cheese.

Per serving: 469 cal., 21 g total fat (10 g sat. fat), 86 mg chol., 1,629 mg sodium, 46 g carbo., 1 g fiber, 25 g pro.

Boiling the water is the most time-consuming part of making this super-fast spin on mac and cheese.

TORTELLINI & CHEESE

1	9-ounce package refrigerated cheese tortellini
1	cup loose-pack frozen peas, corn, or pea pods
1	8-ounce tub cream cheese spread with garden vegetables or chive and onion
½	cup milk
1	9-ounce package frozen chopped cooked chicken breast

START TO FINISH:
20 minutes

MAKES: *4 servings*

1 In a large saucepan cook tortellini according to package directions. Place frozen vegetables in colander. Drain hot pasta over vegetables to thaw; return pasta-vegetable mixture to hot pan.

2 Meanwhile, in a small saucepan combine cream cheese and milk; heat and stir until cheese is melted. Heat chicken according to package directions.

3 Stir cheese mixture into pasta-vegetable mixture. Cook and gently stir until heated through. Spoon into four serving bowls. Top with chicken.

Per serving: 505 cal., 26 g total fat (15 g sat. fat), 130 mg chol., 525 mg sodium, 32 g carbo., 2 g fiber, 32 g pro.

When you're feeding a houseful, it's hard to make everyone happy, but this recipe can! Just start with the big crowd-pleasing bowl of chicken-and-cheese pasta and let diners add the toppers they like to their own servings.

CHEESY CHICKEN & PASTA WITH COLORFUL CONFETTI

START TO FINISH:
30 minutes

MAKES: *6 servings*

1	pound dried pasta (any shape)
¼	cup butter
1	clove garlic, minced
¼	cup all-purpose flour
2	cups milk
½	cup sparkling apple juice or apple juice
8	ounces American cheese, shredded (2 cups)
½	cup shredded Parmesan cheese (2 ounces)
1½	cups chopped cooked chicken or turkey (about 8 ounces)
1	recipe Colorful Confetti

1 Cook pasta according to package directions; drain and keep warm.

2 Meanwhile, in a medium saucepan melt butter over medium heat. Add garlic; cook and stir for 30 seconds. Stir in flour. Stir in milk. Cook and stir until thickened and bubbly. Stir in apple juice. Reduce heat to low; stir in American cheese and Parmesan cheese until melted. Stir in chicken; heat through. Pour over pasta, tossing to coat. Serve pasta with Colorful Confetti.

COLORFUL CONFETTI: In individual bowls place ⅓ cup finely diced cooked ham, ⅓ cup finely diced green sweet pepper, ⅓ cup finely diced seeded plum tomato, ⅓ cup finely chopped pitted ripe olives, and ⅓ cup finely shredded Parmesan cheese. Cover and chill until ready to serve.

Per serving: 696 cal., 29 g total fat (17 g sat. fat), 106 mg chol., 1,036 mg sodium, 69 g carbo., 3 g fiber, 37 g pro.

Agnolotti is a crescent-shaped filled pasta. You'll find it at Italian food specialty stores. If you can't find it, try dried tortellini instead.

THAI CURRY AGNOLOTTI & CHICKEN BOWL

1	14-ounce package dried cheese-filled agnolotti or mezzaluna (half-moon-shaped miniature ravioli)
1	tablespoon cooking oil
¾	cup coarsely chopped carrot
1	cup sliced fresh shiitake mushrooms, stems removed
¾	cup coarsely chopped red sweet pepper
2	green onions, cut into ¼-inch-thick slices
1	14-ounce can regular or light unsweetened coconut milk
3	to 4 teaspoons red curry paste
1½	teaspoons sugar
2	cups cooked chicken or turkey cut or pulled into bite-size pieces
1	tablespoon lime juice
¼	cup chopped dry roasted peanuts
2	tablespoons snipped fresh cilantro

START TO FINISH:
30 minutes

MAKES: *4 servings*

1 Cook pasta according to package directions. Drain; return pasta to hot pan.

2 Meanwhile, in a large skillet heat oil over medium-high heat. Add carrot; cook and stir for 3 minutes. Add mushrooms, sweet pepper, and green onion; cook and stir for 2 minutes more. Add coconut milk, curry paste, and sugar. Reduce heat to medium, stirring until combined. Stir in chicken, lime juice, and cooked and drained pasta; heat through. Remove from heat. Add peanuts and cilantro. Toss gently to mix. (Mixture will thicken as it stands.)

3 Transfer pasta mixture to a warm serving bowl. Serve immediately.

Per serving: 640 cal., 38 g total fat (24 g sat. fat), 96 mg chol., 542 mg sodium, 43 g carbo., 4 g fiber, 37 g pro.

If you prefer to make a wrap sandwich, encase the tortillas in foil and bake them in a 350°F oven about 10 minutes or until warm. Then wrap each tortilla around some of the slaw and chicken mixture. (Recipe pictured on page 112.)

CHICKEN & SLAW TOSTADAS

PREP: *25 minutes*
BAKE: *8 minutes*
MAKES: *6 servings*

3 ounces firm silken-style tofu (fresh bean curd), cut into 1-inch cubes (½ cup)

½ teaspoon finely shredded lime peel (set aside)

¼ cup lime juice

1 tablespoon red wine vinegar

1 tablespoon honey

1 tablespoon Dijon-style mustard

1 canned chipotle chile pepper in adobo sauce (see tip, page 19)

2 tablespoons cooking oil

⅛ teaspoon salt

⅛ teaspoon black pepper

1½ cups packaged shredded broccoli (broccoli slaw)

1½ cups packaged shredded cabbage with carrot (coleslaw mix)

2 tablespoons snipped fresh cilantro

2 cups shredded roasted chicken or turkey (skin removed)

6 6-inch corn tortillas

Lime wedges (optional)

1 Preheat oven to 425°F. For dressing, in a food processor or blender combine tofu, lime juice, red wine vinegar, honey, mustard, and chile pepper; cover and process or blend until smooth. Add oil; process or blend until creamy. Transfer to a small bowl. Stir in lime peel, salt, and black pepper.

2 In a large bowl toss together shredded broccoli, shredded cabbage, cilantro, and ¼ cup of the dressing. In another bowl combine chicken and another ¼ cup of the dressing.

3 For tostadas, place corn tortillas on an ungreased baking sheet; bake about 8 minutes or until lightly browned and crisp, turning once.

4 To assemble tostadas, place tortillas on six dinner plates; divide broccoli mixture among tortillas. Top with chicken mixture. If desired, garnish with lime wedges. Serve with the remaining dressing.

Per serving: 235 cal., 9 g total fat (2 g sat. fat), 42 mg chol., 179 mg sodium, 21 g carbo., 2 g fiber, 18 g pro.

To shorten last-minute preparation, stop by your supermarket's salad bar and select an assortment of cut-up vegetables. (Recipe pictured on page 112.)

PEANUT-CHICKEN BOWL

2	3-ounce packages Oriental-flavor ramen noodles
8	cups water
3	cups cut-up fresh vegetables (such as broccoli florets, halved pea pods, thinly sliced carrots, and/or red sweet pepper strips)
1¼	cups water
¼	cup peanut butter
¼	cup soy sauce
2	tablespoons packed brown sugar
1	tablespoon cornstarch
½	teaspoon crushed red pepper
2	cups chopped cooked chicken or turkey (10 ounces)
1	8-ounce can sliced water chestnuts, drained
1	8-ounce can bamboo shoots, drained
¼	cup chopped peanuts
¼	cup sliced green onions

START TO FINISH:
25 minutes

MAKES: *4 servings*

1 Set aside one of the seasoning packets from ramen noodles to use in recipe; discard remaining packet or save for another use. In a large saucepan bring the 8 cups water to boiling. Break up noodles slightly and add to water along with cut-up vegetables. Return to boiling; reduce heat. Boil gently, uncovered, for 3 minutes. Drain and return to hot saucepan.

2 Meanwhile, for sauce, in a medium saucepan whisk together the 1¼ cups water, the peanut butter, soy sauce, brown sugar, cornstarch, crushed red pepper, and the reserved seasoning packet until smooth. Cook and stir over medium heat until thickened and bubbly. Cook and stir for 2 minutes more.

3 Stir chicken, water chestnuts, and bamboo shoots into sauce; heat through. Add to noodle mixture in saucepan. Toss to combine. Top with peanuts and green onion. Serve immediately.

Per serving: 646 cal., 30 g total fat (4 g sat. fat), 82 mg chol., 1,511 mg sodium, 64 g carbo., 6 g fiber, 38 g pro.

The flavors of Italy fuse in this creamy mix of veggies and chicken. The small amount of half-and-half adds just the right amount of richness.

CHICKEN-VEGETABLE PASTA

START TO FINISH:
25 minutes

MAKES: *5 servings*

8   ounces dried penne

8   ounces fresh asparagus, trimmed and cut into
     1½-inch-long pieces

1   tablespoon olive oil

3   cups sliced fresh shiitake or cremini mushrooms

1   medium leek, thinly sliced, or ½ cup chopped onion

3   cloves garlic, minced

⅓   cup mushroom broth or vegetable broth

¼   cup half-and-half or light cream

¼   teaspoon salt

⅛   teaspoon black pepper

12   ounces shredded cooked chicken or turkey (about 2½ cups)

1   cup chopped plum tomatoes

1   tablespoon finely shredded fresh basil

1   tablespoon finely shredded fresh oregano

     Finely shredded Parmesan cheese (optional)

1 Cook penne according to package directions, adding asparagus for the last 2 minutes of cooking; drain. Return pasta mixture to hot saucepan; cover and keep warm.

2 Meanwhile, in a large skillet heat oil over medium-high heat. Add mushrooms, leek or onion, and garlic; cook for 4 to 5 minutes or until most of the liquid has evaporated. Stir in broth, half-and-half, salt, and pepper. Bring to boiling. Boil gently, uncovered, for 4 to 5 minutes or until mixture is slightly thickened. Stir in chicken, tomato, basil, and oregano; heat through.

3 Spoon the mushroom mixture over pasta mixture; toss gently to coat. Serve immediately. If desired, serve with Parmesan cheese.

Per serving: 396 cal., 8 g total fat (2 g sat. fat), 62 mg chol., 199 mg sodium, 53 g carbo., 4 g fiber, 30 g pro.

Chicken and noodles ready in less than 30 minutes and with just one pot? This recipe is delicious proof it can be done.

CREAMY CHICKEN & NOODLES

2   cups frozen stir-fry vegetables (such as broccoli, carrots, onion, red sweet peppers, celery, water chestnuts, and mushrooms)

1   10¾-ounce can condensed cheddar cheese soup

¾   cup milk

½   teaspoon dried thyme, crushed

    Several dashes bottled hot pepper sauce

2   cups cubed cooked chicken or turkey (10 ounces)

    Hot cooked noodles

START TO FINISH:
25 minutes

MAKES: *4 servings*

1 In a large skillet or saucepan cook frozen vegetables according to package directions. Drain, if necessary; set aside.

2 In same skillet or saucepan stir together cheddar cheese soup, milk, thyme, and hot pepper sauce. Add cooked vegetables and chicken. Cook and stir over medium heat about 10 minutes or until heated through. Serve over hot cooked noodles.

Per serving: 352 cal., 12 g total fat (4 g sat. fat), 102 mg chol., 702 mg sodium, 35 g carbo., 2 g fiber, 29 g pro.

Keep the ingredients for this no-fuss pot pie on hand for a scrumptious last-minute meal.

EASY TURKEY-PESTO POT PIE

PREP: *15 minutes*
BAKE: *15 minutes*
MAKES: *6 servings*

1¾ cups bottled turkey gravy

¼ cup purchased basil or dried tomato pesto

3 cups cubed cooked turkey or chicken (about 1 pound)

1 16-ounce package loose-pack frozen peas and carrots

½ of an 11-ounce package (6) refrigerated breadsticks

1 Preheat oven to 375°F. In a large saucepan combine gravy and pesto; stir in turkey and frozen vegetables. Bring to boiling, stirring frequently. Divide mixture among six 8-ounce au gratin dishes.

2 Unroll and separate breadsticks. Arrange a breadstick on top of each dish. Bake about 15 minutes or until breadsticks are golden.

Per serving: 372 cal., 14 g total fat (2 g sat. fat), 59 mg chol., 988 mg sodium, 30 g carbo., 3 g fiber, 30 g pro.

DINNERTIME DELIGHTS

You'll find the perfect dish for every occasion in this tasty sampling of fried, simmered, broiled, or roasted poultry recipes.

It's easy to add "wow" to oven-fried chicken with a coating of rye crackers. It gives a rich brown color and great flavor. The chicken is delicious cold too, if you want to make it the night before.

OVEN-FRIED BUTTERMILK CHICKEN

PREP: *25 minutes*
MARINATE: *4 to 24 hours*
BAKE: *45 minutes*
MAKES: *12 servings*

5 to 6 pounds meaty chicken pieces (breast halves,* thighs, and/or drumsticks), skinned if desired
2 cups buttermilk
1½ teaspoons salt
1 8-ounce package crisp rye crackers**
2 tablespoons Greek seasoning**
½ cup butter, melted
3 eggs, beaten
2 tablespoons water

1 Place chicken in a resealable plastic bag set in a bowl. For marinade, in a small bowl stir together buttermilk and salt. Pour over chicken. Seal bag; turn to coat chicken. Marinate in the refrigerator for 4 to 24 hours, turning bag occasionally.

2 Drain chicken, discarding marinade. In a blender or food processor combine half of the crackers and half of the Greek seasoning. Blend or process until crackers are crushed; transfer to a shallow dish. Repeat with remaining crackers and Greek seasoning.

3 Preheat oven to 400°F. Lightly grease two 13×9×2-inch aluminum foil baking pans; set aside. Add melted butter to crushed crackers; toss together. In another shallow dish combine eggs and the water. Dip chicken pieces, one at a time, in egg mixture, then roll in cracker mixture to coat. Arrange chicken in prepared baking pans, making sure pieces do not touch.

4 Bake for 45 to 50 minutes or until chicken pieces are tender and no longer pink (170°F for breasts; 180°F for thighs and drumsticks). Serve warm or cover and chill for up to 24 hours.

Per serving: 388 cal., 20 g total fat (8 g sat. fat), 162 mg chol., 476 mg sodium, 18 g carbo., 5 g fiber, 33 g pro.

*****TEST KITCHEN TIP:** If breast halves are large, cut them in half again before marinating.

******TEST KITCHEN TIP:** You can substitute two 4¼-ounce packages water crackers with cracked pepper for the crisp rye crackers and the Greek seasoning. Continue as directed above.

Fried chicken lovers will ask for this sour cream- and chile-seasoned dish time and again. It's a satisfying meal when served with baked beans and potato salad.

GREEN CHILE FRIED CHICKEN

1	8-ounce carton dairy sour cream
¼	cup milk
1	4-ounce can diced green chile peppers
2	tablespoons snipped fresh cilantro
2	tablespoons lime juice
1	clove garlic, minced
¾	teaspoon ground cumin
½	teaspoon salt
¼	teaspoon black pepper
1	2½- to 3-pound cut-up broiler-fryer chicken, skinned if desired
¾	cup all-purpose flour
	Cooking oil
	Bottled hot pepper sauce (optional)
	Lime wedges (optional)

PREP: *25 minutes*
MARINATE: *overnight*
COOK: *40 minutes*
MAKES: *4 to 6 servings*

1 In a small bowl combine sour cream, milk, chile peppers, cilantro, lime juice, garlic, cumin, salt, and black pepper. Place chicken pieces in a resealable plastic bag set in a shallow dish. Pour sour cream mixture over chicken. Seal bag; turn to coat chicken. Marinate in the refrigerator overnight, turning bag occasionally.

2 Place flour in a shallow dish. Remove chicken from sour cream mixture, discarding sour cream mixture. Add chicken pieces to flour, a few at a time, turning to coat.

3 Pour oil into a heavy 12-inch skillet to a depth of ¼ to ½ inch. Heat over medium-high heat until hot (350°F); reduce heat. Carefully add chicken to the skillet. Cook over medium heat about 40 minutes or until chicken is tender and no longer pink (170°F for breasts; 180°F for thighs and drumsticks), turning occasionally to brown evenly. Drain on paper towels. If desired, serve with bottled hot pepper sauce and lime wedges.

Per serving: 608 cal., 42 g total fat (14 g sat. fat), 125 mg chol., 501 mg sodium, 22 g carbo., 1 g fiber, 36 g pro.

A liberal splash of hot pepper sauce on this moist fried chicken zips up the flavor. (Recipe pictured on page 273.)

EGG-BATTERED FRIED CHICKEN

PREP: *25 minutes*

COOK: *30 minutes*

MAKES: *6 servings*

½ of a 10-ounce package all-purpose batter fry mix* (about ¾ cup)

4 eggs

2½ to 3 pounds meaty chicken pieces (breast halves, thighs, and/or drumsticks), skinned if desired

Salt

Black pepper

Peanut oil or cooking oil

Bottled hot pepper sauce

1 Place the batter fry mix in a shallow bowl; set aside. In another shallow bowl lightly beat eggs; set aside.

2 Sprinkle chicken with salt and pepper. Dip chicken pieces, one at a time, into egg mixture, then coat with fry mix. Dip again in the egg mixture and coat again with fry mix.

3 Pour oil into a heavy 12-inch skillet to a depth of ⅓ to ½ inch. Heat over medium-high heat until hot enough to sizzle a drop of water. Carefully add chicken to skillet. (Do not crowd chicken. If necessary, use two skillets.) Reduce heat to medium; cook about 30 minutes or until chicken is tender and no longer pink (170°F for breasts; 180°F for thighs and drumsticks), turning about halfway through to brown evenly. Drain chicken pieces on paper towels. Serve chicken with hot pepper sauce.

Per serving: 546 cal., 38 g total fat (9 g sat. fat), 249 mg chol., 417 mg sodium, 14 g carbo., 1 g fiber, 35 g pro.

*TEST KITCHEN TIP: If you can't find batter fry mix, you can make your own. In a shallow bowl combine ⅔ cup all-purpose flour, 3 tablespoons cornmeal, ¼ teaspoon salt, and ¼ teaspoon black pepper.

If you can't find pesto seasoning, substitute dried Italian seasoning.

TUSCAN CHICKEN

2	tablespoons olive oil
2	to 2½ pounds meaty chicken pieces (breast halves, thighs, and/or drumsticks)
1¼	teaspoons pesto seasoning
½	cup kalamata olives
½	cup dry white wine or chicken broth

PREP: *25 minutes*
COOK: *30 minutes*
MAKES: *4 servings*

1 In a 12-inch skillet heat oil over medium heat. Add chicken; cook for 15 minutes, turning to brown evenly. Reduce heat. Drain off excess oil.

2 Sprinkle pesto seasoning evenly over the chicken. Add olives. Pour white wine or chicken broth over all. Cover tightly and cook for 25 minutes. Uncover and cook for 5 to 10 minutes more or until chicken is tender and no longer pink (170°F for breasts; 180°F for thighs and drumsticks).

Per serving: 334 cal., 18 g total fat (4 g sat. fat), 104 mg chol., 280 mg sodium, 2 g carbo., 1 g fiber, 34 g pro.

Most of the heat in chile peppers is in the membranes and seeds. If you prefer your chicken spicy hot, do not remove the membranes or seed the pepper.

THREE-PEPPER CHICKEN

PREP: *20 minutes*
BAKE: *45 minutes*
MAKES: *6 servings*

2½   to 3 pounds meaty chicken pieces
      (breast halves, thighs, and/or drumsticks), skinned

3   tablespoons butter, melted

1   fresh jalapeño chile pepper, seeded and finely chopped
      (see tip, page 19)

¼   teaspoon salt

¼   teaspoon black pepper

¼   teaspoon cayenne pepper

4   cloves garlic, minced

1 Preheat oven to 375°F. Place chicken pieces, bone sides up, in a lightly greased 15×10×1-inch baking pan. Bake for 25 minutes.

2 Meanwhile, in a small bowl stir together butter, chile pepper, salt, black pepper, cayenne pepper, and garlic. Brush some of the pepper mixture onto chicken. Turn chicken bone sides down; brush with the remaining pepper mixture.

3 Bake for 20 to 30 minutes more or until chicken is tender and no longer pink (170°F for breasts; 180°F for thighs and drumsticks).

Per serving: 272 cal., 17 g total fat (7 g sat. fat), 103 mg chol., 235 mg sodium, 1 g carbo., 0 g fiber, 28 g pro.

An equal mix of sweet-and-sour sauce and hot-style barbecue sauce makes this chicken a finger-licking treat.

SAUCY SWEET & SPICY CHICKEN

2	tablespoons cooking oil
3	cloves garlic, minced
¾	cup bottled sweet-and-sour sauce
¾	cup bottled hot-style barbecue sauce
3	pounds meaty chicken pieces (breast halves, thighs, and/or drumsticks), skinned if desired

PREP: *15 minutes*
COOK: *45 minutes*
MAKES: *6 servings*

1 In a 12-inch skillet heat 1 tablespoon of the oil over medium heat. Add garlic; cook for 1 minute. Using a slotted spoon, transfer garlic to a medium bowl. Stir sweet-and-sour sauce and barbecue sauce into garlic in bowl; set sauce mixture aside.

2 Add the remaining 1 tablespoon oil to skillet. Add chicken; cook over medium heat for 10 minutes, turning to brown evenly (add more oil during cooking, if necessary). Reduce heat; cover tightly. Cook for 25 minutes.

3 Uncover; pour the sauce mixture over the chicken. Bring to boiling. Cook, uncovered, over medium heat about 10 minutes more or until chicken is tender and no longer pink (170°F for breasts; 180°F for thighs and drumsticks), spooning sauce over chicken occasionally. Transfer chicken to a serving platter. Stir sauce and spoon over chicken.

Per serving: 399 cal., 18 g total fat (4 g sat. fat), 104 mg chol., 606 mg sodium, 21 g carbo., 0 g fiber, 33 g pro.

Chipotle chili powder is made from ground chipotle chile peppers and has a fiery, smoky flavor. You'll find it at Mexican food markets or spice specialty stores.

CHIPOTLE-RUBBED BAKED CHICKEN

PREP: *20 minutes*

BAKE: *45 minutes*

MAKES: *6 servings*

2½ to 3 pounds meaty chicken pieces (breast halves, thighs, and/or drumsticks), skinned

2 tablespoons butter or margarine, melted

1 to 1½ teaspoons chipotle chili powder

1 teaspoon packed brown sugar

Dash salt

Dash black pepper

¼ cup sliced green onions

1 Preheat oven to 375°F. Place chicken pieces, bone sides down, in a lightly greased 15×10×1-inch baking pan.

2 In a small bowl combine melted butter, chili powder, brown sugar, salt, and pepper; brush onto chicken pieces.

3 Bake for 45 to 55 minutes or until chicken is tender and no longer pink (170°F for breasts; 180°F for thighs and drumsticks). Sprinkle green onion over chicken pieces.

Per serving: 201 cal., 10 g total fat (4 g sat. fat), 88 mg chol., 139 mg sodium, 1 g carbo., 0 g fiber, 25 g pro.

Fricassee is a French word for meat or poultry (usually chicken or veal) slowly simmered with vegetables in a sauce to form a thick, chunky, stewlike dish.

CHICKEN FRICASSEE

2	3- to 3½-pound cut-up broiler-fryer chickens, skinned if desired
½	cup all-purpose flour
¼	cup olive oil
4	medium carrots, bias-sliced ¼ inch thick
1	pint pearl onions, peeled*
12	cloves garlic, peeled
¼	cup red wine vinegar
¼	cup champagne vinegar
4	cups chicken broth
¼	cup snipped fresh thyme
1	pound small Yukon gold potatoes, quartered

PREP: *50 minutes*
COOK: *30 minutes*
MAKES: *10 servings*

1 Sprinkle chicken with salt and pepper. Place flour in a shallow dish; add chicken pieces, a few at a time, to the dish and turn to lightly coat chicken with flour. Heat two 10- to 12-inch skillets over medium-high heat. Add 2 tablespoons of the oil to each skillet. Divide chicken pieces between the two skillets; cook in the hot oil for 10 to 15 minutes or until browned, turning to brown evenly. Remove chicken from skillets and set one skillet aside.

2 Add carrots and pearl onions to other skillet, adding more oil if necessary. Cook and stir vegetables for 4 minutes. Add garlic cloves; cook for 1 minute more. Add the red wine vinegar and champagne vinegar to skillet. Cook about 3 minutes or until most of the liquid has evaporated, stirring occasionally. Transfer half of the vegetable mixture to the empty skillet. Add 2 cups of the chicken broth and 1 tablespoon of the thyme to each skillet. Bring mixture in each skillet to boiling.

3 Add the light-meat chicken pieces to one skillet and the dark-meat chicken pieces to the second skillet. Divide potatoes between the two skillets. Return to boiling; reduce heat. Cover and simmer for 30 to 40 minutes or until an instant-read thermometer inserted in the light-meat pieces registers 170°F and in the dark-meat pieces registers 180°F. (Light-meat pieces may be done a few minutes before dark-meat.)

4 Transfer chicken and vegetables to a serving platter. Cover with foil and keep warm. For sauce, boil liquid in both skillets, uncovered, until desired consistency. Skim off fat. Spoon sauce over chicken and vegetables. Sprinkle with the remaining 2 tablespoons fresh thyme.

Per serving: 535 cal., 33 g total fat (9 g sat. fat), 138 mg chol., 517 mg sodium, 19 g carbo., 2 g fiber, 38 g pro.

*TEST KITCHEN TIP: To peel pearl onions, in a medium saucepan cook onions in boiling water for 30 seconds. Drain; rinse with cold water. When cool enough to handle, cut a small slice from the root end of each onion. Squeeze from the other end to remove the onion from the peel.

With nine different seasonings, this recipe boasts all the terrific flavor of classic chicken curry.

CHICKEN CURRY

PREP: *40 minutes*
COOK: *20 minutes*
MAKES: *6 servings*

2½ to 3 pounds meaty chicken pieces (breast halves, thighs, and/or drumsticks), skinned
2 tablespoons cooking oil
1 medium onion, finely chopped
4 cloves garlic, minced
2 teaspoons finely chopped fresh ginger
1 teaspoon ground cumin
1 medium tomato, finely chopped
1 tablespoon ground coriander
1 teaspoon coarsely ground black pepper
½ teaspoon salt
½ teaspoon ground turmeric
¼ to ½ teaspoon cayenne pepper (optional)
½ cup plain low-fat yogurt
½ cup water
1 tablespoon lemon juice
3 cups hot cooked brown or white basmati rice

① Cut two or three slits in each chicken piece, making each slit 1 inch long and ½ inch deep.

② In a very large skillet heat oil over medium-high heat. Add chicken; cook for 5 to 8 minutes or until chicken is lightly browned, turning to brown evenly. Using a slotted spoon or tongs, remove chicken from skillet. Set aside.

③ Add onion, garlic, ginger, and cumin to skillet. Reduce heat to medium. Cook for 6 to 8 minutes or until onion is golden brown, stirring frequently. Add tomato, coriander, black pepper, salt, turmeric, and, if desired, cayenne pepper. Cook for 2 minutes, stirring occasionally.

④ Meanwhile, in a small bowl beat yogurt lightly with a whisk or fork. Stir yogurt into tomato mixture.

⑤ Add chicken and the water to the skillet. Bring to boiling; reduce heat. Spoon liquid over chicken to coat. Cover and simmer for 20 to 25 minutes or until chicken is tender and no longer pink (170°F for breasts; 180°F for thighs and drumsticks).

⑥ Transfer chicken to a serving platter. Spoon yogurt-tomato mixture over chicken. Drizzle with lemon juice. Serve with hot cooked rice.

Per serving: 336 cal., 12 g total fat (3 g sat. fat), 78 mg chol., 285 mg sodium, 27 g carbo., 2 g fiber, 29 g pro.

When using the chicken broth option, increase the tomato paste to 3 tablespoons.

BRAISED HUNTER-STYLE CHICKEN

3	pounds meaty chicken pieces (breast halves, thighs, and/or drumsticks), skinned
	Kosher salt or salt
	Freshly ground black pepper
1	tablespoon olive oil
8	ounces fresh mushrooms, sliced
1½	cups chopped onion
2	cloves garlic, minced
½	cup dry red wine or chicken broth
2	tablespoons tomato paste
1	14-ounce can stewed tomatoes
1	tablespoon finely snipped fresh thyme or 1 teaspoon dried thyme, crushed
1	bay leaf
1	tablespoon snipped fresh flat-leaf parsley
1	to 2 tablespoons lemon juice

PREP: *45 minutes*
BAKE: *25 minutes*
MAKES: *6 servings*

1 Preheat oven to 350°F. Sprinkle chicken with kosher salt and freshly ground black pepper. In a 12-inch ovenproof skillet cook chicken in hot oil about 10 minutes or until lightly browned, turning to brown evenly. Drain, reserving 1 tablespoon drippings. Remove chicken and set aside.

2 In the same skillet cook mushrooms, onion, and garlic in the reserved 1 tablespoon drippings until tender. Stir in wine or chicken broth and tomato paste. Cook and stir for 1 to 2 minutes or until most of the liquid has evaporated. Stir in undrained stewed tomatoes, thyme, and bay leaf. Arrange chicken pieces on the tomato mixture. Season chicken with additional kosher salt and freshly ground black pepper. Bring mixture to boiling over medium heat.

3 Cover and bake for 25 to 30 minutes or until chicken is tender and no longer pink (170°F for breasts; 180°F for thighs and drumsticks).

4 To serve, arrange chicken on a platter. Spoon tomato mixture over chicken. Sprinkle with parsley and drizzle with lemon juice.

Per serving: 281 cal., 10 g total fat (2 g sat. fat), 92 mg chol., 278 mg sodium, 11 g carbo., 2 g fiber, 32 g pro.

Lemon- and herb-seasoned chicken quarters roast with a mélange of potatoes, carrots, fennel, and shallots in this impressive yet no-fuss one-dish meal.

LEMON CHICKEN WITH AUTUMN VEGETABLES

PREP: *40 minutes*

ROAST: *50 minutes*

MAKES: *4 to 6 servings*

1	tablespoon dried thyme, crushed
1	tablespoon dried rosemary, crushed
1	tablespoon dried oregano, crushed
1	teaspoon fennel seeds or coriander seeds, crushed
1	teaspoon finely shredded lemon peel
1	teaspoon kosher salt or coarse salt
½	teaspoon coarsely ground black pepper
⅓	cup lemon juice
⅓	cup olive oil
4	chicken quarters (2½ to 3 pounds total) or one 2½- to 3-pound whole broiler-fryer chicken, cut into quarters
12	tiny new potatoes or 4 medium round red or white potatoes, cut into eighths
4	medium carrots and/or parsnips, peeled and quartered
1	large fennel bulb, trimmed and cut into wedges*
4	large shallots, quartered, or 1 medium onion, cut into wedges

1 In a small bowl combine thyme, rosemary, and oregano. In a dry small skillet cook and stir herb mixture over medium heat for 2 to 3 minutes or until fragrant. (Do not burn.) Return to bowl; add fennel seeds, lemon peel, kosher salt, and black pepper. Whisk in lemon juice and olive oil.

2 Preheat oven to 375°F. Skin chicken, if desired. Liberally brush lemon-herb mixture over all sides of the chicken quarters. Place chicken, bone sides down, on a rack in a shallow roasting pan. Arrange potatoes, carrots and/or parsnips, fennel, and shallots in the bottom of roasting pan. Brush some of the remaining lemon-herb mixture over vegetables and chicken.

3 Roast for 50 to 55 minutes or until an instant-read thermometer inserted into an inside thigh muscle registers 180°F (the thermometer should not touch bone). (Do not turn chicken while roasting.) Up to last 5 minutes of roasting, occasionally brush chicken and vegetables with the remaining lemon-herb mixture and spoon pan drippings over chicken and vegetables. Discard any remaining lemon-herb mixture.

Per serving: 587 cal., 34 g total fat (7 g sat. fat), 99 mg chol., 628 mg sodium, 35 g carbo., 14 g fiber, 35 g pro.

***TEST KITCHEN TIP:** To prepare the fennel bulb, use a sharp knife to carefully cut about 1 inch above the bulb; discard the stalks. Remove any wilted outer layers and cut a thin slice from the fennel base. Wash fennel and cut into quarters lengthwise; remove core. Cut into wedges.

These coriander-seasoned hens are equally good with hot-style or sweet paprika.

SPICED GAME HENS

¼   cup lemon juice

2   tablespoons olive oil

1   tablespoon paprika

1   teaspoon salt

1   teaspoon ground coriander

½   teaspoon ground turmeric

¼   teaspoon black pepper

4   cloves garlic, minced

2   1½-pound Cornish game hens

½   cup reduced-sodium chicken broth

     Salt

     Black pepper

PREP: *25 minutes*

MARINATE: *2 hours*

ROAST: *1 hour*

MAKES: *4 servings*

1 In a small bowl combine lemon juice, oil, paprika, the 1 teaspoon salt, the coriander, turmeric, the ¼ teaspoon pepper, and the garlic; set aside.

2 Using a long, heavy knife or kitchen shears, halve Cornish hens lengthwise, cutting through the breast bone of each hen, just off center, and then through the center of the backbone. (Or ask the butcher to cut hens into halves.) If desired, remove backbone of each hen. Twist wing tips under backs.

3 Place game hen halves in a resealable plastic bag. Pour lemon juice mixture over hen halves. Seal bag; turn to coat hen halves. Marinate in the refrigerator for 2 hours, turning bag once.

4 Preheat oven to 375°F. Remove hen halves from bag, reserving marinade. Place hen halves, cut sides down, in a 3-quart rectangular baking dish. Pour reserved marinade over hen halves. Pour broth around hen halves in baking dish. Sprinkle hen halves with additional salt and pepper.

5 Roast, covered, for 40 minutes. Uncover and continue roasting for 20 to 35 minutes more or until an instant-read thermometer inserted into the inside thigh muscle of each hen half registers 180°F (the thermometer should not touch bone).

Per serving: 410 cal., 30 g total fat (7 g sat. fat), 173 mg chol., 813 mg sodium, 4 g carbo., 1 g fiber, 31 g pro.

Bottled barbecue sauce goes in a grand new direction when simmered with chopped rhubarb.
The tangy sauce provides the Cornish game hens with spectacular flavor and color.

GAME HENS WITH RHUBARB GLAZE

PREP: *30 minutes*
ROAST: *55 minutes*
MAKES: *6 servings*

3 1¼- to 1½-pound Cornish game hens
   Olive oil
   Salt
   Black pepper
3½ to 4 cups chopped fresh or frozen rhubarb
1 cup bottled barbecue sauce
¼ cup water
8 ounces dried orzo pasta (rosamarina)
1 cup shredded carrot
¼ cup sliced green onions

1 Use a long, heavy knife or kitchen shears to halve Cornish hens lengthwise, cutting through the breast bone of each hen, just off-center, and through the center of the backbone. (Or ask the butcher to cut hens into halves.) Twist wing tips under backs.

2 Preheat oven to 375°F. Rub oil over the surface and in the cavity of each hen half; sprinkle with salt and pepper. Place hen halves, cut sides down, in a 15×10×1-inch baking pan. Roast for 40 minutes.

3 Meanwhile, for sauce, in a medium saucepan combine rhubarb, barbecue sauce, and the water; bring to boiling over medium-high heat. Reduce heat to medium-low. Cover and cook about 20 minutes or until the rhubarb loses its shape. Remove from the heat; coarsely mash the rhubarb in the saucepan. Set aside 1 cup of the sauce for orzo mixture.

4 Brush the surface of the game hens with some of the remaining sauce. Roast for 15 to 20 minutes more or until an instant-read thermometer inserted into the inside thigh muscle of each hen half registers 180°F (the thermometer should not touch bone); brush with sauce every 5 minutes.

5 Meanwhile, cook orzo according to package directions; drain. Transfer orzo to a large bowl. Stir in the reserved 1 cup sauce, the shredded carrot, and green onion. Season to taste with additional salt and pepper. Mound orzo mixture on a large platter; top with game hen halves. Reheat the remaining sauce and pass with the game hens.

Per serving: 375 cal., 10 g total fat (2 g sat. fat), 111 mg chol., 609 mg sodium, 39 g carbo., 4 g fiber, 31 g pro.

Game hens are always impressive—and yet they're easy as can be to roast. A flavorful tapenade tucked under the skin makes the birds really scrumptious!

CITRUS TAPENADE GAME HENS

½ cup finely chopped pitted niçoise or kalamata olives

1 tablespoon capers, drained and finely chopped

1 clove garlic, minced

1 teaspoon anchovy paste (optional)

½ teaspoon finely shredded orange peel

1 tablespoon olive oil

2 1¼- to 1½-pound Cornish game hens, split lengthwise into halves (see Step 1, page 232)

1 tablespoon olive oil

Salt

Freshly ground black pepper

2 tablespoons finely chopped shallots

1 cup dry white wine or dry vermouth

¼ cup chicken broth

1 tablespoon butter

1 tablespoon snipped fresh thyme

Fresh thyme sprigs

PREP: *40 minutes*

ROAST: *35 minutes*

MAKES: *4 servings*

1 Preheat oven to 425°F. For tapenade, in a bowl combine olives, capers, garlic, anchovy paste (if desired), and orange peel. Stir in 1 tablespoon olive oil.

2 Loosen skin on hens. Using your fingers, carefully spread tapenade evenly under skin of each hen half. Brush hens with 1 tablespoon olive oil; sprinkle both sides of each hen half with salt and pepper. Arrange hens, cut sides down, in a large ovenproof skillet. Roast about 35 minutes or until an instant-read thermometer inserted into inside thigh muscle of each hen half registers 180°F (the thermometer should not touch bone).

3 Remove hens from oven. Transfer to a warm serving platter; cover and keep warm. For sauce, drain all but about 1 tablespoon of the drippings from the skillet. Add shallot to drippings in skillet; cook and stir over medium heat for 2 to 3 minutes or until shallot is tender. Remove skillet from heat. Add wine and chicken broth. Return skillet to heat. Cook and stir to loosen browned bits from skillet. Bring mixture to boiling; reduce heat. Simmer, uncovered, for 4 to 5 minutes to reduce slightly. (Should have about ½ cup sauce.) Remove from heat and whisk in butter until melted. Stir in snipped thyme. Spoon sauce over hens. If desired, garnish with thyme sprigs.

Per serving: 566 cal., 41 g total fat (10 g sat. fat), 177 mg chol., 570 mg sodium, 9 g carbo., 2 g fiber, 29 g pro.

Purchased pesto makes this recipe a breeze. Serve these flavor-packed chicken breasts on a bed of your favorite pasta.

PESTO-STUFFED CHICKEN BREASTS

PREP: *20 minutes*

BAKE: *45 minutes*

MAKES: *4 servings*

4   bone-in chicken breast halves (about 2½ pounds total)

½   cup roasted red sweet peppers, drained and chopped

⅓   cup purchased basil pesto

2   tablespoons finely shredded Parmesan cheese

Salt

Black pepper

1   tablespoon butter, melted

1 Preheat oven to 375°F. Using your fingers, gently separate the chicken skin from the meat of each breast along the rib edge.

2 For stuffing, in a small bowl combine sweet peppers, pesto, and Parmesan cheese. Spoon a rounded tablespoon of the stuffing between the skin and meat of each breast half. Sprinkle stuffed chicken breast halves with salt and pepper.

3 Place breast halves, bone sides down, in a lightly greased 2-quart rectangular baking dish. Drizzle with melted butter. Bake for 45 to 55 minutes or until chicken is tender and no longer pink (170°F).

Per serving: 421 cal., 27 g total fat (8 g sat. fat), 124 mg chol., 407 mg sodium, 4 g carbo., 1 g fiber, 39 g pro.

At the grocery store, you'll find two kinds of paprika: Hungarian and Spanish. Hungarian paprika is generally more pungent than Spanish paprika and can be either sweet or hot. Spanish paprika is only slightly sweet with a slightly bitter undertone.

CHICKEN PAPRIKASH

4	bone-in chicken breast halves or 8 small chicken thighs (about 2 pounds total), skinned
½	teaspoon Hungarian paprika
½	teaspoon garlic powder
½	teaspoon seasoned salt
2	tablespoons olive oil
2	cups vegetable juice
2	tablespoons snipped fresh parsley
1	tablespoon Hungarian paprika
	Few dashes bottled hot pepper sauce
1	8-ounce carton dairy sour cream
½	teaspoon freshly ground black pepper
	Hot cooked spaetzle or noodles

PREP: *30 minutes*
COOK: *30 minutes*
MAKES: *4 servings*

1 Sprinkle chicken with the ½ teaspoon paprika, the garlic powder, and seasoned salt. In a 12-inch skillet heat oil over medium-high heat. Add chicken; cook about 10 minutes or until browned, turning to brown evenly. Add vegetable juice; stir in parsley and the 1 tablespoon paprika. Bring to boiling; reduce heat. Cover and simmer for 30 to 35 minutes or until chicken is tender and no longer pink (170°F for breasts; 180°F for thighs). Remove chicken. Cover with foil and keep warm. Remove skillet from heat.

2 In a small bowl stir hot pepper sauce into sour cream. Gradually whisk 1 cup of the hot vegetable juice mixture into sour cream mixture. Return to remaining vegetable juice mixture in skillet. Stir in black pepper. Add cooked chicken to sauce; heat through (do not boil). Serve with hot cooked spaetzle or noodles.

Per serving: 579 cal., 23 g total fat (9 g sat. fat), 145 mg chol., 1,094 mg sodium, 46 g carbo., 64 g fiber, 45 g pro.

Slice into a golden-roasted chicken breast and discover a sumptuous filling of goat cheese, prosciutto, artichoke hearts, and just the right seasonings. This entrée makes the perfect dinner-party dish—it's easy to make, and guests truly feel treated to something special.

ARTICHOKE-CHÈVRE-STUFFED CHICKEN BREASTS

PREP: *45 minutes*

BAKE: *40 minutes*

MAKES: *8 servings*

¼ cup olive oil

2 teaspoons dried thyme, crushed

¼ teaspoon crushed red pepper

2 6-ounce jars marinated artichoke hearts, drained and chopped

4 ounces prosciutto, cut into thin strips

3 cloves garlic, minced

6 ounces chèvre or other creamy goat cheese

8 large bone-in chicken breast halves (about 5 pounds total)

Salt

Black pepper

1 Preheat oven to 350°F. For filling, in a medium skillet heat 2 tablespoons of the oil over medium heat. Add thyme and crushed red pepper; cook for 1 minute. Stir in artichokes, prosciutto, and garlic; cook and stir for 4 minutes. Remove from heat; stir in chèvre until melted and well mixed. Cool filling completely.

2 Cut a horizontal pocket into each breast half by cutting from one side almost to, but not through, the other side. Stuff pockets with cooled filling. Secure with wooden toothpicks. Sprinkle with salt and black pepper.

3 In a large nonstick skillet heat the remaining 2 tablespoons oil over medium-high heat. Brown chicken breasts, a few at a time, in hot oil. Transfer chicken to a large baking dish. Bake for 40 to 45 minutes or until tender and no longer pink (170°F). Remove toothpicks before serving.

Per serving: 479 cal., 35 g total fat (9 g sat. fat), 103 mg chol., 640 mg sodium, 3 g carbo., 0 g fiber, 38 g pro.

Your family will ask for this homey old-fashioned favorite again and again. It owes its mild licorice flavor to the strips of fresh fennel. (Recipe pictured on page 274.)

CHICKEN & DUMPLINGS

4	bone-in chicken breast halves or 8 small chicken thighs (about 2 pounds total), skinned
2½	cups water
1	medium onion, sliced and separated into rings
1	teaspoon instant chicken bouillon granules
1	teaspoon snipped fresh thyme or ¼ teaspoon dried thyme, crushed
¼	teaspoon black pepper
2	cups sliced carrot
1	medium fennel bulb, cut into bite-size strips (1½ cups)
¼	cup cold water
2	tablespoons cornstarch
1	recipe Dumplings
	Fresh herb sprigs (optional)

PREP: *35 minutes*
COOK: *45 minutes*
MAKES: *4 servings*

1 In a large saucepan combine chicken, the 2½ cups water, the onion, bouillon granules, dried thyme (if using), and pepper. Bring to boiling; reduce heat. Cover and simmer for 25 minutes. Add carrot and fennel. Return to boiling; reduce heat. Cover and simmer for 10 minutes more.

2 Remove chicken from saucepan; set aside. Skim fat from broth in pan. In a small bowl stir together the ¼ cup cold water and the cornstarch; stir into broth in saucepan. Cook and stir until thickened and bubbly. Return chicken to pan; stir in fresh thyme (if using).

3 Drop Dumplings batter from a tablespoon into eight mounds on top of the hot chicken mixture. Cover and simmer about 10 minutes or until a wooden toothpick inserted into a dumpling comes out clean. If desired, garnish with herb sprigs.

DUMPLINGS: In a small bowl stir together 1 cup all-purpose flour, 1½ teaspoons baking powder, ⅛ teaspoon salt, and ⅛ teaspoon coarsely ground black pepper. In another small bowl stir together 1 egg, beaten; ¼ cup milk; and 1 tablespoon cooking oil. Pour egg mixture into flour mixture; stir with a fork until combined.

Per serving: 480 cal., 19 g total fat (5 g sat. fat), 147 mg chol., 562 mg sodium, 39 g carbo., 4 g fiber, 37 g pro.

The refreshing tang of lemon juice, the bold piney taste of rosemary, and the sharp accent of Dijon-style mustard make this roasted chicken incredibly good.

LEMON ROSEMARY CHICKEN

PREP: *15 minutes*

MARINATE: *2 to 4 hours*

ROAST: *25 minutes*

MAKES: *6 servings*

6   large bone-in chicken breast halves (about 4½ pounds total)

1   cup lemon juice

¼   cup olive oil

1   tablespoon snipped fresh rosemary or 1 teaspoon dried rosemary, crushed

2   tablespoons honey

2   tablespoons Dijon-style mustard

2   cloves garlic, minced

¼   teaspoon salt

¼   teaspoon freshly ground black pepper

1 Place chicken breasts in a resealable plastic bag set in a shallow dish. For marinade, in a small bowl combine lemon juice, oil, rosemary, honey, mustard, garlic, salt, and pepper; mix well. Pour over chicken. Seal bag; turn to coat chicken. Marinate in the refrigerator for 2 to 4 hours, turning bag occasionally.

2 Preheat oven to 425°F. Drain chicken, discarding marinade. Place chicken, bone sides down, in a shallow roasting pan. Roast for 25 to 30 minutes or until chicken is golden brown, tender, and no longer pink (170°F).

Per serving: 490 cal., 26 g total fat (7 g sat. fat), 173 mg chol., 195 mg sodium, 3 g carbo., 0 g fiber, 57 g pro.

Düsseldorf, Germany's most famous mustard, is usually dark in color and has a sweet-and-sour flavor. It's equally delicious on chicken, sausage, or cold meats.

GERMAN-STYLE CHICKEN

¼   cup Düsseldorf or horseradish mustard

2   tablespoons dry sherry

½   teaspoon sweet Hungarian paprika or ¼ teaspoon hot Hungarian paprika

4   large bone-in chicken breast halves (about 2½ pounds total), skinned

½   cup soft rye bread crumbs

PREP: *15 minutes*

BAKE: *45 minutes*

MAKES: *4 servings*

1 Preheat oven to 375°F. In a small bowl combine mustard, sherry, and paprika. Transfer 2 tablespoons of the mustard mixture to another small bowl; brush evenly over tops of chicken breast halves. Set aside remaining mustard mixture. Place the chicken breast halves, mustard sides up, in a 3 quart rectangular baking dish. Sprinkle with bread crumbs. Lightly pat onto chicken.

2 Bake for 45 to 50 minutes or until chicken is tender and no longer pink (170°F). Serve with reserved mustard mixture.

Per serving: 243 cal., 4 g total fat (1 g sat. fat), 107 mg chol., 363 mg sodium, 4 g carbo., 1 g fiber, 44 g pro.

Team this brimming-with-seafood chicken with steamed asparagus and hot buttered noodles.

CRAB-STUFFED CHICKEN

PREP: *25 minutes*
COOK: *25 minutes*
MAKES: *4 servings*

1   medium orange
½   of an 8-ounce tub cream cheese
⅛   teaspoon salt
⅛   teaspoon black pepper
1   6- to 6½-ounce can crabmeat, drained, flaked, and cartilage removed
4   skinless, boneless chicken breast halves (about 1¼ pounds total)
     Salt
     Black pepper
1   tablespoon butter

1 Finely shred 1 teaspoon peel from the orange. Cut orange in half; squeeze out 1 tablespoon juice. Discard orange halves.

2 For filling, in a small bowl combine the 1 teaspoon orange peel, the 1 tablespoon orange juice, the cream cheese, the ⅛ teaspoon salt, and the ⅛ teaspoon pepper. Gently stir in crabmeat; set filling aside.

3 Place each chicken breast half between two pieces of plastic wrap. Using the flat side of a meat mallet, pound chicken lightly into a rectangle about ⅛ inch thick. Remove plastic wrap. Sprinkle chicken with additional salt and pepper. Spread one-fourth of the filling evenly in the center of each chicken piece. Fold narrow ends over filling; fold in sides. Starting from a short side, roll up each chicken breast. Secure with wooden toothpicks.

4 In a medium skillet melt butter over medium-low heat. Add chicken; cook about 25 minutes or until chicken is tender and no longer pink (170°F), turning to brown evenly. Remove toothpicks before serving.

Per serving: 327 cal., 15 g total fat (9 g sat. fat), 161 mg chol., 467 mg sodium, 2 g carbo., 0 g fiber, 43 g pro.

If you like veal or chicken piccata, you'll love this lemony pasta, chicken, and caper medley.

LEMON CHICKEN PASTA TOSS

2 cups dried multigrain penne pasta (6 ounces)

12 ounces skinless, boneless chicken breasts, cut into 1-inch pieces

2 tablespoons all-purpose flour

2 tablespoons olive oil

⅓ cup finely chopped shallot

2 cloves garlic, minced

¾ cup chicken broth

3 tablespoons lemon juice

¼ teaspoon salt

¼ teaspoon black pepper

3 tablespoons capers, drained

3 tablespoons snipped fresh flat-leaf parsley

Freshly grated Parmesan cheese (optional)

START TO FINISH:
40 minutes

MAKES: *4 servings*

1 Cook pasta according to package directions; drain. Return pasta to hot saucepan; cover and keep warm.

2 Meanwhile, in a medium bowl toss together chicken and flour until chicken is lightly coated. In a large skillet heat 1 tablespoon of the oil over medium-high heat. Add chicken; cook for 6 to 8 minutes or until chicken is no longer pink. Remove chicken from skillet; set aside.

3 Reduce heat to medium. Add the remaining 1 tablespoon oil to the skillet. Add shallot and garlic; cook and stir about 1 minute or until tender. Carefully stir in chicken broth, lemon juice, salt, and pepper. Cook for 2 to 3 minutes or until reduced to about ⅔ cup. Stir in chicken, capers, and parsley; heat through.

4 Toss pasta with chicken mixture. If desired, serve with Parmesan cheese.

Per serving: 339 cal., 9 g total fat (1 g sat. fat), 50 mg chol., 589 mg sodium, 36 g carbo., 4 g fiber, 29 g pro.

Mushrooms, white wine, shallots, and dried tomatoes give old-time gravy an appealing new edge.

CHICKEN WITH MUSHROOM~TOMATO PAN SAUCE

START TO FINISH:
40 minutes

MAKES: *4 servings*

4 skinless, boneless chicken breast halves
(about 1¼ pounds total)

Salt

Black pepper

5 tablespoons butter

1 cup sliced fresh shiitake, porcini, or button mushrooms

⅔ cup dry white wine

½ cup chicken broth

¼ cup finely chopped shallots or onion

3 tablespoons snipped drained oil-packed dried tomatoes

2 tablespoons whipping cream

2 teaspoons snipped fresh basil or parsley

1 Place each chicken breast half between two pieces of plastic wrap. Using the flat side of a meat mallet, pound the chicken lightly into rectangles about ¼ inch thick. Discard plastic wrap. Sprinkle with ¼ teaspoon salt and ¼ teaspoon pepper.

2 In a large skillet melt 1 tablespoon of the butter over medium-high heat. Add mushrooms; cook and stir until tender. Remove mushrooms from skillet. Melt 1 tablespoon of the remaining butter in skillet. Reduce heat to medium. Add chicken to skillet; cook for 6 to 8 minutes or until no longer pink; turn once. Transfer to a platter; cover with foil to keep warm.

3 For sauce, add wine, chicken broth, and shallot to the hot skillet. Cook and stir to scrape up the browned bits from the bottom of the skillet. Bring to boiling. Boil gently for 10 to 15 minutes or until liquid is reduced to ¼ cup.*

4 Reduce heat to medium-low. Stir in mushrooms, tomatoes, and whipping cream. Add the remaining 3 tablespoons butter, 1 tablespoon at a time, stirring until butter is melted after each addition. (Sauce should be slightly thickened.) Stir in basil. Season to taste with additional salt and pepper. Serve sauce over chicken.

Per serving: 437 cal., 26 g total fat (15 g sat. fat), 146 mg chol., 578 mg sodium, 10 g carbo., 1 g fiber, 35 g pro.

*TEST KITCHEN TIP: It is important to reduce the liquid to ¼ cup in Step 3 because otherwise the sauce will be too thin.

These tantalizing chicken bundles have honey-sweetened apricots and cranberries on the inside and a crispy Parmesan cheese coating on the outside. (Recipe pictured on page 275.)

APRICOT-CHICKEN ROLL-UPS

Nonstick cooking spray
1 6- or 7-ounce package dried apricots, snipped
½ cup dried cranberries
3 tablespoons honey
1½ teaspoons ground ginger
⅔ cup fine dry bread crumbs
2 tablespoons snipped fresh parsley
1 tablespoon all-purpose flour
1 tablespoon finely shredded Parmesan cheese
1 teaspoon paprika
½ teaspoon sugar
½ teaspoon dried oregano, crushed
½ teaspoon salt
¼ teaspoon garlic powder
¼ teaspoon onion powder
2 tablespoons shortening
2 eggs
6 skinless, boneless chicken breast halves (about 2 pounds total)

PREP: *40 minutes*
BAKE: *35 minutes*
MAKES: *6 servings*

1 Preheat oven to 350°F. Lightly coat a 3-quart rectangular baking dish with nonstick cooking spray; set aside. In a small bowl stir together dried apricots, cranberries, honey, and ginger; set aside.

2 In a medium bowl stir together bread crumbs, parsley, flour, cheese, paprika, sugar, oregano, salt, garlic powder, onion powder, and ¼ teaspoon black pepper. Using a pastry blender, cut in shortening until mixture resembles fine crumbs. Transfer to a shallow dish; set aside. Place eggs in another shallow dish; beat lightly with a fork and set aside.

3 Place each chicken breast between two pieces of plastic wrap. Using the flat side of a meat mallet, pound chicken lightly into rectangles slightly less than ¼ inch thick. Discard plastic wrap. Spoon a scant ¼ cup of the apricot mixture onto the center of each chicken breast. Fold in bottom and sides and roll up. Secure with wooden toothpicks. Dip each chicken roll in egg, then coat with bread crumb mixture. Place in prepared dish.

4 Bake for 35 to 40 minutes or until chicken is tender and no longer pink (170°F). Remove toothpicks before serving.

Per serving: 405 cal., 9 g total fat (2 g sat. fat), 159 mg chol., 546 mg sodium, 43 g carbo., 4 g fiber, 40 g pro.

Marsala, available both dry and sweet, is a Sicilian wine used mostly for cooking. In this recipe it lends a smoky flavor to the chicken and vegetables.

THYME CHICKEN MARSALA

START TO FINISH:
40 minutes

MAKES: *2 servings*

2   skinless, boneless chicken breast halves (about 10 ounces total)

1   tablespoon all-purpose flour

2   tablespoons olive oil

1   medium carrot, cut into thin strips

1   small red or yellow sweet pepper, cut into thin strips

2   cloves garlic, minced

¼   teaspoon salt

¼   teaspoon black pepper

⅓   cup dry Marsala

1   tablespoon snipped fresh thyme or ¼ teaspoon dried thyme, crushed

     Hot cooked linguine or other pasta (optional)

1 Place each chicken breast half between two pieces of plastic wrap. Using the flat side of a meat mallet, pound lightly into rectangles about ¼ inch thick. Discard plastic wrap. Coat breasts lightly with flour, shaking off excess. Set aside.

2 In a large skillet heat 1 tablespoon of the oil over medium heat. Add carrot strips; cook for 3 minutes. Add sweet pepper strips, garlic, salt, and black pepper to the skillet. Cook and stir about 5 minutes or until crisp-tender. Arrange vegetable mixture on two dinner plates. Cover with foil and keep warm.

3 In the same skillet heat the remaining 1 tablespoon oil over medium heat. Add chicken; cook for 4 to 6 minutes or until chicken is tender and no longer pink, turning once. Place chicken on top of vegetables; keep warm.

4 Add Marsala and thyme to the skillet. Cook and stir for 1 minute, scraping up any browned bits from the bottom of the skillet. Pour over chicken. If desired, serve with hot cooked linguine or other pasta.

Per serving: 311 cal., 17 g total fat (3 g sat. fat), 59 mg chol., 350 mg sodium, 10 g carbo., 2 g fiber, 23 g pro.

If you like, skip the chilling and enjoy this hoisin-sauced chicken warm.

ASIAN CHICKEN

6   skinless, boneless chicken breast halves
    (2 to 2½ pounds total)

    Salt

    Black pepper

2   tablespoons hoisin sauce or plum sauce

1   6-ounce package rice sticks

1   6-ounce package fresh baby spinach

1   recipe Asian Dressing

1   tablespoon sesame seeds, toasted

    Slivered green onions (optional)

PREP: *20 minutes*
BAKE: *35 minutes*
CHILL: *1 hour*
MAKES: *6 servings*

1 Preheat oven to 375°F. Arrange chicken breast halves in a 3-quart rectangular baking dish or a 13×9×2-inch baking pan. Sprinkle with salt and pepper. Brush tops with hoisin sauce. Bake for 35 to 40 minutes or until chicken is tender and no longer pink (170°F). Cool slightly; cover and chill for at least 1 hour or until ready to serve (up to 2 days).

2 Meanwhile, cook rice sticks according to package directions. Drain; rinse with cold water. Drain well. Snip rice sticks a few times. Place rice sticks in a resealable plastic bag. Seal bag. Chill until ready to serve.

3 To serve, arrange spinach on six dinner plates. Arrange cooked rice sticks on top of spinach. Place chilled chicken breasts on top of rice sticks. Drizzle with Asian Dressing. Sprinkle with sesame seeds and, if desired, green onion.

ASIAN DRESSING: In a screw-top jar combine ¾ cup rice vinegar, ⅓ cup salad oil, 3 tablespoons hoisin sauce or plum sauce, 2 tablespoons soy sauce, 1½ teaspoons grated fresh ginger or ¼ teaspoon ground ginger, and ¼ teaspoon crushed red pepper. Cover and shake well; chill until ready to serve (up to 1 week).

Per serving: 434 cal., 16 g total fat (3 g sat. fat), 88 mg chol., 733 mg sodium, 30 g carbo., 1 g fiber, 38 g pro.

These succulent chicken breasts cradle a zesty feta cheese, tomato, and basil filling.

FETA-STUFFED CHICKEN BREASTS

START TO FINISH:
40 minutes

MAKES: *4 servings*

1   tablespoon snipped dried tomatoes (not oil-packed)

4   skinless, boneless chicken breast halves
    (about 1¼ pounds total)

¼   cup crumbled feta cheese (1 ounce)

2   tablespoons softened cream cheese (1 ounce)

2   teaspoons snipped fresh basil or ½ teaspoon dried basil,
    crushed

⅛   teaspoon black pepper

1   teaspoon olive oil or cooking oil

    Fresh basil sprigs (optional)

❶ Place tomato in a small bowl. Pour enough boiling water over the tomato to cover. Let stand for 10 minutes. Drain and pat dry; set aside. Meanwhile, using a sharp knife, cut a pocket in each chicken breast half by cutting horizontally through the thickest portion to, but not through, the opposite side. Set aside.

❷ In a small bowl combine tomato, feta cheese, cream cheese, and the snipped or dried basil. Spoon about 1 rounded tablespoon of the cheese mixture into each chicken breast pocket. If necessary, secure openings with wooden toothpicks. Sprinkle chicken with pepper.

❸ In a large nonstick skillet heat oil over medium-high heat. Add chicken; cook for 12 to 14 minutes or until tender and no longer pink, turning once (reduce heat to medium if chicken browns too quickly). If desired, garnish with basil sprigs.

Per serving: 216 cal., 7 g total fat (3 g sat. fat), 96 mg chol., 195 mg sodium, 1 g carbo., 0 g fiber, 35 g pro.

Caribbean cuisine is known for its jerk seasoning, which generally contains chiles, thyme, garlic, onion, and spices such as cinnamon, ginger, allspice, and/or cloves. This recipe pairs the dynamite spice combination with luscious summer fruits—peaches, plums, and cherries.

SPICY CHICKEN WITH FRUIT

2	teaspoons Jamaican jerk seasoning
2	fresh serrano chile peppers, seeded and finely chopped (see tip, page 19)
4	skinless, boneless chicken breast halves (1¼ to 1½ pounds total)
	Nonstick cooking spray
½	cup peach nectar
3	green onions, bias-sliced into 1-inch pieces
2	cups sliced, peeled peaches
1	cup sliced, pitted plums
1	tablespoon packed brown sugar
⅛	teaspoon salt
½	cup halved pitted dark sweet cherries

START TO FINISH:
35 minutes

MAKES: *4 servings*

1 In a small bowl combine jerk seasoning and one of the chile peppers. Rub mixture onto both sides of each chicken breast half. Lightly coat an unheated large skillet with nonstick cooking spray. Preheat skillet over medium heat. Add chicken; cook for 8 to 12 minutes or until tender and no longer pink (170°F), turning once. Transfer to a serving platter; cover and keep warm.

2 Add 2 tablespoons of the peach nectar and the green onions to the skillet. Cook and stir over medium heat for 4 to 5 minutes or just until green onions are tender.

3 In a medium bowl combine the remaining chile pepper, remaining peach nectar, half of the peaches, half of the plums, the brown sugar, and salt. Add to skillet. Cook and stir over medium heat about 2 minutes or until slightly thickened and bubbly. Remove from heat. Stir in remaining peaches and plums. Stir in cherries. Spoon over chicken.

Per serving: 271 cal., 3 g total fat (1 g sat. fat), 82 mg chol., 323 mg sodium, 27 g carbo., 3 g fiber, 34 g pro.

The pecans give this crispy chicken a deliciously nutty texture while the orange marmalade and maple syrup give it a pleasing sweetness.

PECAN-CRUSTED CHICKEN

PREP: *20 minutes*
COOK: *12 minutes*
MAKES: *4 servings*

2   tablespoons orange marmalade
2   tablespoons pure maple syrup
1   cup finely chopped pecans
3   tablespoons all-purpose flour
¼   teaspoon salt
4   skinless, boneless chicken breast halves
    (about 1¼ pounds total)
2   tablespoons cooking oil
1   tablespoon butter

1 In a small bowl stir together orange marmalade and maple syrup; set aside. In a shallow dish combine pecans, flour, and salt. Brush marmalade mixture onto both sides of each chicken breast half. Dip chicken into pecan mixture to coat, pressing pecan mixture into chicken if necessary.

2 In a 12-inch skillet heat cooking oil and butter over medium heat until the butter melts and the mixture begins to bubble. Add chicken; cook for 12 to 15 minutes or until golden brown and no longer pink (170°F), turning once. Reduce heat if chicken browns too quickly.

Per serving: 506 cal., 32 g total fat (5 g sat. fat), 90 mg chol., 279 mg sodium, 21 g carbo., 3 g fiber, 36 g pro.

From among the many Cajun seasonings on the market, choose a salt-free blend to keep the sodium content in check.

CAJUN CHICKEN PASTA

PREP: *40 minutes*
BAKE: *25 minutes*
MAKES: *8 to 10 servings*

1   pound dried bow tie or rotini pasta

4   skinless, boneless chicken breast halves (about 1¼ pounds total), cut into 1-inch pieces

2   tablespoons all-purpose flour

2   tablespoons salt-free Cajun seasoning

1   tablespoon cooking oil

2   cups whipping cream

2   cups shredded cheddar and Monterey Jack cheese blend (8 ounces)

½   teaspoon salt

3   cups seeded, diced tomatoes

¼   cup sliced green onions

    Bottled hot pepper sauce (optional)

1 Cook pasta according to package directions. Drain; return pasta to hot pan.

2 Meanwhile, in a large resealable plastic bag combine chicken, flour, and 1 tablespoon of the Cajun seasoning; seal and toss to coat. In a large skillet heat oil over medium-high heat. Add chicken; cook and stir until chicken is tender and no longer pink.

3 Preheat oven to 350°F. For sauce, in a medium saucepan heat cream over medium heat just until boiling, stirring occasionally. Remove from heat; add 1 cup of the cheese, the remaining 1 tablespoon Cajun seasoning, and the salt, whisking until cheese is melted and mixture is smooth.

4 In a very large bowl combine cooked pasta, cooked chicken, sauce, tomato, and the remaining 1 cup cheese. Spoon mixture into a greased 3-quart rectangular baking dish.

5 Cover and bake for 25 to 30 minutes or until hot in center. Sprinkle with green onion. If desired, pass bottled hot pepper sauce.

Per serving: 656 cal., 37 g total fat (21 g sat. fat), 207 mg chol., 395 mg sodium, 47 g carbo., 2 g fiber, 34 g pro.

MAKE-AHEAD DIRECTIONS: Prepare as directed through Step 4. Cover with plastic wrap, then foil, and refrigerate for up to 24 hours. To serve, preheat oven to 350°F. Remove plastic wrap. Bake, covered with foil, for 35 to 40 minutes or until hot in center.

Opt for the chile peppers that suit your heat preferences. Ancho peppers range from mild to medium-hot, and pasilla peppers are hot.

CHICKEN WITH PEPPER MOLE

PREP: *25 minutes*

STAND: *20 minutes*

COOK: *12 minutes*

MAKES: *8 servings*

2	dried ancho or pasilla chile peppers (see tip, page 19)
¼	cup water
8	skinless, boneless chicken breast halves (about 2½ pounds total)
	Salt
	Black pepper
1	medium tomato, cut up
1	medium onion, cut up
⅓	cup shelled pumpkin seeds or blanched almonds, toasted
¼	cup reduced-sodium chicken broth
2	cloves garlic
¾	teaspoon salt
½	teaspoon sugar
½	teaspoon ground coriander
¼	teaspoon ground cinnamon
	Shelled pumpkin seeds or blanched almonds, toasted (optional)
	Warmed flour tortillas (optional)
	Lime wedges (optional)

1 Cut up chile peppers; discard stems and seeds. In a small saucepan combine chile peppers and the ¼ cup water. Bring to boiling; remove from heat. Let chile peppers stand for 20 minutes; drain. Set aside.

2 Arrange chicken in an extra-large skillet; add a small amount of water. Sprinkle chicken with salt and black pepper. Bring water to boiling; reduce heat. Cover and simmer about 12 minutes or until chicken is tender and no longer pink (170°F). Drain.

3 Meanwhile, for sauce, in a blender or food processor combine the chile peppers, tomato, onion, the ⅓ cup pumpkin seeds or almonds, the chicken broth, garlic, the ¾ teaspoon salt, the sugar, coriander, and cinnamon. Cover and blend or process until nearly smooth, scraping down side of container as needed. Transfer to a small saucepan; bring to boiling over medium heat. Remove from heat.

4 To serve, spoon the sauce over the chicken. If desired, sprinkle with additional pumpkin seeds and serve with tortillas and lime wedges.

Per serving: 214 cal., 5 g total fat (1 g sat. fat), 82 mg chol., 390 mg sodium, 5 g carbo., 2 g fiber, 35 g pro.

This hearty recipe features a delicious blend of chicken and garden vegetables—all cooked in one skillet!

OZARK MOUNTAIN SUCCOTASH

⅓ cup all-purpose flour

⅓ cup yellow cornmeal

    Salt

    Black pepper

1   egg, lightly beaten

1   tablespoon milk

8   ounces fresh okra, cut into ½-inch-thick pieces (2 cups)

⅓ cup cooking oil

1   medium green sweet pepper, chopped

1   medium onion, chopped

2   cloves garlic, minced

1   small yellow summer squash or zucchini, cut into thin bite-size strips

1   cup loose pack frozen whole kernel corn, thawed

12 ounces skinless, boneless chicken breasts, cut into bite-size strips

START TO FINISH:
50 minutes

MAKES: *4 servings*

1 In a resealable plastic bag combine flour, cornmeal, ¼ teaspoon salt, and ⅛ teaspoon black pepper. In a small bowl combine egg and milk. Dip okra pieces into egg mixture. Add one-fourth of the okra to the plastic bag; seal bag and shake to coat okra well. Remove coated okra. Repeat with remaining okra and flour mixture. Set aside.

2 In a large skillet heat 1 tablespoon of the oil over medium heat. Add sweet pepper, onion, and garlic. Cook and stir for 3 to 4 minutes or until onion is tender. Add squash and corn. Cook and stir for 2 to 3 minutes or until corn is tender. Remove from skillet; drain on paper towels. Set aside.

3 Carefully add another 1 tablespoon oil to hot skillet. Add chicken. Cook and stir over medium-high heat for 2 to 3 minutes or until tender and no longer pink. Add to vegetable mixture; set aside.

4 In the same skillet heat the remaining oil. Test oil by adding one piece of okra; if okra sizzles, oil is hot enough. Fry okra, half at a time, over medium-high heat for 3 to 4 minutes or until golden brown, turning once (add more oil during cooking, if necessary). Using a slotted spoon, remove okra from skillet. When all the okra has been fried, drain all but 2 tablespoons of the oil from the skillet. Return okra to the skillet.

5 Return chicken and vegetables to the skillet. Heat and stir gently until heated through. Season to taste with additional salt and pepper.

Per serving: 427 cal., 21 g total fat (4 g sat. fat), 103 mg chol., 231 mg sodium, 34 g carbo., 5 g fiber, 27 g pro.

Lemongrass is a seasoning often used in Thai and Vietnamese dishes. It has long, thin grayish green leaves and a tangy lemon flavor. You'll find it in Asian food markets, although larger supermarkets also carry it.

LEMONGRASS CHICKEN OVER NOODLES

START TO FINISH:
50 minutes

MAKES: *4 servings*

2 tablespoons sugar

3 tablespoons water

⅓ cup chicken broth

3 tablespoons fish sauce or oyster sauce

1 teaspoon cornstarch

2 tablespoons cooking oil

2 tablespoons finely chopped fresh lemongrass or 1 teaspoon finely shredded lemon peel

3 cloves garlic, minced

1 large onion, halved lengthwise and thinly sliced

1 medium carrot, thinly bias sliced

2 cups broccoli florets

1 medium red or green sweet pepper, cut into 1-inch squares

2 fresh red chile peppers, seeded and cut into thin strips (see tip, page 19)

12 ounces skinless, boneless chicken breasts or thighs, cut into bite-size strips

3 cups hot cooked Chinese egg noodles, vermicelli, capellini, fettuccine, or linguine

1 For sauce, in a small saucepan heat sugar over medium-high heat until sugar begins to melt, shaking saucepan occasionally to heat sugar evenly. Reduce heat to low and cook until sugar is melted and light brown (about 3 minutes more). Stir as necessary after sugar begins to melt. Carefully add the water, stirring until sugar is dissolved. Remove from heat. In a small bowl stir together chicken broth, fish sauce, and cornstarch; stir into sugar mixture. Set aside.

2 Add oil to a wok or 12-inch skillet. Heat over medium-high heat. Stir-fry lemongrass or lemon peel and garlic in hot oil for 15 seconds. Add onion and carrot; stir-fry for 2 minutes (add more oil during cooking, if necessary). Add broccoli; stir-fry for 2 minutes. Add sweet pepper and chile peppers; stir-fry for 2 minutes more or until vegetables are crisp-tender. Remove vegetables from wok.

3 Add chicken to wok; stir-fry about 4 minutes or until no longer pink. Push chicken from center of wok. Stir sauce; add to center of wok. Cook and stir until thickened and bubbly. Return vegetables to wok; cook and stir about 1 minute or until heated through. Serve over hot noodles.

Per serving: 405 cal., 10 g total fat (2 g sat. fat), 89 mg chol., 1,201 mg sodium, 50 g carbo., 5 g fiber, 29 g pro.

Save time by using 4 teaspoons of bottled minced garlic instead of peeling and mincing 8 cloves.

JERK CHICKEN BREASTS

6   skinless, boneless chicken breast halves
    (about 2 pounds total)

4   teaspoons Jamaican jerk seasoning

8   cloves garlic, minced

2   teaspoons snipped fresh thyme or ½ teaspoon
    dried thyme, crushed

2   teaspoons finely shredded lemon peel

2   tablespoons lemon juice

    Olive oil cooking spray or 2 teaspoons olive oil

    Lemon wedges

PREP: *20 minutes*

CHILL: *30 minutes to 24 hours*

BROIL: *6 minutes*

MAKES: *6 servings*

1 Place each chicken breast half between two sheets of plastic wrap. Using the flat side of a meat mallet, pound chicken lightly into rectangles about ½ inch thick. In a small bowl combine jerk seasoning, garlic, thyme, and lemon peel. Brush chicken breast halves with lemon juice. Sprinkle garlic mixture evenly over chicken breasts; rub in with your fingers. Place chicken in a resealable plastic bag; seal bag. Chill in the refrigerator for 30 minutes to 24 hours.

2 Preheat broiler. Lightly coat the unheated rack of a broiler pan with olive oil cooking spray or brush lightly with olive oil.

3 Place chicken on the rack in the broiler pan. Broil 3 to 4 inches from the heat for 6 to 10 minutes or until chicken is tender and no longer pink, turning once halfway through broiling.

4 To serve, slice chicken; pass lemon wedges.

Per serving: 180 cal., 3 g total fat (1 g sat. fat), 88 mg chol., 283 mg sodium, 2 g carbo., 0 g fiber, 35 g pro.

Thai cooks make two kinds of curry: red and green. This green version gets its delightful flavor from green curry paste, fish sauce, coconut milk, Thai basil, and jalapeño chile peppers.

GREEN CURRY CHICKEN

START TO FINISH:
45 minutes

MAKES: *4 servings*

1 tablespoon cooking oil

1 to 3 tablespoons green curry paste

1 pound skinless, boneless chicken breasts, cut into bite-size strips

2 tablespoons fish sauce

1 teaspoon sugar

½ teaspoon salt

1 14-ounce can unsweetened coconut milk

2 cups peeled (if desired) and cubed Thai, Japanese, or regular eggplant

1 8-ounce can bamboo shoots, rinsed and drained

⅓ cup fresh Thai basil or regular basil, snipped or shredded if large

1 to 2 fresh red jalapeño or serrano chile peppers, seeded and cut into thin strips (see tip, page 19)

Hot cooked jasmine, basmati, or long grain rice

1 Pour oil into a wok or very large skillet. Heat over medium heat. Add curry paste; reduce heat to low and cook and stir for 30 seconds or until fragrant. Add chicken to skillet; cook and stir over medium-high heat for 3 to 4 minutes or until chicken is no longer pink. Stir in fish sauce, sugar, and salt.

2 Gradually add coconut milk, stirring until well mixed. Bring to boiling; reduce heat. Simmer, uncovered, for 10 minutes.

3 Add eggplant and bamboo shoots; cover and cook about 8 minutes more or until eggplant is tender. Remove from heat.

4 Transfer mixture to a serving dish. Sprinkle with basil and chile peppers. Serve in shallow bowls with hot cooked rice.

Per serving: 367 cal., 24 g total fat (17 g sat. fat), 66 mg chol., 1,143 mg sodium, 9 g carbo., 30 g pro.

To add even more interest to this dish, choose one of the many varieties of flavored couscous mixes available. Simply cook it according to package directions and serve in place of the plain couscous.

GREEK-STYLE CHICKEN SKILLET

START TO FINISH:
40 minutes

MAKES: *4 servings*

4	skinless, boneless chicken breast halves (about 1¼ pounds total)
	Salt
	Black pepper
1	tablespoon olive oil or cooking oil
1½	cups sliced zucchini
1	medium onion, sliced and separated into rings
¾	cup chopped green sweet pepper
2	cloves garlic, minced
⅛	teaspoon black pepper
¼	cup water
1	10¾-ounce can condensed tomato soup
2	cups hot cooked couscous or orzo pasta (rosamarina)
½	cup crumbled feta cheese (2 ounces)
	Lemon wedges

1 Sprinkle chicken with salt and black pepper. In a large skillet heat oil over medium heat. Add chicken; cook for 12 to 15 minutes or until tender and no longer pink (170°F), turning once. Remove chicken from skillet. Cover with foil and keep warm.

2 Add zucchini, onion, sweet pepper, garlic, and the ⅛ teaspoon black pepper to skillet. Add the water; reduce heat. Cover and cook for 5 minutes, stirring once or twice. Stir in tomato soup. Bring to boiling; reduce heat. Cover and simmer for 5 minutes more, stirring once.

3 Return chicken to skillet, turning to coat. Serve with couscous, feta cheese, and lemon wedges.

Per serving: 401 cal., 10 g total fat (4 g sat. fat), 99 mg chol., 827 mg sodium, 36 g carbo., 4 g fiber, 41 g pro.

Here the intriguing flavors of coq au vin are rolled into pasta rosettes and topped with an opulent cream sauce. It's a great dinner-party dish because you can prepare it just before your guests arrive and then slide it into the oven after you welcome them. (Recipe pictured on page 275.)

COQ AU VIN ROSETTES

PREP: *40 minutes*

BAKE: *35 minutes*

MAKES: *8 servings
(16 rosettes)*

2	tablespoons butter or margarine
3	cups sliced fresh mushrooms
½	cup chopped onion
8	skinless, boneless chicken breast halves (about 2½ pounds total), cut into 1-inch pieces
¾	cup dry white wine
½	teaspoon dried tarragon, crushed
½	teaspoon white pepper
⅛	teaspoon salt
8	dried lasagna noodles
1	8-ounce package cream cheese, cut up
½	cup dairy sour cream
2	tablespoons all-purpose flour
½	cup half-and-half, light cream, or milk
1	cup shredded Gruyère cheese (4 ounces)
1	cup shredded Muenster cheese (4 ounces)
	Slivered almonds, toasted (optional)
	Snipped fresh parsley (optional)

1 In a large skillet melt butter over medium-high heat. Add mushrooms and onion; cook for 4 to 5 minutes or until tender, stirring occasionally. Add chicken, wine, tarragon, white pepper, and salt. Bring just to boiling; reduce heat. Cover and simmer for 5 minutes, stirring once. Remove from heat.

2 Meanwhile, cook lasagna noodles according to package directions. Halve each noodle lengthwise. Curl each noodle half into a 2½-inch-diameter ring; place noodle rings, cut sides down, in a 3-quart rectangular baking dish.

3 Using a slotted spoon, spoon chicken mixture into centers of noodle rings, reserving the liquid in the skillet. Add the cream cheese to reserved liquid; heat and stir just until cream cheese is melted.

4 Preheat oven to 325°F. In a small bowl stir together sour cream and flour; stir in half-and-half. Add the sour cream mixture, Gruyère cheese, and Muenster cheese to the cream cheese mixture in skillet. Cook and stir over medium heat until thickened and bubbly. Spoon cheese mixture over filled rings in baking dish. If desired, sprinkle with slivered almonds.

5 Bake, covered, about 35 minutes or until heated through. If desired, top with snipped parsley.

Per serving: 734 cal., 32 g total fat (18 g sat. fat), 249 mg chol., 494 mg sodium, 22 g carbo., 1 g fiber, 83 g pro.

Crushed gingersnaps make a crispy yet subtly sweet coating for tender strips of baked chicken.

CHICKEN & PINEAPPLE RICE

1   15¼-ounce can or two 8-ounce cans pineapple tidbits
    (juice pack)

¾   cup long grain rice

½   teaspoon salt

½   cup coarsely chopped green sweet pepper
    Nonstick cooking spray

1   cup finely crushed gingersnaps (about 20 cookies)

¼   teaspoon salt

1   egg

1   tablespoon water

4   skinless, boneless chicken breast halves
    (about 1¼ pounds total), cut lengthwise into halves

PREP: *20 minutes*

COOK: *18 minutes*

STAND: *5 minutes*

BAKE: *15 minutes*

MAKES: *4 servings*

1 Preheat oven to 400°F. Drain pineapple, reserving juice. Set pineapple aside. Add enough water to reserved juice to measure 1¾ cups total liquid. In a medium saucepan stir together juice mixture, uncooked rice, and the ½ teaspoon salt. Bring to boiling; reduce heat. Cover and simmer for 18 minutes. Remove from heat. Stir in pineapple and sweet pepper. Let stand, covered, for 5 minutes.

2 Meanwhile, lightly coat a 15×10×1-inch baking pan with nonstick cooking spray; set aside. In a shallow dish combine gingersnaps and the ¼ teaspoon salt. In another shallow dish whisk together egg and the water. Dip chicken breast pieces, one at a time, into egg mixture, then into gingersnap mixture to coat. Arrange chicken in a single layer in prepared baking pan. Lightly coat chicken with nonstick cooking spray.

3 Bake for 15 to 18 minutes or until chicken is tender and no longer pink. Serve chicken with rice mixture.

Per serving: 519 cal., 7 g total fat (2 g sat. fat), 135 mg chol., 763 mg sodium, 73 g carbo., 2 g fiber, 40 g pro.

With turmeric and other earthy spices, as well as couscous, dried fruits, and nuts, this dish is inspired by the cooking of North Africa.

CHICKEN & FRUIT COUSCOUS

PREP: *45 minutes*

CHILL: *1 to 2 hours*

STAND: *5 minutes*

MAKES: *8 to 10 servings*

1 teaspoon salt

1 teaspoon ground cumin

1 teaspoon ground ginger

½ teaspoon ground turmeric

½ teaspoon ground cinnamon

6 boneless, skinless chicken breast halves (about 2 pounds total), cut into 1-inch pieces

1 tablespoon olive oil

2 tablespoons butter

3 medium onions, cut into thin wedges

4 cloves garlic, minced

¼ teaspoon crushed red pepper

1 6-ounce package dried apricots, cut into strips

¾ cup golden raisins

3 14-ounce cans chicken broth

1 10-ounce package quick-cooking couscous

¼ teaspoon black pepper

⅔ cup slivered or sliced almonds, toasted

Snipped fresh flat-leaf parsley

1 For spice mixture, in a small bowl stir together salt, cumin, ginger, turmeric, and cinnamon. Sprinkle 1 tablespoon of the spice mixture over the chicken. Cover and chill for 1 to 2 hours to allow spices to penetrate meat. Set aside the remaining spice mixture.

2 In a 4-quart Dutch oven heat oil over medium-high heat. Add half of the chicken to Dutch oven. Cook and stir for 4 to 5 minutes or until chicken is no longer pink. Remove chicken. (If necessary, add additional oil.) Cook remaining chicken. Remove chicken; set aside.

3 Add butter to Dutch oven and melt over medium-high heat. Add onions, garlic, and crushed red pepper. Cook about 8 minutes or until onions begin to turn golden brown, stirring occasionally. Add remaining spice mixture to onion mixture, stirring to combine. Return chicken to Dutch oven along with apricots and raisins.

4 Add chicken broth to Dutch oven. Bring to boiling. Stir in couscous and black pepper. Cover and remove from heat. Let stand for 5 minutes. Just before serving, sprinkle with almonds and parsley.

Per serving: 485 cal., 12 g total fat (3 g sat. fat), 75 mg chol., 980 mg sodium, 60 g carbo., 6 g fiber, 35 g pro.

Another time try these plump chicken rolls with peach or strawberry jam instead of apricot.

APRICOT-CRANBERRY-STUFFED CHICKEN

6	skinless, boneless chicken breast halves (about 2 pounds total)
1½	cups herb-seasoned stuffing mix
½	cup apricot jam
⅓	cup dried cranberries
¼	cup butter or margarine, melted

PREP: *30 minutes*
BAKE: *25 minutes*
MAKES: *6 servings*

1 Preheat oven to 400°F. Place each chicken breast half between two pieces of plastic wrap. Using the flat side of a meat mallet, pound chicken lightly into rectangles about ⅛ inch thick. Discard plastic wrap. Set chicken aside.

2 In a medium bowl combine stuffing mix, ⅓ cup of the jam, ¼ cup of the cranberries, and 3 tablespoons of the melted butter. Stir until moistened; set aside.

3 For glaze, in a small bowl stir together the remaining jam, cranberries, and 1 tablespoon melted butter. Set glaze aside.

4 Place about ⅓ cup of the stuffing mixture on each chicken piece. Fold in bottom and sides and roll up. Secure with wooden toothpicks. Place chicken rolls in a greased 3-quart rectangular baking dish.

5 Bake for 15 minutes. Brush glaze over chicken. Bake for 10 to 15 minutes more or until chicken is tender and no longer pink. Remove toothpicks before serving.

Per serving: 393 cal., 11 g total fat (6 g sat. fat), 109 mg chol., 374 mg sodium, 35 g carbo., 2 g fiber, 37 g pro.

Spiffed up with chicken, Italian seasoning, smoked cheddar cheese, and sourdough bread crumbs, this tomatoey version of mac and cheese is more at home at a bistro than a diner.

CHICKEN MAC & CHEESE

PREP: *40 minutes*

BAKE: *20 minutes*

STAND: *10 minutes*

MAKES: *6 servings*

1   tablespoon olive oil

1   pound skinless, boneless chicken breasts, cut into bite-size pieces

1   to 2 teaspoons dried Italian seasoning, crushed
    Salt
    Black pepper

8   ounces dried mostaccioli, ziti, or penne pasta

3   tablespoons butter

1   medium onion, chopped

2   cloves garlic, minced

3   tablespoons all-purpose flour

2   tablespoons tomato paste

3   cups milk

8   ounces smoked cheddar, Gruyère, or Swiss cheese, shredded (2 cups)

2   cups soft sourdough or French bread crumbs

½   cup finely shredded Parmesan or Romano cheese (2 ounces)

3   tablespoons butter, melted

1 Preheat oven to 350°F. In a large skillet heat oil over medium heat. Add chicken, Italian seasoning, ⅛ teaspoon salt, and ⅛ teaspoon pepper; cook until chicken is tender and no longer pink. Remove from skillet.

2 Cook pasta according to package directions just until tender. Drain; return pasta to hot pan.

3 Meanwhile, in same skillet melt 3 tablespoons butter over medium heat. Add onion and garlic; cook until tender. Stir in flour. Stir in tomato paste. Add milk. Cook and stir until mixture is thickened and bubbly; reduce heat. Add shredded smoked cheddar cheese, stirring until cheese is almost melted. Remove from heat; season to taste with additional salt and pepper. Add cheese mixture and chicken to cooked pasta, stirring to coat. Spoon mixture into a 2-quart square or rectangular baking dish.

4 In a small bowl stir together bread crumbs, Parmesan cheese, and 3 tablespoons melted butter. Sprinkle crumb mixture over pasta mixture. Bake for 20 to 25 minutes or until crumb mixture is golden brown and edges are bubbly. Let stand for 10 minutes before serving.

Per serving: 670 cal., 33 g total fat (20 g sat. fat), 131 mg chol., 710 mg sodium, 49 g carbo., 2 g fiber, 42 g pro.

A sophisticated twist on classic black-eyed peas and rice, this chicken dish is seasoned with garlic, poultry seasoning, two kinds of pepper, saffron, and thyme.

CHICKEN WITH BLACK-EYED PEAS & RICE

1	tablespoon olive oil
1	cup chopped red onion
1½	pounds chicken breast tenderloins
2	cloves garlic, minced
1	14-ounce can reduced-sodium chicken broth
½	teaspoon poultry seasoning
¼	to ½ teaspoon black pepper
¼	teaspoon crushed red pepper
¾	cup saffron-flavored yellow rice mix*
1	15-ounce can black-eyed peas, rinsed and drained
1	tablespoon snipped fresh thyme or 1 teaspoon dried thyme, crushed
	Finely chopped red onion (optional)
	Snipped fresh thyme (optional)

START TO FINISH:
45 minutes

MAKES: *6 servings*

1 In a 12-inch skillet heat oil over medium heat. Add the 1 cup chopped onion; cook about 4 minutes or until tender. Add chicken and garlic; cook about 4 minutes more or until chicken is browned, turning once.

2 Stir in chicken broth, poultry seasoning, black pepper, and crushed red pepper. Bring to boiling.

3 Stir in uncooked rice mix. Reduce heat. Cover and cook about 10 minutes or until rice is almost tender.

4 Stir in black-eyed peas and the 1 tablespoon fresh thyme or the dried thyme. Cover and cook about 10 minutes more or until heated through and liquid is absorbed. If desired, garnish with additional finely chopped red onion and snipped thyme.

Per serving: 280 cal., 4 g total fat (1 g sat. fat), 66 mg chol., 641 mg sodium, 28 g carbo., 4 g fiber, 32 g pro.

*TEST KITCHEN TIP: You can find saffron-flavored yellow rice mix with other rice mixes in your supermarket. Look for a brand that combines the seasonings and the rice to make it easier to measure out the ¾ cup needed for this recipe. If the brand you buy comes with a separate seasoning packet, mix the seasonings with the rice in a bowl and measure out ¾ cup.

Chicken legs, often a good buy, turn this hearty dish of rather ordinary vegetables into a comforting home-style dinner.

HEARTY CHICKEN & NOODLES

PREP: *45 minutes*

COOK: *30 minutes*

MAKES: *6 servings*

3	chicken legs (drumstick and thigh) (about 2 pounds total), skinned
2¼	cups water
1	14-ounce can reduced-sodium chicken broth
1	bay leaf
1	tablespoon snipped fresh thyme or 1 teaspoon dried thyme, crushed
¾	teaspoon salt
¼	teaspoon black pepper
2	cups sliced carrot
1½	cups chopped onion
3	cups dried wide noodles
2	cups milk
1	cup loose-pack frozen peas
2	tablespoons all-purpose flour

1 In a 4½-quart Dutch oven combine chicken, the water, chicken broth, bay leaf, dried thyme (if using), salt, and pepper. Add carrot and onion. Bring to boiling; reduce heat. Cover and simmer about 30 minutes or until chicken is tender and no longer pink (180°F). Discard bay leaf.

2 Remove chicken from Dutch oven; cool slightly. Remove meat from bones; discard bones. Chop or shred chicken and set aside.

3 Return vegetable mixture to boiling. Add uncooked noodles; cook, uncovered, for 5 minutes. Stir in 1½ cups of the milk and the peas.

4 In a screw-top jar combine the remaining ½ cup milk and the flour. Cover and shake until smooth. Stir into noodle mixture. Cook and stir over medium heat until thickened and bubbly. Stir in chicken and fresh thyme (if using). Cook for 1 to 2 minutes more or until heated through.

Per serving: 316 cal., 6 g total fat (2 g sat. fat), 102 mg chol., 624 mg sodium, 37 g carbo., 4 g fiber, 27 g pro.

When you're in the mood for something tropical, turn to these delicious chicken drumsticks dressed in a buttery-rich macadamia nut crust.

MACADAMIA NUT-CRUSTED CHICKEN

Nonstick cooking spray

1½	cups herb-seasoned stuffing mix, crushed
1	3½-ounce jar macadamia nuts, finely chopped
1	egg
3	tablespoons milk
3	tablespoons honey
2½	to 3 pounds chicken drumsticks, skinned
3	tablespoons butter, melted
½	cup mayonnaise or salad dressing
4	teaspoons Dijon-style mustard or yellow mustard

PREP: *25 minutes*

BAKE: *45 minutes*

MAKES: *8 to 10 servings*

1 Preheat oven to 375°F. Lightly coat a 15×10×1-inch baking pan with nonstick cooking spray; set aside.

2 In a shallow dish stir together crushed stuffing mix and nuts. In another shallow dish whisk together egg, milk, and 2 tablespoons of the honey. Dip chicken drumsticks into egg mixture, then into crumb mixture to coat. Arrange chicken in prepared pan. Drizzle with melted butter.

3 Bake for 45 to 55 minutes or until chicken is tender and no longer pink (180°F). (Do not turn chicken while baking.)

4 Meanwhile, for sauce, in a small bowl stir together the remaining 1 tablespoon honey, the mayonnaise, and mustard. Serve the chicken with sauce.

Per serving: 402 cal., 29 g total fat (7 g sat. fat), 104 mg chol., 416 mg sodium, 17 g carbo., 2 g fiber, 20 g pro.

Barbecue in the winter? Why not—when it's all done in the oven. Chicken drumsticks are coated with a slightly sweet barbecue sauce that offers a taste of summer while winter winds howl.

KICKIN' CHICKEN

PREP: *20 minutes*

BAKE: *45 minutes*

MAKES: *8 servings*

Nonstick cooking spray

8   chicken drumsticks, skinned

¼   teaspoon salt

¼   teaspoon black pepper

2   teaspoons cooking oil

2   cloves garlic, minced

¾   cup bottled barbecue sauce

¼   cup ketchup

¼   cup orange juice or water

2   tablespoons packed brown sugar

2   tablespoons mild-flavored molasses or maple-flavored syrup

Several dashes bottled hot pepper sauce (optional)

1 Preheat oven to 375°F. Lightly coat a 15×10×1-inch baking pan with nonstick cooking spray. Arrange chicken in prepared baking pan. Sprinkle with salt and pepper. Bake for 25 minutes.

2 Meanwhile, for sauce, in a medium saucepan heat oil over medium heat. Add garlic; cook for 30 seconds. Stir in barbecue sauce, ketchup, orange juice, brown sugar, molasses or maple-flavored syrup, and, if desired, hot pepper sauce; heat through.

3 Carefully brush chicken with sauce. Turn chicken and brush with additional sauce. Bake for 20 to 25 minutes more or until chicken is tender and no longer pink (180°F). Reheat any remaining sauce; drizzle some of the sauce over chicken. Pass remaining sauce.

Per serving: 188 cal., 5 g total fat (1 g sat. fat), 78 mg chol., 355 mg sodium, 13 g carbo., 0 g fiber, 22 g pro.

Crushed seasoned croutons make a quick and flavorful coating for these oven-fried drumsticks. To crush the croutons, put them in a resealable plastic bag and smash with a rolling pin.

CROUTON-CRUSTED CHICKEN DRUMSTICKS

⅓	cup buttermilk
1½	cups cheddar and Romano-, sourdough cheese-, or cheese and garlic-flavored croutons
1½	teaspoons garlic-pepper seasoning
¼	teaspoon celery seeds
8	chicken drumsticks, skinned

PREP: *20 minutes*
BAKE: *45 minutes*
MAKES: *4 servings*

1 Preheat oven to 375°F. Place buttermilk in a shallow dish. Finely crush croutons (you should have about 1¼ cups). In another shallow dish combine crushed croutons, garlic-pepper seasoning, and celery seeds. Dip drumsticks into buttermilk, then into crouton mixture to coat.

2 Arrange chicken in a greased 15×10×1-inch baking pan. Bake for 45 to 55 minutes or until chicken is tender and no longer pink (180°F). (Do not turn chicken pieces while baking.)

Per serving: 290 cal., 14 g total fat (4 g sat. fat), 119 mg chol., 632 mg sodium, 7 g carbo., 0 g fiber, 30 g pro.

Osso buco is a dish in which the meat (traditionally veal but in this recipe chicken) is braised in a tomatoey wine sauce. Carrot, celery, and onion are also classic ingredients.

CHICKEN OSSO BUCO WITH LINGUINE

PREP: *50 minutes*

SOAK: *20 minutes*

COOK: *45 minutes*

MAKES: *4 to 6 servings*

1 ounce dried porcini mushrooms

4 ounces thick-sliced pancetta or bacon, chopped

2 tablespoons olive oil

2½ to 3 pounds chicken thighs and drumsticks, skinned

2 cups fresh cremini or other mushrooms, quartered

1 cup finely chopped carrot

1 cup sliced celery

1 cup chopped onion

4 cloves garlic, minced

2 14½-ounce cans petite diced tomatoes

½ cup dry white wine

1 fresh thyme sprig

1 bay leaf

8 ounces dried linguine or spaghetti

¼ cup finely shredded Parmesan cheese (1 ounce)

2 tablespoons snipped fresh basil or oregano

1 teaspoon finely shredded lemon peel

1 Rinse and drain dried porcini mushroom; soak in ½ cup warm water for 20 minutes. Drain mushrooms, reserving liquid. Coarsely chop mushrooms; set aside. Strain liquid; set aside. In a very large skillet cook pancetta or bacon until crisp. Drain pancetta or bacon on paper towels, discarding drippings. Cover pancetta or bacon and chill until needed.

2 In the same skillet heat oil over medium-high heat. Add chicken; cook about 10 minutes or until browned, turning to brown evenly (add more oil during cooking, if necessary). Remove chicken from skillet. Add cremini mushrooms, carrot, celery, onion, and garlic to skillet. Cook and stir about 5 minutes or until almost tender. Carefully add porcini mushrooms, mushroom liquid, undrained tomatoes, wine, thyme sprig, and bay leaf. Bring to boiling. Return chicken to skillet. Reduce heat to low. Cover and simmer for 35 to 40 minutes or until chicken is tender and no longer pink (180°F). Remove chicken from skillet; cover and keep warm. Simmer vegetable mixture, uncovered, about 10 minutes or until desired consistency. Discard bay leaf.

3 Meanwhile, cook pasta according to package directions; drain. In a bowl combine pancetta or bacon, Parmesan cheese, snipped herb, and lemon peel. Serve pasta with chicken and vegetables. Top with cheese mixture.

Per serving: 896 cal., 42 g total fat (12 g sat. fat), 195 mg chol., 1,362 mg sodium, 67 g carbo., 7 g fiber, 56 g pro.

Pancetta, kalamata olives, and goat cheese are the ingredients that make this Mediterranean dish unforgettable. Pancetta is a salt-cured Italian bacon that's sold sliced or in a sausagelike roll. Look for it at Italian specialty stores. (Recipe pictured on page 276.)

CHICKEN THIGHS & ORZO

1   4-ounce package pancetta, chopped, or 4 slices bacon, chopped
    Olive oil (optional)

6   large chicken thighs (about 2¼ pounds total), skinned

2   14½-ounce cans diced tomatoes with garlic and onion

1   cup dried orzo pasta (rosamarina)

1   cup water

2   cloves garlic, minced

⅓   cup pitted kalamata olives

¼   cup snipped fresh basil

1   6-ounce package fresh baby spinach

3   ounces goat cheese with basil and roasted garlic

PREP: *35 minutes*
COOK: *25 minutes*
MAKES: *6 servings*

1 In a 5- to 6-quart Dutch oven cook pancetta or bacon until brown. Remove pancetta or bacon from Dutch oven, reserving 2 tablespoons drippings in Dutch oven (add olive oil if necessary to equal 2 tablespoons drippings). Drain pancetta or bacon on paper towels; set aside.

2 Cook chicken in reserved drippings about 10 minutes or until light brown, turning to brown evenly; drain off fat. Add undrained tomatoes, uncooked orzo, the water, and garlic to chicken in Dutch oven. Bring to boiling; reduce heat. Cover and simmer for 25 to 30 minutes or until chicken is tender and no longer pink (180°F) and orzo is tender. If necessary, cook, uncovered, for 2 to 3 minutes more or until sauce is desired consistency. Stir in pancetta or bacon, olives, and basil and heat through.

3 Divide spinach among six dinner plates. Top spinach with chicken thighs and orzo mixture. Top with cheese.

Per serving: 395 cal., 18 g total fat (5 g sat. fat), 77 mg chol., 1,229 mg sodium, 32 g carbo., 2 g fiber, 26 g pro.

Broccoli slaw and pecans boost the flavor of these tender sweet-and-sour chicken thighs.

CHICKEN WITH BROCCOLI & GARLIC

START TO FINISH:
35 minutes

MAKES: *4 servings*

¼   cup all-purpose flour

¼   teaspoon salt

¼   teaspoon black pepper

4   skinless, boneless chicken thighs (about 12 ounces total)

1   tablespoon olive oil

1   bulb garlic, separated into cloves, peeled, and sliced (about ¼ cup)

1   cup reduced-sodium chicken broth

3   tablespoons white wine vinegar

2   tablespoons honey

1   16-ounce package shredded broccoli (broccoli slaw mix)

2   tablespoons coarsely chopped pecans

1 In a resealable plastic bag combine flour, salt, and pepper. Add chicken; seal bag. Shake to coat.

2 In a large skillet heat oil over medium heat. Add chicken; cook for 10 to 12 minutes or until chicken is tender and no longer pink (180°F), turning once. Transfer chicken to a serving plate; cover and keep warm.

3 Add garlic to skillet. Cook and stir for 1 minute. Add chicken broth, vinegar, and honey. Bring to boiling; reduce heat. Simmer, uncovered, for 5 minutes. Stir in broccoli. Return to boiling; reduce heat. Cover and simmer for 8 to 10 minutes more or until broccoli is crisp-tender. Stir in pecans. Serve the broccoli mixture with the chicken.

Per serving: 272 cal., 10 g total fat (2 g sat. fat), 68 mg chol., 382 mg sodium, 25 g carbo., 3 g fiber, 22 g pro.

Many large supermarkets stock a variety of Asian foods, including red curry paste. If yours doesn't, visit an Asian food store.

COCONUT-CHICKEN CURRY

1½	pounds skinless, boneless chicken thighs, cut into bite-size pieces
¼	cup red curry paste
1	tablespoon olive oil
1	large onion, coarsely chopped
1¼	cups fresh coconut milk* or one 13½-ounce can unsweetened coconut milk
1½	cups purchased matchstick carrots or 3 medium carrots, thinly sliced
1	teaspoon finely shredded lime peel
	Hot cooked rice
	Snipped fresh cilantro

PREP: *35 minutes*

STAND: *30 minutes*

MAKES: *4 servings*

1 In a large bowl combine chicken and curry paste; let stand at room temperature for 30 minutes.

2 In a 12-inch skillet heat oil over medium heat. Add chicken mixture and onion. Cook for 8 to 10 minutes or until chicken is tender and no longer pink, stirring occasionally.

3 Remove chicken mixture from skillet. Carefully add coconut milk to skillet, scraping up any browned bits from the bottom of the skillet. Add carrots and lime peel. Bring to boiling; reduce heat. Simmer, uncovered, about 5 minutes or until carrots are crisp-tender. Return chicken mixture to skillet. Simmer, uncovered, for 3 to 5 minutes or until liquid thickens slightly. Serve with rice; sprinkle with snipped cilantro.

Per serving: 561 cal., 28 g total fat (18 g sat. fat), 136 mg chol., 433 mg sodium, 36 g carbo., 2 g fiber, 39 g pro.

*TEST KITCHEN TIP: To make fresh coconut milk, cut the tip from a young coconut. Pour out coconut liquid; scoop out coconut meat. In blender combine coconut liquid and coconut meat; cover and blend until nearly smooth. Add enough chicken broth to make 1¼ cups.

Meaty chicken thighs, rice-shape orzo pasta, lemon, and kalamata olives make a delectable combination.

KALAMATA LEMON CHICKEN

PREP: *15 minutes*

BAKE: *35 minutes*

MAKES: *4 servings*

1	tablespoon olive oil
1	to 1¼ pounds skinless, boneless chicken thighs
⅔	cup dried orzo pasta (rosamarina)
½	cup pitted kalamata olives
1	14-ounce can chicken broth
½	of a lemon, cut into wedges or chunks
1	tablespoon lemon juice
1	teaspoon dried Greek seasoning
¼	teaspoon salt
¼	teaspoon freshly ground black pepper
	Hot chicken broth (optional)
	Snipped fresh oregano (optional)

1 Preheat oven to 400°F. In a 4-quart Dutch oven heat oil over medium-high heat. Add chicken; cook for 5 minutes, turning once. Stir in uncooked orzo, olives, the can of chicken broth, the lemon wedges, lemon juice, Greek seasoning, salt, and pepper.

2 Bake, covered, about 35 minutes or until chicken is tender and no longer pink (180°F). Serve in shallow bowls; if desired, pour additional chicken broth over individual servings and top with snipped oregano.

Per serving: 309 cal., 11 g total fat (2 g sat. fat), 91 mg chol., 837 mg sodium, 24 g carbo., 2 g fiber, 27 g pro.

Chopped walnuts and fresh sage turn purchased pesto into an enchanting accent for roasted turkey.

SAGE PESTO TURKEY BREAST

Nonstick cooking spray

2　3- to 3½-pound bone-in turkey breast halves

2　7-ounce containers refrigerated basil pesto or one 10-ounce jar pesto

⅓　cup finely snipped fresh sage

¼　cup finely chopped walnuts

½　teaspoon salt

½　teaspoon freshly ground black pepper

PREP: *25 minutes*

ROAST: *1 hour 35 minutes*

STAND: *10 minutes*

MAKES: *10 to 12 servings*

1 Preheat oven to 400°F. Coat a large shallow roasting pan and rack with nonstick cooking spray. Place turkey breast halves, bone sides down, on rack in prepared pan. Set aside.

2 In a medium bowl combine pesto, sage, walnuts, salt, and pepper; mix well. Reserve half of the pesto mixture to pass with the turkey; cover and chill until serving time.

3 Starting at the breast bone of each turkey breast half, slip your fingers between skin and meat to loosen skin, leaving skin attached at top. Rub about two-thirds of the remaining pesto mixture under the skin over the breast meat. Rub remaining pesto mixture over the skin of the breast halves.

4 Insert an oven-going meat thermometer into the thickest part of the turkey breast halves (the thermometer should not touch bone). Roast for 20 minutes. Reduce oven temperature to 350°F. Roast for 1¼ to 1½ hours more or until thermometer registers 170°F, juices run clear, and turkey is no longer pink. If necessary to prevent overbrowning, cover with foil for the last 30 to 45 minutes of roasting.

5 Remove turkey from oven. Let stand, covered with foil, for 10 minutes before carving. Serve with reserved pesto mixture.

Per serving: 519 cal., 27 g total fat (2 g sat. fat), 171 mg chol., 419 mg sodium, 6 g carbo., 0 g fiber, 61 g pro.

This fabulous turkey breast couldn't be more satisfying—the alluring spices rubbed under the skin create an amazing barbecue-inspired flavor.

BBQ SPICE-RUBBED TURKEY BREAST

PREP: *30 minutes*

ROAST: *1 hour 20 minutes*

STAND: *10 minutes*

MAKES: *10 to 12 servings*

Nonstick cooking spray

2　3- to 3½-pound bone-in turkey breast halves

2　tablespoons packed dark brown sugar

2　teaspoons paprika

2　teaspoons garlic powder

1½　teaspoons salt

1　teaspoon ground cumin

1　teaspoon chili powder

¾　teaspoon freshly ground black pepper

1　recipe Cranberry Barbecue Sauce

1 Preheat oven to 400°F. Coat a large shallow roasting pan and rack with nonstick cooking spray. Place turkey breast halves, bone sides down, on roasting rack in prepared pan. In small bowl combine brown sugar, paprika, garlic powder, salt, cumin, chili powder, and pepper.

2 Starting at breast bone of each turkey breast half, slip fingers between skin and meat to loosen skin, leaving skin attached at top. Lift skin and spread spice mixture evenly under skin over breast meat. Insert an oven-going meat thermometer into the thickest part of the turkey breast halves (the thermometer should not touch bone).

3 Roast on lower rack of oven for 20 minutes. Reduce oven temperature to 350°F. Roast for 1 to 1½ hours more or until meat thermometer registers 170°F, juices run clear, and turkey is no longer pink; occasionally spoon pan juices over turkey.

4 Remove turkey from oven. Cover with foil; let stand for 10 minutes before carving. Serve with Cranberry Barbecue Sauce.

CRANBERRY BARBECUE SAUCE: In saucepan heat 1 tablespoon cooking oil over medium heat. Add 1 cup chopped onion; cook and stir about 5 minutes or until tender. Add one 16-ounce can whole cranberry sauce, ⅓ cup bottled chili sauce, 1 tablespoon cider vinegar, 1 teaspoon Worcestershire sauce, and ¼ teaspoon black pepper. Bring to boiling; reduce heat. Simmer about 5 minutes or until thickened, stirring often.

Per serving: 406 cal., 7 g total fat (2 g sat. fat), 167 mg chol., 724 mg sodium, 25 g carbo., 1 g fiber, 57 g pro.

TEST KITCHEN TIP: To simplify, you can rub the spice mixture onto the outside of each turkey breast for a crusty spice appearance. Place foil over turkey breasts for the last 30 minutes of roasting to prevent burning.

DINNERTIME DELIGHTS

**EGG-
BATTERED
FRIED
CHICKEN**

(Recipe on page 222)

**CHICKEN &
DUMPLINGS**

(Recipe on page 237)

DINNERTIME DELIGHTS

APRICOT-CHICKEN ROLL-UPS

(Recipe on page 243)

COQ AU VIN ROSETTES

(Recipe on page 256)

CHICKEN THIGHS & ORZO
(Recipe on page 267)

DINNERTIME DELIGHTS

TURKEY-ASPARAGUS BAKE

(Recipe on page 294)

DINNERTIME DELIGHTS

CHICKEN-TOFU STIR-FRY

(Recipe on page 300)

MOCK CHICKEN POT PIE

(Recipe on page 301)

PIZZAS & SANDWICHES

**MOP
SAUCE
PIZZA**

(Recipe on page 312)

ITALIAN TURKEY SANDWICHES

(Recipe on page 316)

PIZZAS & SANDWICHES

PULLED CHICKEN SANDWICHES

(Recipe on page 317)

WRAP 'N' ROLL CHICKEN

(Recipe on page 319)

TURKEY ON LEAF-CUTOUT BISCUITS

(Recipe on page 328)

HOT OFF THE GRILL

TANDOORI-SPICED CHICKEN

(Recipe on page 342)

DOUBLE CHERRY-CHICKEN ROLL-UPS

(Recipe on page 346)

HOT OFF THE GRILL

GLAZED CHICKEN WITH WILTED SPINACH
(Recipe on page 355)

CHICKEN FAJITAS

(Recipe on page 357)

CHIPOTLE PEACH-GLAZED CHICKEN

(Recipe on page 367)

HOT OFF THE GRILL

**SOUTHWEST
CHICKEN
BURGERS**

(Recipe on page 380)

THE WHOLE BIRD

CHICKEN WITH ROSEMARY & GARLIC POTATOES
(Recipe on page 384)

THE WHOLE BIRD

ROASTED HERBED TURKEY

(Recipe on page 395)

The tangy citrus and cilantro mixture serves as both a marinade and a sauce, infusing the turkey with mouthwatering flavor.

CITRUS TURKEY WITH CILANTRO SAUCE

2	3- to 3½-pound bone-in turkey breast halves
2	cups lightly packed fresh cilantro leaves
1⅓	cups orange juice
½	cup lemon juice
12	cloves garlic, halved
1	fresh jalapeño chile pepper, seeded and cut up (see tip, page 19)
2	teaspoons salt
2	teaspoons ground cumin
½	teaspoon freshly ground black pepper
1½	cups olive oil
	Nonstick cooking spray

PREP: *30 minutes*

MARINATE: *8 to 24 hours*

ROAST: *1 hour 20 minutes*

STAND: *10 minutes*

MAKES: *10 to 12 servings*

1 Using the tip of a sharp knife, prick turkey breast halves in several spots. Place turkey breast halves, skin sides down, in a very large resealable plastic bag set in a baking dish. Set aside.

2 For cilantro sauce, in a food processor or blender combine cilantro, orange juice, lemon juice, garlic, chile pepper, salt, cumin, and black pepper. Cover and process until almost smooth. With processor or blender running, slowly add oil in thin stream. Pour 2 cups of the cilantro sauce into a covered container; refrigerate until serving time. Pour remaining cilantro sauce over turkey breast halves. Seal bag; turn to coat turkey. Marinate in refrigerator for 8 to 24 hours, turning bag occasionally.

3 Preheat oven to 400°F. Coat shallow roasting pan and roasting rack with nonstick cooking spray. Remove turkey from marinade; discard marinade. Place turkey, bone sides down, on rack in prepared roasting pan. Insert an oven-going meat thermometer into the thickest part of the turkey breast halves (the thermometer should not touch bone). Roast for 20 minutes. Reduce oven temperature to 350°F. Roast turkey 1 to 1½ hours more or until thermometer registers 170°F, juices run clear, and turkey is no longer pink. If necessary to prevent overbrowning, cover with foil for the last 30 to 45 minutes of roasting.

4 Remove turkey from oven. Cover with foil; let stand for 10 minutes before carving. Stir reserved cilantro sauce; pass with turkey.

Per serving: 578 cal., 35 g total fat (5 g sat. fat), 167 mg chol., 504 mg sodium, 6 g carbo., 1 g fiber, 58 g pro.

The delectable glaze mixes apricot spreadable fruit with brown mustard and roasted garlic. It's equally delicious on roasted chicken or Cornish game hen.

MUSTARD & GARLIC ROASTED TURKEY BREAST

PREP: *15 minutes*

ROAST: *1¼ hours*

STAND: *10 minutes*

MAKES: *4 to 6 servings*

1	2-pound bone-in turkey breast portion
2	tablespoons butter, melted
¼	teaspoon salt
¼	teaspoon black pepper
¼	cup apricot or peach spreadable fruit
2	tablespoons coarse-grain brown mustard
1½	teaspoons bottled roasted minced garlic

1 Preheat oven to 325°F. Place turkey breast, bone side down, on a rack in a shallow roasting pan. Brush with 1 tablespoon of the melted butter; sprinkle with salt and pepper. Insert an oven-going meat thermometer into the thickest part of the turkey breast portion (the thermometer should not touch bone).

2 For glaze, in a small bowl combine the remaining 1 tablespoon melted butter, the spreadable fruit, mustard, and garlic; set glaze aside.

3 Roast turkey for 1¼ to 1½ hours or until thermometer registers 170°F, juices run clear, and turkey is no longer pink; brush with glaze several times during the last 15 minutes of roasting. Transfer turkey to a cutting board; let stand for 10 to 15 minutes before carving.

Per serving: 235 cal., 8 g total fat (3 g sat. fat), 104 mg chol., 254 mg sodium, 9 g carbo., 0 g fiber, 32 g pro.

The pleasing maple-and-mustard sauce is the perfect counterpoint for the peppery roasted turkey.

PEPPERED MAPLE TURKEY BREAST

3 tablespoons cracked black peppercorns
1 tablespoon kosher salt
2 2- to 2½-pound boneless, skinless turkey breast halves
1 cup pure maple syrup
4½ teaspoons Dijon-style mustard
¼ cup butter, cut up

1 Preheat oven to 325°F. In a small bowl combine peppercorns and kosher salt. Sprinkle peppercorn mixture on all sides of turkey breast halves; rub in with your fingers. Place turkey on a rack in a roasting pan. Roast for 45 minutes.

2 Meanwhile, in a small saucepan combine maple syrup and mustard; heat just until boiling. Brush some of the syrup mixture over turkey; dot with half of the butter. Roast for 30 minutes more. Brush with more of the syrup mixture; dot with the remaining butter. Roast for 20 to 30 minutes more or until an instant-read thermometer inserted in the center registers 170°F, juices run clear, and turkey is no longer pink.

3 Remove turkey from oven. Cover with foil; let stand for 10 minutes before carving. Reheat the remaining syrup mixture until boiling; serve over sliced turkey.

Per serving: 514 cal., 21 g total fat (8 g sat. fat), 161 mg chol., 937 mg sodium, 28 g carbo., 1 g fiber, 49 g pro.

PREP: *15 minutes*
ROAST: *1 hour 35 minutes*
STAND: *10 minutes*
MAKES: *8 to 10 servings*

It's the mustard sauce that sets this dish apart from the rest—a sour cream base is revved up with white wine, tarragon, and (what else?) Dijon-style mustard.

TURKEY WITH MUSTARD SAUCE

START TO FINISH:
45 minutes

MAKES: *4 servings*

2	turkey breast tenderloins or 4 skinless, boneless chicken breast halves (about 1 pound total)
1	tablespoon olive oil or cooking oil
½	cup sliced leeks or shallots
½	cup dry white wine
½	cup reduced-sodium chicken broth
1	teaspoon snipped fresh tarragon or ¼ teaspoon dried tarragon, crushed
	Dash black pepper
1	pound fresh asparagus spears
¼	cup dairy sour cream
2	tablespoons Dijon-style mustard

1 If using turkey breast tenderloins, split each tenderloin in half horizontally to make four ½-inch-thick portions. In a large nonstick skillet heat oil over medium heat. Add turkey or chicken and leeks or shallots; cook about 5 minutes or until turkey is brown, turning once. Stir in wine, chicken broth, dried tarragon (if using), and pepper. Bring to boiling; reduce heat. Cover and simmer about 5 minutes or until turkey is tender and no longer pink (170°F).

2 Meanwhile, wash asparagus and break off woody bases where spears break easily. In a covered large saucepan cook asparagus in a small amount of boiling water for 3 to 5 minutes or until crisp-tender. Drain well.

3 Transfer turkey to a serving platter, reserving liquid in skillet; cover turkey and keep warm. Bring liquid in skillet to boiling. Continue boiling about 5 minutes or until wine mixture is reduced to ½ cup.

4 For sauce, in a small bowl stir together sour cream and mustard; stir in hot wine mixture. Return to skillet. Heat through, but do not boil. Stir in fresh tarragon (if using). Arrange cooked asparagus alongside turkey; spoon sauce over the turkey and asparagus.

Per serving: 237 cal., 8 g total fat (3 g sat. fat), 73 mg chol., 315 mg sodium, 6 g carbo., 1 g fiber, 29 g pro.

There are two varieties of sweet potatoes—moist and dry. The dry type has cream-colored to yellow meat and is less sweet than the moist version, which has bright orange meat. Either will work in this tempting turkey dish.

TURKEY NUGGETS & SWEET POTATOES

3   tablespoons olive oil

2   teaspoons snipped fresh rosemary

2   medium sweet potatoes, peeled and cut into 1-inch pieces (3 cups)

12 ounces turkey breast tenderloin, cut into 1-inch pieces

⅓   cup finely crushed stone-ground wheat crackers (8 to 10)

PREP: *20 minutes*

BAKE: *20 minutes*

MAKES: *4 servings*

1 Preheat oven to 400°F. In a medium bowl combine oil and rosemary. Toss sweet potatoes in oil mixture; transfer potatoes to a 15×10×1-inch baking pan, reserving oil mixture in bowl. Toss turkey with the reserved oil mixture. Add crushed crackers to turkey and toss to coat. Add turkey to sweet potatoes in pan. Arrange in a single layer.

2 Bake about 20 minutes or until turkey and sweet potatoes are tender and turkey is no longer pink.

Per serving: 327 cal., 13 g total fat (2 g sat. fat), 51 mg chol., 102 mg sodium, 30 g carbo., 4 g fiber, 22 g pro.

Remember this company-pleasing entrée the next time you're hosting a weekend brunch.
Add a fruit compote and your favorite muffins for a no-fuss menu. (Recipe pictured on page 277.)

TURKEY-ASPARAGUS BAKE

PREP: *25 minutes*

BAKE: *23 minutes*

MAKES: *6 servings*

1 pound fresh asparagus or one 10-ounce package frozen cut asparagus or cut broccoli

1 pound uncooked ground turkey or chicken

1 cup chopped onion

½ cup chopped red sweet pepper

3 eggs

2 cups milk

1 cup all-purpose flour

¼ cup grated Parmesan cheese

1 teaspoon lemon-pepper seasoning

½ teaspoon dried tarragon, basil, or thyme, crushed

1 cup shredded Swiss cheese (4 ounces)

1 Preheat oven to 425°F. To cook fresh asparagus, wash and scrape off scales. Break off and discard woody bases of asparagus. Cut asparagus into 1½-inch-long pieces. In a covered saucepan cook asparagus in a small amount of boiling water for 4 to 8 minutes or until crisp-tender; drain. (For frozen asparagus or broccoli, cook according to package directions; drain.) Set aside.

2 In a large skillet cook turkey, onion, and sweet pepper just until turkey is done and vegetables are tender. Remove from heat; drain. Arrange turkey mixture in a greased 3-quart rectangular baking dish; top with cooked asparagus.

3 In a large bowl combine eggs, milk, flour, Parmesan cheese, lemon-pepper seasoning, and tarragon; beat with a wire whisk or rotary beater until smooth. (Or combine these ingredients in a blender container; cover and blend for 20 seconds.) Pour egg mixture evenly over the layers in baking dish.

4 Bake about 20 minutes or until a knife inserted near the center comes out clean. Sprinkle with the Swiss cheese; bake for 3 to 5 minutes more or until the cheese is melted.

Per serving: 355 cal., 17 g total fat (8 g sat. fat), 161 mg chol., 417 mg sodium, 24 g carbo., 2 g fiber, 26 g pro.

Old-time cooks roasted the chicken, stirred together the soup base, and made dumpling batter from scratch. You can use a deli-roasted chicken, condensed soup, and refrigerated corn bread twists.

EASY CHICKEN & DUMPLINGS

1	2- to 2½-pound purchased roasted chicken
1	16-ounce package frozen mixed vegetables
1¼	cups reduced-sodium chicken broth or water
1	10¾-ounce can condensed cream of chicken soup
⅛	teaspoon black pepper
1	11.5-ounce package refrigerated corn bread twists

PREP: *25 minutes*
COOK: *15 minutes*
MAKES: *4 to 6 servings*

1 Remove string from chicken, if present. Remove and discard skin from chicken. Remove meat from bones, discarding bones. Chop or shred chicken (you should have 3½ to 4 cups chopped chicken). In a large saucepan stir together chicken, frozen vegetables, chicken broth, cream of chicken soup, and pepper. Bring to boiling; reduce heat. Cover and simmer about 15 minutes or until vegetables are tender.

2 Meanwhile, remove the corn bread twists from package; cut along perforations. Lay twists on a baking sheet; roll two twists together to make a spiral. Repeat with remaining twists. Bake according to package directions.

3 To serve, spoon chicken mixture into bowls and serve with corn bread spirals.

Per serving: 683 cal., 32 g total fat (9 g sat. fat), 106 mg chol., 1,553 mg sodium, 56 g carbo., 5 g fiber, 44 g pro.

All it takes are four simple ingredients to dress up a store-bought roasted chicken for a Mexican fiesta. Serve guacamole and Spanish rice on the side.

MEXICAN CHICKEN CASSEROLE

PREP: *15 minutes*

BAKE: *15 minutes*

MAKES: *4 servings*

1   15-ounce can black beans, rinsed and drained

½   cup purchased chunky salsa

½   teaspoon ground cumin

1   2- to 2¼-pound purchased roasted chicken

¼   cup shredded Monterey Jack cheese with jalapeño chile peppers (1 ounce)

Dairy sour cream (optional)

1 Preheat oven to 350°F. In a small bowl stir together beans, ¼ cup of the salsa, and the cumin. Divide bean mixture among four au gratin dishes or casseroles. Set aside.

2 Cut chicken into quarters. Place one chicken quarter on top of the bean mixture in each dish or casserole. Spoon the remaining ¼ cup salsa evenly over chicken. Sprinkle with cheese. Bake for 15 to 20 minutes or until heated through. If desired, top with sour cream.

Per serving: 468 cal., 23 g total fat (7 g sat. fat), 140 mg chol., 596 mg sodium, 16 g carbo., 5 g fiber, 50 g pro.

Tradition has it that shepherd's pie was the frugal cook's way to use up leftovers from Sunday's dinner. You won't need leftovers for this version. It takes advantage of frozen mashed potatoes and roasted chicken from your supermarket's deli.

CHUCKWAGON SHEPHERD'S PIE

2¼	cups milk
1	22-ounce package frozen mashed potatoes
¼	cup snipped fresh parsley
½	teaspoon salt
1	2- to 2½-pound purchased roasted chicken
1	28-ounce can baked beans
1	11-ounce can whole kernel corn with sweet peppers, drained
½	cup purchased salsa

PREP: *25 minutes*
BAKE: *30 minutes*
MAKES: *6 servings*

1 Preheat oven to 350°F. In a large saucepan heat milk to a simmer over medium heat. Stir in frozen mashed potatoes. Cook over medium-low heat for 5 to 8 minutes or until heated through and smooth, stirring often. Stir in 2 tablespoons of the parsley and the salt; set aside.

2 Remove string from chicken, if present. Remove and discard skin from chicken. Remove meat from bones, discarding bones. Using two forks, shred chicken. In a large bowl stir together chicken, the remaining 2 tablespoons parsley, the beans, corn, and salsa. Spoon into a 3-quart rectangular baking dish. Spoon potatoes over chicken mixture and spread evenly.

3 Bake for 30 to 35 minutes or until heated through.

Per serving: 645 cal., 22 g total fat (7 g sat. fat), 106 mg chol., 1,200 mg sodium, 70 g carbo., 11 g fiber, 42 g pro.

To add extra heat, choose serrano chile peppers—they provide more kick than jalapeño peppers.

CHICKEN & ORZO CASSEROLE

PREP: *15 minutes*

BAKE: *20 minutes*

STAND: *10 minutes*

MAKES: *4 to 6 servings*

2   teaspoons cumin seeds

1   14-ounce can chicken broth

1   14½-ounce can Mexican-style stewed tomatoes or one 10-ounce can diced tomatoes and green chile peppers

¼   cup oil-packed dried tomatoes, cut up

1   cup dried orzo pasta (rosamarina)

2   9-ounce packages Southwest-flavored frozen cooked chicken breast strips, thawed, or two 6-ounce packages refrigerated Southwest-flavored cooked chicken breast strips

Smoked paprika (optional)

Seeded and chopped fresh jalapeño or serrano chile peppers (see tip, page 19) (optional)

1 Preheat oven to 350°F. In a large saucepan heat cumin seeds over medium heat for 3 to 4 minutes or until seeds are toasted and aromatic, shaking pan occasionally. Carefully stir in chicken broth, undrained stewed or diced tomatoes, dried tomatoes, and uncooked orzo. Bring to boiling. Transfer mixture to a 2-quart baking dish. Top with chicken breast strips.

2 Cover with foil. Bake about 20 minutes or until orzo is tender. Let stand, covered, for 10 minutes before serving. If desired, sprinkle with smoked paprika and top with chopped chile pepper.

Per serving: 388 cal., 7 g total fat (2 g sat. fat), 60 mg chol., 1,227 mg sodium, 44 g carbo., 3 g fiber, 35 g pro.

To save a step, omit heating the sauce and add 10 minutes to the baking time.

LEMON CHICKEN LASAGNA

Nonstick cooking spray

1   16-ounce jar roasted garlic Alfredo pasta sauce

1   tablespoon capers, drained

6   no-boil lasagna noodles

½   of a 15-ounce carton ricotta cheese

6   ounces fontina cheese or mozzarella, shredded (1½ cups)

1½   teaspoons finely shredded lemon peel

¼   cup finely shredded Parmesan cheese (1 ounce)

1   9-ounce package refrigerated or thawed frozen cooked chicken breast strips

PREP: *25 minutes*
BAKE: *40 minutes*
STAND: *20 minutes*
MAKES: *6 servings*

1 Preheat oven to 350°F. Lightly coat a 2-quart square baking dish with nonstick cooking spray; set aside. In a saucepan combine Alfredo sauce and capers. Bring to boiling over medium heat, stirring occasionally.

2 Spoon ⅓ cup of the sauce mixture into the prepared dish. Top with two of the uncooked lasagna noodles. In a medium bowl stir together ricotta cheese, 1 cup of the fontina cheese, and 1 teaspoon of the lemon peel. Spoon half of the ricotta mixture over noodles. Sprinkle with 2 tablespoons of the Parmesan cheese. Top with half of the chicken. Spoon half of the remaining sauce over chicken layer.

3 Top with two more noodles, the remaining ricotta mixture, and the remaining chicken. Add the remaining two noodles and sauce; sprinkle with the remaining ½ cup fontina cheese and 2 tablespoons Parmesan cheese.

4 Cover with foil. Bake for 40 minutes. Let stand, covered, on a wire rack for 20 minutes before serving. Sprinkle with the remaining ½ teaspoon lemon peel.

Per serving: 529 cal., 34 g total fat (19 g sat. fat), 159 mg chol., 1,522 mg sodium, 20 g carbo., 0 g fiber, 35 g pro.

Create a unique dish every time you make this stir-fry by mixing and matching the vegetables. (Recipe pictured on page 278.)

CHICKEN-TOFU STIR-FRY

PREP: *40 minutes*

MARINATE: *1 to 4 hours*

MAKES: *6 servings*

2 tablespoons olive oil

2 tablespoons orange juice

1 tablespoon reduced-sodium soy sauce

1 tablespoon Worcestershire sauce

1 tablespoon grated fresh ginger or 1 teaspoon ground ginger

1 teaspoon dry mustard

1 teaspoon ground turmeric

8 ounces cooked chicken breast, cubed

8 ounces tub-style extra-firm tofu (fresh bean curd), drained and cubed

2 medium carrots, bias-sliced, or 2 stalks celery, thinly sliced

1 cup fresh pea pods and/or sliced fresh mushrooms

3 green onions, cut into ½-inch-long pieces

1 medium red or green sweet pepper, cut into thin bite-size strips

2 cups chopped baby bok choy and/or fresh bean sprouts

3 cups hot cooked brown rice or long grain rice

1 In a large bowl stir together 1 tablespoon of the oil, the orange juice, soy sauce, Worcestershire sauce, ginger, mustard, and turmeric. Add cooked chicken and tofu cubes; stir to coat. Cover and marinate in the refrigerator for 1 to 4 hours.

2 In a very large nonstick skillet heat the remaining 1 tablespoon oil over medium-high heat. Add carrots or celery; cook and stir for 2 minutes. Add pea pods and/or mushrooms; cook and stir for 2 minutes. Add green onions and sweet pepper; stir in bok choy and/or bean sprouts. Cook and stir for 2 minutes. Add undrained chicken mixture; heat through. Serve with hot cooked rice.

Per serving: 288 cal., 9 g total fat (2 g sat. fat), 32 mg chol., 195 mg sodium, 31 g carbo., 4 g fiber, 20 g pro.

By baking the pastry strips in the oven and cooking the creamy chicken filling in a saucepan, this mock chicken pot pie goes together quickly and easily. (Recipe pictured on page 278.)

MOCK CHICKEN POT PIE

½   of a 15-ounce package rolled refrigerated unbaked piecrust (1 crust)

1   10¾-ounce can condensed cream of onion soup

1⅓   cups milk

1   3-ounce package cream cheese, cut up

½   teaspoon dried sage, crushed

¼   teaspoon black pepper

1½   cups chopped cooked chicken (about 8 ounces)

1   10-ounce package frozen mixed vegetables

½   cup instant rice

PREP: *30 minutes*
BAKE: *6 minutes*
MAKES: *4 servings*

1 Preheat oven to 450°F. Let piecrust stand at room temperature as directed on package. Unroll piecrust. Using a pizza cutter or sharp knife, cut piecrust into strips ½ to 1 inch wide. Place piecrust strips on an ungreased baking sheet. Bake for 6 to 8 minutes or until golden brown.

2 Meanwhile, for filling, in a large saucepan combine cream of onion soup, milk, cream cheese, sage, and pepper. Cook and stir over medium-high heat until cream cheese melts. Stir in chicken, frozen vegetables, and uncooked rice. Bring to boiling; reduce heat. Cover and simmer about 10 minutes or until vegetables and rice are tender.

3 Transfer filling to a serving dish. Top with piecrust strips.

Per serving: 603 cal., 30 g total fat (14 g sat. fat), 93 mg chol., 933 mg sodium, 57 g carbo., 3 g fiber, 25 g pro.

From cupboard and refrigerator to oven is a 15-minute trip for this layered casserole. While it bakes, set the table and fix a salad or vegetable side dish.

QUICK CHICKEN TORTILLA BAKE

PREP: *15 minutes*

BAKE: *45 minutes*

MAKES: *8 servings*

2   10¾-ounce cans condensed cream of chicken soup

1   10-ounce can diced tomatoes and green chile peppers

12   6- or 7-inch corn tortillas, cut into thin bite-size strips

3   cups cubed cooked chicken or turkey (about 1 pound)

1   cup shredded Mexican blend cheese (4 ounces)

1 Preheat oven to 350°F. In a medium bowl combine cream of chicken soup and undrained tomatoes; set aside. Sprinkle one-third of the tortilla strips over the bottom of an ungreased 3-quart rectangular baking dish. Layer half of the chicken over tortilla strips; spoon half of the soup mixture on top. Repeat layers, ending with a layer of tortilla strips.

2 Bake, covered, about 40 minutes or until bubbly around edges and center is hot. Uncover; sprinkle with cheese. Bake about 5 minutes more or until cheese is melted.

Per serving: 325 cal., 14 g total fat (6 g sat. fat), 66 mg chol., 819 mg sodium, 26 g carbo., 4 g fiber, 23 g pro.

Comfort food is never so easy as this quick-to-fix pot pie. It gets a jump-start from purchased mashed potatoes, frozen vegetables, and cooked chicken.

SMASHED POTATO CHICKEN POT PIE

3	tablespoons butter or margarine
⅓	cup all-purpose flour
½	teaspoon seasoned pepper
¼	teaspoon salt
1	14-ounce can reduced-sodium chicken broth
¾	cup milk
2½	cups chopped cooked chicken or turkey (about 12 ounces)
2	cups loose-pack frozen peas and carrots, thawed
2	cups loose-pack frozen cut green beans, thawed
1	20-ounce package refrigerated mashed potatoes (about 2⅔ cups)
2	tablespoons grated Parmesan cheese
1	clove garlic, minced

PREP: *25 minutes*
BAKE: *30 minutes*
STAND: *5 minutes*
MAKES: *6 servings*

1 Preheat oven to 375°F. In a large saucepan melt butter over medium heat. Stir in flour, ¼ teaspoon of the seasoned pepper, and the salt. Add chicken broth and milk all at once. Cook and stir over medium heat until thickened and bubbly. Stir in cooked chicken and thawed vegetables. Pour into a 3-quart rectangular baking dish.

2 In a medium bowl combine mashed potatoes, cheese, garlic, and the remaining ¼ teaspoon seasoned pepper. Using a spoon, drop potato mixture in large mounds over chicken mixture in baking dish.

3 Bake for 30 to 40 minutes or until heated through. Let stand for 5 minutes before serving.

Per serving: 330 cal., 13 g total fat (6 g sat. fat), 72 mg chol., 616 mg sodium, 29 g carbo., 4 g fiber, 25 g pro.

These boat-shaped peppers are brimming with a luscious chicken, cheese, and cilantro filling and are topped with a fiery cumin-seasoned tomato sauce.

CHICKEN CHILE RELLENOS

PREP: *45 minutes*

BAKE: *22 minutes*

MAKES: *6 servings*

6	fresh poblano chile peppers (3 to 4 ounces each) (see tip, page 19)
2	cups shredded or chopped cooked chicken (10 ounces)
1	cup shredded Monterey Jack cheese (4 ounces)
½	cup loose-pack frozen corn, thawed
½	of an 8-ounce tub cream cheese with chives
2	tablespoons snipped fresh cilantro
1	tablespoon olive oil
1	cup thinly sliced sweet onion (such as Vidalia, Walla Walla, or Maui)
3	cloves garlic, thinly sliced
1	15-ounce can tomato sauce
1½	teaspoons ground cumin
½	teaspoon ground coriander
¼	teaspoon salt
¼	teaspoon cayenne pepper
2	tablespoons snipped fresh cilantro

1 Preheat oven to 350°F. Lay each chile pepper on its side and cut a lengthwise slice from one side, leaving the stem intact on the pepper. (The pepper will now be boat shaped.) Chop each slice of pepper which was just removed; set aside. Remove seeds and membranes from chile peppers. In a large saucepan cook chile peppers, half at a time, in boiling water for 2 minutes. Drain well; set aside.

2 For filling, in a medium bowl combine chicken, ½ cup of the shredded cheese, the corn, cream cheese, and 2 tablespoons cilantro. Spoon filling into chile peppers and place in a greased 3-quart rectangular baking dish.

3 For sauce, in a large skillet heat oil over medium-low heat. Add the reserved chopped chile pepper, the onion, and garlic; cook about 5 minutes or until tender, stirring occasionally. Stir in tomato sauce, cumin, coriander, salt, and cayenne pepper. Cook and stir until bubbly. Spoon sauce over stuffed peppers in baking dish.

4 Bake, covered, for 20 to 25 minutes or until heated through. Sprinkle with the remaining ½ cup shredded cheese. Bake, uncovered, about 2 minutes more or until cheese is melted. Sprinkle with 2 tablespoons cilantro.

Per serving: 329 cal., 18 g total fat (8 g sat. fat), 78 mg chol., 658 mg sodium, 20 g carbo., 2 g fiber, 23 g pro.

Take your choice of sage, marjoram, or thyme to season these savory pies—each one creates a deliciously unique flavor.

CHICKEN ALFREDO POT PIES

½	of a 15-ounce package rolled refrigerated unbaked piecrust (1 crust)
3	cups frozen mixed vegetable blend (any combination)
3	cups cubed cooked chicken or turkey (about 1 pound)
1	10-ounce container refrigerated Alfredo pasta sauce
½	teaspoon dried sage, marjoram, or thyme, crushed

PREP: *25 minutes*
BAKE: *12 minutes*
MAKES: *4 servings*

1 Preheat oven to 450°F. Let piecrust stand at room temperature as directed on package. In a large skillet cook the vegetables in a small amount of boiling water for 5 minutes; drain. Return to skillet. Stir in chicken, Alfredo sauce, and sage. Cook and stir until bubbly. Divide mixture among four 10-ounce casseroles or custard cups.

2 On a lightly floured surface, roll piecrust into a 13-inch round. Cut four 5-inch circles from piecrust round; place on top of the casseroles. Press edges of pastry firmly against sides of casseroles. Cut slits in the tops for steam to escape. Place casseroles in a foil-lined shallow baking pan. Bake for 12 to 15 minutes or until pastry is golden brown.

Per serving: 709 cal., 41 g total fat (19 g sat. fat), 143 mg chol., 596 mg sodium, 45 g carbo., 4 g fiber, 38 g pro.

Stash some cooked chicken or turkey in the freezer—in 1½-cup portions—so you'll have the meat on hand for this lively bake. You can freeze cooked poultry for up to 4 months.

TEX-MEX CHICKEN BAKE

PREP: *25 minutes*

BAKE: *35 minutes*

MAKES: *4 to 6 servings*

1½	cups chopped cooked chicken or turkey (about 8 ounces)
1	10¾-ounce can condensed cream of chicken or cream of mushroom soup
½	cup dairy sour cream
1	4-ounce can diced green chile peppers
1	2¼-ounce can sliced pitted ripe olives
2	green onions, sliced
1½	cups coarsely crushed tortilla chips or corn chips
1½	cups shredded Monterey Jack cheese with jalapeño chile peppers or Monterey Jack cheese (6 ounces)
1	cup chopped tomatoes

1 Preheat oven to 375°F. In a large bowl combine chicken or turkey, cream of chicken or mushroom soup, sour cream, undrained chile peppers, undrained olives, and green onions.

2 Sprinkle one-third of the chips over the bottom of a greased 2-quart square baking dish. Spoon half of the chicken or turkey mixture over chips. Top with half of the cheese. Repeat layers, ending with a layer of chips.

3 Bake about 35 minutes or until heated through. Sprinkle with tomato just before serving.

Per serving: 455 cal., 30 g total fat (14 g sat. fat), 101 mg chol., 1,088 mg sodium, 17 g carbo., 2 g fiber, 30 g pro.

Two cheeses, rice mix, and cream of chicken soup transform leftover chicken into a rich oven meal.

CHICKEN-WILD RICE BAKE

1	6-ounce package long grain and wild rice mix
1	tablespoon butter or margarine
1	large onion, chopped
3	cloves garlic, minced
1	10¾-ounce can condensed cream of chicken soup
1	cup milk
1½	teaspoons dried basil, crushed
2	cups shredded Swiss cheese (8 ounces)
3	cups chopped cooked chicken or turkey (about 1 pound)
1	4-ounce can (drained weight) sliced mushrooms, drained
½	cup shredded Parmesan cheese (2 ounces)
⅓	cup sliced almonds, toasted

PREP: *35 minutes*
BAKE: *15 minutes*
MAKES: *6 servings*

1 Preheat oven to 350°F. Prepare long grain and wild rice mix according to package directions, except discard the seasoning packet. Set aside.

2 In a 12-inch skillet melt butter over medium heat. Add onion and garlic; cook until onion is tender. Stir in cream of chicken soup, milk, and basil; heat through. Slowly add Swiss cheese, stirring until cheese is melted. Stir in cooked long grain and wild rice, the turkey, and mushrooms.

3 Transfer to a 3-quart rectangular baking dish. Sprinkle with Parmesan cheese. Bake for 15 to 20 minutes or until heated through. Sprinkle with almonds before serving.

Per serving: 565 cal., 28 g total fat (13 g sat. fat), 120 mg chol., 1,128 mg sodium, 36 g carbo., 3 g fiber, 42 g pro.

The original version of this famous casserole calls for making a rich mushroom-studded cream sauce. The canned soup in this version trims the preparation time.

QUICK TURKEY TETRAZZINI

PREP: *20 minutes*

BAKE: *12 minutes*

MAKES: *4 servings*

Nonstick cooking spray

6 ounces dried spaghetti

1 19-ounce can ready-to-serve chunky creamy chicken with mushroom soup

6 ounces cooked turkey breast or chicken breast, chopped (about 1 cup)

½ cup finely shredded Parmesan cheese (2 ounces)

2 tablespoons sliced almonds

1 Lightly coat a 2-quart square baking dish with nonstick cooking spray; set aside. Cook spaghetti according to package directions. Drain; return to hot pan. Add creamy chicken with mushroom soup, turkey, and half of the cheese to hot spaghetti, stirring until combined. Heat through.

2 Preheat oven to 425°F. Transfer spaghetti mixture to prepared baking dish. Sprinkle with almonds and the remaining cheese. Bake for 12 to 15 minutes or until top is golden brown.

Per serving: 413 cal., 13 g total fat (5 g sat. fat), 59 mg chol., 752 mg sodium, 43 g carbo., 2 g fiber, 28 g pro.

PIZZAS & SANDWICHES

7

Serving a top-notch meal is
easy with these dynamite
pizzas, sandwiches, and wraps.

This pizza with a Mexican twist features picante sauce—that's Spanish for spicy! A short list of the ingredients includes chicken, sweet pepper, red onion, and cheese.

SPICY CHICKEN PIZZA

PREP: *25 minutes*

BAKE: *13 minutes*

MAKES: *6 servings*

2   teaspoons cooking oil

12   ounces skinless, boneless chicken breasts, cut into thin strips

1   medium red sweet pepper, cut into thin strips

½   of a medium red onion, thinly sliced
     Nonstick cooking spray

1   13.8-ounce package refrigerated pizza dough

½   cup bottled mild picante sauce

½   cup shredded sharp cheddar cheese (2 ounces)

1 Preheat oven to 400°F. In a large nonstick skillet heat oil over medium-high heat. Add chicken; cook about 5 minutes or until no longer pink. Remove from skillet. Add sweet pepper and red onion to skillet; cook about 5 minutes or until tender. Remove from skillet; set aside.

2 Coat a 15×10×1-inch baking pan with nonstick cooking spray. Unroll pizza dough into pan; press with fingers to form a 12×8-inch rectangle. Pinch edges of dough to form crust.

3 Spread crust with picante sauce. Top with chicken and vegetables; sprinkle with cheddar cheese. Bake for 13 to 18 minutes or until crust is brown and cheese is melted.

Per serving: 305 cal., 9 g total fat (3 g sat. fat), 43 mg chol., 527 mg sodium, 34 g carbo., 2 g fiber, 21 g pro.

If you'd rather use leftover cooked chicken instead of the refrigerated cooked chicken breast strips, simply cut the cooked chicken into strips and sprinkle with dried Italian seasoning.

MUSHROOM-TOMATO PESTO PIZZA

1	12-inch Italian bread shell (such as Boboli brand)
½	cup purchased dried tomato pesto
1	cup shredded 4-cheese pizza blend (4 ounces)
1	6-ounce package refrigerated Italian-seasoned cooked chicken breast strips
1½	cups sliced fresh mushrooms (such as shiitake, cremini, and/or button)

PREP: *15 minutes*

BAKE: *10 minutes*

MAKES: *4 servings*

1 Preheat oven to 400°F. Place the bread shell on a 12-inch pizza pan. Spread pesto over bread shell. Sprinkle with half of the cheese. Top with chicken and mushrooms. Sprinkle with the remaining cheese.

2 Bake for 10 to 15 minutes or until pizza is heated through and cheese is melted.

Per serving: 585 cal., 24 g total fat (8 g sat. fat), 55 mg chol., 1,382 mg sodium, 64 g carbo., 4 g fiber, 33 g pro.

Another time use the Mop Sauce (without tomatoes) as a basting sauce for grilled chicken. Follow the sauce recipe up to the addition of the tomatoes and tomato paste. (Recipe pictured on page 279.)

MOP SAUCE PIZZA

PREP: *50 minutes*

BAKE: *15 minutes*

MAKES: *6 servings*

1　recipe Mop Sauce

1　2- to 2¼-pound purchased roasted chicken

1　12-inch prebaked pizza crust or Italian bread shell (such as Boboli brand)

¼　cup chopped green sweet pepper

4　ounces smoked provolone cheese, shredded (1 cup)

4　slices pepper bacon or regular bacon, cooked, drained, and crumbled

1 Prepare Mop Sauce. Meanwhile, remove string from chicken, if present. Remove skin from chicken and discard. Remove meat from bones; discard bones. Use two forks to pull chicken into small pieces (you should have 3 to 4 cups). Set 2 cups of the meat aside (save remaining meat for another use).

2 Preheat oven to 450°F. Place bread shell or pizza crust on a large greased baking sheet. Bake for 5 minutes. Remove from oven. Spread Mop Sauce over bread shell or crust to within ½ to 1 inch of the edge. Sprinkle with the 2 cups chicken and the sweet pepper. Sprinkle with cheese and bacon. Bake for 10 to 12 minutes more or until the cheese is melted and bubbly. Serve immediately.

MOP SAUCE: In a small saucepan stir together 1 cup apple juice or apple cider; 1 cup cider vinegar; 1 teaspoon packed brown sugar; 1 clove garlic, minced; ½ to 1 teaspoon bottled hot pepper sauce; ½ teaspoon dry mustard; ½ teaspoon paprika; and ½ teaspoon ground cumin. Bring to boiling; reduce heat. Boil gently, uncovered, about 30 minutes or until mixture is reduced to 1 cup. Add 2 tomatoes, seeded and chopped, and half of a 6-ounce can (⅓ cup) tomato paste; stir to combine. Return to boiling; reduce heat. Boil gently, uncovered, about 10 minutes more or until slightly thickened, stirring occasionally. Use immediately or cool, cover, and store in the refrigerator for up to 1 week.

Per serving: 433 cal., 15 g total fat (5 g sat. fat), 64 mg chol., 806 mg sodium, 47 g carbo., 1 g fiber, 30 g pro.

This is a fun new way to enjoy leftover turkey. It's super easy because it calls for some terrific convenience products—packaged mixed greens, bottled salad dressing, bottled roasted minced garlic, Italian bread shells, and bottled roasted red sweet peppers.

TURKEY & GREENS PIZZAS

PREP: *20 minutes*
BROIL: *4 minutes*
MAKES: *8 servings*

4	cups mesclun or other mixed baby greens
¼	cup bottled olive oil vinaigrette salad dressing
1	tablespoon olive oil
½	teaspoon bottled roasted minced garlic or bottled minced garlic
4	8-inch Italian bread shells (such as Boboli brand)
3	cups chopped cooked turkey or chicken (about 1 pound)
¾	cup bottled roasted red sweet peppers, drained and chopped
1½	cups shredded mozzarella cheese (6 ounces)
	Bottled olive oil vinaigrette salad dressing (optional)

1 Preheat broiler. In a large bowl combine greens and the ¼ cup salad dressing; toss to coat. Set aside.

2 In a small bowl combine olive oil and roasted minced garlic. Lightly brush the top side of each bread shell with the oil mixture. Place bread shells, oiled sides up, on a very large baking sheet or two large baking sheets. Broil 4 to 5 inches from the heat for 2 to 3 minutes or until bread shells are lightly browned (if using two sheets, broil one sheet at a time).

3 Top bread shells with turkey and roasted red sweet peppers. Sprinkle with cheese. Broil about 2 minutes more or until cheese melts. Top with greens mixture. If desired, pass additional salad dressing.

Per serving: 514 cal., 20 g total fat (4 g sat. fat), 65 mg chol., 832 mg sodium, 52 g carbo., 1 g fiber, 34 g pro.

Take your choice: Serve this zesty chicken-and-cheese mixture on bread for a traditional sandwich or on tortillas for a wrap.

CHICKEN ENCHILADA SANDWICHES

PREP: *25 minutes*

CHILL: *up to 24 hours*

MAKES: *6 servings*

2 skinless, boneless chicken breast halves (10 to 12 ounces total), finely chopped

1 tablespoon butter

1 teaspoon chili powder

½ teaspoon ground cumin

1 clove garlic, minced

Dash cayenne pepper

1 3-ounce package cream cheese, softened

½ cup shredded sharp cheddar cheese (2 ounces)

¼ cup dairy sour cream

1 10-ounce can diced tomatoes and green chile peppers, drained

2 green onions, thinly sliced

2 tablespoons snipped fresh cilantro

12 slices white sandwich bread, crusts removed, or six 8-inch flour tortillas

Cucumber slices, avocado slices, or tomato slices (optional)

12 leaves butterhead (Boston or Bibb) or green leaf lettuce

1 In a large skillet cook chicken in hot butter until lightly browned and no longer pink. Stir in chili powder, cumin, garlic, and cayenne pepper; cook for 1 minute more. Cool slightly.

2 In a medium bowl combine cream cheese, cheddar cheese, and sour cream; beat with an electric mixer on low to medium speed until creamy and combined. Fold in chicken mixture, drained tomatoes and peppers, green onions, and cilantro. Cover and chill for up to 24 hours.

3 Spread chicken mixture on six slices of the bread. If desired, top with cucumber, avocado, or tomato slices. Add lettuce and the remaining six slices bread. (Or spread chicken mixture evenly over tortillas; top with lettuce and, if desired, cucumber, avocado, or tomato. Roll up tortillas.)

Per serving: 324 cal., 15 g total fat (8 g sat. fat), 62 mg chol., 543 mg sodium, 28 g carbo., 2 g fiber, 20 g pro.

This po' boy is made with spice-crusted chicken thighs that turn a crispy black on the outside when sautéed. The coleslaw provides a cooling counterpoint to the spicy chicken.

SPICY CHICKEN PO' BOYS WITH RANCH SLAW

3	cups packaged shredded cabbage with carrot (coleslaw mix)
3	tablespoons bottled ranch salad dressing
1	teaspoon ground chipotle chile pepper or chili powder
½	teaspoon sugar
½	teaspoon kosher salt or salt
⅓	teaspoon garlic powder
½	teaspoon ground cumin
2	pounds skinless, boneless chicken thighs
1	tablespoon olive oil
8	individual ciabatta or French rolls, split

PREP: *25 minutes*
CHILL: *1 hour*
MAKES: *8 servings*

1 For slaw, in a medium bowl combine coleslaw mix and ranch salad dressing. Cover and chill for 1 hour.

2 For chicken, in a shallow dish combine chipotle chile pepper or chili powder, sugar, salt, garlic powder, and cumin. Sprinkle both sides of each chicken thigh with spice mixture, coating lightly.

3 In a large nonstick skillet heat oil over medium-high heat. Add chicken; cook for 10 to 14 minutes or until chicken is lightly blackened and no longer pink (180°F), turning once.

4 To serve, slice chicken thighs and place on bottom halves of split rolls. Top with slaw and top halves of split rolls.

Per serving: 504 cal., 14 g total fat (3 g sat. fat), 92 mg chol., 941 mg sodium, 59 g carbo., 4 g fiber, 33 g pro.

An aromatic basil-flavored spread boosts these sandwiches from ordinary to extraordinary. Fresh basil is the key here; dried simply doesn't work. (Recipe pictured on page 280.)

ITALIAN TURKEY SANDWICHES

START TO FINISH:
20 minutes

MAKES: *4 servings*

⅓ cup fine dry bread crumbs

2 teaspoons dried Italian seasoning, crushed

2 turkey breast tenderloins (about 1 pound total)

2 teaspoons olive oil

2 tablespoons snipped and/or shredded fresh basil

¼ cup mayonnaise or salad dressing

8 ½-inch-thick slices Italian bread, toasted

1 cup bottled roasted red and/or yellow sweet peppers, cut into thin strips

   Fresh basil leaves (optional)

1 In a large resealable plastic bag combine bread crumbs and Italian seasoning. Split each turkey tenderloin in half horizontally to make a total of four ½-inch-thick portions. Place a turkey portion in the bag; seal and shake to coat. Remove turkey portion from bag. Repeat with remaining turkey portions.

2 In a 12-inch nonstick skillet heat oil over medium heat. Add turkey; cook about 10 minutes or until tender and no longer pink (170°F), turning once.

3 Meanwhile, in a small bowl stir 1 tablespoon of the snipped and/or shredded basil into mayonnaise. Spread mayonnaise mixture onto one side of each of four of the bread slices.

4 Top with turkey, sweet pepper strips, and the remaining 1 tablespoon snipped and/or shredded basil. If desired, garnish with basil leaves. Top with remaining bread slices.

Per serving: 416 cal., 17 g total fat (3 g sat. fat), 73 mg chol., 630 mg sodium, 32 g carbo., 3 g fiber, 32 g pro.

There's no need to go to the trouble of cooking chicken at home, just stop by the supermarket and pick up a roasted bird. You'll have great-tasting chicken barbecue sandwiches in minutes. (Recipe pictured on page 281.)

PULLED CHICKEN SANDWICHES

1	2½-pound purchased roasted chicken
1	tablespoon olive oil
1	medium onion, cut into ¼-inch-thick slices
⅓	cup cider vinegar or white wine vinegar
½	cup tomato sauce
3	to 4 tablespoons seeded and finely chopped fresh red and/or green hot chile peppers (see tip, page 19)
2	tablespoons snipped fresh thyme
2	tablespoons molasses
2	tablespoons water
½	teaspoon salt
4	sandwich buns, split

START TO FINISH:
35 minutes

MAKES: *6 servings*

1 Remove string from chicken, if present. Remove skin from chicken and discard. Remove meat from bones; discard bones. Use two forks or your fingers to pull chicken into shreds. Set aside.

2 In a large skillet heat oil over medium heat. Add onion; cook about 5 minutes or until tender, stirring occasionally to separate into rings. Add vinegar; cook and stir for 1 minute more.

3 Stir in tomato sauce, chile peppers, thyme, molasses, the water, and salt. Bring to boiling. Add the chicken; tossing gently to coat. Heat through. Serve on buns.

Per serving: 445 cal., 12 g total fat (3 g sat. fat), 84 mg chol., 990 mg sodium, 51 g carbo., 2 g fiber, 33 g pro.

If you like, substitute hoagie buns or tortillas for the croissants.

HONEY-CHICKEN SANDWICHES

START TO FINISH:
20 minutes

MAKES: *4 servings*

1   small red onion, halved lengthwise and thinly sliced

3   tablespoons honey

2   teaspoons snipped fresh thyme or ½ teaspoon dried thyme, crushed

12 ounces thinly sliced cooked chicken or turkey, halved crosswise

4   croissants, halved horizontally and toasted

1 In a medium skillet combine red onion, honey, and thyme. Cook and stir over medium-low heat just until hot (do not boil). Stir in chicken; heat through. Arrange chicken mixture in halved croissants.

Per serving: 445 cal., 18 g total fat (8 g sat. fat), 118 mg chol., 498 mg sodium, 40 g carbo., 2 g fiber, 29 g pro.

Try this fruity curried chicken in flavored tortillas, if you can find them; otherwise plain will do. (Recipe pictured on page 281.)

WRAP 'N' ROLL CHICKEN

½ cup plain yogurt

½ to 1 teaspoon curry powder (optional)

¼ teaspoon salt

¼ teaspoon black pepper

1 small cucumber, seeded and finely chopped (about ⅔ cup)

1 8-ounce can crushed pineapple, well drained

6 7- to 8-inch flour tortillas

1½ cups cooked chicken breast or turkey breast strips

START TO FINISH:
20 minutes

MAKES: *6 servings*

1 In a medium bowl stir together yogurt, curry powder (if desired), salt, and pepper. Stir in cucumber and pineapple.

2 Spread tortillas with cucumber mixture. Divide chicken strips among tortillas, placing chicken near edge of each tortilla. Roll up tortillas. Cut each tortilla in half diagonally. if desired, secure with wooden toothpicks.

Per serving: 184 cal., 4 g total fat (1 g sat. fat), 31 mg chol., 258 mg sodium, 23 g carbo., 1 g fiber, 14 g pro.

Pepperoncini are pickled peppers that have a sweet yet spicy flavor. They often are included as part of antipasto trays. Look for them with the pickles at the supermarket or in the ethnic food section.

GREEK CHICKEN SALAD SUB WITH OLIVE SALSA

START TO FINISH:
25 minutes

MAKES: *4 servings*

½   cup pitted kalamata olives

½   cup pepperoncini, stems and seeds removed

¼   cup chopped red onion

¼   cup olive oil

2   tablespoons red wine vinegar

2   teaspoons snipped fresh oregano

⅛   teaspoon salt

⅛   teaspoon black pepper

1   medium tomato, diced

1   16-ounce loaf French bread

1   9-ounce package frozen cooked chicken breast strips, thawed

¾   cup thinly sliced cucumber

3   ounces feta cheese, coarsely crumbled

1 For the olive salsa, in a food processor* combine olives, pepperoncini, red onion, olive oil, red wine vinegar, oregano, salt, and pepper. Cover and process until coarsely chopped. Stir in tomato; set aside.

2 Horizontally split loaf of bread. Hollow out inside of each half, leaving ¾-inch-thick shells. Fill the bottom half of the loaf with chicken, cucumber, feta cheese, and the olive salsa. Top with top half of the loaf.

Per serving: 611 cal., 24 g total fat (6 g sat. fat), 60 mg chol., 2,206 mg sodium, 65 g carbo., 5 g fiber, 13 g pro.

***TEST KITCHEN TIP:** If you don't have a food processor, finely chop the ingredients and combine by hand.

This recipe is a great way to get your kids to eat some veggies without even knowing it. The yellow squash looks like cheese.

CHICKEN & BISCUIT POCKETS

2   10.2-ounce packages refrigerated large flaky biscuits
    (5 per package)

1   cup finely chopped cooked chicken or turkey (5 ounces)

⅔   cup coarsely shredded yellow summer squash

½   cup shredded Monterey Jack or cheddar cheese (2 ounces)

½   cup mayonnaise or salad dressing

1   tablespoon honey mustard

PREP: *25 minutes*
BAKE: *12 minutes*
MAKES: *5 servings*

1 Preheat oven to 400°F. Separate biscuits and flatten each with the palm of your hand to a 4-inch circle. Divide chicken, squash, and cheese among dough circles, placing filling on one side of each dough circle. Fold the other sides of dough circles over filling; pinch edges well to seal.* Arrange filled biscuits about 2 inches apart on an ungreased baking sheet. Bake about 12 minutes or until biscuit tops are golden brown and edges are set.

2 Meanwhile, in a small bowl stir together mayonnaise and mustard. Serve as dipping sauce for warm biscuits.

Per serving: 626 cal., 39 g total fat (10 g sat. fat), 43 mg chol., 1,359 mg sodium, 48 g carbo., 0 g fiber, 19 g pro.

***TEST KITCHEN TIP:** For a tighter seal, press edges with the tines of a fork.

Serve these tender chicken-filled bundles with a crisp tossed salad or a bowl of your favorite soup.

CHEESY CORN & CHICKEN TURNOVERS

PREP: *25 minutes*

BAKE: *15 minutes*

MAKES: *4 servings*

1   15-ounce package rolled refrigerated unbaked piecrust (2 crusts)

2   cups chopped cooked chicken or turkey (10 ounces)

1   11-ounce can whole kernel corn with sweet peppers, drained

1   10¾-ounce can condensed cream of chicken and herbs soup or cream of mushroom soup

1   cup shredded cheddar cheese (4 ounces)

1 Let piecrusts stand at room temperature according to package directions. Preheat oven to 400°F. In a medium bowl combine chicken, corn, soup, and cheese. Unroll piecrusts on a lightly floured surface or pastry cloth; roll each piecrust into a 13-inch circle. Cut each piecrust into quarters.

2 Spoon about ½ cup of the chicken mixture along one straight side of a piecrust triangle about ¾ inch from edge. Brush edges of triangle with a little water. Fold other straight side of triangle over the chicken mixture. Seal edges with a fork. Prick the top of the triangle several times with a fork. Repeat with remaining chicken mixture and pastry triangles. Place wedges on a greased large baking sheet.

3 Bake about 15 minutes or until wedges are golden brown. Serve hot.

Per serving: 862 cal., 47 g total fat (21 g sat. fat), 118 mg chol., 1,625 mg sodium, 73 g carbo., 3 g fiber, 33 g pro.

If you prefer, serve the creamy medley in hollowed-out tomato shells.

CURRY CHICKEN SALAD WRAPS

½ cup mayonnaise or salad dressing

½ teaspoon curry powder

⅛ teaspoon black pepper

2 cups chopped cooked chicken breast or turkey breast (10 ounces)

¼ cup sliced green onions

4 romaine lettuce leaves or 8 fresh spinach leaves

4 7-inch whole wheat flour tortillas

1 medium tomato, chopped

PREP: *20 minutes*

CHILL: *2 to 24 hours*

MAKES: *4 servings*

1 In a medium bowl combine mayonnaise, curry powder, and pepper. Stir in chicken and green onion. Cover and chill for 2 to 24 hours.

2 To assemble, place a romaine leaf or two spinach leaves on each tortilla. Top with chicken mixture and chopped tomato. Roll up; cut in half to serve.

Per serving: 469 cal., 27 g total fat (5 g sat. fat), 70 mg chol., 587 mg sodium, 29 g carbo., 3 g fiber, 26 g pro.

CURRY CHICKEN SALAD TOMATOES: Prepare as directed in Step 1. To serve, cut a thin slice from the top of each of 4 large tomatoes. Using a spoon, scoop out center of each tomato, leaving a shell. Spoon about ½ cup of the chicken mixture into each tomato shell.

Per serving: 341 cal., 25 g total fat (5 g sat. fat), 70 mg chol., 209 mg sodium, 5 g carbo., 2 g fiber, 23 g pro.

Hoagie buns cradle traditional Cobb salad ingredients, including avocado, cooked chicken, tomato, bacon, blue cheese, and hard-cooked eggs.

COBB SALAD HOAGIES

START TO FINISH:
35 minutes

MAKES: *4 servings*

3	tablespoons olive oil
1	tablespoon white wine vinegar
1	teaspoon Dijon-style mustard
½	teaspoon salt
½	teaspoon black pepper
1	avocado, halved, seeded, peeled, and finely chopped
1⅓	cups cubed cooked chicken or turkey (about 7 ounces)
2	plum tomatoes, chopped
4	slices bacon, crisp-cooked, drained, and crumbled
½	cup crumbled blue cheese (2 ounces)
4	leaves butterhead (Boston or Bibb) lettuce
4	hoagie buns, split, hollowed out, and toasted
2	hard-cooked eggs, chopped

1 For dressing, in a small bowl whisk together olive oil, vinegar, mustard, salt, and pepper. Stir in avocado; set aside.

2 In a medium bowl combine chicken, tomatoes, bacon, and blue cheese. Pour dressing over chicken mixture; toss to coat. Place lettuce leaves on the bottom halves of the hollowed-out hoagie buns. Spoon chicken mixture over lettuce. Sprinkle with chopped eggs. Add top halves of the buns.

Per serving: 659 cal., 35 g total fat (9 g sat. fat), 165 mg chol., 1,214 mg sodium, 55 g carbo., 5 g fiber, 32 g pro.

Mango chutney and curry powder give this chicken salad a deliciously exotic twist.

CHICKEN SALAD SANDWICHES

¼ cup mango chutney (snip any large fruit pieces)

2 tablespoons mayonnaise or salad dressing

1 teaspoon curry powder

2 cups cubed cooked chicken or turkey (10 ounces)

1 cup seedless red grapes, halved

¼ cup sliced or slivered almonds, toasted

4 croissants, split, or four 6-inch pita bread rounds, halved crosswise

Lettuce leaves

START TO FINISH:
20 minutes

MAKES: *4 servings*

1 In a small bowl combine chutney, mayonnaise, and curry powder. Stir in chicken, grapes, and almonds.

2 Top each croissant bottom or line each pita bread half with lettuce; top or fill with chicken mixture. Add tops of croissants.

Per serving: 547 cal., 27 g total fat (9 g sat. fat), 103 mg chol., 541 mg sodium, 49 g carbo., 4 g fiber, 27 g pro.

Keep these ingredients on hand for your little ones' lunches. They'll love the sweet surprise of cherries or raisins in the spread.

LUNCH BOX SUB SANDWICHES

START TO FINISH:
15 minutes

MAKES: *4 servings*

¼ cup mayonnaise or salad dressing

¼ cup finely snipped dried tart cherries or raisins

1 teaspoon Dijon-style mustard

4 hamburger buns, split

4 slices mozzarella cheese (3 ounces total)

6 ounces thinly sliced cooked turkey breast or chicken breast

1 medium tomato, thinly sliced

1 In a small bowl stir together mayonnaise, cherries or raisins, and mustard. Spread the bottoms of the buns with the mayonnaise mixture. Top with cheese, turkey, and tomato. Add bun tops.

Per serving: 355 cal., 18 g total fat (5 g sat. fat), 37 mg chol., 949 mg sodium, 30 g carbo., 2 g fiber, 18 g pro.

MAKE-AHEAD DIRECTIONS: Prepare as directed. Wrap each sandwich in plastic wrap. Chill for up to 24 hours. To tote, place in insulated lunch boxes with ice packs.

Gone are the corned beef and Swiss cheese in this tropical version of the classic sandwich. Instead ham, turkey, cheddar cheese, and pineapple take center stage.

ISLAND REUBENS

8   slices dark rye bread, toasted

½   cup bottled Thousand Island salad dressing

6   ounces sliced cooked turkey or chicken

6   ounces sliced cooked ham

4   slices Swiss cheese

1   cup canned or bottled sauerkraut, well drained

½   cup canned crushed pineapple, well drained

4   slices sharp cheddar cheese

4   slices red onion

PREP: *15 minutes*

BROIL: *5 minutes*

MAKES: *4 servings*

1 Preheat broiler. Place bread slices on a very large baking sheet. Spread one side of each of the bread slices with Thousand Island salad dressing. Top half of the bread slices with turkey, ham, and Swiss cheese. Top the remaining half of the bread slices with sauerkraut, pineapple, cheddar cheese, and onion.

2 Broil 5 inches from the heat about 5 minutes or until cheese is melted. Carefully top ham- and turkey-topped bread slices with the sauerkraut-topped slices, onion sides down.

Per serving: 677 cal., 36 g total fat (15 g sat. fat), 120 mg chol., 2,948 mg sodium, 44 g carbo., 9 g fiber, 40 g pro.

A buttermilk biscuit slathered with apple butter, piled high with turkey, and sprinkled with almonds—now that's a mighty fine sandwich. (Recipe pictured on page 282.)

TURKEY ON LEAF-CUTOUT BISCUITS

PREP: *20 minutes*
BAKE: *10 minutes*
MAKES: *8 servings*

4	cups all-purpose flour*
4	teaspoons baking powder
½	teaspoon baking soda
½	teaspoon salt
1⅓	cups buttermilk
½	cup cooking oil
2	tablespoons butter, melted
½	teaspoon paprika
1	recipe Pear-Sage Butter or 1 cup purchased apple butter
10	ounces shaved smoked turkey or smoked chicken
¼	cup sliced almonds, toasted
	White cheddar cheese or provolone cheese slices (optional)
	Leaf lettuce (optional)

1 Preheat oven to 450°F. In a medium bowl combine flour, baking powder, baking soda, and salt. In a small bowl stir together buttermilk and oil. Pour into flour mixture; stir just until moistened.

2 On a lightly floured surface, knead dough by folding and gently pressing it for 10 to 12 strokes. Roll out or pat dough to 1-inch thickness. Cut dough with a 3-inch leaf-shape or round cookie cutter, dipping cutter in flour between cuts. Transfer biscuits to an ungreased baking sheet. In a bowl combine melted butter and paprika. Brush biscuit tops with butter mixture.

3 Bake for 10 to 12 minutes or until bottoms are browned. Transfer to a wire rack; cool. Using a serrated knife or sharp knife, carefully split biscuits in half horizontally.

4 Top bottom half of each biscuit with smoked turkey and almonds. Top with 2 tablespoons of the Pear-Sage Butter or apple butter. If desired, add cheese and lettuce. Cover with biscuit tops.

Per serving: 655 cal., 22 g total fat (5 g sat. fat), 29 mg chol., 813 mg sodium, 97 g carbo., 4 g fiber, 15 g pro.

***TEST KITCHEN TIP:** If desired, substitute ½ cup whole wheat flour or oat bran for ½ cup of the all-purpose flour.

PEAR-SAGE BUTTER: In a medium saucepan combine 2 cups peeled, finely chopped fresh pears, ¼ cup water, and ½ cup sugar. Cook and stir over medium-low heat until bubbly. Boil gently, uncovered, for 20 to 25 minutes or until mixture is very thick and liquid is nearly evaporated, mashing fruit after 15 minutes of cooking. (Adjust heat as needed to maintain a gentle boil.) Remove saucepan from heat. Stir in 1 tablespoon snipped fresh sage. Cool completely. Use immediately or cover and store in the refrigerator got up to 3 days. Makes about 1 cup.

For easy biting, look for slender asparagus spears, which are more tender than thick spears.

CLASSY CUBAN SANDWICHES

8 ounces fresh thin asparagus spears, trimmed

2 tablespoons water

4 hoagie buns or torpedo rolls, split

2 to 3 tablespoons coarse-grain mustard

6 ounces thinly sliced cooked turkey breast or chicken breast

6 ounces thinly sliced serrano ham or other cooked ham

Dill pickle slices

8 ounces sliced Swiss cheese

1 tablespoon olive oil

START TO FINISH:
25 minutes

MAKES: *4 servings*

1 In a microwave-safe 9-inch pie plate or shallow baking dish combine asparagus and the water; cover with vented plastic wrap. Microwave on 100% power (high) for 3 minutes; drain and set aside.

2 Spread bottom halves of buns with mustard. Top with asparagus, turkey, ham, pickle slices, and cheese. Add bun tops.

3 Heat oil in a very large skillet or grill pan over medium heat (or preheat a covered electric indoor grill and brush with oil). Place sandwiches in skillet or grill pan or on electric grill (cook in batches if necessary); cover sandwiches in skillet or grill pan with a large heavy plate and press gently (or close lid of electric grill). Cook for 2 to 3 minutes per side (3 to 4 minutes total in covered grill) or until bread is toasted and cheese is melted.

Per serving: 799 cal., 35 g total fat (15 g sat. fat), 109 mg chol., 2,224 mg sodium, 79 g carbo., 5 g fiber, 42 g pro.

Peppered turkey adds a tantalizing bite to these quick-fixing subs.

TURKEY SUBS WITH CITRUS MAYONNAISE

START TO FINISH:
15 minutes

MAKES: *4 servings*

1   orange

½   cup mayonnaise or salad dressing

4   sourdough rolls or one 8-ounce loaf baguette-style French bread, cut crosswise into quarters

8   to 12 ounces thinly sliced cooked peppered turkey, smoked turkey, or smoked chicken

4   slices Swiss or provolone cheese (3 to 4 ounces total)

1 Finely shred 1 teaspoon peel from the orange. Cut the orange in half; squeeze 2 tablespoons juice from orange halves. Discard seeds and any remaining orange. For citrus mayonnaise, in a small bowl combine orange peel, orange juice, and mayonnaise.

2 Split rolls or bread quarters horizontally; toast, if desired. Spread citrus mayonnaise on the cut sides of each roll or bread quarter. Place bottom halves of the rolls or bread quarters on a serving platter, mayonnaise sides up. Layer turkey and cheese on rolls or bread quarters. Top with remaining halves of rolls or bread quarters, mayonnaise sides down. Cover and store any remaining citrus mayonnaise in the refrigerator for up to 3 days.

Per serving: 436 cal., 30 g total fat (7 g sat. fat), 61 mg chol., 1,123 mg sodium, 21 g carbo., 1 g fiber, 21 g pro.

A cheese-and-honey mustard spread serves as the irresistible and innovative base for sliced ham, turkey, and colby cheese in this super-satisfying sandwich.

DELI SANDWICH STACKS

½   of a 4-ounce container light semisoft cheese with garlic and herb

2   tablespoons honey mustard

¼   teaspoon lemon-pepper seasoning

6   slices marble rye, cracked wheat, or seven-grain bread

2   small plum tomatoes, thinly sliced

⅓   cup sliced canned banana peppers, well drained

1   cup loosely packed fresh spinach leaves or 4 lettuce leaves

4   thin slices colby or Monterey Jack cheese

4   ounces thinly sliced cooked turkey breast or chicken breast

4   ounces low-fat, reduced-sodium thinly sliced cooked ham

Fresh banana peppers (optional)

1 In a small bowl combine semisoft cheese, honey mustard, and lemon-pepper seasoning. Spread the cheese mixture evenly onto one side of each of four of the bread slices.

2 To assemble sandwiches, divide tomatoes, sliced banana peppers, spinach or lettuce, and colby cheese evenly among the four bread slices, spread sides up. Top two stacks with turkey and two stacks with ham. Arrange the stacks with ham on top of the stacks with turkey, bread sides down. Top with the remaining two bread slices. Cut stacks in half. If desired, garnish each half with a banana pepper and secure with a wooden pick.

Per serving: 315 cal., 12 g total fat (6 g sat. fat), 51 mg chol., 1,245 mg sodium, 31 g carbo., 4 g fiber, 22 g pro.

START TO FINISH:
20 minutes

MAKES: *4 servings*

Shredded cheddar cheese and taco seasoning make everyday turkey salad sandwiches into out-of-the-ordinary fare.

TURKEY TACO SANDWICHES

PREP: *15 minutes*

CHILL: *1 to 4 hours*

MAKES: *8 servings*

3   cups chopped cooked turkey or chicken (about 1 pound)

½   cup shredded cheddar cheese (2 ounces)

½   cup mayonnaise or salad dressing

1   tablespoon milk

2   teaspoons taco seasoning mix

8   hamburger buns, split

1   cup shredded lettuce

⅓   cup finely chopped tomato

1 In a medium bowl combine turkey and cheese. For dressing, in a small bowl stir together mayonnaise, milk, and taco seasoning. Pour over turkey mixture; toss lightly to coat. Cover and chill for 1 to 4 hours.

2 To serve, spoon about ⅓ cup of the turkey mixture onto bottom half of each bun. Top with lettuce and tomato. Add bun tops. Serve immediately.

Per serving: 344 cal., 18 g total fat (5 g sat. fat), 52 mg chol., 421 mg sodium, 22 g carbo., 1 g fiber, 22 g pro.

HOT OFF THE GRILL

For a sensational meal, fire up
the grill and cook one of these
stick-to-the-ribs poultry favorites.

The blend of five different spices lends an appetizing golden color and dynamite flavor to this succulent grilled chicken.

CURRY-GRILLED CHICKEN

PREP: *20 minutes*
GRILL: *1¼ hours*
STAND: *10 minutes*
MAKES: *5 servings*

1	3- to 4-pound whole broiler-fryer chicken
2	tablespoons olive oil
1	teaspoon salt
1	teaspoon ground cumin
1	teaspoon ground turmeric
½	teaspoon ground mustard
¼	teaspoon ground cardamom
¼	teaspoon cayenne pepper
	Salt
	Black pepper
1	recipe Minted Cucumber Sauce

1 Remove neck and giblets from chicken; discard or save for another use. Twist wing tips under back. In a small bowl combine oil, the 1 teaspoon salt, the cumin, turmeric, mustard, cardamom, and cayenne pepper. Brush over chicken. Season body cavity with additional salt and black pepper.

2 For a charcoal grill, arrange medium-hot coals around a drip pan. Test for medium heat above the pan. Place chicken, breast side up, on grill rack over drip pan. Cover; grill for 1¼ to 1¾ hours or until an instant-read thermometer inserted into one of the inside thigh muscles registers 180°F (the thermometer should not touch bone). The juices should run clear, and the drumsticks should move easily in their sockets. (For a gas grill, preheat grill. Reduce heat to medium. Adjust for indirect cooking. Grill as above, except place chicken on a rack in a roasting pan.)

3 Remove chicken from grill. Cover with foil; let stand for 10 minutes before carving. Serve with Minted Cucumber Sauce.

MINTED CUCUMBER SAUCE: In a small bowl combine 1 cup chopped seeded cucumber; one 6-ounce carton plain low-fat yogurt; 1 plum tomato, seeded and chopped; 2 tablespoons snipped fresh mint; 1 tablespoon olive oil; and ¼ teaspoon salt. Cover and chill while grilling chicken or for up to 2 hours. If desired, let stand at room temperature for 30 minutes before serving.

Per serving: 504 cal., 36 g total fat (9 g sat. fat), 141 mg chol., 838 mg sodium, 6 g carbo., 1 g fiber, 37 g pro.

The bird looks odd sitting upright on the grill, but the moist, herb-seasoned chicken tastes sublime.

BEER CAN CHICKEN

2	teaspoons packed brown sugar
2	teaspoons paprika
2	teaspoons salt
1	teaspoon dry mustard
½	teaspoon black pepper
½	teaspoon dried thyme, crushed
¼	teaspoon garlic powder
1	12-ounce can beer
1	3½- to 4-pound whole broiler-fryer chicken
2	tablespoons butter or margarine, softened
¼	of a lemon

PREP: *30 minutes*
GRILL: *1¼ hours*
STAND: *10 minutes*
MAKES: *4 to 6 servings*

1 In a small bowl combine brown sugar, paprika, salt, dry mustard, pepper, thyme, and garlic powder. Discard about half of the beer from the can. Add 1 teaspoon of the spice mixture to the half empty can (beer will foam up).

2 Remove neck and giblets from chicken; discard or save for another use. Sprinkle another 1 teaspoon of the spice mixture inside the body cavity. Rub the outside of the chicken with butter and sprinkle the remaining spice mixture evenly over chicken.

3 Hold the chicken upright with the opening of the body cavity at the bottom and lower it onto the beer can so the can fits into the body cavity. Pull the chicken legs forward so the bird rests on its legs and the can. Twist wing tips behind back. Stuff the lemon quarter in the neck cavity to seal in steam.

4 For a charcoal grill, arrange medium-hot coals around a drip pan. Test for medium heat above pan. Stand chicken upright on grill rack over drip pan. Cover and grill for 1¼ to 1¾ hours or until an instant-read thermometer inserted into one of the inside thigh muscles registers 180°F (the thermometer should not touch bone). The juices should run clear, and the drumsticks should move easily in their sockets. If necessary, tent chicken with foil to prevent overbrowning. (For a gas grill, preheat grill. Reduce heat to medium. Adjust for indirect cooking. If necessary, remove upper grill racks so chicken will stand upright. Grill as above.)

5 Remove chicken from grill, holding by the can. Cover with foil; let stand for 10 minutes. Use a hot pad to grasp the can; use heavy tongs to carefully remove the chicken.

Per serving: 635 cal., 45 g total fat (15 g sat. fat), 217 mg chol., 1,180 mg sodium, 3 g carbo., 0 g fiber, 51 g pro.

Originally from China, star anise is the pod of a small evergreen tree. Although unrelated to anise seed, it has a similar licorice flavor. Look for star anise in Asian specialty stores or the spice section of your supermarket.

ASIAN-SPICED CHICKEN

PREP: *15 minutes*
CHILL: *6 to 8 hours*
GRILL: *1 1/4 hours*
STAND: *10 minutes*
MAKES: *4 servings*

8	cups water
1/3	cup coarse kosher salt
1/4	cup soy sauce
1/4	cup rice vinegar or white vinegar
8	star anise, broken
2	3-inch-long pieces stick cinnamon, broken
1	tablespoon sugar
2	teaspoons fennel seeds, crushed
1	3- to 3 1/2-pound whole broiler-fryer chicken

1 For brine, in a deep stainless-steel or enamel stock pot or plastic container stir together the water, kosher salt, soy sauce, vinegar, star anise, cinnamon, sugar, and fennel seeds until salt is dissolved.

2 Remove neck and giblets from chicken; discard or save for another use. Rinse inside of chicken. Submerge chicken in brine. Cover and refrigerate for 6 to 8 hours, turning chicken occasionally.

3 Remove chicken from brine. Pat chicken dry with paper towels. Pull neck skin to the back; fasten with a skewer. Use 100%-cotton kitchen string to tie drumsticks securely to tail; twist wing tips under back.

4 For a charcoal grill, arrange medium-hot coals around a drip pan. Test for medium heat above the pan. Place chicken, breast side up, on grill rack over drip pan. Cover; grill for 1 1/4 to 1 1/2 hours or until an instant-read thermometer inserted into one of the inside thigh muscles registers 180°F (the thermometer should not touch bone). The juices should run clear, and the drumsticks should move easily in their sockets. (For a gas grill, preheat grill. Reduce heat to medium. Adjust for indirect cooking. Grill as above.)

5 Remove chicken from grill. Cover with foil; let stand for 10 minutes before carving.

Per serving: 485 cal., 33 g total fat (10 g sat. fat), 172 mg chol., 1,874 mg sodium, 0 g carbo., 0 g fiber, 43 g pro.

Due to the large amount of turkey drippings, you may prefer to omit the drip pan and place the turkey on a rack in a roasting pan. Place the pan in the center of the grill, not directly over the heat.

NEW ENGLAND GRILLED TURKEY

1¼	cups kosher salt
1	cup pure maple syrup
1	6-ounce can frozen apple juice concentrate, thawed
3	cloves garlic, crushed
4	whole cloves
¼	teaspoon whole black peppercorns
1	8- to 10-pound whole turkey
½	cup butter, softened
1	teaspoon ground sage
1	recipe Gingered Cranberry Sauce

PREP: *45 minutes*
CHILL: *12 to 24 hours*
GRILL: *2½ hours*
STAND: *15 minutes*
MAKES: *8 to 12 servings*

1 For brine, in a deep pot stir together 4 cups hot water, kosher salt, maple syrup, and juice concentrate until salt is dissolved. Add 1 gallon (16 cups) cold water, garlic, cloves, and peppercorns. Remove neck and giblets from turkey; discard or save for another use. Rinse inside of turkey. Submerge turkey in brine and weight it to keep it submerged. Cover and refrigerate for 12 to 24 hours.

2 Remove turkey from brine. Pat turkey dry with paper towels. In a small bowl combine butter and sage; set aside. Starting at the neck on one side of the breast, slip your fingers between skin and meat, loosening the skin as you work toward the tail end. Once your entire hand is under the skin, free the skin around the thigh and leg area up to, but not around, the tip of the drumstick. Repeat on the other side of the breast. Rub sage-butter mixture under the skin directly onto meat. Sprinkle surface and cavity of turkey with salt and black pepper. Pull neck skin to back; fasten with a skewer. If a band of skin crosses the tail, tuck the ends of the drumsticks under the band. If no band, use 100%-cotton kitchen string to tie drumsticks securely to tail. Twist wing tips under back.

3 For a charcoal grill, arrange medium-hot coals around a drip pan. Test for medium heat above the pan. Place turkey on grill rack over drip pan. Cover; grill for 2½ to 3 hours or until an instant-read thermometer inserted into one of the inside thigh muscles registers 180°F (the thermometer should not touch bone). The juices should run clear, and the drumsticks should move easily in their sockets. Add coals every 45 to 60 minutes and cut band of skin or string between drumsticks for the last hour of grilling so thighs cook evenly. (For a gas grill, preheat grill. Reduce heat to medium. Adjust for indirect cooking. Grill as above.) Remove turkey from grill. Cover with foil; let stand for 15 minutes. Serve with Gingered Cranberry Sauce.

Per serving: 676 cal., 26 g total fat (11 g sat. fat), 308 mg chol., 1,223 mg sodium, 31 g carbo., 2 g fiber, 76 g pro.

GINGERED CRANBERRY SAUCE: In a medium saucepan combine 1 cup sugar and 1 cup water. Bring to boiling, stirring to dissolve sugar. Boil rapidly for 5 minutes. Add 2 cups fresh cranberries, ½ cup snipped dried apples, 1½ teaspoons grated fresh ginger, and 1 teaspoon finely shredded lemon peel. Return to boiling; reduce heat to medium. Boil gently for 3 to 4 minutes or until cranberry skins pop, stirring occasionally. Remove from heat. Serve warm or chilled.

It doesn't matter which fresh herb is your favorite. Any one will shine in this simple recipe.

HERB- & LEMON-CRUSTED GAME HENS

PREP: *30 minutes*

CHILL: *12 to 24 hours*

GRILL: *50 minutes*

STAND: *10 minutes*

MAKES: *4 servings*

2	lemons
1½	cups snipped fresh herbs (such as oregano and basil)
2	teaspoons kosher salt or sea salt or 1½ teaspoons salt
½	teaspoon freshly ground black pepper
4	1¼- to 1½-pound Cornish game hens

1 Finely shred 2 teaspoons peel from one of the lemons. In a small bowl combine lemon peel, herbs, salt, and pepper; set aside. Cut 1½ of the lemons into slices; cut remaining lemon half into four wedges.

2 Remove necks and giblets from Cornish game hens; discard or save for another use. If desired, remove skin from hens. Place hens on a plate or baking dish. Place one lemon wedge into each hen cavity. Use 100%-cotton kitchen string to tie drumsticks securely to tails; twist wing tips under the backs. Generously pat outside of birds with herb mixture. Lay lemon slices over tops. Cover tightly with plastic wrap and chill in the refrigerator for 12 to 24 hours.

3 For a charcoal grill, arrange medium-hot coals around a drip pan. Test for medium heat above the pan. Place Cornish hens, breast sides up, on grill rack over drip pan. Cover; grill for 50 to 60 minutes or until an instant-read thermometer inserted into one of the inside thigh muscles registers 180°F (the thermometer should not touch bone). The juices should run clear, and the drumsticks should move easily in their sockets. (For a gas grill, preheat grill. Reduce heat to medium. Adjust for indirect cooking. Grill as above.)

4 Remove hens from grill. Cover with foil; let stand for 10 minutes before carving.

Per serving: 676 cal., 45 g total fat (12 g sat. fat), 346 mg chol., 1,134 mg sodium, 3 g carbo., 0 g fiber, 60 g pro.

A technique first used by Native Americans in the Pacific Northwest, plank cooking utilizes cedar or alder wood to impart smoky wood flavor. Look for the planks wherever grilling supplies are sold.

PLANK-SMOKED GAME HENS

PREP: *30 minutes*

SOAK: *1 hour*

GRILL: *55 minutes*

MAKES: *4 servings*

1   14×6×¾-inch cedar or alder grill plank

2   teaspoons cooking oil

¼   cup finely chopped onion

1   clove garlic, minced

½   cup apricot spreadable fruit

1   fresh serrano chile pepper, seeded and finely chopped (see tip, page 19)

½   teaspoon finely shredded lime peel

1   tablespoon lime juice

2   1¼- to 1½-pound Cornish game hens, halved

    Salt

    Black pepper

1   recipe Tipsy Fruit Salad

1 Before grilling, soak plank in enough water to cover for at least 1 hour. Place a weight on plank so it stays submerged during soaking. Drain plank.

2 For glaze, in a medium skillet heat oil over medium heat. Add onion and garlic; cook until tender. In a small bowl combine onion mixture, spreadable fruit, chile pepper, lime peel, and lime juice. Set aside.

3 For a charcoal grill, place plank on the grill rack directly over medium coals; heat about 5 minutes or until plank begins to crackle and smoke. Place hens, cut sides down, on the plank. Sprinkle hens lightly with salt and black pepper. Cover; grill for 25 minutes. Carefully spoon glaze over hens. Cover; grill for 25 to 35 minutes more or until an instant-read thermometer inserted into one of the inside thigh muscles registers 180°F (the thermometer should not touch bone). The juices should run clear, and the drumsticks should move easily in their sockets. (For a gas grill, preheat grill. Reduce heat to medium. Heat plank and grill hens as above.)

4 Transfer plank with Cornish game hens to a serving platter. Serve with Tipsy Fruit Salad.

TIPSY FRUIT SALAD: In a medium bowl combine 1 large nectarine, pitted and chopped; 1½ cups cubed honeydew melon; 1 cup halved red seedless grapes; ½ cup fresh blueberries; 2 tablespoons rum or unsweetened pineapple juice; 1 tablespoon honey; ½ teaspoon finely shredded lime peel; and 1 tablespoon lime juice. Cover and chill for up to 24 hours.

Per serving: 554 cal., 25 g total fat (7 g sat. fat), 173 mg chol., 167 mg sodium, 50 g carbo., 2 g fiber, 31 g pro.

This perfectly smoked mahogany-brown bird is a beauty that's sure to please whenever you serve it.

GARLIC-LOADED LEMON CHICKEN

PREP: *15 minutes*

MARINATE: *4 to 8 hours*

SOAK: *1 hour*

SMOKE: *1½ hours*

MAKES: *4 servings*

1	3½- to 4-pound whole broiler-fryer chicken, quartered
⅓	cup olive oil
2	tablespoons finely shredded lemon peel (set aside)
3	tablespoons lemon juice
1	tablespoon Dijon-style mustard
12	cloves garlic, minced
2	teaspoons dried rosemary, crushed
1	teaspoon salt
1	teaspoon coarsely ground black pepper
6	to 8 hickory or oak wood chunks

1 Place chicken in a resealable plastic bag set in a shallow dish. For marinade, whisk together oil, lemon juice, and mustard. Stir in lemon peel, garlic, rosemary, salt, and pepper; pour over chicken. Seal bag; turn to coat chicken. Marinate in the refrigerator for 4 to 8 hours, turning the bag occasionally.

2 Before smoke cooking, soak wood chunks in enough water to cover for at least 1 hour. Drain chunks before using. Drain chicken, discarding the marinade.

3 In a smoker arrange preheated coals, drained wood chunks, and water pan according to the manufacturer's directions. Pour water into water pan. Place chicken quarters, bone sides down, on grill rack over the water pan. Cover and smoke for 1½ to 2 hours or until tender and juices run clear (170°F for breasts; 180°F for thighs and drumsticks). Add additional coals and water as needed to maintain temperature and moisture.

Per serving: 692 cal., 52 g total fat (13 g sat. fat), 201 mg chol., 603 mg sodium, 3 g carbo., 1 g fiber, 51 g pro.

Toasting the coriander and fennel seeds takes only minutes and repays your extra effort with a lovely toasted aroma and taste.

CITRUS CHICKEN WITH HERBS & SPICES

1	teaspoon coriander seeds
1	teaspoon fennel seeds
2½	to 3 pounds meaty chicken pieces (breast halves, thighs, and/or drumsticks), skinned if desired
½	cup orange juice
¼	cup thinly sliced green onions
3	tablespoons honey
1	tablespoon snipped fresh thyme
1	tablespoon snipped fresh sage
1	tablespoon snipped fresh rosemary
½	teaspoon salt
½	teaspoon cracked black pepper

PREP: *25 minutes*

MARINATE: *4 to 8 hours*

GRILL: *50 minutes*

MAKES: *4 servings*

1 In a small skillet cook coriander seeds and fennel seeds over medium heat about 5 minutes or until seeds are fragrant and toasted, stirring constantly. Remove from heat; let cool. Grind seeds with a mortar and pestle.

2 Place chicken in a resealable plastic bag set in a shallow dish. For marinade, in a small bowl combine orange juice, green onion, honey, thyme, sage, rosemary, salt, and pepper. Stir in ground seeds. Pour over chicken. Seal bag; turn to coat chicken. Marinate in the refrigerator for 4 to 8 hours, turning bag occasionally.

3 Drain chicken, discarding marinade. For a charcoal grill, arrange medium-hot coals around a drip pan. Test for medium heat above the pan. Place chicken pieces, bone sides down, on grill rack over drip pan. Cover; grill for 50 to 60 minutes or until chicken is tender and no longer pink (170°F for breasts; 180°F for thighs and drumsticks). (For a gas grill, preheat grill. Reduce heat to medium. Adjust for indirect cooking. Grill as above.)

Per serving: 357 cal., 16 g total fat (4 g sat. fat), 129 mg chol., 261 mg sodium, 9 g carbo., 1 g fiber, 42 g pro.

This buttermilk-bathed chicken borrows seasonings used in traditional East Indian tandoori cooking. The cucumber sauce cools the heat. (Recipe pictured on page 283.)

TANDOORI-SPICED CHICKEN

PREP: *25 minutes*
MARINATE: *2 to 4 hours*
GRILL: *50 minutes*
MAKES: *6 servings*

3 cups buttermilk

¼ cup kosher salt

2 tablespoons sugar

4 cloves garlic, minced

1 tablespoon ground ginger

1 tablespoon curry powder

1½ teaspoons onion powder

¾ teaspoon cayenne pepper

2½ to 3 pounds meaty chicken pieces (breast halves, thighs, and/or drumsticks), skinned

1 recipe Curry-Cucumber Sauce

1 For brine, in a large bowl combine buttermilk, kosher salt, sugar, and garlic. In a small bowl combine ginger, curry powder, onion powder, and cayenne pepper; set aside 2 teaspoons of the ginger mixture. Stir remaining ginger mixture into buttermilk mixture; stir until salt and sugar are dissolved. Place chicken in a resealable plastic bag set in a shallow dish. Pour brine over chicken. Seal bag; turn to coat chicken. Marinate in the refrigerator for 2 to 4 hours, turning bag occasionally.

2 Drain chicken, discarding brine. Sprinkle chicken evenly with the reserved 2 teaspoons ginger mixture.

3 For a charcoal grill, arrange medium-hot coals around a drip pan. Test for medium heat above the pan. Place chicken pieces, bone sides down, on greased grill rack over drip pan. Cover; grill for 50 to 60 minutes or until chicken is tender and no longer pink (170°F for breast halves; 180°F for thighs and drumsticks). (For a gas grill, preheat grill. Reduce heat to medium. Adjust for indirect cooking. Grill as above.)

4 Serve chicken with Curry-Cucumber Sauce.

CURRY-CUCUMBER SAUCE: In a medium bowl combine 1 cup chopped seeded cucumber, ½ cup mayonnaise or salad dressing, ⅓ cup buttermilk, ½ teaspoon curry powder, and ¼ teaspoon ground ginger. Cover and chill until serving time. Makes about 1½ cups.

Per serving: 315 cal., 21 g total fat (5 g sat. fat), 85 mg chol., 421 mg sodium, 3 g carbo., 0 g fiber, 26 g pro.

Another time brush grilled or broiled chicken breasts with the sweet-and-savory glaze.

ORANGE-CORIANDER GLAZED CHICKEN

⅓   cup orange marmalade

1   tablespoon soy sauce

1   tablespoon Oriental chili sauce

1½   teaspoons ground coriander

2½   to 3 pounds meaty chicken pieces (breast halves, thighs, and/or drumsticks), skinned if desired

       Salt

       Black pepper

1   orange, cut into thin wedges

       Snipped fresh cilantro (optional)

PREP: *20 minutes*

GRILL: *50 minutes*

MAKES: *4 servings*

1 For glaze, in a small saucepan combine marmalade, soy sauce, chili sauce, and coriander. Heat and stir over low heat until marmalade is melted. Set aside.

2 Sprinkle chicken with salt and pepper. For a charcoal grill, arrange medium-hot coals around a drip pan. Test for medium heat above the pan. Place chicken pieces, bone sides up, on grill rack over drip pan. Cover; grill for 50 to 60 minutes or until chicken is tender and no longer pink (170°F for breast halves; 180°F for thighs and drumsticks), turning once halfway through grilling and brushing occasionally with glaze during the last 10 minutes of grilling. (For a gas grill, preheat grill. Reduce heat to medium. Adjust for indirect cooking. Grill as above.)

3 Serve with orange wedges. If desired, sprinkle chicken with cilantro.

Per serving: 411 cal., 16 g total fat (4 g sat. fat), 130 mg chol., 700 mg sodium, 23 g carbo., 1 g fiber, 43 g pro.

Use a small, sharp, pointed knife to cut the pockets into the chicken breasts before marinating them.

CHICKEN STUFFED WITH SPINACH & SWEET PEPPERS

PREP: *30 minutes*

MARINATE: *2 to 4 hours*

GRILL: *45 minutes*

MAKES: *6 servings*

6	medium bone-in chicken breast halves (about 3¾ pounds total)
¼	cup honey mustard
2	tablespoons mayonnaise or salad dressing
1	tablespoon olive oil
1	tablespoon red wine vinegar
1	teaspoon dried oregano, crushed
1	teaspoon dried basil, crushed
1	teaspoon dried rosemary, crushed
1	cup finely shredded mozzarella cheese (4 ounces)
1	cup chopped fresh spinach
½	cup finely chopped red sweet pepper
¼	teaspoon black pepper
3	cloves garlic, minced
	Plum tomatoes, cut up (optional)

1 Make a horizontal pocket in each chicken breast half by cutting from one side almost to, but not through, the other side. Place chicken in a resealable plastic bag set in a shallow dish. For marinade, in a small bowl combine mustard, mayonnaise, oil, vinegar, oregano, basil, and rosemary. Pour over chicken. Seal bag; turn to coat chicken. Marinate in the refrigerator for 2 to 4 hours, turning bag occasionally.

2 Meanwhile, for stuffing, in a medium bowl combine mozzarella cheese, spinach, sweet pepper, black pepper, and garlic. Drain chicken, discarding marinade. Spoon stuffing into pockets in chicken breast halves. If necessary, fasten pockets with wooden toothpicks.

3 For a charcoal grill, arrange medium-hot coals around a drip pan. Test for medium heat above the pan. Place chicken breast halves, bone sides up, on grill rack over drip pan. Cover; grill for 45 to 55 minutes or until chicken is tender and no longer pink (170°F), turning once halfway through grilling. (For a gas grill, preheat grill. Reduce heat to medium. Adjust for indirect cooking. Grill as above.) If desired, serve with tomatoes.

Per serving: 373 cal., 23 g total fat (7 g sat. fat), 105 mg chol., 309 mg sodium, 4 g carbo., 0 g fiber, 35 g pro.

Prosciutto is an Italian ham that is salt-cured and air-dried, not smoked. It usually is sold in very thin slices. In a pinch, you can substitute thinly sliced smoked ham.

CHICKEN STUFFED WITH MUSHROOMS & PROSCIUTTO

1	15×7×½-inch cedar or alder grill plank
1	tablespoon olive oil
½	cup sliced fresh mushrooms
¼	cup finely chopped onion
1	clove garlic, minced
¾	cup chopped fresh spinach
½	cup shredded fontina or Gouda cheese (2 ounces)
1	ounce prosciutto, chopped
4	medium bone-in chicken breast halves (about 2½ pounds total)
	Olive oil
	Freshly ground black pepper
	Hot cooked spinach or plain fettuccine (optional)

PREP: *30 minutes*

SOAK: *1 hour*

GRILL: *25 minutes*

STAND: *5 minutes*

MAKES: *4 servings*

1 Before grilling, soak plank in enough water to cover for at least 1 hour. Place a weight on plank so it stays submerged during soaking. Drain plank.

2 In a medium skillet heat 1 tablespoon olive oil over medium-high heat. Add mushrooms, onion, and garlic. Cook until tender. Remove from heat. Let stand about 5 minutes to cool slightly. Stir in spinach, cheese, and prosciutto. Set aside.

3 Remove bones from chicken breast halves, leaving skin intact. Spoon mushroom mixture between the skin and flesh of breast halves. Brush the chicken breast halves with additional olive oil and sprinkle with pepper.

4 For a charcoal grill, place plank on grill rack directly over medium coals; heat about 5 minutes or until plank begins to crackle and smoke. Place chicken, skin sides up, on plank. Cover; grill chicken about 20 minutes or until tender and no longer pink (170°F). (For a gas grill, preheat grill. Reduce heat to medium. Heat plank and grill chicken as above.)

5 Remove chicken from grill. Let chicken stand for 5 minutes. Slice chicken diagonally. If desired, serve over hot cooked pasta.

Per serving: 514 cal., 31 g total fat (9 g sat. fat), 165 mg chol., 424 mg sodium, 2 g carbo., 0 g fiber, 54 g pro.

Sink your fork into one of these plump rolls, and the creamy, cherry-dotted filling oozes out. (Recipe pictured on page 283.)

DOUBLE CHERRY-CHICKEN ROLL-UPS

PREP: *30 minutes*
GRILL: *20 minutes*
MAKES: *4 servings*

½ of an 8-ounce container mascarpone cheese or ½ of an 8-ounce tub cream cheese

⅓ cup snipped dried cherries

3 tablespoons thinly sliced green onions

4 skinless, boneless chicken breast halves (about 1¼ pounds total)

1 tablespoon packed brown sugar

½ teaspoon salt

¼ teaspoon black pepper

1 recipe Cherry-Orange Sauce

1 For filling, in a small bowl combine mascarpone cheese, dried cherries, and green onion. Set filling aside.

2 Place each chicken breast half between two pieces of plastic wrap. Using the flat side of a meat mallet, pound the chicken lightly into rectangles about ¼ inch thick. Remove plastic wrap. Divide filling evenly among chicken breast halves, spreading over each to within ½ inch of edges. Fold in sides of each chicken piece; roll up from a short end. Secure with wooden toothpicks.

3 For rub, in a small bowl combine brown sugar, salt, and pepper. Sprinkle over chicken roll-ups; rub in with your fingers.

4 For a charcoal grill, arrange medium-hot coals around a drip pan. Test for medium heat above the pan. Place chicken on grill rack over drip pan. Cover; grill for 20 to 25 minutes or until chicken is tender and no longer pink (170°F). (For a gas grill, preheat grill. Reduce heat to medium. Adjust for indirect cooking. Grill as above.)

5 Serve with Cherry-Orange Sauce.

CHERRY-ORANGE SAUCE: Finely shred enough peel from 1 orange to equal 1 teaspoon. Set aside. Peel and section the orange over a bowl to catch
the juices. Add enough additional orange juice to measure ¼ cup total liquid. In a small saucepan combine the ¼ cup orange juice and ½ cup cherry preserves; heat and stir until melted. Remove from heat. Coarsely chop the orange sections; stir into preserves mixture along with the 1 teaspoon peel.

Per serving: 459 cal., 15 g total fat (8 g sat. fat), 118 mg chol., 400 mg sodium, 45 g carbo., 2 g fiber, 40 g pro.

Be sure you're using a plain rice mix instead of one with salty seasonings.

CHICKEN & WILD RICE SALAD

1	6-ounce package long grain and wild rice mix
⅔	cup bottled Italian salad dressing
6	skinless, boneless chicken breast halves (about 2 pounds total)
1	cup loose-pack frozen French-style green beans
1	14-ounce can artichoke hearts, drained and quartered
2½	cups packaged shredded cabbage with carrot (coleslaw mix)
	Lettuce leaves (optional)

PREP: *30 minutes*
CHILL: *2 hours*
GRILL: *12 minutes*
MAKES: *6 servings*

1 Prepare long grain and wild rice mix according to package directions. Transfer to a medium bowl. Cover and refrigerate about 2 hours or until chilled.

2 Place 3 tablespoons of the Italian salad dressing in a small bowl. Set aside remaining Italian salad dressing.

3 For a charcoal grill, place chicken on the rack of an uncovered grill directly over medium coals. Grill for 12 to 15 minutes or until chicken is tender and no longer pink (170°F), turning once and brushing chicken with the 3 tablespoons dressing during the last 2 minutes of grilling. (For a gas grill, preheat grill. Reduce heat to medium. Place chicken on grill rack over heat. Cover; grill as above.)

4 Meanwhile, rinse green beans with cool water for 30 seconds; drain well. In a large bowl toss together green beans, chilled cooked rice, artichoke hearts, and coleslaw mix. Pour the reserved Italian salad dressing over rice mixture; toss gently to coat.

5 Transfer chicken to a cutting board; slice chicken. Serve chicken with rice mixture. If desired, garnish with lettuce leaves.

Per serving: 374 cal., 10 g total fat (2 g sat. fat), 88 mg chol., 1,124 mg sodium, 30 g carbo., 4 g fiber, 40 g pro.

This Greek-inspired dish features lemon- and oregano-marinated grilled chicken tossed with a crunchy mix of cucumbers, tomatoes, and onion. In keeping with the Greek theme, there's also creamy cucumber salad dressing, feta cheese, and kalamata olives.

GREEK CHICKEN SALAD

PREP: *30 minutes*
MARINATE: *4 to 24 hours*
GRILL: *12 minutes*
MAKES: *4 servings*

4   skinless, boneless chicken breast halves (about 1¼ pounds total)

1   tablespoon lemon juice

1   tablespoon olive oil

1   tablespoon snipped fresh oregano or 1 teaspoon dried oregano, crushed

¼   teaspoon black pepper

2   cloves garlic, minced

3   medium cucumbers, seeded and cut into ½-inch pieces

2   medium tomatoes, cut into ½-inch pieces

½   cup chopped red onion

     Mixed salad greens (optional)

⅓   cup bottled creamy cucumber salad dressing

½   cup crumbled feta cheese (2 ounces)

¼   cup chopped pitted kalamata olives or ripe olives

1 Place chicken in a resealable plastic bag set in a shallow dish. For marinade, in a small bowl combine lemon juice, oil, oregano, pepper, and garlic. Pour over chicken. Seal bag; turn to coat chicken. Marinate in the refrigerator for 4 to 24 hours, turning bag occasionally.

2 Meanwhile, in a medium bowl toss together cucumbers, tomatoes, and red onion. Set aside.

3 Drain chicken, discarding marinade. For a charcoal grill, place chicken on the rack of uncovered grill directly over medium coals. Grill for 12 to 15 minutes or until tender and no longer pink (170°F), turning once halfway through grilling. (For a gas grill, preheat grill. Reduce heat to medium. Place chicken on grill rack over heat. Cover; grill as above.)

4 Transfer chicken to a cutting board; cut into bite-size pieces. Toss chicken with cucumber mixture. If desired, serve on greens. Drizzle salad dressing over chicken-cucumber mixture. Sprinkle with feta cheese and olives.

Per serving: 391 cal., 20 g total fat (5 g sat. fat), 95 mg chol., 483 mg sodium, 16 g carbo., 3 g fiber, 37 g pro.

The spicy Thai-inspired glaze dresses up the skewered chicken. Leaving at least a ¹/₄-inch space between the pieces on the kabobs allows the chicken to cook evenly.

THAI-SPICED CHICKEN KABOBS

1   small fresh pineapple (3 to 3½ pounds)
    Nonstick cooking spray or cooking oil
1   pound skinless, boneless chicken breasts, cut into 1-inch pieces
1   recipe Thai Brushing Sauce
1   tablespoon butter, melted
1   tablespoon packed brown sugar (optional)
    Hot cooked rice (optional)

PREP: *30 minutes*
GRILL: *13 minutes*
MAKES: *4 servings*

1 Cut off ends of pineapple. Halve pineapple lengthwise; cut each half crosswise into four slices. Lightly coat pineapple slices with nonstick cooking spray or brush with oil. Set aside.

2 Thread chicken pieces onto four long metal skewers, leaving a ¼-inch space between pieces.

3 For a charcoal grill, place skewers on the rack of uncovered grill directly over medium coals. Grill for 7 minutes; turn skewers. Remove ¼ cup of the Thai Brushing Sauce and brush over chicken. Discard the remainder of the sauce used to brush chicken. Arrange pineapple slices on grill rack directly over medium coals. Grill chicken and pineapple for 6 to 8 minutes more or until chicken is no longer pink and pineapple is heated through, turning once. (For a gas grill, preheat grill. Reduce heat to medium. Place skewers [and later pineapple] on grill rack over heat. Cover; grill as above.)

4 In a small bowl combine the remaining Thai Brushing Sauce, the melted butter, and, if desired, brown sugar; serve with chicken and pineapple. If desired, serve with rice.

THAI BRUSHING SAUCE: In a small bowl combine ²/₃ cup bottled sweet-and-sour sauce, 2 tablespoons snipped fresh basil, 1 teaspoon Thai seasoning or five-spice powder, and 1 clove garlic, minced. Makes about ¾ cup.

Per serving: 285 cal., 5 g total fat (2 g sat. fat), 73 mg chol., 332 mg sodium, 34 g carbo., 2 g fiber, 27 g pro.

Fresh pineapple gives this Asian-inspired chicken tropical freshness, but you can also use canned pineapple slices for convenience.

PINEAPPLE CHICKEN

PREP: *25 minutes*

GRILL: *12 minutes*

MAKES: *4 servings*

1   small fresh pineapple, peeled (3 to 3½ pounds)*

3   tablespoons hoisin sauce

⅛   to ¼ teaspoon crushed red pepper

4   skinless, boneless chicken breast halves (about 1¼ pounds total)

2   tablespoons snipped fresh cilantro

1 Cut four ½-inch-thick slices from pineapple; core slices and set aside. For hoisin glaze, chop enough of the remaining pineapple to make 1¼ cups. In a blender or small food processor combine chopped pineapple, hoisin sauce, and crushed red pepper. Cover and blend or process until nearly smooth. Set aside.

2 For a charcoal grill, place chicken on the rack of uncovered grill directly over medium coals. Grill for 6 minutes. Turn chicken and place pineapple slices on grill. Brush chicken and pineapple with half of the hoisin glaze. Grill for 6 to 9 minutes more or until chicken is tender and no longer pink (170°F) and pineapple is warm. (For a gas grill, preheat grill. Reduce heat to medium. Place chicken [and later pineapple] on grill rack over heat. Cover; grill as above.)

3 In a small saucepan heat remaining hoisin glaze over low heat until mixture comes to boiling. To serve, arrange chicken breast halves and pineapple rings on four dinner plates. Sprinkle with snipped cilantro. Pass warmed hoisin glaze.

Per serving: 245 cal., 3 g total fat (1 g sat. fat), 83 mg chol., 273 mg sodium, 20 g carbo., 2 g fiber, 34 g pro.

*TEST KITCHEN TIP: For an even quicker meal, substitute a 20-ounce can pineapple slices (juice pack) for the fresh pineapple. Remove and reserve four of the slices. Chop remaining pineapple slices (should have about 1¼ cups). Grill pineapple slices for only 4 minutes.

Marinating is a terrific way to flavor foods. This marinade features a mix of garlic, lemon, and herbs that marries perfectly with the chicken.

LEMON-HERB CHICKEN

6   skinless, boneless chicken breast halves (about 2 pounds total)
¼   cup olive oil
6   cloves garlic, minced
1   tablespoon finely shredded lemon peel
2   teaspoons snipped fresh thyme
1   teaspoon snipped fresh rosemary
¼   to ½ teaspoon crushed red pepper
¼   teaspoon salt
⅛   to ¼ teaspoon black pepper
     Fresh thyme sprigs (optional)
     Lemon wedges (optional)

PREP: *15 minutes*
MARINATE: *2 to 4 hours*
GRILL: *12 minutes*
MAKES: *6 servings*

1 Place chicken in a resealable plastic bag set in a shallow dish. For marinade, in a small bowl combine oil, garlic, lemon peel, the snipped thyme, rosemary, crushed red pepper, salt, and black pepper. Pour marinade over chicken. Seal bag; turn to coat chicken. Marinate in the refrigerator for 2 to 4 hours, turning bag occasionally.

2 Drain chicken, discarding marinade. For a charcoal grill, place chicken on the rack of uncovered grill directly over medium coals. Grill for 12 to 15 minutes or until chicken is tender and no longer pink (170°F), turning once halfway through grilling. (For a gas grill, preheat grill. Reduce heat to medium. Place chicken on grill rack over heat. Cover; grill as above.) If desired, garnish with fresh thyme sprigs and lemon wedges.

Per serving: 216 cal., 7 g total fat (1 g sat. fat), 88 mg chol., 132 mg sodium, 1 g carbo., 0 g fiber, 35 g pro.

If you prefer, peel the cucumber for the sauce before you chop it.

CHICKEN WITH CUCUMBER-YOGURT SAUCE

PREP: *20 minutes*

GRILL: *12 minutes*

MAKES: *4 servings*

1   6-ounce carton plain low-fat yogurt

¼   cup thinly sliced green onions

2   teaspoons snipped fresh mint

½   teaspoon ground cumin

¼   teaspoon salt

¼   teaspoon black pepper

1   cup chopped, seeded cucumber

4   skinless, boneless chicken breast halves (about 1¼ pounds total)

1 In a medium bowl combine yogurt, green onion, mint, cumin, salt, and ⅛ teaspoon of the pepper. Transfer half of the yogurt mixture to a small bowl; set aside. For cucumber-yogurt sauce, stir cucumber into remaining yogurt mixture. Cover and chill until serving time.

2 Sprinkle chicken breast halves with the remaining ⅛ teaspoon pepper.

3 For a charcoal grill, place chicken on the rack of uncovered grill directly over medium coals. Grill for 12 to 15 minutes or until chicken is tender and no longer pink (170°F), turning once halfway through grilling and brushing occasionally with reserved yogurt mixture for the last half of grilling. Discard any remaining yogurt mixture. (For a gas grill, preheat grill. Reduce heat to medium. Place chicken on grill rack over heat. Cover; grill as above.)

4 Serve chicken with the cucumber-yogurt sauce.

Per serving: 193 cal., 3 g total fat (1 g sat. fat), 85 mg chol., 254 mg sodium, 5 g carbo., 0 g fiber, 35 g pro.

Add some gusto to the lime dressing by stirring in ⅛ teaspoon cayenne pepper before chilling.

CHICKEN & ZUCCHINI SANDWICHES

¼   cup mayonnaise or salad dressing

½   teaspoon finely shredded lime peel or lemon peel

1   medium zucchini or yellow summer squash,*
     cut lengthwise into ¼-inch-thick slices

3   tablespoons Worcestershire sauce for chicken

4   skinless, boneless chicken breast halves (about 1¼ pounds total)

4   whole wheat hamburger buns, split and toasted

PREP: *20 minutes*

GRILL: *12 minutes*

MAKES: *4 servings*

1 For lime dressing, in a small bowl combine mayonnaise and lime peel. Cover and chill until serving time.

2 Brush zucchini slices with 1 tablespoon of the Worcestershire sauce; set aside. Brush all sides of chicken breast halves with the remaining 2 tablespoons Worcestershire sauce.

3 For a charcoal grill, place chicken on the rack of uncovered grill directly over medium coals. Grill for 12 to 15 minutes or until chicken is tender and no longer pink (170°F), turning once halfway through grilling. Add zucchini slices to grill for the last 6 minutes of grilling time for chicken, turning once and grilling until zucchini slices are softened and lightly browned. (For a gas grill, preheat grill. Reduce heat to medium. Place chicken [and later zucchini] on grill rack over heat. Cover; grill as above.)

4 To serve, spread lime dressing onto cut sides of toasted buns. If desired, halve zucchini slices crosswise. Place chicken breast halves and zucchini slices on bun bottoms; add bun tops.

Per serving: 380 cal., 14 g total fat (3 g sat. fat), 87 mg chol., 564 mg sodium, 25 g carbo., 3 g fiber, 37 g pro.

*TEST KITCHEN TIP: For added color, use half of a medium zucchini and half of a medium yellow summer squash.

Stop by a local farmer's market to pick up the fresh veggies for this enticing pasta dish.

CHICKEN & GARDEN VEGETABLE PENNE PASTA

PREP: *25 minutes*

ROAST: *30 minutes*

GRILL: *12 minutes*

MAKES: *4 servings*

12	plum tomatoes, cored and halved
1	pound baby squash (such as pattypan, sunburst, and/or zucchini) (halve any large squash)
1	red sweet pepper, cut into bite-size strips
4	green onions, sliced into 1-inch pieces
3	tablespoons olive oil
1	tablespoon snipped fresh rosemary
	Kosher salt
	Black pepper
1	pound skinless, boneless chicken breast halves
8	ounces dried penne or bow tie pasta (2½ cups)
¼	cup snipped fresh flat-leaf parsley
2	to 3 tablespoons snipped fresh basil
¼	cup grated Parmesan cheese

1 Preheat oven to 450°F. Place tomatoes in a 13×9×2-inch baking pan or shallow roasting pan. Place squash, sweet pepper, and green onions in another shallow baking pan. Drizzle tomatoes and squash mixture with 2 tablespoons of the olive oil; season with rosemary, ½ teaspoon kosher salt, and ½ teaspoon black pepper. Roast about 20 minutes for squash mixture or just until tender and about 30 minutes for tomatoes or until very soft and skins are beginning to brown, stirring occasionally.

2 Meanwhile, brush chicken with the remaining 1 tablespoon olive oil; sprinkle lightly with kosher salt and black pepper. For a charcoal grill, place chicken on the rack of uncovered grill directly over medium coals. Grill for 12 to 15 minutes or until chicken is tender and no longer pink (170°F), turning once halfway through grilling. (For a gas grill, preheat grill. Reduce heat to medium. Place chicken on grill rack over heat. Cover; grill as above.) Let stand for 5 minutes. Slice chicken into strips.

3 Meanwhile, in a large saucepan cook pasta according to package directions in lightly salted boiling water. Drain pasta and transfer to a very large bowl.

4 To serve, stir tomatoes, squash mixture, chicken, parsley, and basil into hot pasta. Season to taste with kosher salt and black pepper. Transfer to a serving platter; sprinkle or serve with Parmesan cheese.

Per serving: 524 cal., 15 g total fat (3 g sat. fat), 70 mg chol., 399 mg sodium, 60 g carbo., 7 g fiber, 40 g pro.

Apple jelly and ginger combine in an easy-to-fix glaze for chicken. (Recipe pictured on page 284.)

GLAZED CHICKEN WITH WILTED SPINACH

1	recipe Ginger-Apple Glaze
4	skinless, boneless chicken breast halves (about 1¼ pounds total)
	Nonstick cooking spray
2	medium apples, cored and sliced
1	medium leek, sliced, or ⅓ cup chopped onion
2	cloves garlic, minced
2	tablespoons apple juice, apple cider, or chicken broth
1	10 ounce bag fresh spinach, stems removed (about 10 cups)
	Salt
	Black pepper

PREP: *20 minutes*
GRILL: *12 minutes*
MAKES: *4 servings*

❶ Measure ¼ cup of the Ginger-Apple Glaze; set aside remaining glaze. For a charcoal grill, place chicken on the rack of uncovered grill directly over medium coals. Grill for 12 to 15 minutes or until chicken is tender and no longer pink (170°F), turning once halfway through grilling and brushing often with the ¼ cup Ginger-Apple Glaze during the last 5 minutes of grilling. (For a gas grill, preheat grill. Reduce heat to medium. Place chicken on grill rack over heat. Cover; grill as above.)

❷ Meanwhile, lightly coat an unheated large saucepan or Dutch oven with nonstick cooking spray. Preheat over medium heat. Add apples, leek, and garlic; cook for 3 minutes. Stir in the reserved Ginger-Apple Glaze and the apple juice; bring to boiling. Add spinach; toss just until wilted. Season to taste with salt and pepper.

❸ To serve, slice each chicken breast half crosswise into six to eight pieces. Arrange spinach mixture on four dinner plates; top with chicken.

GINGER-APPLE GLAZE: In a small saucepan combine ½ cup apple jelly; 2 tablespoons soy sauce; 1 tablespoon snipped fresh thyme or 1 teaspoon dried thyme, crushed; 1 teaspoon finely shredded lemon peel; and 1 teaspoon grated fresh ginger. Heat and stir just until jelly is melted. Makes ⅔ cup.

Per serving: 346 cal., 2 g total fat (1 g sat. fat), 82 mg chol., 819 mg sodium, 47 g carbo., 4 g fiber, 36 g pro.

To cut cilantro or any fresh herb in a flash, put the leaves in a glass measuring cup and use kitchen shears to snip them into tiny pieces.

GINGER CHICKEN KABOBS

PREP: *25 minutes*

CHILL: *2 to 6 hours*

GRILL: *8 minutes*

MAKES: *4 servings*

1	pound skinless, boneless chicken breasts, cut into 1-inch pieces
2	tablespoons snipped fresh cilantro
1	tablespoon grated fresh ginger
2	cloves garlic, minced
1	fresh serrano or jalapeño chile pepper, seeded and finely chopped (see tip, page 19)
1	teaspoon cooking oil
½	teaspoon ground coriander
½	teaspoon ground cumin
¼	teaspoon salt
¼	teaspoon garam masala (optional)
⅛	teaspoon ground nutmeg
1	cup fresh pineapple cubes
1	medium red or green sweet pepper, cut into 1-inch pieces

1 Place chicken in a resealable plastic bag set in a shallow dish. Add cilantro, ginger, garlic, chile pepper, oil, coriander, cumin, salt, garam masala (if desired), and nutmeg to plastic bag. Seal bag; turn and press bag to coat chicken. Chill for 2 to 6 hours.

2 On eight 10- to 12-inch skewers,* alternately thread chicken, pineapple, and sweet pepper, leaving a ¼-inch space between pieces.

3 For a charcoal grill, place skewers on the rack of uncovered grill directly over medium coals. Grill for 8 to 12 minutes or until chicken is no longer pink, turning occasionally to brown evenly. (For a gas grill, preheat grill. Reduce heat to medium. Place skewers on grill rack over heat. Cover; grill as above.)

Per serving: 175 cal., 3 g total fat (1 g sat. fat), 66 mg chol., 212 mg sodium, 8 g carbo., 1 g fiber, 27 g pro.

BROILER DIRECTIONS: Preheat broiler. Place skewers on the unheated rack of a broiler pan. Broil 4 to 5 inches from the heat for 8 to 12 minutes or until chicken is no longer pink, turning occasionally to brown evenly.

***TEST KITCHEN TIP:** If using wooden skewers, soak in enough water to cover for at least 1 hour before using.

The black bean, jicama, tomato, and avocado relish gives old-fashioned fajitas a brand-new taste and look. (Recipe pictured on page 285.)

CHICKEN FAJITAS

4	skinless, boneless chicken breast halves (about 1¼ pounds total)
½	cup bottled Italian salad dressing
½	teaspoon chili powder
½	teaspoon ground cumin
2	small red, green, and/or yellow sweet peppers, quartered lengthwise
1	small red onion, cut into ½-inch-thick slices
1	15-ounce can black beans, rinsed and drained
1	cup chopped, peeled jicama
1	large tomato, chopped
1	medium avocado, halved, seeded, peeled, and chopped
½	cup snipped fresh cilantro
8	10-inch flour tortillas, warmed*
1	16-ounce jar salsa
	Shredded cheese (optional)
	Dairy sour cream (optional)

PREP: *45 minutes*

MARINATE: *1 to 24 hours*

GRILL: *12 minutes*

MAKES: *8 servings*

1 Place chicken in a resealable plastic bag set in a shallow dish. For marinade, combine Italian dressing, chili powder, and cumin. Pour over chicken. Seal bag; turn to coat chicken. Marinate in the refrigerator for 1 to 24 hours, turning bag occasionally.

2 Drain chicken, reserving marinade. Brush marinade over sweet peppers and red onion. Discard remaining marinade. In a large bowl toss together black beans, jicama, tomato, avocado, and cilantro; set aside.

3 For a charcoal grill, place chicken, sweet peppers, and red onion on the rack of uncovered grill directly over medium coals. Grill until chicken is tender and no longer pink (170°F) and vegetables are crisp-tender, turning once halfway through grilling (allow 12 to 15 minutes for chicken and 8 to 10 minutes for vegetables). (For a gas grill, preheat grill. Reduce heat to medium. Place chicken and vegetables on grill rack over heat. Cover; grill as above.)

4 Remove chicken and vegetables from grill; carefully slice into thin bite-size strips. Spoon chicken and vegetables onto warmed tortillas. Top with black bean mixture and salsa. If desired, top with shredded cheese and sour cream. Roll up.

Per serving: 396 cal., 16 g total fat (3 g sat. fat), 41 mg chol., 720 mg sodium, 42 g carbo., 6 g fiber, 25 g pro.

*TEST KITCHEN TIP: To warm the tortillas, preheat oven to 350°F. Wrap stacked tortillas tightly in foil. Bake about 10 minutes or until heated through. (Or place on edge of grill and heat about 10 minutes or until heated through; turn once.)

These chicken kabobs owe their captivating flavor to the trio of tangy lime, lively garlic-herb seasoning, and tongue-tingling ancho chile pepper.

CHILE-LIME CHICKEN SKEWERS

PREP: *20 minutes*

GRILL: *10 minutes*

MAKES: *4 servings*

1   pound skinless, boneless chicken breasts, cut into 1-inch-wide strips

2   limes

1½   teaspoons ground ancho chile pepper

1   teaspoon garlic-herb seasoning

1 Place chicken strips in a shallow dish; set aside. Finely shred enough peel from one of the limes to measure 1 teaspoon (chill lime and use for juice another time). Cut the remaining lime into wedges and set aside. For rub, combine lime peel, ancho chile pepper, and garlic-herb seasoning. Sprinkle evenly over chicken; rub in with your fingers.

2 On four long metal skewers, thread chicken, accordion-style, leaving a ¼-inch space between pieces. For a charcoal grill, place skewers on the rack of uncovered grill directly over medium coals. Grill for 10 to 12 minutes or until chicken is tender and no longer pink, turning once. (For a gas grill, preheat grill. Reduce heat to medium. Place skewers on grill rack over heat. Cover; grill as above.) Serve with lime wedges.

Per serving: 132 cal., 2 g total fat (0 g sat. fat), 66 mg chol., 62 mg sodium, 1 g carbo., 0 g fiber, 26 g pro.

Capers and minced garlic freshen the flavor of bottled salad dressing. Another time drizzle the versatile vinaigrette over grilled or broiled fish.

CHICKEN WITH CAPER VINAIGRETTE

¼ cup oil-packed dried tomato strips

4 skinless, boneless chicken breast halves (about 1¼ pounds total)

¼ cup bottled clear Italian salad dressing

2 tablespoons capers, rinsed and drained

¼ teaspoon black pepper

1 clove garlic, minced

PREP: *15 minutes*

GRILL: *12 minutes*

MAKES: *4 servings*

1 Drain tomato strips, reserving oil. Set tomato strips aside. Brush chicken with some of the reserved oil.

2 For a charcoal grill, place chicken on the rack of uncovered grill directly over medium coals. Grill for 12 to 15 minutes or until chicken is tender and no longer pink (170°F), turning once and brushing with remaining reserved oil halfway through grilling. Discard any remaining oil. (For a gas grill, preheat grill. Reduce heat to medium. Place chicken on grill rack over heat. Cover; grill as above.)

3 Meanwhile, for vinaigrette, in a small bowl whisk together salad dressing, capers, pepper, and garlic.

4 To serve, diagonally slice each chicken breast. Spoon vinaigrette over chicken. Top with tomato strips.

Per serving: 218 cal., 4 g total fat (1 g sat. fat), 99 mg chol., 447 mg sodium, 3 g carbo., 1 g fiber, 40 g pro.

Apricot spreadable fruit and jerk seasoning team up to give these chicken skewers a delightful zing. Another time try strawberry spreadable fruit instead.

APRICOT CHICKEN KABOBS

PREP: *25 minutes*

GRILL: *8 minutes*

MAKES: *4 servings*

1	pound skinless, boneless chicken breasts, cut into 1-inch pieces
1½	teaspoons Jamaican jerk seasoning
1	cup fresh sugar snap peas or pea pods, strings and tips removed
1	cup fresh or canned pineapple chunks
1	medium red sweet pepper, cut into 1-inch pieces
¼	cup apricot spreadable fruit

1 In a large bowl sprinkle chicken with about half of the jerk seasoning; toss gently to coat. Cut any large sugar snap peas in half crosswise.

2 On long skewers,* alternately thread chicken, sugar snap peas, pineapple, and sweet pepper, leaving a ¼-inch space between pieces. Set aside.

3 For sauce, in a small saucepan combine remaining jerk seasoning and the spreadable fruit. Cook and stir just until spreadable fruit is melted; set aside.

4 For a charcoal grill, place skewers on the rack of uncovered grill directly over medium coals. Grill for 8 to 12 minutes or until chicken is no longer pink and vegetables are crisp-tender, turning once and brushing occasionally with sauce during the last 2 minutes of grilling. (For a gas grill, preheat grill. Reduce heat to medium. Place skewers on grill rack over heat. Cover; grill as above.)

Per serving: 199 cal., 2 g total fat (0 g sat. fat), 66 mg chol., 173 mg sodium, 20 g carbo., 2 g fiber, 27 g pro.

*TEST KITCHEN TIP: If using wooden skewers, soak in enough water to cover for at least 1 hour before using.

Heating the tortillas on the grill gives them a warm, toasty flavor. Both corn and flour tortillas work well, but the corn tortillas puff less when they're grilled so are easier to layer.

CHICKEN & AVOCADO TOSTADOS

4   6-inch corn or flour tortillas

2   tablespoons cooking oil

3   tablespoons taco seasoning

4   skinless, boneless chicken breast halves (about 1¼ pounds total)

4   cups fresh baby spinach

1   avocado, halved, seeded, peeled, and sliced

½   cup purchased thick and chunky salsa

PREP: *20 minutes*

GRILL: *14 minutes*

MAKES: *4 servings*

1 Brush tortillas on both sides with 1 tablespoon of the oil; sprinkle with half of the taco seasoning. Brush chicken breast halves on both sides with remaining 1 tablespoon oil and sprinkle with remaining taco seasoning.

2 For a charcoal grill, place tortillas on greased rack of uncovered grill directly over medium coals. Grill about 2 minutes or until crisp, turning once halfway through grilling. Transfer to four dinner plates.

3 Place chicken on the greased grill rack directly over medium coals. Grill for 12 to 15 minutes or until tender and no longer pink (170°F), turning once halfway through grilling. (For a gas grill, preheat grill. Reduce heat to medium. Place tortillas [and later chicken] on greased grill rack over heat. Cover; grill as above.)

4 Divide spinach and avocado among grilled tortillas. Shred chicken with a fork. Arrange shredded chicken over avocado. Spoon salsa over the chicken.

Per serving: 386 cal., 16 g total fat (3 g sat. fat), 82 mg chol., 825 mg sodium, 23 g carbo., 6 g fiber, 37 g pro.

Bottled salad dressing makes marinating the chicken for these Italian-style kabobs super easy.

CHICKEN SPIEDINI

PREP: *35 minutes*

MARINATE: *2 to 24 hours*

GRILL: *10 minutes*

MAKES: *4 servings*

1¼   pounds chicken breast tenderloins

⅔   cup bottled sweet Italian salad dressing or bottled clear Italian salad dressing

¾   cup seasoned fine dry bread crumbs

¾   cup halved fresh mushrooms

2   cloves garlic, minced

1   tablespoon butter

¼   cup coarsely chopped prosciutto

¾   cup shredded mozzarella cheese (3 ounces)

1   lemon, quartered

1 Place chicken in a resealable plastic bag set in a shallow dish. Pour salad dressing over chicken. Seal bag; turn to coat chicken. Marinate in the refrigerator for 2 to 24 hours, turning bag occasionally.

2 Drain chicken, discarding marinade. Place bread crumbs in a shallow dish. Dip chicken in bread crumbs to coat. On five to six long metal skewers, thread chicken, accordion-style, leaving a ¼-inch space between pieces.

3 For a charcoal grill, place skewers on the rack of uncovered grill directly over medium coals. Grill for 10 to 12 minutes or until chicken is tender and no longer pink, turning once halfway through grilling. (For a gas grill, preheat grill. Reduce heat to medium. Place skewers on grill rack over heat. Cover; grill as above.)

4 In a large skillet cook mushrooms and garlic in hot butter about 5 minutes or just until mushrooms are tender, stirring occasionally. Add prosciutto; cook and stir for 2 minutes more.

5 Remove chicken from skewers; arrange on a serving plate. Sprinkle chicken with half of the cheese. Spoon mushroom mixture over chicken. Sprinkle with remaining cheese. Serve with lemon quarters.

Per serving: 471 cal., 22 g total fat (6 g sat. fat), 113 mg chol., 1,820 mg sodium, 22 g carbo., 0 g fiber, 46 g pro.

Oriental chili sauce has a lot more kick than the regular version. It is made with chile peppers, vinegar, and spices and can vary in hotness depending on the brand and the country of origin. It is sold in the Asian food section of larger supermarkets and in Asian food specialty shops.

PINEAPPLE-GLAZED CHICKEN

1	15×7×½-inch cedar or alder grill plank
1	tablespoon olive oil
¼	cup finely chopped onion
1	clove garlic, minced
½	cup pineapple preserves
1	tablespoon soy sauce
1	tablespoon Oriental chili sauce
½	teaspoon finely shredded lemon peel
1	tablespoon lemon juice
4	whole chicken legs (thigh-drumstick portion)
	Salt
	Freshly ground black pepper
8	fresh pineapple wedges*
	Snipped fresh cilantro (optional)

PREP: *25 minutes*

SOAK: *1 hour*

GRILL: *55 minutes*

MAKES: *4 servings*

1 Before grilling, soak plank in enough water to cover for at least 1 hour. Place a weight on plank so it stays submerged during soaking. Drain plank.

2 For glaze, in a small saucepan heat oil over medium heat. Add onion and garlic; cook until tender. Stir in pineapple preserves, soy sauce, chili sauce, lemon peel, and lemon juice. Cook and stir over low heat just until preserves melt. Remove from heat; set aside.

3 For a charcoal grill, place plank on grill rack directly over medium coals; heat about 5 minutes or until plank begins to crackle and smoke. Place chicken on plank. Sprinkle chicken lightly with salt and pepper. Carefully spoon glaze over chicken. Discard any remaining glaze. Cover; grill for 25 minutes. Arrange pineapple wedges, overlapping slightly, on plank. Cover; grill for 25 to 30 minutes more or until chicken is no longer pink (180°F in thigh). (For a gas grill, preheat grill. Reduce heat to medium. Heat plank and grill chicken and pineapple as above.)

4 Serve chicken with pineapple wedges. If desired, sprinkle chicken with cilantro.

Per serving: 478 cal., 23 g total fat (6 g sat. fat), 138 mg chol., 535 mg sodium, 35 g carbo., 1 g fiber, 31 g pro.

*TEST KITCHEN TIP: Cut a whole fresh unpeeled pineapple into quarters lengthwise. From one of the quarters, cut ½ inch-thick crosswise slices.

Jalapeño jelly provides both sweetness and heat. For a little more heat, use the red version.

SMOKIN' DRUMSTICKS

PREP: *15 minutes*
SOAK: *1 hour*
GRILL: *50 minutes*
MAKES: *5 servings*

2   cups mesquite wood chips
2½   to 3 pounds chicken drumsticks, skinned if desired
     Salt
     Black pepper
½   cup jalapeño chile pepper jelly
1   recipe Dipping Sauce

1 Before grilling, soak mesquite wood chips in enough water to cover for at least 1 hour.

2 Sprinkle drumsticks with salt and pepper. For a charcoal grill, arrange medium-hot coals around a drip pan. Test for medium heat above pan. Drain wood chips and add to coals. Place drumsticks on grill rack over drip pan. Cover; grill for 50 to 60 minutes or until chicken is tender and no longer pink (180°F). (For a gas grill, preheat grill. Reduce heat to medium. Adjust for indirect cooking. Grill as above.)

3 Meanwhile, in a small saucepan heat jelly until melted. Brush drumsticks with jelly occasionally during the last 10 minutes of grilling. Serve with Dipping Sauce.

DIPPING SAUCE: In a small bowl combine one 8-ounce carton dairy sour cream, 2 tablespoons snipped fresh cilantro, ½ teaspoon finely shredded lime peel, 2 tablespoons lime juice, and ⅛ teaspoon salt. Cover and chill until ready to serve.

Per serving: 488 cal., 29 g total fat (11 g sat. fat), 157 mg chol., 313 mg sodium, 24 g carbo., 0 g fiber, 32 g pro.

A marinade that blends rosemary, dry mustard, orange peel, and orange juice imparts a fruity flavor to the chicken that complements the fresh taste of the peach-and-pepper topper.

ROSEMARY CHICKEN WITH PEACH SALSA

12	chicken drumsticks, skinned
2	teaspoons finely shredded orange peel
½	cup orange juice
2	tablespoons olive oil or cooking oil
2	teaspoons snipped fresh rosemary or ½ teaspoon dried rosemary, crushed
1	teaspoon dry mustard
¼	teaspoon salt
2	medium peaches or nectarines or 1⅓ cups loose-pack frozen unsweetened peach slices, thawed
½	cup coarsely chopped red or yellow sweet pepper
2	green onions, sliced
1	fresh jalapeño chile pepper, seeded and chopped (see tip, page 19)
2	tablespoons orange juice

PREP: *30 minutes*

MARINATE: *1 to 4 hours*

GRILL: *50 minutes*

MAKES: *6 servings*

1 Place chicken in a resealable plastic bag set in a shallow dish. For marinade, in a small bowl combine orange peel, the ½ cup orange juice, the oil, rosemary, dry mustard, and salt; pour over chicken. Seal bag; turn to coat chicken. Marinate in the refrigerator for 1 to 4 hours, turning the bag occasionally.

2 Meanwhile, for salsa, pit and coarsely chop fresh peaches or nectarines. In a medium bowl combine peaches or nectarines, sweet pepper, green onions, chile pepper, and the 2 tablespoons orange juice. Cover and chill until serving time.

3 Drain chicken, reserving marinade. For a charcoal grill, arrange medium-hot coals around a drip pan. Test for medium heat above pan. Place chicken on grill rack over drip pan. Cover; grill for 50 to 60 minutes or until chicken is tender and no longer pink (180°F), turning once and brushing with reserved marinade after 25 minutes of grilling. Discard any remaining marinade. (For a gas grill, preheat grill. Reduce heat to medium. Adjust for indirect cooking. Grill as above.) Serve the chicken with salsa.

Per serving: 198 cal., 7 g total fat (2 g sat. fat), 82 mg chol., 133 mg sodium, 6 g carbo., 1 g fiber, 26 g pro.

Time to rethink cranberries—they aren't just for the holidays. Here cranberry-orange sauce joins forces with barbecue sauce and Dijon-style mustard to glaze grilled drumsticks.

CRANBERRY GRILLED CHICKEN

PREP: *20 minutes*

GRILL: *35 minutes*

MAKES: *4 servings*

½ teaspoon finely shredded orange peel

¼ teaspoon black pepper

8 chicken drumsticks or thighs, skinned

½ of a 10-ounce container frozen cranberry-orange sauce, thawed (½ cup)

¼ cup bottled barbecue sauce

2 teaspoons Dijon-style mustard

Lettuce leaves (optional)

1 medium orange, sectioned (optional)

1 In a small bowl stir together orange peel and pepper. Sprinkle evenly over chicken; rub in with your fingers. For a charcoal grill, place chicken on the rack of uncovered grill directly over medium coals. Grill for 25 minutes, turning occasionally.

2 Meanwhile, in a small saucepan stir together cranberry-orange sauce, barbecue sauce, and mustard. Cook and stir until heated through. Remove from heat. (Mixture will be thick.)

3 Brush cranberry mixture onto chicken. Grill for 10 to 20 minutes more or until tender and no longer pink (180°F), turning and brushing occasionally with the cranberry mixture up until the last 5 minutes of grilling. Discard any remaining cranberry mixture. (For a gas grill, preheat grill. Reduce heat to medium. Place chicken on grill rack over heat. Cover; grill as above.) If desired, serve with lettuce and orange.

Per serving: 318 cal., 7 g total fat (2 g sat. fat), 157 mg chol., 335 mg sodium, 17 g carbo., 0 g fiber, 42 g pro.

Chipotle chile peppers in adobo sauce create fabulous firepower in this chunky peach brush-on for chicken. (Recipe pictured on page 285.)

CHIPOTLE PEACH-GLAZED CHICKEN

½   teaspoon salt

¼   teaspoon black pepper

¼   teaspoon ground nutmeg

8   chicken thighs (about 2½ pounds total), skinned*

⅓   cup peach preserves

2   tablespoons white wine vinegar

2   to 3 teaspoons chopped canned chipotle chile peppers
     in adobo sauce (see tip, page 19)

PREP: *20 minutes*

GRILL: *50 minutes*

MAKES: *4 servings*

1 In a small bowl combine salt, black pepper, and ⅛ teaspoon of the nutmeg; sprinkle evenly over chicken thighs. For glaze, in a small saucepan combine peach preserves, vinegar, chipotle chile pepper, and the remaining ⅛ teaspoon nutmeg; heat and stir just until preserves are melted. Set aside.

2 For a charcoal grill, arrange medium-hot coals around a drip pan. Test for medium heat above pan. Place chicken thighs on grill rack over drip pan. Cover; grill for 50 to 60 minutes or until tender and no longer pink (180°F), brushing with glaze during the last 10 minutes of grilling. (For a gas grill, preheat grill. Reduce heat to medium. Adjust for indirect cooking. Grill as above.)

Per serving: 459 cal., 27 g total fat (8 g sat. fat), 156 mg chol., 426 mg sodium, 19 g carbo., 0 g fiber, 33 g pro.

***TEST KITCHEN TIP:** If you prefer, use 4 skinless, boneless chicken breast halves (about 1¼ pounds total). Prepare as directed in Step 1. For a charcoal grill, place chicken breast halves on rack of uncovered grill directly over medium coals. Grill for 12 to 15 minutes or until tender and no longer pink (170°F), turning once halfway through grilling and brushing often with glaze during the last 2 minutes of grilling. (For a gas grill, preheat grill. Reduce heat to medium. Place chicken breast halves on grill rack over heat. Cover; grill as above.)

This buttermilk marinade gives chicken thighs the same moistness and tang that makes buttermilk fried chicken so popular.

CHICKEN THIGHS IN BUTTERMILK-CHIVE MARINADE

PREP: *15 minutes*
MARINATE: *4 to 6 hours*
GRILL: *50 minutes*
MAKES: *4 servings*

8   chicken thighs (about 2½ pounds total), skinned if desired
¾   cup buttermilk
3   tablespoons snipped fresh chives
1   tablespoon finely shredded lemon peel
3   tablespoons lemon juice
3   cloves garlic, minced
    Lemon wedges
    Snipped fresh chives

1 Place chicken in a resealable plastic bag set in a shallow dish. For marinade, in a medium bowl combine buttermilk, the 3 tablespoons chives, the lemon peel, lemon juice, and garlic. Pour over chicken. Seal bag; turn to coat chicken. Marinate in the refrigerator for 4 to 6 hours, turning the bag occasionally.

2 Drain chicken, discarding marinade. For a charcoal grill, arrange medium-hot coals around a drip pan. Test for medium heat above pan. Place chicken thighs on grill rack over drip pan. Cover; grill for 50 to 60 minutes or until chicken is tender and no longer pink (180°F), turning once halfway through grilling. (For a gas grill, preheat grill. Reduce heat to medium. Adjust for indirect cooking. Grill as above.) Serve with lemon wedges and sprinkle with additional chives.

Per serving: 556 cal., 39 g total fat (11 g sat. fat), 224 mg chol., 180 mg sodium, 2 g carbo., 0 g fiber, 47 g pro.

The shape of boneless chicken thighs makes them naturals for stuffing and shaping into tidy rolls.

PAPAYA-STUFFED CHICKEN THIGHS

1   tablespoon toasted sesame oil

1   teaspoon grated fresh ginger or ½ teaspoon ground ginger

¼   teaspoon salt

6   skinless, boneless chicken thighs (about 1½ pounds total)
    Salt
    Black pepper

¼   cup sliced green onions

6   2×½-inch pieces peeled, seeded papaya or mango
    (¼ of a medium papaya or ½ of a medium mango)

2   tablespoons snipped fresh cilantro ·

PREP: *30 minutes*
GRILL: *20 minutes*
MAKES: *6 servings*

1 In a small bowl combine sesame oil, ginger, and the ¼ teaspoon salt. Place each chicken thigh, boned side up, on a flat surface, spreading thigh open. Season with salt and pepper and brush with some of the oil mixture. Sprinkle thighs with green onion. Place one papaya piece crosswise near a short side of each thigh. Starting from side with fruit, roll up; secure with wooden toothpicks. Brush with remaining oil mixture.

2 For a charcoal grill, arrange medium-hot coals around a drip pan. Test for medium heat above pan. Place chicken on grill rack over drip pan. Cover; grill for 20 to 25 minutes or until chicken is tender and no longer pink (180°F), turning once halfway through grilling. (For a gas grill, preheat grill. Reduce heat to medium. Adjust for indirect cooking. Grill as above.)

3 To serve, sprinkle with cilantro.

Per serving: 169 cal., 8 g total fat (1 g sat. fat), 86 mg chol., 366 mg sodium, 3 g carbo., 1 g fiber, 21 g pro.

If you're wary of splitting a whole turkey breast, ask your butcher to halve the breast for you or buy two turkey breast halves of about the same size.

JERK-RUBBED TURKEY BREAST

PREP: *35 minutes*

GRILL: *1¼ hours*

STAND: *10 minutes*

MAKES: *12 servings*

1	tablespoon cooking oil
1	large red onion, finely chopped
3	cloves garlic, minced
1	fresh jalapeño chile pepper, seeded and finely chopped (see tip, page 19)
1	teaspoon snipped fresh thyme
½	teaspoon salt
½	teaspoon ground allspice
¼	teaspoon ground nutmeg
⅛	teaspoon ground cloves
¼	cup dark rum
2	tablespoons lime juice
1	4- to 5-pound whole bone-in turkey breast, split
	Salt
	Black pepper

1 In a large skillet heat oil over medium heat. Add onion, garlic, and chile pepper; cook about 4 minutes or until tender. Add thyme, the ½ teaspoon salt, the allspice, nutmeg, and cloves. Cook and stir for 1 minute. Remove from heat; add rum and lime juice. Return to heat. Bring to boiling; reduce heat. Simmer, uncovered, for 1 to 2 minutes or until liquid is evaporated. Remove from heat; cool.

2 Starting at the breast bone of each turkey breast half, slip your fingers between the skin and the meat to loosen the skin, leaving skin attached at the sides to make a pocket. Lift skin and spread onion mixture evenly under skin. Sprinkle turkey breast halves with additional salt and pepper. Insert an oven-going meat thermometer into the thickest part of a turkey breast half (the thermometer should not touch bone).

3 For a charcoal grill, arrange medium-hot coals around a drip pan. Test for medium heat above pan. Place turkey breast halves, bone sides down, on grill rack over drip pan. Cover; grill for 1¼ to 2 hours or until thermometer registers 170°F. (For a gas grill, preheat grill. Reduce heat to medium. Adjust for indirect cooking. Grill as above.)

4 Remove turkey breast halves from grill. Cover with foil; let stand for 10 minutes before carving.

Per serving: 236 cal., 11 g total fat (3 g sat. fat), 84 mg chol., 203 mg sodium, 2 g carbo., 0 g fiber, 28 g pro.

This recipe is the answer when you want to make a delicious meal that looks impressive but is actually very simple to fix.

TURKEY WITH DRIED TOMATO PESTO

⅓   cup purchased basil pesto

3   tablespoons chopped, drained oil-packed dried tomatoes

1   2- to 2½-pound bone-in turkey breast half

Salt

Black pepper

12   ounces dried fettuccine, cooked and drained

PREP: *25 minutes*

GRILL: *1¼ hours*

STAND: *10 minutes*

MAKES: *8 servings*

1 In a small bowl stir together pesto and dried tomato; set aside. Starting at the breast bone, slip your fingers between the turkey skin and meat to loosen skin, leaving skin attached at the side to make a pocket. Lift skin and spoon half of the pesto mixture over the meat; rub with your fingers to spread evenly. Fold skin back over meat, covering as much as possible. Sprinkle breast with salt and pepper. Insert an oven-going meat thermometer into the thickest part of the breast half (the thermometer should not touch bone).

2 For a charcoal grill, arrange medium-hot coals around a drip pan. Test for medium heat above the pan. Place turkey, bone side down, on grill rack over drip pan. Cover; grill for 1¼ to 2 hours or until thermometer registers 170°F. (For a gas grill, preheat grill. Reduce heat to medium. Adjust for indirect cooking. Grill as above.)

3 Remove turkey from grill. Cover with foil; let stand for 10 minutes before carving. Meanwhile, toss remaining pesto mixture with hot fettuccine. Slice turkey. Serve with fettuccine.

Per serving: 328 cal., 9 g total fat (1 g sat. fat), 50 mg chol., 196 mg sodium, 34 g carbo., 1 g fiber, 26 g pro.

Showcase these colorful kabobs on a bed of aromatic rice, such as jasmine or wild pecan.

TURKEY, PORTOBELLO MUSHROOM & VEGETABLE KABOBS

PREP: *35 minutes*
MARINATE: *2 to 24 hours*
GRILL: *12 minutes*
MAKES: *8 servings*

½ cup sliced green onions

⅓ cup olive oil

¼ cup balsamic vinegar

1 tablespoon Worcestershire sauce

4 cloves garlic, minced

1 teaspoon dried rosemary, crushed

1 teaspoon dried tarragon, crushed

1½ to 2 pounds boneless turkey breast or thigh,
cut into 1-inch cubes

8 ounces fresh baby bella or button mushrooms, quartered, or
portobello mushrooms, stemmed and cut into 1-inch pieces

1 medium red sweet pepper, cut into 1-inch pieces

1 small yellow summer squash, cut into 1-inch pieces

1 small zucchini, cut into 1-inch pieces

1 For marinade, in a small bowl combine green onion, olive oil, balsamic vinegar, Worcestershire sauce, garlic, rosemary, and tarragon. In a large resealable plastic bag set in a shallow dish combine turkey, mushrooms, sweet pepper, summer squash, and zucchini. Pour marinade over turkey mixture in bag. Seal bag; toss to coat. Marinate in the refrigerator for 2 to 24 hours, turning bag occasionally.

2 Drain turkey and vegetables, discarding marinade. On eight 10- to 12-inch metal skewers, alternately thread turkey and vegetables, leaving a ¼-inch space between pieces.

3 For a charcoal grill, place skewers on greased rack of uncovered grill directly over medium coals. Grill for 12 to 14 minutes or until turkey is no longer pink, turning once halfway through grilling. (For a gas grill, preheat grill. Reduce heat to medium. Place skewers on greased grill rack over heat. Cover; grill as above.)

Per serving: 142 cal., 4 g total fat (1 g sat. fat), 51 mg chol., 54 mg sodium, 4 g carbo., 1 g fiber, 22 g pro.

The crisp texture of the warm slaw is a pleasant surprise and an appealing contrast to the turkey.

TERIYAKI TURKEY TENDERLOINS

2	turkey breast tenderloins (about 1 pound total)
¼	cup soy sauce
2	tablespoons packed brown sugar
2	tablespoons lemon juice
1	tablespoon cooking oil
1	teaspoon grated fresh ginger
1	clove garlic, minced
1	recipe Hot Pineapple Slaw

PREP: *30 minutes*

MARINATE: *1 to 2 hours*

GRILL: *12 minutes*

MAKES: *4 servings*

1 Split each turkey breast tenderloin in half horizontally to make a total of four ½-inch-thick portions. Place turkey in a resealable plastic bag set in a shallow dish. For marinade, in a small bowl combine soy sauce, brown sugar, lemon juice, oil, ginger, and garlic. Pour marinade over turkey. Seal bag; turn to coat turkey. Marinate in the refrigerator for 1 to 2 hours, turning bag once.

2 Drain turkey, reserving marinade. For a charcoal grill, place turkey on the rack of uncovered grill directly over medium coals. Grill for 12 to 15 minutes or until turkey is no longer pink (170°F), turning once and brushing with reserved marinade halfway through grilling. Discard any remaining marinade. (For a gas grill, preheat grill. Reduce heat to medium. Place turkey on grill rack over heat. Cover and grill as above.)

3 Serve with Hot Pineapple Slaw.

HOT PINEAPPLE SLAW: In a medium saucepan cook ¼ cup thinly sliced green onions and ⅛ teaspoon crushed red pepper in 1 tablespoon cooking oil for 2 minutes. Stir in 2 cups shredded napa cabbage, 1 cup bite-size fresh pineapple pieces, ¼ cup green sweet pepper cut into thin strips, 1 teaspoon toasted sesame oil, and dash salt. Cook and stir just until cabbage is wilted.

Per serving: 239 cal., 8 g total fat (1 g sat. fat), 68 mg chol., 557 mg sodium, 12 g carbo., 2 g fiber, 29 g pro.

Think of these kabobs as Thanksgiving dinner on a skewer. They combine turkey and sweet potatoes with sage and onion.

SAGE TURKEY KABOBS

PREP: *35 minutes*

MARINATE: *2 to 8 hours*

GRILL: *12 minutes*

MAKES: *4 servings*

1   pound turkey breast tenderloins

1   small red onion, cut into 8 wedges

½   cup cider vinegar

¼   cup olive oil

2   tablespoons sugar

2   cloves garlic, minced

1   teaspoon snipped fresh thyme or ½ teaspoon dried thyme, crushed

1   teaspoon salt

20   fresh sage leaves

   Salt

   Black pepper

2   medium sweet potatoes

1 Cut turkey breast tenderloins lengthwise into ½-inch-thick strips. Place turkey strips and onion wedges in a resealable plastic bag set in a shallow dish.

2 For marinade, in a small bowl combine vinegar, oil, sugar, garlic, thyme, and salt. Snip four of the sage leaves; stir into marinade. Pour half of the marinade over turkey and onion. Cover remaining marinade and chill. Seal bag; turn to coat turkey and onion. Marinate in the refrigerator for 2 to 8 hours, turning bag occasionally.

3 Drain turkey and onion, discarding marinade. On a flat surface, spiral each turkey strip into an "S" shape. On eight metal skewers, alternately thread the remaining 16 sage leaves, the onion wedges, and turkey spirals, leaving a ¼-inch space between pieces. Sprinkle with salt and pepper.

4 Scrub sweet potatoes but do not peel. Cut potatoes diagonally into ½-inch-thick slices. Brush with some of the reserved marinade.

5 For a charcoal grill, place skewers and sweet potatoes on the rack of uncovered grill directly over medium coals. Grill for 12 to 14 minutes or until turkey is no longer pink and sweet potatoes are tender, turning once and brushing occasionally with the remainder of the reserved marinade during the last 2 minutes of grilling. (For a gas grill, preheat grill. Reduce heat to medium. Place turkey and sweet potatoes on grill rack over heat. Cover; grill as above.)

Per serving: 370 cal., 15 g total fat (2 g sat. fat), 70 mg chol., 780 mg sodium, 30 g carbo., 3 g fiber, 30 g pro.

Meyer lemons, a cousin to Mandarin oranges, are darker and sweeter than regular lemons, but you can substitute regular lemons if you like.

PESTO TURKEY PLATTER

3   turkey breast tenderloins (about 1½ pounds total)
6   small tomatoes, halved lengthwise
    Salt
    Freshly ground black pepper
½   cup purchased pesto
1   tablespoon olive oil
3   Meyer lemons, lemons, or limes, halved
2   avocados, halved, seeded, peeled, and sliced

PREP: *20 minutes*
GRILL: *16 minutes*
MAKES: *6 servings*

1 Sprinkle turkey and tomatoes with salt and pepper. For a charcoal grill, place turkey on the rack of uncovered grill directly over medium coals. Grill for 16 to 20 minutes or until an instant-read thermometer inserted near the center registers 170°F, brushing with pesto during the last 5 minutes of grilling.

2 Meanwhile, in a large bowl toss tomatoes with olive oil. Grill tomatoes, cut sides down, over medium coals about 10 minutes or until slightly charred, turning once. Add lemon halves, cut sides down, for the last 5 minutes of grilling. (For a gas grill, preheat grill. Reduce heat to medium. Place turkey [and later tomatoes and lemons] on grill rack over heat. Cover; grill as above.)

3 Slice turkey; arrange on platter with tomato halves and avocado slices. Squeeze juice from lemon halves over tomatoes and avocado.

Per serving: 401 cal., 25 g total fat (2 g sat. fat), 78 mg chol., 305 mg sodium, 13 g carbo., 5 g fiber, 32 g pro.

Make a well-rounded meal of taco salad by filling the tortilla shells with grilled turkey strips, Spanish rice, and a creamy dressing spiked with adobo sauce.

ADOBO TURKEY TACO SALAD

PREP: *40 minutes*
MARINATE: *1 to 24 hours*
GRILL: *25 minutes*
MAKES: *6 servings*

¼ cup adobo sauce from canned chipotle chile peppers in adobo sauce

3 tablespoons honey

1 tablespoon lime juice

1 cup purchased black bean and corn salsa

½ cup Mexican crema or dairy sour cream

1½ pounds turkey breast tenderloins

1 4.3-ounce package Spanish rice mix

6 cups spring mix salad greens or 6 cups shredded lettuce

6 purchased baked crisp salad shells

½ cup crumbled queso blanco or queso fresco or shredded farmer's cheese (2 ounces)

2 limes, cut into wedges

1 In a small bowl combine adobo sauce, honey, and lime juice. For dressing, remove 2 tablespoons of the adobo sauce mixture and place in a medium bowl; stir in salsa and crema or sour cream. Cover and chill dressing until ready to serve.

2 Place turkey breast tenderloins in a resealable plastic bag set in a shallow dish; add remaining adobo sauce mixture. Seal bag; turn to coat turkey. Marinate in the refrigerator for 1 to 24 hours, turning the bag occasionally.

3 Prepare Spanish rice mix according to package directions; set aside.

4 Drain turkey, discarding marinade. For a charcoal grill, arrange medium-hot coals around a drip pan. Test for medium heat above pan. Place turkey on grill rack over drip pan. Cover; grill for 25 to 30 minutes or until turkey is tender and no longer pink (170°F). (For a gas grill, preheat grill. Reduce heat to medium. Adjust for indirect cooking. Grill as above.)

5 Transfer turkey to a cutting board; cool slightly. Slice turkey diagonally into thin strips.

6 To assemble salads, divide greens among the salad shells. Top with Spanish rice and turkey; drizzle with dressing. Sprinkle with cheese and serve with lime wedges.

Per serving: 491 cal., 17 g total fat (5 g sat. fat), 78 mg chol., 889 mg sodium, 50 g carbo., 4 g fiber, 35 g pro.

At first the sweetness of the glaze dominates, then the peppery heat sneaks up on you.

SWEET & SPICY TURKEY DRUMSTICKS

1	teaspoon onion salt
½	teaspoon garlic salt
½	teaspoon black pepper
¼	teaspoon cayenne pepper
¼	teaspoon dry mustard
¼	teaspoon ground allspice
⅛	teaspoon ground cloves
6	turkey drumsticks (5½ to 6 pounds total)
2	tablespoons olive oil
½	cup jalapeño chile pepper jelly

PREP: *15 minutes*

GRILL: *45 minutes*

MAKES: *6 servings*

1 For rub, in a small bowl combine onion salt, garlic salt, black pepper, cayenne pepper, dry mustard, allspice, and cloves. Brush turkey drumsticks with oil. Sprinkle evenly with rub; rub in with your fingers.

2 In a small saucepan heat jalapeño jelly until melted.

3 For a charcoal grill, arrange medium-hot coals around a drip pan. Test for medium heat above the pan. Place turkey drumsticks on grill rack over drip pan. Cover; grill for 45 minutes to 1¼ hours or until turkey is tender and no longer pink (180°F), turning occasionally and brushing frequently with jalapeño jelly during the last 10 minutes of grilling. (For a gas grill, preheat grill. Reduce heat to medium. Adjust for indirect cooking. Grill as above.)

Per serving: 478 cal., 15 g total fat (4 g sat. fat), 277 mg chol., 520 mg sodium, 18 g carbo., 0 g fiber, 65 g pro.

Pineapple and mustard combine to make a tangy sauce for turkey thighs, and the island-style noodle salad is the perfect accompaniment.

ALOHA TURKEY THIGHS

PREP: *30 minutes*

GRILL: *50 minutes*

MAKES: *4 servings*

¾ cup unsweetened pineapple juice

2 tablespoons honey

1 tablespoon Dijon-style mustard

1 tablespoon soy sauce

1½ teaspoons cornstarch

1 clove garlic, minced

2 turkey thighs (about 2 pounds total), skinned if desired

Salt

Black pepper

1 recipe Hawaiian Noodle Salad

1 For sauce, in a small saucepan combine pineapple juice, honey, mustard, soy sauce, cornstarch, and garlic. Cook and stir over medium heat until thickened and bubbly. Cook and stir for 1 minute more. Remove from heat. Transfer half of the sauce to a bowl; cover and set aside.

2 Sprinkle turkey with salt and pepper. For a charcoal grill, arrange medium-hot coals around a drip pan. Test for medium heat above pan. Place turkey on grill rack over drip pan. Cover; grill for 50 to 60 minutes or until turkey is tender and no longer pink (180°F), brushing turkey frequently with remaining sauce during the last 20 minutes of grilling. (For a gas grill, preheat grill. Reduce heat to medium. Adjust for indirect cooking. Grill as above.)

3 To serve, cut turkey meat from bones. Serve with reserved sauce and Hawaiian Noodle Salad.

HAWAIIAN NOODLE SALAD: Cook one 3-ounce package broken ramen noodles according to package directions, except omit spice packet. Run under cold water until chilled; drain. For dressing, in a small screw-top jar combine 2 tablespoons lime juice; 1 tablespoon salad oil; 2 teaspoons toasted sesame oil; 1 fresh jalapeño chile pepper, seeded and finely chopped (see tip, page 19); 2 teaspoons finely chopped crystallized ginger; and ¼ teaspoon salt. Cover and shake well to combine. In a large bowl combine chilled noodles; the dressing; one 8-ounce can crushed pineapple, drained; ½ cup finely chopped red sweet pepper; 4 green onions, thinly sliced; and ¼ cup chopped macadamia nuts, toasted. Toss to coat.

Per serving: 533 cal., 22 g total fat (4 g sat. fat), 151 mg chol., 584 mg sodium, 44 g carbo., 2 g fiber, 40 g pro.

Rich-flavored tahini is a little lighter in color than peanut butter but is much thicker. Use a whisk when combining it with the other ingredients.

TAHINI TURKEY THIGHS

½   cup tahini (sesame seed paste)
¼   cup water
2   tablespoons soy sauce
1   tablespoon lemon juice
1   tablespoon honey
1   tablespoon Asian chile garlic sauce
1   teaspoon grated fresh ginger
4   turkey thighs (3½ to 4 pounds total), skinned if desired
1   recipe Garbanzo Bean Salad

PREP: *40 minutes*
GRILL: *50 minutes*
MAKES: *6 servings*

1 For sauce, in a medium bowl whisk together tahini, the water, soy sauce, lemon juice, honey, chile garlic sauce, and ginger until combined; set aside.

2 For a charcoal grill, arrange medium-hot coals around a drip pan. Test for medium heat above pan. Place turkey thighs on grill rack over drip pan. Cover; grill for 50 to 60 minutes or until turkey is tender and no longer pink (180°F), turning once halfway through grilling and brushing frequently with sauce during the last 20 minutes of grilling. Discard any remaining sauce. (For a gas grill, preheat grill. Reduce heat to medium. Adjust for indirect cooking. Grill as above.)

3 To serve, cut turkey meat from bones. Serve with Garbanzo Bean Salad.

GARBANZO BEAN SALAD: For dressing, in a small screw-top jar combine 3 tablespoons olive oil, 3 tablespoons lemon juice, ¼ teaspoon salt, and ⅛ teaspoon black pepper. Cover and shake well. Rinse and drain two 15-ounce cans garbanzo beans (chickpeas). In a large bowl combine the beans; ¾ cup finely chopped yellow or red sweet pepper; ⅔ cup snipped fresh parsley; ½ cup finely chopped, seeded cucumber; ⅓ cup snipped fresh mint; 2 plum tomatoes, seeded and chopped; and ¼ cup finely chopped red onion. Add dressing; toss to combine. Cover and chill until ready to serve.

Per serving: 600 cal., 32 g total fat (6 g sat. fat), 119 mg chol., 985 mg sodium, 34 g carbo., 8 g fiber, 44 g pro.

This Tex-Mex sensation showcases tortilla chip-seasoned chicken patties, pepper cheese, avocado, and salsa, all piled on slabs of toasted corn bread. (Recipe pictured on page 286.)

SOUTHWEST CHICKEN BURGERS

PREP: 25 minutes

BAKE: 30 minutes

COOL: 10 minutes

GRILL: 15 minutes

MAKES: 4 servings

CHEESY CORN BREAD SLICES: Preheat oven to 400°F. In a large bowl combine 1½ cups all-purpose flour, 1 cup yellow cornmeal, ¼ cup sugar, 4 teaspoons baking powder, and 1 teaspoon salt. In a small bowl whisk together 3 eggs, 1½ cups milk, and ⅓ cup cooking oil; add all at once to flour mixture. Stir just until moistened. Fold in 1 cup shredded cheddar cheese (4 ounces). Pour batter into a well-greased 8×4×2-inch loaf pan. Bake about 30 minutes or until a toothpick inserted in center comes out clean. Cool in pan on a wire rack for 10 minutes. Remove from pan; cool completely. Wrap and store corn bread overnight before slicing. Cut corn bread in half crosswise. Reserve half of the corn bread for another use (if desired, freeze in an airtight freezer container or bag for up to 3 months). Cut remaining half of the corn bread into four pieces.

4 Cheesy Corn Bread Slices or 4 hamburger buns, split and toasted

1 egg

¼ cup crushed nacho cheese-flavor or plain tortilla chips

3 tablespoons finely chopped green sweet pepper

¾ teaspoon chili powder

¼ teaspoon salt

¼ teaspoon black pepper

1 pound uncooked ground chicken

4 ounces Monterey Jack cheese with jalapeño chile peppers, shredded (1 cup)

1 medium avocado, halved, seeded, peeled, and sliced

Purchased salsa

1 Prepare Cheesy Corn Bread Slices (if using). In a large bowl beat egg with a whisk; stir in crushed tortilla chips, sweet pepper, chili powder, salt, and black pepper. Add chicken; mix well. Shape the chicken mixture into four ¾-inch-thick patties.

2 For a charcoal grill, place patties on the rack of uncovered grill directly over medium coals. Grill for 14 to 18 minutes or until done (165°F),* turning once halfway through grilling. If using Cheesy Corn Bread Slices, add them for the last 2 minutes of grilling, turning slices once. Top patties with cheese. Grill for 1 to 2 minutes more or until cheese is melted. (For a gas grill, preheat grill. Reduce heat to medium. Place patties [and later Cheesy Corn Bread Slices] on grill rack over heat. Cover; grill as above.)

3 Serve patties on toasted Cheesy Corn Bread Slices or buns with avocado and salsa.

Per serving: 801 cal., 50 g total fat (12 g sat. fat), 176 mg chol., 1,056 mg sodium, 48 g carbo., 6 g fiber, 41 g pro.

*TEST KITCHEN TIP: The internal color of a burger is not a reliable doneness indicator. A chicken patty cooked to 165°F is safe, regardless of color. To measure the doneness of a patty, insert an instant-read thermometer through the side of the patty to a depth of 2 to 3 inches.

These delicate turkey patties get a flavorful accent from spinach and roasted red peppers.

MEDITERRANEAN TURKEY BURGERS

1	pound uncooked ground turkey or chicken
½	cup crushed rich round crackers (about 13 crackers)
½	of a 10-ounce package frozen chopped spinach, thawed and well drained
⅓	cup chopped onion
2	tablespoons Dijon-style mustard
¼	teaspoon salt
4	ounces drained fresh mozzarella cheese or mozzarella cheese, cut into 4 slices
¼	cup bottled roasted red sweet peppers, drained and cut into strips
4	white or whole wheat kaiser rolls, split and toasted

PREP: *20 minutes*
GRILL: *16 minutes*
MAKES: *4 servings*

1 In a large bowl combine turkey, crushed crackers, spinach, onion, mustard, and salt. Shape mixture into four ¾-inch-thick patties. If necessary, cover and chill about 30 minutes or until firm.

2 For a charcoal grill, place patties on the rack of uncovered grill directly over medium coals. Grill for 14 to 18 minutes or until done (165°F),* turning once halfway through grilling.

3 Top patties with mozzarella cheese and roasted red pepper strips. Grill for 2 to 3 minutes more or until cheese melts. (For a gas grill, preheat grill. Reduce heat to medium. Place patties on grill rack over heat. Cover; grill as above.) Serve burgers on rolls.

Per serving: 492 cal., 20 g total fat (8 g sat. fat), 110 mg chol., 965 mg sodium, 41 g carbo., 3 g fiber, 34 g pro.

*TEST KITCHEN TIP: The internal color of a burger is not a reliable doneness indicator. A turkey patty cooked to 165°F is safe, regardless of color. To measure the doneness of a patty, insert an instant-read thermometer through the side of the patty to a depth of 2 to 3 inches.

Tired of the same old burgers with pickles, ketchup, and mustard? For a change of pace, try these cilantro- and garlic-seasoned turkey burgers topped with a citrusy mayonnaise.

CILANTRO-TURKEY BURGERS

PREP: *25 minutes*
GRILL: *14 minutes*
MAKES: *4 servings*

1 pound uncooked ground turkey or chicken
¼ cup snipped fresh cilantro or ¼ cup snipped fresh flat-leaf parsley plus 1 tablespoon dried cilantro, crushed
¼ cup finely chopped onion
4 cloves garlic, minced
¾ teaspoon salt
¼ teaspoon black pepper
1 tablespoon olive oil
4 kaiser rolls, split and toasted
1 recipe Orange-Cilantro Mayonnaise
4 lettuce leaves
   Sliced red onion (optional)

1 In a large bowl gently combine turkey, fresh cilantro or parsley plus dried cilantro, chopped onion, garlic, salt, and pepper. Shape mixture into four ¾-inch-thick patties. Brush tops of patties with oil.

2 For a charcoal grill, place patties on the rack of uncovered grill directly over medium coals. Grill for 14 to 18 minutes or until done (165°F),* turning once halfway through grilling. (For a gas grill, preheat grill. Reduce heat to medium. Place patties on grill rack over heat. Cover; grill as above.)

3 Spread cut sides of rolls with Orange-Cilantro Mayonnaise. Serve patties on rolls with lettuce and, if desired, sliced onion.

ORANGE-CILANTRO MAYONNAISE: In a small bowl combine ½ cup mayonnaise or salad dressing; 2 tablespoons snipped fresh cilantro or 2 tablespoons snipped fresh flat-leaf parsley plus 1½ teaspoons dried cilantro, crushed; ½ teaspoon finely shredded orange peel; and 1 teaspoon orange juice. Makes about ½ cup.

Per serving: 600 cal., 40 g total fat (8 g sat. fat), 100 mg chol., 1,042 mg sodium, 33 g carbo., 2 g fiber, 26 g pro.

TEST KITCHEN TIP: Orange-Cilantro Mayonnaise may be made up to 3 days ahead. Store, covered, in the refrigerator.

*TEST KITCHEN TIP: The internal color of a burger is not a reliable doneness indicator. A turkey patty cooked to 165°F is safe, regardless of color. To measure the doneness of a patty, insert an instant-read thermometer through the side of the patty to a depth of 2 to 3 inches.

THE WHOLE BIRD

If you're looking for terrific flavor, try any of these enticing ideas for whole chickens and turkeys.

Using a basting brush made from rosemary sprigs lends tremendous herbed flavor to the chicken and potatoes. For a pretty garnish, sprinkle the roasted chickens and potatoes with fresh rosemary leaves and lemon peel strips. (Recipe pictured on page 287.)

CHICKEN WITH ROSEMARY & GARLIC POTATOES

PREP: *30 minutes*

CHILL: *6 to 8 hours*

ROAST: *1¼ hours*

STAND: *10 minutes*

MAKES: *8 servings*

¼ cup snipped fresh rosemary

2 3½- to 3¾-pound whole broiler-fryer chickens

8 sprigs fresh rosemary

1 small lemon

⅓ cup olive oil

4 cloves garlic, crushed

2 pounds red, white, and/or gold new potatoes

1 For brine, in a large Dutch oven stir together 1 gallon (16 cups) water, ½ cup salt, and the snipped rosemary until salt is dissolved. Rinse insides of chickens. Submerge chickens in brine. Make a brush by using 100%-cotton kitchen string to tie together 6 of the rosemary sprigs. Add rosemary brush to brine mixture. Cover and refrigerate for 6 to 8 hours.

2 Using a vegetable peeler or zester, remove lemon peel, being careful not to remove any white pith. Cut lemon in half; set aside. In a small saucepan combine the lemon peel, the oil, and 2 cloves of the garlic. Cook over low heat just until warm to the touch; remove from heat and set aside.

3 Preheat oven to 425°F. Remove chickens and rosemary brush from brine. Pat chickens dry with paper towels. Pull neck skin to back of each chicken; fasten with skewers. Twist wing tips under backs. In body cavity of each chicken, place a lemon half, a sprig of the remaining rosemary, and a garlic clove. Use 100%-cotton kitchen string to tie drumsticks securely to tails.

4 Cut large potatoes into ½-inch-thick slices and halve small potatoes. Place in a large shallow roasting pan. Sprinkle with ¼ teaspoon salt and ¼ teaspoon black pepper. Using rosemary brush, baste potatoes with some of the oil mixture. Place chickens, breast sides up, on potatoes in pan. Using rosemary brush, baste chickens with oil mixture.

5 Roast for 30 minutes. Reduce oven temperature to 375°F. Roast for 45 to 60 minutes more or until potatoes are tender and an instant-read thermometer inserted into one of the inside thigh muscles registers 180°F (the thermometer should not touch bone), brushing twice with remaining oil mixture during first hour of roasting. The juices should run clear, and the drumsticks should move easily in their sockets. Discard any remaining oil mixture and the rosemary brush.

6 Remove chicken from oven; discard cavity ingredients. Cover with foil; let stand for 10 minutes before carving. Transfer chickens to a serving platter; surround with potatoes.

Per serving: 585 cal., 27 g total fat (7 g sat. fat), 243 mg chol., 431 mg sodium, 22 g carbo., 4 g fiber, 65 g pro

Get a jump-start on meal prep by roasting two chickens. Serve one for dinner and use the other during the week in soups, salads, or sandwiches.

CITRUS-HERB SLOW-ROASTED CHICKEN

1	4½- to 5-pound whole roasting chicken
4	teaspoons salt
2	teaspoons paprika (if available, use sweet smoked paprika)
1	teaspoon onion powder
1	teaspoon garlic powder
1	teaspoon white pepper
1	teaspoon dried thyme, crushed
1	teaspoon black pepper
½	teaspoon ground sage
½	teaspoon cayenne pepper
1	large lemon, cut into 8 wedges
1	small onion, cut into 8 wedges
4	cloves garlic, minced
1	teaspoon sugar

PREP: *30 minutes*
CHILL: *8 to 24 hours*
ROAST: *3¾ hours*
STAND: *10 minutes*
MAKES: *8 servings*

1 Remove neck and giblets from chicken; discard or save for another use. Pull neck skin to back; fasten with skewer. Use 100%-cotton kitchen string to tie drumsticks securely to tail. Twist wing tips under back. Set aside.

2 For spice rub, in a small bowl combine salt, paprika, onion powder, garlic powder, white pepper, thyme, black pepper, sage, and cayenne pepper. In a medium bowl combine 1 tablespoon of the spice rub, the lemon, onion, garlic, and sugar. Squeeze a wedge of lemon over the lemon mixture. Cover and refrigerate for 8 to 24 hours.

3 Use your fingers to rub the remaining spice rub all over the chicken's skin and inside the body cavity. If possible, reach under the skin. Place chicken in a resealable plastic bag. Seal bag. Refrigerate for 8 to 24 hours.

4 Preheat oven to 425°F. Remove chicken from bag. Place chicken, breast side up, on a rack in a shallow roasting pan. Stuff the chicken's cavity with the lemon mixture. Roast for 15 minutes.

5 Reduce the oven temperature to 250°F. Roast for 1 hour. Use a squeeze-style baster or a pastry brush to baste the chicken with the pan juices. Roast for 2½ to 3 hours more or until an instant-read thermometer inserted into one of the inside thigh muscles registers 180°F (the thermometer should not touch bone), basting chicken with pan juices about every 30 minutes. The juices should run clear, and the drumsticks should move easily in their sockets. Remove chicken from oven. Cover with foil; let stand for 10 minutes before carving.

Per serving: 278 cal., 12 g total fat (4 g sat. fat), 156 mg chol., 1,366 mg sodium, 4 g carbo., 1 g fiber, 40 g pro.

Roasted chicken gets a crunchy twist with this buttery thyme-and-pecan coating.

FRESH GARLIC & PECAN CHICKEN

PREP: *30 minutes*

ROAST: *1¼ hours*

STAND: *10 minutes*

MAKES: *4 servings*

1	3- to 3½-pound whole broiler-fryer chicken
6	cloves garlic, thinly sliced
⅔	cup finely chopped pecans
¼	cup butter, melted
1	tablespoon snipped fresh thyme or 1 teaspoon dried thyme, crushed
½	teaspoon black pepper
¼	teaspoon salt

1 Preheat oven to 375°F. Remove neck and giblets from chicken; discard or save for another use. Pull neck skin to back; fasten with skewer. Use 100%-cotton kitchen string to tie drumsticks securely to tail; twist wing tips under back. Using a small sharp knife, cut numerous slits about 1 inch wide and ½ inch deep in the breast portion of the chicken. Using your fingers, insert a slice of garlic into each slit.

2 In a small bowl combine pecans, melted butter, thyme, pepper, and salt. Pat mixture onto top of chicken.

3 Place chicken, breast side up, on a rack in a shallow roasting pan. Roast for 1¼ to 1½ hours or until an instant-read thermometer inserted into the center of one of the inside thigh muscles registers 180°F (the thermometer should not touch bone). The juices should run clear, and the drumsticks should move easily in their sockets. If necessary, cover chicken loosely with foil for the last 10 to 15 minutes of roasting to prevent pecans from overbrowning.

4 Remove chicken from oven. Cover with foil; let stand for 10 minutes before carving. If desired, spoon any pecans from roasting pan over individual servings.

Per serving: 725 cal., 59 g total fat (18 g sat. fat), 205 mg chol., 400 mg sodium, 4 g carbo., 2 g fiber, 45 g pro.

A blend of herbs placed under the skin adds a lot of flavor to this roasted chicken while working like a marinade.

ROASTED ITALIAN CHICKEN

2	tablespoons balsamic vinegar
2	tablespoons olive oil
1	tablespoon lemon juice
3	cloves garlic, minced
1	tablespoon snipped fresh oregano or 1 teaspoon dried oregano, crushed
1	tablespoon snipped fresh basil or 1 teaspoon dried basil, crushed
1½	teaspoons snipped fresh thyme or ½ teaspoon dried thyme, crushed
½	teaspoon salt
½	teaspoon coarsely ground black pepper
1	3- to 3½-pound whole broiler-fryer chicken

PREP: *15 minutes*
ROAST: *1¼ hours*
STAND: *10 minutes*
MAKES: *6 servings*

1 Preheat oven to 375°F. In a small bowl whisk together balsamic vinegar, oil, lemon juice, garlic, oregano, basil, thyme, salt, and pepper; set aside.

2 Remove neck and giblets from chicken; discard or save for another use. Place chicken, breast side up, on a rack in a shallow roasting pan. Pull neck skin to back; fasten with skewer. Use 100%-cotton kitchen string to tie drumsticks securely to tail; twist wing tips under back. Slip your fingers between the skin and the breast and leg meat of the chicken, forming a pocket. Spoon herb mixture into pocket. Brush remaining herb mixture over outside of the chicken.

3 Roast for 1¼ to 1½ hours or until an instant-read thermometer inserted into an inside thigh muscle registers 180°F (the thermometer should not touch bone). The juices should run clear, and the drumsticks should move easily in their sockets. If necessary to prevent overbrowning, cover with foil during the last 15 minutes of roasting.

4 Remove chicken from oven. Cover with foil; let stand for 10 minutes before carving.

Per serving: 374 cal., 27 g total fat (7 g sat. fat), 115 mg chol., 282 mg sodium, 2 g carbo., 0 g fiber, 29 g pro.

Seven different seasonings make this roasted bird a cut above grandma's Sunday chicken.

HERB-ROASTED CHICKEN & VEGETABLES

PREP: *35 minutes*
ROAST: *1¼ hours*
STAND: *10 minutes*
MAKES: *4 servings*

1   pound red potatoes, quartered (or halved, if small)
3   carrots, halved lengthwise and cut into 1-inch-long pieces
1   medium turnip, peeled and cut into 1½-inch pieces
1   3½- to 4-pound whole broiler-fryer chicken
2   tablespoons butter or margarine, melted
2   cloves garlic, minced
1   teaspoon dried basil, crushed
½   teaspoon ground sage
½   teaspoon dried thyme, crushed
½   teaspoon salt
¼   teaspoon lemon-pepper seasoning
1   medium onion, cut into 1-inch chunks
2   tablespoons butter or margarine, melted
¼   teaspoon black pepper

1   In a large saucepan bring lightly salted water to boiling. Add potatoes, carrots, and turnip. Return to boiling; reduce heat. Cover and simmer for 5 minutes; drain. Set aside.

2   Preheat oven to 375°F. Remove neck and giblets from chicken; discard or save for another use. Pull neck skin to back; fasten with skewer. Use 100%-cotton kitchen string to tie drumsticks securely to tail; twist wing tips under back. Place chicken, breast side up, on a rack in a shallow roasting pan. Brush with 2 tablespoons melted butter; rub garlic over chicken.

3   In a small bowl stir together basil, sage, thyme, ¼ teaspoon of the salt, and the lemon-pepper seasoning. Sprinkle basil mixture evenly over chicken; rub in with your fingers.

4   Add drained vegetables and the onion to bottom of the roasting pan around chicken. Drizzle vegetables with 2 tablespoons melted butter; sprinkle with remaining ¼ teaspoon salt and the black pepper.

5   Roast for 1¼ to 1¾ hours or until an instant-read thermometer inserted into the center of one of the inside thigh muscles registers 180°F (the thermometer should not touch bone), stirring vegetables once or twice during roasting. The juices should run clear, and the drumsticks should move easily in their sockets.

6   Remove chicken from oven. Cover with foil; let stand for 10 minutes. To serve, place chicken on a serving platter. Surround with vegetables.

Per serving: 799 cal., 51 g total fat (17 g sat. fat), 233 mg chol., 657 mg sodium, 28 g carbo., 4 g fiber, 54 g pro.

Your choice of garden-fresh herbs gives this home-style classic sophisticated new flavor.

LEMONY ROASTED CHICKEN

1	3- to 3½-pound whole broiler-fryer chicken
3	cloves garlic, thinly sliced
2	tablespoons snipped assorted fresh herbs (such as flat-leaf parsley, thyme, and sage)
2	tablespoons olive oil
1½	teaspoons finely shredded lemon peel
¼	teaspoon black pepper
½	to 1 teaspoon sea salt or coarse salt
1	small onion, quartered

PREP: *20 minutes*
ROAST: *1¼ hours*
STAND: *10 minutes*
MAKES: *4 servings*

1 Preheat oven to 375°F. Using a small sharp knife, cut 8 to 10 small slits in the chicken skin, especially on the breasts and hindquarters. Using your fingers, insert a slice of garlic into each slit, just under the skin. Mince remaining garlic and set aside.

2 In a small bowl combine minced garlic, herbs, olive oil, lemon peel, and pepper. Spread herb mixture evenly over chicken; rub in with your fingers. Sprinkle chicken, including body cavity, with salt. Place onion quarters in body cavity. Use 100%-cotton kitchen string to tie drumsticks securely to tail; twist wing tips under back. Place chicken, breast side up, on a rack in a shallow roasting pan.

3 Roast for 1¼ to 1¾ hours or until an instant-read thermometer inserted into one of the inside thigh muscles registers 180°F (the thermometer should not touch bone). The juices should run clear, and the drumsticks should move easily in their sockets.

4 Remove chicken from oven. Remove the onion from the cavity. Cover chicken with foil; let stand for 10 minutes before carving.

Per serving: 278 cal., 12 g total fat (2 g sat. fat), 119 mg chol., 375 mg sodium, 4 g carbo., 1 g fiber, 37 g pro.

Get this bird ready for the oven the night before you plan to serve it. The next day all you have to do is pile potatoes around the chicken and put everything in the oven.

PROVENÇAL HERB-RUBBED ROASTER

PREP: *20 minutes*

CHILL: *2 to 24 hours*

ROAST: *1¼ hours*

STAND: *10 minutes*

MAKES: *6 servings*

1   3½- to 4-pound whole broiler-fryer chicken

¼   cup olive oil

2   tablespoons herbes de Provence

1   teaspoon smoked salt or salt

1   teaspoon crushed red pepper

¾   teaspoon coarsely ground black pepper

1½   pounds tiny yellow and purple potatoes and/or fingerling potatoes, halved

1 Remove neck and giblets from chicken; discard or save for another use. Pull neck skin to back; fasten with skewer. Use 100%-cotton kitchen string to tie drumsticks securely to tail; twist wing tips under back. Brush chicken with 2 tablespoons of the olive oil.

2 In a small bowl stir together herbes de Provence, smoked salt or salt, crushed red pepper, and black pepper. Rub 2 tablespoons of the pepper mixture onto the chicken. Cover the remaining pepper mixture; set aside. Place chicken in a resealable plastic bag. Seal bag. Refrigerate for 2 to 24 hours.

3 Preheat oven to 375°F. Remove chicken from bag. Place chicken, breast side up, on a rack in a shallow roasting pan. Insert an oven-going meat thermometer into the center of one of the inside thigh muscles (the thermometer should not touch bone).

4 In a large bowl combine the remaining 2 tablespoons oil and the remaining pepper mixture. Add the potatoes and toss to combine. Arrange potatoes around the chicken in pan. Roast for 1¼ to 1¾ hours or until thermometer registers 180°F. The juices should run clear, and the drumsticks should move easily in their sockets.

5 Remove chicken from oven. Cover with foil; let stand for 10 minutes before carving. To serve, place the chicken on a large serving platter. Surround with potatoes.

Per serving: 543 cal., 35 g total fat (9 g sat. fat), 134 mg chol., 492 mg sodium, 18 g carbo., 3 g fiber, 37 g pro.

This gobbler gets sensational flavor from homemade jam that includes Granny Smith apples, sweet onion, and lots of roasted garlic.

ROASTED TURKEY WITH SWEET ONION JAM

1	10- to 12-pound turkey
	Cooking oil
1	recipe Sweet Onion Jam or 1 cup purchased roasted onion jam
6	medium red and/or white onions, peeled and cut into wedges
10	to 12 cloves unpeeled garlic
	Chicken broth
¼	cup dry white wine or apple juice
3	tablespoons all-purpose flour

PREP: *15 minutes*
ROAST: *2¾ hours*
STAND: *15 minutes*
MAKES: *12 to 14 servings*

1 Preheat oven to 325°F. Remove neck and giblets from turkey; discard or save for another use. Rinse inside of turkey; pat dry with paper towels. If desired, season body cavity with salt. Pull neck skin to back; fasten with skewer. If a band of skin crosses the tail, tuck the ends of the drumsticks under the band. If no band, use 100% cotton kitchen string to tie the drumsticks securely to tail. Twist wing tips under back.

2 Place turkey, breast side up, on a rack in a shallow roasting pan. Brush with oil. Insert an oven-going meat thermometer into the center of one of the inside thigh muscles (the thermometer should not touch bone).

3 Cover turkey loosely with foil. Roast for 1 hour. Meanwhile, roast garlic for Sweet Onion Jam, if using.

4 In a large bowl combine onion wedges, unpeeled garlic cloves, and 2 tablespoons oil; toss lightly to coat. Spoon onion mixture around turkey. Roast about 1¼ hours more or until thermometer registers 160°F. Meanwhile, finish preparing the Sweet Onion Jam. Remove foil from turkey. Cut band of skin or string between drumsticks so thighs cook evenly. Carefully spread Sweet Onion Jam over turkey. Roast for 30 to 45 minutes more or until thermometer registers 180°F. The juices should run clear, and the drumsticks should move easily in their sockets.

5 Remove turkey from oven. Transfer turkey and onion wedges to a serving platter. Cover with foil; let stand for 15 to 20 minutes before carving.

6 Meanwhile, pour pan drippings into a large measuring cup. Skim fat from drippings and strain remaining drippings. Add chicken broth, if necessary, to measure 1¾ cups liquid total. In a medium saucepan combine wine and flour. Stir in strained drippings. Cook and stir until thickened and bubbly; cook and stir for 1 minute more. Serve with turkey.

SWEET ONION JAM: Preheat oven to 325°F. Slice about ¼ inch off the pointed end of 1 bulb garlic so that the individual cloves show. Place garlic bulb in a small baking dish, cut side up, and drizzle with 1 tablespoon olive oil. Cover and roast for 45 to 60 minutes or until the garlic cloves have softened. Cool. Gently squeeze garlic cloves and juices into a medium saucepan. Stir in 1 large sweet onion, finely chopped; ½ cup sugar; ½ cup finely chopped Granny Smith apple; and ½ cup balsamic vinegar. Bring to boiling over medium-high heat, stirring occasionally; reduce heat. Simmer, uncovered, about 30 minutes or until onion and apple have softened and turned transparent and the mixture has thickened, stirring occasionally. (The jam can be prepared and refrigerated for up to 3 days before use.) Makes about 1 cup.

Per serving: 590 cal., 27 g total fat (7 g sat. fat), 202 mg chol., 199 mg sodium, 19 g carbo., 1 g fiber, 62 g pro.

Tarragon is used both in the turkey and in the glaze. A 1-ounce package of fresh tarragon is enough for both recipes. Start by chopping the ¼ cup for the glaze; then use the remainder in the bird.

MAPLE-TARRAGON GLAZED TURKEY

PREP: *45 minutes*
ROAST: *2¾ hours*
STAND: *15 minutes*
MAKES: *10 servings*

1	10- to 12-pound turkey
2	or 3 sprigs fresh tarragon or 2 teaspoons dried tarragon, crushed
1	tablespoon butter or margarine, melted
1	recipe Maple-Tarragon Glaze
2	blood oranges or regular oranges, quartered
2	large bunches seedless red or purple grapes
1	recipe Orange Gravy

MAPLE-TARRAGON GLAZE: In a medium saucepan combine 1½ teaspoons finely shredded orange peel; 1½ cups orange juice; ¾ cup pure maple syrup; ⅓ cup tarragon vinegar; ¼ cup snipped fresh tarragon or 1½ teaspoons dried tarragon, crushed; 1 teaspoon dry mustard; ½ teaspoon salt; and ¼ teaspoon black pepper. Bring to boiling, stirring frequently (watch carefully as mixture will bubble up); reduce heat. Boil gently, uncovered, for 30 to 35 minutes or until mixture reaches a glazing consistency, stirring occasionally. (You should have about 1 cup.)

1 Preheat oven to 325°F. Remove neck and giblets from turkey; discard or save for another use. Rinse inside of turkey; pat dry with paper towels. Place the fresh tarragon sprigs in body cavity (if using dried tarragon, rub in cavity). Pull neck skin to back; fasten with skewer. If a band of skin crosses the tail, tuck the ends of the drumsticks under the band. If no band, use 100%-cotton kitchen string to tie drumsticks securely to tail. Twist wing tips under back.

2 Place turkey, breast side up, on a rack in a shallow roasting pan. Brush with butter. Sprinkle with salt and black pepper. Insert an oven-going meat thermometer into the center of one of the inside thigh muscles (the thermometer should not touch bone). Cover turkey loosely with foil.

3 Roast for 2 to 2¼ hours or until thermometer registers 160°F. Meanwhile, prepare Maple-Tarragon Glaze.

4 Remove foil and cut band of skin or string between drumsticks so thighs cook evenly. Add oranges to roasting pan; brush oranges and turkey with half of the Maple-Tarragon Glaze. Roast, uncovered, for 30 minutes more.

5 Add grapes to roasting pan; brush fruit and turkey with remaining glaze. Roast about 15 minutes more or until thermometer registers 180°F. The juices should run clear, and the drumsticks should move easily in their sockets.

6 Remove turkey from oven; reserve drippings. Transfer turkey to a serving platter. Cover turkey with foil; let stand for 15 to 20 minutes before carving. Meanwhile, prepare Orange Gravy. Arrange roasted oranges and grapes around turkey. Serve with Orange Gravy.

ORANGE GRAVY: Pour the drippings from turkey into a 2-cup glass measuring cup. Add enough orange juice to measure 1½ cups liquid total; place in a medium saucepan. Combine one 14-ounce can chicken broth and 2 tablespoons cornstarch; stir into orange juice mixture. Cook and stir over medium heat until thickened and bubbly. Cook and stir for 2 minutes more. Season with salt and black pepper. Makes about 3 cups.

Per serving: 384 cal., 8 g total fat (3 g sat. fat), 141 mg chol., 379 mg sodium, 36 g carbo., 1 g fiber, 39 g pro.

Jellied cranberry sauce, honey, and apple jelly add a festive glisten as well as a sweet fruit flavor to this moist, tender turkey.

ROASTED TURKEY WITH CRANBERRY GLAZE

1	10- to 12-pound turkey
	Salt
	Black pepper
1	medium onion, cut into quarters
1	medium orange, cut into quarters
4	sprigs fresh sage
4	sprigs fresh thyme
	Cooking oil
1	8-ounce can jellied cranberry sauce
¼	cup apple jelly
2	tablespoons honey or light-colored corn syrup
1	tablespoon lemon juice or cider vinegar
½	teaspoon snipped fresh thyme or ¼ teaspoon dried thyme, crushed

PREP: *20 minutes*

ROAST: *2¾ hours*

STAND: *15 minutes*

MAKES: *12 to 14 servings*

1 Preheat oven to 325°F. Remove neck and giblets from turkey; discard or save for another use. Rinse inside of turkey; pat dry with paper towels. Season body cavity with salt and pepper. Sprinkle outside of turkey with pepper. Place onion, orange, sage sprigs, and thyme sprigs in body cavity. Pull neck skin to back; fasten with skewer. If a band of skin crosses the tail, tuck the ends of the drumsticks under the band. If no band, use 100%-cotton kitchen string to tie drumsticks securely to tail. Twist wing tips under back.

2 Place turkey, breast side up, on a rack in a shallow roasting pan. Brush with oil. Insert an oven-going meat thermometer into the center of one of the inside thigh muscles (the thermometer should not touch bone). Cover turkey loosely with foil.

3 Roast for 2¾ to 3 hours or until thermometer registers 180°F. The juices should run clear, and the drumsticks should move easily in their sockets. During the last 45 minutes of roasting, remove foil and cut band of skin or string between drumsticks so thighs cook evenly.

4 Meanwhile, for glaze, in a small saucepan combine cranberry sauce, apple jelly, honey, lemon juice, and snipped or dried thyme; cook and stir until cranberry sauce and jelly are melted and mixture is smooth. During the last 25 minutes of roasting, brush turkey often with glaze.

5 Remove turkey from oven; discard cavity ingredients. Cover turkey with foil; let stand for 15 to 20 minutes before carving.

Per serving: 442 cal., 12 g total fat (3 g sat. fat), 229 mg chol., 225 mg sodium, 15 g carbo., 0 g fiber, 63 g pro.

Get ready for some "oohs" and "aahs" as you bring this golden-brown beauty to your table. Everyone will love the way the turkey and apples combine to create a double dose of incredible taste. Plus, the apple-tinged drippings make a gravy like none other!

BUTTERY CIDER-GLAZED TURKEY

PREP: *45 minutes*
ROAST: *3 hours 20 minutes*
STAND: *15 minutes*
MAKES: *16 to 18 servings*

CIDER GLAZE: In a small saucepan combine 2 cups apple cider or apple juice and five 3-inch-long sticks cinnamon, broken. Bring to boiling; reduce heat. Boil steadily about 30 minutes or until cider is reduced to ⅔ cup. Add ⅓ cup butter, ⅓ cup packed brown sugar, and 1 teaspoon dried thyme, crushed. Cook and stir until sugar is dissolved. Discard cinnamon sticks.

1	12- to 14-pound turkey
4	large cloves garlic, halved
7	medium baking apples, cored and cut into eighths
1	small onion, cut into wedges
2	tablespoons butter, melted
2	tablespoons lemon juice
1	recipe Cider Glaze
⅓	cup all-purpose flour
	Chicken broth

1 Preheat oven to 325°F. Remove neck and giblets from turkey; discard or save for another use. Rinse inside of turkey; pat dry with paper towels. Season body cavity with salt and pepper. Rub 2 garlic clove halves in cavity. Place remaining 6 garlic clove halves, 8 of the apple wedges, and onion in cavity.

2 Pull neck skin to back; fasten with skewer. If band of skin crosses tail, tuck the ends of the drumsticks under the band. If no band, use 100%-cotton kitchen string to tie drumsticks securely to tail. Twist wing tips under back. Brush turkey with melted butter. Season with salt and black pepper. Place turkey, breast side up, on a rack in a shallow roasting pan. Insert an oven-going meat thermometer into the center of one of the inside thigh muscles (the thermometer should not touch bone). Cover turkey with foil. Roast for 2½ to 3¼ hours or until thermometer registers 160°F. Cut band of skin or string between drumsticks after 2½ hours.

3 Toss remaining apple wedges with lemon juice. Place apples around turkey; cover apples with foil. Roast for 30 minutes more. Remove foil from turkey and apples; brush turkey and drizzle apples with Cider Glaze. Roast, uncovered, about 20 minutes more or until thermometer registers 180°F, brushing turkey and drizzling apples with Cider Glaze once more.

4 Remove turkey from oven; discard cavity ingredients. Transfer turkey to a serving platter. Surround with apples. Cover with foil; let stand for 15 to 20 minutes before carving. Meanwhile, for gravy, pour pan drippings into a large measuring cup. Scrape browned bits from pan into the cup. Skim and reserve fat from the drippings. Pour ¼ cup of the reserved fat into a medium saucepan (discard remaining fat). Stir in flour. Add enough chicken broth to drippings in cup to measure 2½ cups total liquid; add to flour mixture in saucepan. Cook and stir over medium heat until thickened and bubbly. Cook and stir for 1 minute more. Season to taste with salt and pepper. Serve gravy with turkey.

Per serving: 544 cal., 26 g total fat (9 g sat. fat), 196 mg chol., 359 mg sodium, 18 g carbo., 2 g fiber, 55 g pro.

Spiced Sweet Potato Stuffing, made with raisin bread, sweet potatoes, and jerk seasoning, is the perfect complement to this sage- and citrus-accented bird. (Recipe pictured on page 288.)

ROASTED HERBED TURKEY

1   10- to 12-pound turkey
3   tablespoons snipped fresh sage
½   teaspoon salt
½   teaspoon black pepper
1   recipe Spiced Sweet Potato Stuffing (optional)
1   tablespoon olive oil
1   orange
1   tablespoon honey
     Oranges, halved (optional)
     Fresh sage leaves (optional)

PREP: *30 minutes*
ROAST: *2¾ hours*
STAND: *15 minutes*
MAKES: *12 servings*

1 Remove neck and giblets from turkey; discard or save for another use. Rinse inside of turkey; pat dry with paper towels. Season body cavity with 1 tablespoon of the snipped sage, the salt, and pepper. If desired, lightly pack Spiced Sweet Potato Stuffing into cavity.

2 Preheat oven to 325°F. Pull neck skin to back; fasten with skewer. If a band of skin crosses the tail, tuck the ends of the drumsticks under the band. If no band, use 100%-cotton kitchen string to tie the drumsticks securely to tail. Twist wing tips under back.

3 Place turkey, breast side up, on a rack in a shallow roasting pan. Brush turkey with oil. Insert an oven-going meat thermometer into the center of one of the inside thigh muscles (the thermometer should not touch bone). Roast for 2¾ to 3 hours or until thermometer registers 180°F and center of stuffing (if using) registers 165°F. The juices should run clear, and the drumsticks should move easily in their sockets.

4 Remove turkey from oven. Halve and squeeze juice from the one orange. In a small bowl combine the remaining 2 tablespoons snipped sage, the orange juice, and the honey. Brush on the hot turkey.

5 Cover turkey with foil; let stand for 15 to 20 minutes before carving. If desired, garnish turkey with orange halves and sage leaves.

Per serving: 394 cal., 12 g total fat (3 g sat. fat), 229 mg chol., 221 mg sodium, 3 g carbo., 0 g fiber, 64 g pro.

SPICED SWEET POTATO STUFFING: In a medium saucepan bring ¾ cup reduced-sodium chicken broth to boiling. Add 2 cups chopped, peeled sweet potatoes. Return to boiling; reduce heat. Cover and cook for 7 to 10 minutes or just until tender. Do not drain. Add 12 slices raisin bread, lightly toasted and cubed, and 2 teaspoons Jamaican jerk seasoning; stir until mixed. Add additional broth, if necessary, to moisten.

These pecan- and leek-stuffed hens make a sensational meal for four. Complete your menu with buttered green beans and corn muffins.

MAPLE-GLAZED STUFFED HENS

PREP: *30 minutes*

ROAST: *1 hour*

STAND: *10 minutes*

MAKES: *4 servings*

2	slices bacon
1	small leek or 2 green onions, thinly sliced
2	tablespoons chopped pecans or walnuts
⅛	teaspoon dried thyme or marjoram, crushed
1	cup dry bread cubes (1½ slices)
1	to 2 tablespoons water
2	1¼- to 1½-pound Cornish game hens
1	teaspoon butter or margarine, melted
2	tablespoons maple-flavored syrup or pure maple syrup
1	tablespoon butter or margarine, melted
2	teaspoons Dijon-style mustard or 1 teaspoon brown mustard

1 In a medium skillet cook bacon until crisp. Remove bacon and drain on paper towels. Crumble bacon and set aside. Reserve 1 tablespoon of the bacon drippings in skillet.

2 Cook leek and nuts in reserved bacon drippings over medium heat until leek is tender and nuts are toasted; remove from heat. Stir in bacon, thyme, and a dash black pepper. Stir in bread cubes. Drizzle enough of the water over bread mixture to moisten, tossing lightly until mixed.

3 Preheat oven to 375°F. Lightly season the cavity of each hen with salt and pepper. Lightly stuff the hens with the bread mixture. Skewer neck skin, if present, to back of each hen. Use 100%-cotton kitchen string to tie drumsticks securely to tails; twist wing tips under backs. Place hens, breast sides up, on a rack in a shallow roasting pan. Brush with the 1 teaspoon melted butter. Cover loosely with foil. Roast for 1 to 1¼ hours or until an instant-read thermometer inserted into one of the inside thigh muscles registers 180°F (the thermometer should not touch bone). Juices should run clear, and the drumsticks should move easily in their sockets.

4 Meanwhile, for glaze, in a small bowl stir together syrup, the 1 tablespoon melted butter, and the mustard. Uncover hens and brush with glaze frequently during the last 15 minutes of roasting.

5 Remove hens from oven. Let stand, covered, for 10 minutes before serving. To serve, use kitchen shears or a long heavy knife to carefully cut each hen in half lengthwise.

Per serving: 511 cal., 35 g total fat (11 g sat. fat), 191 mg chol., 385 mg sodium, 16 g carbo., 1 g fiber, 32 g pro.

If you're looking for a company-special entrée, these cherry-glazed game hens are fabulous. Team them with a rice pilaf and some steamed asparagus or broccoli.

CRIMSON CHERRY-GLAZED HOLIDAY HENS

2	cloves garlic
4	1½-pound Cornish game hens
1	tablespoon olive oil
½	teaspoon salt
¼	teaspoon black pepper
2	tablespoons butter
⅓	cup sliced or chopped shallot
1	12-ounce jar red cherry preserves (with whole cherries)
¼	cup red wine vinegar
½	teaspoon ground allspice
¼	teaspoon ground cloves

PREP: *20 minutes*
ROAST: *1 hour*
COOK: *20 minutes*
STAND: *10 minutes*
MAKES: *8 servings*

1 Preheat oven to 375°F. Cut one of the garlic cloves in half and rub the skin of each hen with cut side of garlic clove. Mince the remaining garlic clove and set aside. Brush hens with oil and sprinkle with the salt and pepper. Use 100%-cotton kitchen string to tie drumsticks securely to tails; twist wing tips under backs. Place hens, breast sides up, on a rack in a shallow roasting pan. Roast for 1 to 1¼ hours or until an instant-read thermometer inserted into one of the inside thigh muscles registers 180°F (the thermometer should not touch bone). The juices should run clear, and the drumsticks should move easily in their sockets.

2 Meanwhile, for glaze, in a small saucepan melt butter over medium heat. Add minced garlic and shallot; cook about 3 minutes or until tender, stirring often. Stir in preserves, red wine vinegar, allspice, and cloves. Bring to boiling; reduce heat. Boil gently, uncovered, about 20 minutes or until desired glazing consistency.

3 Remove hens from oven. Cover with foil; let stand for 10 minutes before serving. To serve, use kitchen shears or a long heavy knife to carefully cut each hen in half lengthwise. Spoon glaze over hen halves.

Per serving: 510 cal., 27 g total fat (7 g sat. fat), 128 mg chol., 271 mg sodium, 31 g carbo., 1 g fiber, 36 g pro.

Balsamic vinegar lends a subtly sweet accent to the roasted vegetables while garlic and rosemary boost the flavor of the succulent game hen.

GAME HEN WITH ROASTED VEGETABLES

PREP: *20 minutes*
ROAST: *1½ hours*
STAND: *10 minutes*
MAKES: *2 servings*

1   medium carrot, cut into large chunks
1   medium russet potato, cut into large chunks
1   medium parsnip or turnip, peeled and cut into large chunks
1   small onion, cut into wedges
1   tablespoon olive oil
1   tablespoon balsamic vinegar
1   1½-pound Cornish game hen or poussin
2   cloves garlic, minced
2   teaspoons snipped fresh rosemary or ½ teaspoon dried rosemary, crushed
¼   teaspoon salt
⅛   teaspoon coarsely ground black pepper

1 Preheat oven to 400°F. In a large bowl combine carrot, potato, parsnip or turnip, and onion. Add oil and balsamic vinegar; toss lightly to coat. Spread in a 9×9×2-inch baking pan; cover with foil. Roast for 30 minutes. Reduce oven temperature to 375°F.

2 Meanwhile, gently separate the skin from the hen breast and tops of drumsticks by slipping a paring knife or your fingers between the skin and the meat to make two pockets that extend all the way to the neck cavity and the drumsticks. In a small bowl combine garlic, rosemary, salt, and pepper. Rub 2 teaspoons of the fresh rosemary mixture (½ teaspoon of the dried rosemary mixture) under the skin onto the breast and drumstick meat. Use 100%-cotton kitchen string to tie drumsticks securely to tail; twist wing tips under back. Rub remaining rosemary mixture onto skin. Stir vegetables. Place hen, breast side up, in baking pan with vegetables.

3 Roast hen and vegetables, uncovered, for 1 to 1¼ hours or until vegetables are tender and an instant-read thermometer inserted into the center of one of the inside thigh muscles registers 180°F (the thermometer should not touch bone), stirring vegetables once or twice. The juices should run clear, and the drumsticks should move easily in their sockets.

4 Remove hen from oven. Transfer roasted hen to a serving platter. Surround with vegetables. Cover with foil; let stand for 10 minutes before serving. To serve hen, use kitchen shears or a long heavy knife to carefully cut hen in half lengthwise.

Per serving: 345 cal., 12 g total fat (2 g sat. fat), 133 mg chol., 399 mg sodium, 27 g carbo., 5 g fiber, 32 g pro.

Mix and match the vegetables and fruit you use in the stuffing that bakes inside this juicy full-flavored bird.

DUCKLING WITH SIMPLE HONEY-ALMOND SAUCE

1   4- to 5-pound domestic duckling or whole roasting chicken

1   cup chopped mixed fresh vegetables
(such as celery, carrots, and/or onions)

1   cup chopped mixed fresh fruit
(such as apples, pears, and/or oranges)

6   cloves garlic, minced

6   sprigs fresh rosemary

2   tablespoons Dijon-style mustard

1   tablespoon soy sauce

1   recipe Simple Honey-Almond Sauce

PREP: *25 minutes*
COOK: *15 minutes*
ROAST: *1 hour 55 minutes*
STAND: *30 minutes*
MAKES: *4 servings*

1 If using duckling, cut shallow slits every 2 inches across the skin. In an 8- to 10-quart pot bring 6 quarts (24 cups) water to boiling. Immerse duckling or chicken in the boiling water; reduce heat. Boil gently, uncovered, for 15 minutes. Remove bird and drain well; discard water. Let duckling or chicken stand until cool enough to handle (about 15 minutes).

2 Preheat oven to 450°F. Sprinkle body cavity of bird with 1 teaspoon salt and 1 teaspoon coarsely ground black pepper. In a small bowl combine chopped mixed vegetables, chopped mixed fruit, garlic, and rosemary sprigs. Stuff body cavity with vegetable mixture. Pull neck skin to back; fasten with skewer. Use 100%-cotton kitchen string to tie drumsticks to tail; twist wing tips under back. Place bird, breast side up, on a rack in a shallow roasting pan. Roast duckling for 1¼ hours (chicken for 45 minutes). Remove from oven; reduce oven temperature to 350°F.

3 In a small bowl combine mustard and soy sauce. Spread mixture over duckling or chicken. Insert an oven-going meat thermometer into center of one of the inside thigh muscles (the thermometer should not touch bone). Roast duckling about 30 minutes more (chicken about 20 minutes more) or until thermometer registers 180°F. Juices should run clear, and drumsticks move easily in their sockets. Discard hot fat as it accumulates.

4 Remove duckling or chicken from oven; increase oven temperature to 500°F. Let bird stand for 15 minutes. Spoon stuffing from cavity and transfer to a foil-lined baking sheet. Using paper towels to protect your hand from the heat, hold bird and use kitchen shears to halve the bird lengthwise, cutting along the backbone. Cut halves in half crosswise. Place duckling or chicken quarters on top of stuffing. Roast for 10 minutes more. Serve with Simple Honey-Almond Sauce.

SIMPLE HONEY-ALMOND SAUCE: In a small saucepan melt 3 tablespoons butter over medium heat. Add ½ cup sliced almonds. Cook and stir about 5 minutes or until almonds turn a deep golden brown. Stir in 2 tablespoons honey; heat through. Makes about ½ cup.

Per serving: 740 cal., 61 g total fat (23 g sat. fat), 170 mg chol., 1,162 mg sodium, 18 g carbo., 3 g fiber, 32 g pro.

INDEX

C

Cajun Chicken Pasta, 249
Caraway Chicken Stew, 35
Carrots
Caraway Chicken Stew, 35
Chicken & Artichoke Soup, 28
Chicken & Dumplings, 237
Chicken, Artichoke & Brie Soup, 49
Chicken, Broccoli & Carrot Salad, 84
Chicken Fricassee, 227
Chicken Linguine with Pesto
Sauce, 203
Chicken Osso Buco with Linguine, 266
Chicken-Tofu Stir-Fry, 300
Chicken with Mushroom
Stuffing, 115
Chicken with Sourdough
Stuffing, 113
Coconut-Chicken Curry, 269
Confetti Chicken Soup, 30
Creamy Chicken & Rice Soup, 47
Easy Sausage & Chicken Stew, 154
Easy Turkey-Pesto Pot Pie, 218
Game Hens with Rhubarb Glaze, 232
Game Hen with Roasted
Vegetables, 398
Ground Chicken & Barley Soup, 38
Herbed Chicken Noodle Soup, 138
Herb-Roasted Chicken &
Vegetables, 388
Italian Chicken with White
Beans, 139
Kale, Lentil & Chicken Soup, 45
Lemon Chicken with Autumn
Vegetables, 230
Lemongrass Chicken over
Noodles, 252
Lemon-Tarragon Chicken Toss, 185
Mediterranean Chicken & Pasta, 157

Carrots *(continued)*
Mexican Chef's Salad, 78
Mulligatawny Soup, 43
Potato-Topped Chicken &
Vegetables, 142
Smashed Potato Chicken Pot Pie, 303
Sweet & Sour Chicken, 171
Tandoori Chicken & Vegetables, 127
Thai Chicken & Vegetable Soup, 136
Thai Curry Agnolotti & Chicken
Bowl, 213
Thyme Chicken Marsala, 244
Towering Tostadas, 209
Turkey & Dumplings, 147
Turkey & Rice Soup, 55
Vegetable-Wild Rice Soup, 51
Yucatan-Style Turkey Soup, 53
Cheese
Adobo Turkey Taco Salad, 376
Apricot-Chicken Roll-Ups, 243
Artichoke-Chèvre-Stuffed Chicken
Breasts, 236
Barbecued Chicken, Apple & Onion
Pizza, 14
Basil-Cream Chicken Thighs, 135
BBQ Chicken & Cheese
Quesadillas, 210
BBQ Chicken Burgers & Waffle
Fries, 195
Blue Cheese Chicken, 119
Cajun Chicken Pasta, 249
Cheesy Chicken & Pasta with
Colorful Confetti, 212
Cheesy Corn & Chicken
Turnovers, 322
Cheesy Corn Bread Slices, 380
Chicken & Artichoke Soup, 28
Chicken & Biscuit Pockets, 321
Chicken & Garden Vegetable Penne
Pasta, 354

Cheese *(continued)*
Chicken & Poblano-Stuffed Buns, 19
Chicken & Raisin-Stuffed
Mushrooms, 17
Chicken, Artichoke & Brie Soup, 49
Chicken Breasts with Brandy
Sauce, 116
Chicken, Broccoli & Rice, 122
Chicken Chile Rellenos, 304
Chicken Chili, 126
Chicken Enchilada Sandwiches, 314
Chicken, Goat Cheese & Greens, 201
Chicken Linguine with Pesto
Sauce, 203
Chicken Mac & Cheese, 260
Chicken Osso Buco with
Linguine, 266
Chicken Quesadillas, 204
Chicken Salad with Olives &
Peppers, 82
Chicken Spiedini, 362
Chicken Stuffed with Mushrooms &
Prosciutto, 345
Chicken Stuffed with Spinach &
Sweet Peppers, 344
Chicken Thighs & Orzo, 267
Chicken Tossed Salad, 60
Chicken Tostadas, 144
Chicken-Wild Rice Bake, 307
Chicken with Smoky Paprika
Sauce, 117
Chipotle Chili with Hominy, 39
Choose-a-Vegetable Chicken Soup, 48
Classy Cuban Sandwiches, 329
Cobb Salad Hoagies, 324
Colorful Confetti, 212
Coq au Vin Rosettes, 256
Crab-Stuffed Chicken, 240
Creamy Ranch Chicken, 178
Deli Sandwich Stacks, 331

METRIC MEASUREMENTS

The charts on this page provide a guide for converting measurements from the U.S. customary system, which is used throughout this book, to the metric system.

Product Differences

Most of the ingredients called for in the recipes in this book are available in most countries. However, some are known by different names. Here are some common American ingredients and their possible counterparts:

All-purpose flour is enriched, bleached or unbleached white household flour. When self-rising flour is used in place of all-purpose flour in a recipe that calls for leavening, omit the leavening agent (baking soda or baking powder) and salt.

Baking soda is bicarbonate of soda.

Cornstarch is cornflour.

Golden raisins are sultanas.

Green, red, or yellow sweet peppers are capsicums or bell peppers.

Light-colored corn syrup is golden syrup.

Powdered sugar is icing sugar.

Sugar (white) is granulated, fine granulated, or castor sugar.

Vanilla or vanilla extract is vanilla essence.

Volume and Weight

The United States traditionally uses cup measures for liquid and solid ingredients. The chart below shows the approximate imperial and metric equivalents. If you are accustomed to weighing solid ingredients, the following approximate equivalents will be helpful.

1 cup butter, castor sugar, or rice = 8 ounces = $\frac{1}{2}$ pound = 250 grams

1 cup flour = 4 ounces = $\frac{1}{4}$ pound = 125 grams

1 cup icing sugar = 5 ounces = 150 grams

Canadian and U.S. volume for a cup measure is 8 fluid ounces (237 ml), but the standard metric equivalent is 250 ml.

1 British imperial cup is 10 fluid ounces.

In Australia, 1 tablespoon equals 20 ml, and there are 4 teaspoons in the Australian tablespoon.

Spoon measures are used for smaller amounts of ingredients. Although the size of the tablespoon varies slightly in different countries, for practical purposes and for recipes in this book, a straight substitution is all that's necessary. Measurements made using cups or spoons always should be level unless stated otherwise.

Common Weight Range Replacements

Imperial / U.S.	Metric
$\frac{1}{2}$ ounce	15 g
1 ounce	25 g or 30 g
4 ounces ($\frac{1}{4}$ pound)	115 g or 125 g
8 ounces ($\frac{1}{2}$ pound)	225 g or 250 g
16 ounces (1 pound)	450 g or 500 g
$1\frac{1}{4}$ pounds	625 g
$1\frac{1}{2}$ pounds	750 g
2 pounds or $2\frac{1}{4}$ pounds	1,000 g or 1 Kg

Oven Temperature Equivalents

Fahrenheit Setting	Celsius Setting*	Gas Setting
300°F	150°C	Gas Mark 2 (very low)
325°F	160°C	Gas Mark 3 (low)
350°F	180°C	Gas Mark 4 (moderate)
375°F	190°C	Gas Mark 5 (moderate)
400°F	200°C	Gas Mark 6 (hot)
425°F	220°C	Gas Mark 7 (hot)
450°F	230°C	Gas Mark 8 (very hot)
475°F	240°C	Gas Mark 9 (very hot)
500°F	260°C	Gas Mark 10 (extremely hot)
Broil	Broil	Grill

*Electric and gas ovens may be calibrated using Celsius. However, for an electric oven, increase Celsius setting 10 to 20 degrees when cooking above 160°C. For convection or forced air ovens (gas or electric), lower the temperature setting 25°F/10°C when cooking at all heat levels.

Baking Pan Sizes

Imperial / U.S.	Metric
9×1$\frac{1}{2}$-inch round cake pan	22- or 23×4-cm (1.5 L)
9×1$\frac{1}{2}$-inch pie plate	22- or 23×4-cm (1 L)
8×8×2-inch square cake pan	20×5-cm (2 L)
9×9×2-inch square cake pan	22- or 23×4.5-cm (2.5 L)
11×7×1$\frac{1}{2}$-inch baking pan	28×17×4-cm (2 L)
2-quart rectangular baking pan	30×19×4.5-cm (3 L)
13×9×2-inch baking pan	34×22×4.5-cm (3.5 L)
15×10×1-inch jelly roll pan	40×25×2-cm
9×5×3-inch loaf pan	23×13×8-cm (2 L)
2-quart casserole	2 L

U.S. / Standard Metric Equivalents

$\frac{1}{8}$ teaspoon = 0.5 ml	
$\frac{1}{4}$ teaspoon = 1 ml	
$\frac{1}{2}$ teaspoon = 2 ml	
1 teaspoon = 5 ml	
1 tablespoon = 15 ml	
2 tablespoons = 25 ml	
$\frac{1}{4}$ cup = 2 fluid ounces = 50 ml	
$\frac{1}{3}$ cup = 3 fluid ounces = 75 ml	
$\frac{1}{2}$ cup = 4 fluid ounces = 125 ml	
$\frac{2}{3}$ cup = 5 fluid ounces = 150 ml	
$\frac{3}{4}$ cup = 6 fluid ounces = 175 ml	
1 cup = 8 fluid ounces = 250 ml	
2 cups = 1 pint = 500 ml	
1 quart = 1 litre	

HEALTHY, FAST & FLAVORFUL RECIPES

FOR NO-HASSLE MEALS!

THE BIGGEST BOOK SERIES INCLUDES:

30-Minute Meals
Bread Machine Recipes
Casseroles
Cookies
Diabetic Recipes
Easy Canned Soup Recipes
Grilling
Italian Recipes
Low-Carb Recipes
Slow Cooker Recipes
Slow Cooker Recipes Volume 2
Soups & Stews

Available where quality books are sold.

FAMILY-FRIENDLY RECIPES
TO SATISFY EVERY APPETITE.

Better Homes and Gardens
BIGGEST BOOK OF
GRILLING
Hundreds of Sizzlin' Recipes for Ch...
PLUS: Sassy Sauces, Rubs, a...

Better Homes and Gardens,
BIGGEST BOOK OF
30 MINUTE MEALS

All-new sequel to the #1 national bestseller!
Better Homes and Gardens,
BIGGEST BOOK OF
SLOW COOKER RECIPES
VOLUME 2
More than 400 great-tasting recipes
featuring main dishes, sides, and desserts

Meredith® BOOKS

ADT0143_0406